een, and

7585

The Empress, the Queen, and the Nun

The Johns Hopkins University Studies
in Historical and Political Science
116th Series (1998)

THE EMPRESS, THE QUEEN, AND THE NUN

Women and Power at the Court of Philip III of Spain

MAGDALENA S. SÁNCHEZ

The Johns Hopkins University Press
Baltimore and London

This book has been brought to publication with the generous assistance
of the Program for Cultural Cooperation between Spain's Ministry of
Culture and Education and United States' Universities.

The Johns Hopkins University Press
2715 North Charles Street
Baltimore, Maryland 21218-4363
The Johns Hopkins Press Ltd., London

Library of Congress Cataloging-in-Publication Data
will be found at the end of this book.
A catalog record for this book is available from the British Library.

ISBN 0-8018-5791-0

Contents

Illustrations

Preface and Acknowledgments

HISTORIANS have long overlooked the three women who are at the center of this book. Nevertheless, Empress María, Margaret of the Cross, and Margaret of Austria formed the core of the Austrian Habsburg diplomatic network in Spain during the reign of Philip III. When I began my research, I was interested in the diplomatic ties between the Spanish and Austrian Habsburgs in the period directly preceding the Thirty Years' War (1618–48). I sought to discover the importance of familial ties in the making of political decisions, particularly during a reign that was marked by financial strain.

In reading Spanish ambassadorial reports and the minutes of the Spanish Council of State meetings, I found that the influence of Empress María, Margaret of the Cross, and Margaret of Austria was scarcely recorded. Nevertheless, the Austrian Habsburgs regularly wrote to these women asking for their assistance in numerous issues. Imperial ambassadors noted that they had met with these women and discussed political matters with them. Court chroniclers and foreign ambassadors also recorded isolated attempts by all three women to influence political decisions. I therefore became intrigued about how these women might have influenced politics at the Spanish court, what issues concerned them, how they gained access to Philip III and to the Duke of Lerma, and what their actions might tell us about how women expressed a political voice in the early modern period. Moreover, an examination of the maneuvering of these three women could greatly broaden our understanding of how court politics and diplomatic networks functioned in early modern Europe. Thus, what began as a project on diplomatic relations evolved into a study of court politics and court intrigue during the reign of Philip III.

A common thread that ran through the lives of Empress María, Margaret of the Cross, and Margaret of Austria was their piety and their connection to religious institutions. It is, in fact, the religious aspect of the lives of Empress María and Margaret of the Cross in particular that has caused historians to discount their political influence. In the case of Margaret of Austria, historians have argued that her frequent pregnancies and young age limited her ability to affect court politics. As I researched the activities of these women at the Spanish court, I continued to ask myself if religious life and maternal responsibilities were obstacles to the political influence of these Habsburg women. It was clear that pious deeds were essential to the lives of all three women, central to their self-definition and central to the way biographers chose to portray them. However, far from isolating them from the male political world, piety brought these royal women attention and gave them a means to participate in political decision making at the Spanish court. Margaret of Austria's pregnancies gained her the affection and attention of Philip III and acted as a means for her to ensure that her husband stayed close to her. My research caused me continuously to rethink how historians have understood the avenues to political power and, specifically, what access women had to that power.

In conceiving of the political world of Philip III's court, I was greatly aided by conversations with numerous individuals. Mack Walker's offhand comment as we walked through the streets of Vienna, that the history of court politics could best be understood by looking at hairdressers, confessors, and mistresses, remained in the back of my mind as I developed this project. Orest Ranum's keen insight into the early modern court and his continued support of my interest in diplomatic history have aided me greatly. Barbara Harris's work on Tudor women and her informative comments about English court politics have also helped to shape my own ideas about how the Spanish court functioned. From the inception of this research project I have continuously benefited from Richard Kagan's thorough knowledge of Spanish history and Spanish archives and libraries. His encouragement, assistance, and friendship have made him an ideal mentor.

I would like to thank the archivists and staff at the archives and libraries in which I worked: the Archivo General de Simancas, the Biblioteca Nacional, the Archivo Histórico Nacional, the Archivo del Palacio Real, the Real Academia de la Historia, el Instituto Valencia de Don Juan, the Archivo and Biblioteca Zabálburu, the Archivo Histórico de Protocoles, the Haus-, Hof-, und Staatsarchiv, the Österreichische Nationalbibliothek, the British Library, the

Archives Générales du Royaume, the Archivio Segreto Vaticano, and the Archivios di Stato in Florence and Venice. I would also like to thank the nuns of the Real Monasterio de la Encarnación, who allowed me to look at their material on Sor Mariana de San José.

I have had the good fortune to work at three academic institutions that have supported and encouraged my research financially. I would like to acknowledge Gettysburg College, the University of North Carolina at Charlotte, and Texas Christian University for the generous faculty research grants they awarded me. I was able to take a semester's leave from teaching and devote myself exclusively to research and writing in Madrid because of a very generous fellowship from the Spanish Joint Committee for Cultural and Educational Cooperation. A grant from the International Telephone and Telegraph corporation (ITT) allowed me to conduct the initial research in Spain, Austria, and Italy, and fellowships from the Johns Hopkins University made it possible for me to extend my stays in Italy and in Vienna.

Some sections of chapters three and four appeared in an essay entitled "Pious and Political Images of a Habsburg Woman at the Court of Philip III (1598–1621)," in *Spanish Women in the Golden Age: Images and Realities*, ed. Magdalena S. Sánchez and Alain Saint-Saëns (Greenwood Press, an imprint of Greenwood Publishing Group, Inc., Westport, Connecticut: 1996), 91–107. Chapter eight was originally published in a modified fashion as "Melancholy and Female Illness: Habsburg Women and Politics at the Court of Philip III," in the *Journal of Women's History* 8, no. 2 (Summer 1996): 81–102. I would like to thank Greenwood Press and the *Journal of Women's History* for allowing me to use this material.

I would also like to thank Henry Tom, executive editor at the Johns Hopkins University Press. He took an interest in my project at an early stage and shepherded it through to completion. His comments and suggestions about the manuscript have helped to make this a stronger book. I am grateful to Sue Spittle for enhancing the floorplans of the Alcázar, to Margie Towery for preparing the index, and especially to Celestia Ward for copyediting the manuscript.

Completing this book would have been impossible without the support of numerous friends and colleagues in the United States, Spain, and Austria. In particular I would like to thank Bernardo José García García, whose own work on the Duke of Lerma and whose detailed knowledge of Philip III's reign have helped me enormously. His assistance has been, for me, the model of open, scholarly cooperation, and his friendship has made my trips to Madrid all the more enjoyable. I would also like to thank Jodi Bilinkoff, Robert Bireley, S.J., Fernando Bouza Álvarez, Friedrich Edelmayer, Antonio Feros, Gernot Heiß, Helen Nader, and Mary Elizabeth Perry.

During my extended trips to Madrid and Vienna, I enjoyed the hospitality of several friends. For their assistance in Madrid, I would like to thank the late Yvonne López von Wallenstein, Alain Saint-Saëns, and Anne McCall; in Vienna, I have Robert Brandstetter to thank for an ideal setting in which to think and write about these Habsburg women. I would also like to thank the extended Sánchez-Bowman clan for their indirect and direct support of my research, even when they had little understanding of what it was all about. In that clan I would especially like to express my gratitude to James Bowman, Nancy Bowman Holt, Carolina and Rosa Sánchez, Guillermo Sánchez Fornaris, and Carolina Parladé de Sánchez for assistance both abroad and in the United States, assistance that allowed me to concentrate on my research and gave me a break from the daily concerns of a house and a son.

This book would not have taken its current shape had it not been for the continued encouragement and support of William Bowman. Bill encouraged me to pursue my interest in the Habsburg women even when it meant beginning my research almost from scratch after completing my dissertation. He constantly urged me to write and gave up valuable research and writing time to allow me to work on this book. His assistance in the final preparation of this manuscript has been invaluable. Perhaps especially commendable was his willingness in numerous Viennese cafés and *Bierstuben* to put up with my never-ending conversations about court politics, when he would have preferred to take a break from academics and talk about soccer. Finally, a word about our son, Lucas. I have to say that this book has been written despite him. His birth postponed its completion and his activities for the past three and a half years have continuously thwarted my efforts to devote my mental and physical energies to the manuscript. In the end, however, Lucas has also put academics into proper perspective for me and has helped me to understand that life should take precedence over scholarly agendas. Perhaps, like the Habsburg women, I have learned that maternal duties translate into a lifetime of informal influence and responsibilities, a prospect that for me (but probably not for Empress María, Margaret of Austria, and Margaret of the Cross) is almost too frightening to contemplate.

Introduction

The king and queen, having returned from their wedding to Madrid, went to visit the empress, rekindling the duke's [Lerma's] jealousy, who feared that the warnings which the new queen would hear from the empress and her daughter, the infanta doña Margaret [of the Cross], would damage his position as royal favorite [*privanza*]. In particular, he very much disliked that the two cousins [Margaret of Austria and Margaret of the Cross] would speak to each other in German, and not being able to block this, he ensured that at the very least they saw each other the least possible, something which greatly bothered the empress because she understood that this would not end well for her grandson [Philip III].[1]

THIS COMMENTARY, written by Hans Khevenhüller, imperial ambassador to the Spanish court, epitomizes the rivalry that existed between the Duke of Lerma and the three Habsburg women who are at the heart of this study of Spain during the reign of Philip III (1598–1621). Khevenhüller understood that the Habsburg women and Lerma were mutually suspicious of one another. The situation had grown so bad that, by 1606, the papal nuncio in Madrid could report that there was "almost a civil war" at the Spanish court.[2] The conflict among all these individuals was grounded in the realization that access to Philip III was the principal means of exercising power at the Spanish court; thus Lerma sought to block the access of others to the monarch while the women tried to ensure that the avenues of communication remained open. Lerma also feared what occurred when the three women met together: they threatened to create an organized network of opposition to his power. Yet the Habsburg women felt that they had a duty to voice their concerns to the monarch because his own reputation and the future of the House of Austria were at stake. Together with Hans Khevenhüller, these three women positioned themselves as opponents to the Duke of Lerma and as the voice of the Austrian Habsburgs in Spain.

During the reign of Philip III the Austrian Habsburgs were strongly represented in Spain. Philip III married his second cousin, Margaret of Austria (1584–1611), who came from the Styrian branch of the Austrian Habsburg family. Two other Habsburg women, Empress María (1528–1603) and her daughter, Margaret of the Cross (1567–1633), resided in Madrid for all or part of Philip III's reign. Empress María was Charles V's daughter and Philip III's aunt; she was the widow of Emperor Maximilian II.[3] Margaret of the Cross, daughter of Empress María and Emperor Maximilian II, lived as a Franciscan nun in the convent of the Descalzas Reales for the whole of Philip III's reign. These three women served as the unofficial agents of the Austrian Habsburgs at the Spanish court and worked consistently to encourage Philip III to provide financial assistance to the Austrian Habsburgs. Yet the women's importance at the Spanish court has long been overlooked by historians, who have associated this period exclusively with the onset of Spanish political and economic decline.

Historians have tended to dismiss Philip III as a weak, dimwitted monarch who preferred hunting and traveling to governing and therefore turned over the reins of power to his royal favorite (*privado*), Don Francisco Gómez de Sandoval y Rojas, first Duke of Lerma. Philip III has fared much worse than his son, Philip IV, whose reputation has been rehabilitated by such historians as R. A. Stradling and John Elliott.[4] It is quite telling that, although Stradling dedicates himself to improving the image historians have of Philip IV, he insists on retaining and even emphasizing the negative impression of Philip III. Stradling has described Philip III as "that miserable monarch."[5] This negative view of Philip III's character and leadership qualities has also led historians to see the reign as that of the Duke of Lerma, who supposedly wielded such influence and power over Philip III that he virtually controlled all political dealings at the Spanish court. Thus, when examining Spanish policies during Philip III's reign, historians have tended to ascribe them to Lerma rather than to Philip III. In turn, Lerma is thought to have used his influence over the monarch to enrich himself and his family. He supposedly failed to make good use of the power with which Philip III invested him. Several historians have gone so far as to claim that this period was characterized not so much by poor government as by an "absence of government."[6]

The Duke of Lerma has so dominated the historiographical view of Philip III's court that all other individuals at that court have been considered and defined almost exclusively in relationship to Lerma. Thus, Empress María was important only in explaining why Lerma encouraged Philip III to transfer the Spanish court from Madrid to Valladolid in 1601; the transfer was part of Lerma's effort to limit the influence of Empress María upon Philip III.[7] Historians have noted that Queen Margaret of Austria was one of the Duke of Lerma's sharpest critics at the Spanish court; the queen encouraged Philip III to act independently of his royal favorite.[8] Yet the queen is often used as an example of how Lerma silenced and controlled any possible competitors for power. In this way, the reign of Philip III is the extended story of how Lerma alone wielded governmental authority. No one has examined the political voice of Empress María and Margaret of Austria or even analyzed the basis of our assumptions about their influence or their problems with the Duke of Lerma. Historians have virtually ignored the influence of Margaret of the Cross even though she served as one of the Austrian Habsburg's chief diplomatic representatives at the Spanish court until her death, in 1633. The case of Margaret of the Cross is particularly telling. Because she lived as a cloistered nun for her last forty-eight years, historians have assumed that she could not have influenced governmental policy at the Spanish court. She is remembered strictly as a pious nun.

If one looks to the end of Philip III's reign and particularly to the beginning of the Thirty Years' War, in 1618, one can see that Philip III decided to assist the Austrian Habsburgs financially and militarily in putting down the Bohemian revolt. This was a course of action which went along with the cause the Habsburg women had consistently represented at Philip III's court and which went against the policies of the Duke of Lerma. The standard interpretation of Philip III's actions in 1618 has been that it signaled Lerma's fall from royal favor as well as the growing influence of Baltasar de Zúñiga, who had formerly been the Spanish ambassador to the imperial court.[9] While this interpretation is certainly correct, it tells only a small part of the story. In fact, the events of 1618 were the culmination of a power struggle that had begun at the Spanish court as early as the beginning of Philip III's reign. Lerma's influence at that court was continuously challenged by numerous individuals, but primarily by Empress María, Margaret of Austria, Margaret of the Cross, and by individuals around these women. Many people competed for Philip III's attention, and there were signs that Lerma's influence over the monarch had begun to wane as early as 1608. Moreover, although Philip III was heavily influenced by the Duke of Lerma in the first years of his reign, he gradually developed his own ideas, and by 1612 he was relying far less than before on the recommendations of his privado.[10]

We know very little about the precise ways in which people exercised power over Philip III or over early modern monarchs in general. We certainly know little about the exact nature of Lerma's *privanza* (favor with the monarch).[11] Antonio Feros's work on the Duke of Lerma begins to address this issue. Feros explains the relationship between Lerma and the king in terms of early modern friendship. Lerma's influence with the monarch was grounded in the affection, reciprocal duties, and personal ties that came with such a friendship. Feros has also carefully analyzed Lerma's use of patronage to attempt to cement his control over court networks.[12] In a similar fashion, we need to have a better understanding of how the three Habsburg women exercised influence over Philip III. We need to view these women apart from the Duke of Lerma, as historical subjects who deserve to be examined in their own right. In order to do so, I consider the biographies and eulogies written about these three women, but I go far beyond the type of hagiographic, devotional images that biographers and eulogists presented to consider other, less flattering views that contemporaries had of them. In this way, I tackle what I consider to be the greatest obstacle to understanding the political roles these women played: that is, the constant, one-dimensional, simplified portrayal of these women as pious individuals for whom prayer was the only avenue for effecting political change.

Although historians have overlooked these Habsburg women (and Spanish royal women in general) and have argued that their role in politics was minimal, it was clear to their contemporaries that women had political roles. However, these political roles were thought to be subordinate to those of men; women were to express their political sentiments only when and if these sentiments were in the service of the traditional male hierarchy. For example, Philip III's queen, Margaret of Austria, could write her relatives in Central Europe to pressure them for specific demands that were favorable to the Spanish king and his government; in fact, this was the accepted function of the queen. However, councillors of state and government officials did not ask *her* opinion on these issues and worried when she in turn tried to use her influence at the Spanish court to help her Austrian Habsburg relatives. Moreover, in those cases in which the queen's intervention helped secure the Spanish monarchy's requests in Central Europe, the Spanish government never officially recognized the queen's crucial role in the negotiations, and in the diplomatic correspondence her role was scarcely, if ever, mentioned. Ministers expected the queen to use her familial connections to the advantage of the Spanish monarchy, but they did not accept that she had a political voice of her own.

Royal women did not calmly accept their proscribed political roles but instead found ways to voice their opinions in a fashion that was more acceptable to the male hierarchy. To break male-imposed political boundaries, women exploited religious patronage and familial concerns, areas in which men acknowledged and tolerated female power. Although royal women framed their requests in religious and familial terms, these requests frequently were political in nature. This was a conscious effort on the part of women to bypass the traditional governmental networks and to use the male notions of acceptable female behavior to their own and their relatives' advantage. It was also a conscious effort to have a role in political life, the life which affirmed men's social and personal worth but which was increasingly closed to women. Royal women, because of their lineage and upbringing, were political creatures. Their marriages were politically motivated, and they served in foreign countries as unofficial diplomatic representatives for their relatives. The moral tracts prepared for them by confessors and moralists did not cause royal women to accept subordination to men easily, especially when their lives and training had prepared them to fulfill important official functions.

This attitude was particularly true of Habsburg women, such as Margaret of Austria, Charles V's aunt, or María of Hungary, sister of Charles V, who historically served as regents or governesses of important territories.[13] Habsburg women such as Margaret of the Cross, who had less formal claims to governmental authority, still found indirect ways of exercising a political role. The continued political impact of Empress María, Margaret of the Cross, and Margaret of Austria exemplifies the manner in which female relatives of kings, emperors, and other rulers influenced policy despite male attempts to eliminate or at least circumscribe women's involvement in politics. Each of these women had very definite ways of reaching and influencing Philip III. They knew how to negotiate for the Austrian Habsburgs and how to gain the attention of Philip III and his court. In particular, the three women exploited the influence afforded them by familial connections, their reputations for piety, and even frequent illnesses.

In relying on their familial ties to gain them Philip III's ear, the Habsburg women employed techniques which were freely used by all members of the House of Austria. The Austrian Habsburgs generously sprinkled their letters to Philip III, Empress María, Margaret of the Cross, and Margaret of Austria with notes of familial affection and responsibilities. These references were designed to remind the recipient of the letter that membership in the House of Austria demanded that one place the dynasty above all else. Empress María, Margaret of the Cross, and Margaret of Austria recognized the efficacy of such arguments and knew that their familial connections to the monarch placed them above everyone else, including the Duke of Lerma.

Their reputations as devout women also gave these three great leverage with a monarch as pious as Philip III. Their piety attracted attention and served as a direct foil to the supposedly corrupt political and financial practices of the Spanish court. In a monarchy that made royal confessors councillors of state, piety could serve as a direct avenue to political power. While a reputation for piety was not exclusive to women, and especially not to Habsburg women, it served as a particularly fruitful way for these women to exercise influence. Religious devotion gained them the favor and sympathy of the Spanish populace, the respect of ambassadors and nuncios, and the continued affection and regard of their relatives. Ultimately, their spiritual practices (which were both private and public) lent greater weight to their petitions and their arguments.

The use of illness as a tool for political power was certainly not the exclusive domain of women, either. In fact, the Duke of Lerma consistently used melancholy as a means to escape the pressures of the court when he could no longer deal with criticism. Yet illness (and pregnancy) was often associated with women's frail bodies and was used as possible grounds to exclude them from any share in public power. By using complaints of illness to win Philip III's attention, the three Habsburg women inverted these arguments and employed the strong means available to them to maneuver politically at the Spanish court.

Ultimately, in considering the mechanisms used by all three women to exercise influence over Philip III, Empress María, Margaret of Austria, and Margaret of the Cross emerge as politically astute women. They were savvy about how to play the complicated game of court politics and about how best to pierce the strong armor with which Lerma attempted to shield his influence at the Spanish court. These women were far from the naive, incompetent players that some historians have imagined them to be. They knew the means used by men to negotiate policies or to circumvent the authority of possible rivals. They employed these and other methods in order to constitute a strong and effective network of opposition to the Duke of Lerma.

Historians have ignored the political influence of the three Habsburg women and have concentrated exclusively on the Duke of Lerma, in part because the sources for writing political history are too often limited to official reports of state councils, minutes of conciliar meetings, and diplomatic correspondence. Yet all of these records were generated by and for men, who constituted the official male hierarchy of the court. Thus, their reports did not consider unofficial influence on the making of policy, that is, the influence of royal confessors or family members, especially women.

Such influence does appear, however, in other historical documents: court chronicles, records of religious foundations, wills, and private correspondence. These documents refer to the influence that individuals exerted by pressuring the king or his ministers in an indirect or direct fashion. These documents often provide excellent information about women's use of patronage, a chief vehicle through which elite women exerted control in the early modern period.[14] While governmental bodies generated reports designed to affirm that decision making was in the hands of a select group of men and that the process functioned through rational governmental organs, observers noted that negotiations often took place in such unlikely places as cloistered convents, gardens of summer homes, and at royal lunches. The imperial ambassador Hans Khevenhüller recorded that he negotiated issues with Philip III in the cloistered royal convent of the Descalzas Reales in Madrid.[15] Diego de Guzmán, Philip III's royal almoner, reported that after having lunch with the king at the Duke of Lerma's house, they discussed state matters. Guzmán also noted that the king habitually gave audiences after the midday meal he often ate at the Duke of Lerma's house, which was situated in front of the Descalzas Reales convent.[16]

Political decision making was not, therefore, solely the domain of councillors of state; the organized minutes of the meetings of the Council of State, with the detailed opinions of specific councillors, often hide the complicated negotiating process that took place long before the king met with his councillors. Our evaluation of the formation of political policy in the early modern period, and of the manner in which early modern diplomacy functioned, must begin to take these informal influences into consideration. When one examines the informal negotiations, a wider picture of the Spanish court emerges, complete with complex diplomatic networks in which royal women figured prominently. This broader picture of court politics and diplomatic networks provides a way of studying the political influence of royal women in early modern Spain.

My study of the way the three Habsburg women exercised authority at Philip III's court also illustrates how early modern diplomacy worked. Although so-called modern diplomacy, with its resident diplomats and regular diplomatic reports, began in Italy during the Renaissance, the official ambassador continued to function through established private (and often familial) networks.[17] In some cases, these networks were much more important for gathering information and exercising power than was the diplomat himself. Therefore, ambassadors were valued according to their skills in establishing intricate informational links at a court.[18] The Austrian Habsburgs were often reluctant to establish formal diplomatic ties with other rulers. Instead, they relied heavily on informal diplomatic networks primarily revolving around relatives, many of whom were women. The principal representative of the Austrian Habsburgs in the early modern period always held the title of Holy Roman Emperor, a title that, in Europe, was second only to that of the pope. For this reason, the emperors often believed themselves to be above sending diplomatic representatives to European courts where kings ruled.[19] In the complicated game of diplomatic precedence, the imperial ambassadors claimed superiority over all other diplomats except papal nuncios. Rather than admit that their representatives would not always receive preferential treatment, Habsburg emperors merely refrained from appointing regular ambassadors to other countries. This tendency reinforced the creation of informal diplomatic networks, principally centered on royal women, to negotiate matters for the Austrian Habsburgs.

Moreover, the early modern Austrian Habsburg political system was a model of a decentralized, politically disorganized state. Each of the Austrian Habsburg archdukes had a separate court with its own diplomatic representatives. In the early seventeenth century, for example, Emperor Rudolf II was based in Prague, Archduke Matthias in Vienna, Archduke Ferdinand in Graz, and Archduke Maximilian in Innsbruck. The Austrian Habsburgs, at least in the late sixteenth and early seventeenth centuries, failed to agree on one diplomatic corps to represent all of their diverse interests. This is not surprising given the degree of hostility between several of the Austrian Habsburgs, especially Emperor Rudolf II and his successor, Archduke Matthias.[20] The one constant in the diplomatic practice of all the Austrian Habsburg archdukes was their reliance upon relatives to negotiate matters informally for them.

With the Spanish monarchy, the Austrian Habsburgs had the additional problem of deciding whether territories ruled by relatives should negotiate with each other as foreign countries. The Austrian Habsburgs demanded preferential treatment from the Spanish monarch. They cited the Spanish monarch's familial, political, and economic interests in the maintenance of the Habsburg dynasty. Establishing an intricate, expensive diplomatic network in the Spanish kingdoms implied that familial connections were not as strong as they should be. Moreover, the Austrian Habsburgs could and did rely on their relatives in Spain to negotiate with the Spanish monarch and his ministers. It was advantageous to work through family members because they were technically able to bypass official diplomatic channels and could also reach the monarch in private moments. So the Austrian Habsburg diplomatic network at the Spanish court, both by design and by default, functioned primarily through relatives, most of whom were women.

The focus of this network exemplifies the intersection and overlapping of familial and political concerns in the early modern period. While the Habsburg women in Madrid argued that by speaking for the Austrian Habsburgs they were merely protecting the needs of family and religion, in fact they were speaking about "political" subjects that affected the financial and economic concerns of the Spanish state. Their continual pressure for Spanish financial assistance to the Austrian Habsburgs in Central Europe and Flanders ignored the Spanish monarchy's limited financial resources and went against the plans of the Duke of Lerma and some councillors of state to concentrate these resources on the Iberian peninsula. While Lerma sought to focus the monarchy's attention on the Mediterranean and to bring about a rapprochement with France, the Habsburg women and their supporters at the Spanish court wanted cooperation with the Austrian Habsburgs in Central Europe.[21] Hence the demands of the Habsburg women often met with the disapproval of the Duke of Lerma and of councillors of state.

The particular requests made by these women and the arguments they used in making these requests also allow us to examine the degree to which women manipulated the accepted feminine spheres of family and religion to mask—and even justify—entrance into difficult political debates and to affect the outcome of those debates. Their actions and petitions also lead us to consider whether these women followed an agenda set for them by their male relatives or whether they fashioned their strategies to suit their own specific needs and preferences. Ultimately, the stories of Empress María, Margaret of Austria, and Margaret of the Cross show women as strong and deft political players who could effectively pursue goals in the interest of their family but who could also pursue independent political and personal objectives. Women, especially royal women, were at the center of the early modern European political world.

1

Expanding the Spanish Court
Private Homes and Public Spaces

ACCESS TO PHILIP III was a mark of privilege. The Spanish king, like other Spanish monarchs before and after him, was a private individual who jealously guarded his solitude.[1] He did not mix openly with other people, and even on those occasions when he went out in public, elaborate rituals separated him from contact with many other individuals. Those who were able to reach the monarch could claim his attention and influence his decisions. Philip III's daily routine included a wide variety of religious events—daily mass, visits to convents and churches, participation in religious processions—as well as private midday meals, afternoon audiences, meetings of the Council of State, visits to private homes, and regular hunting trips. The monarch's daily activities, therefore, took him out of the royal apartments in the palace and into convents, churches, and private homes. Philip III's routine also brought him into regular contact with his female relatives: Margaret of Austria accompanied him on his visits to convents and churches; Empress María visited with him in private homes and the monarch's palaces outside Madrid; and both the empress and Margaret of the Cross met with him in the Descalzas convent.

This extended world in which Philip III, his relatives, his councillors, and foreign ambassadors moved constituted his royal court. Historians who have studied the Spanish court have concentrated in general on the royal palace, the king, and his immediate entourage. There has been no in-depth account of exactly what constituted the Spanish Habsburg court—that is, its physical layout and its patronage networks. A large, dynamic court with numerous dependent individuals who relied on royal patronage and support began to develop during Philip III's reign, despite the monarch's personal desire for privacy.[2] Yet, Philip III's physical court—the place where he lived, made political decisions, and met with councillors and attendants—was not a clearly defined and delineated space.[3] The king regularly went from his royal apartments in Madrid to the convent of the Descalzas Reales, to numerous churches and convents in Madrid, to the Escorial, and to hunting lodges and palaces such as El Pardo outside Madrid. He frequently went to the homes of individuals such as his *privado* (favorite), the Duke of Lerma, and Juan de Borja, *mayordomo mayor* (Lord High Steward) of Empress María, uncle to the Duke of Lerma, and member of the Councils of Portugal and Finance (*hazienda*).[4]

The fluid nature of Philip III's court allowed for informal contact between the monarch and private individuals, in particular his female relatives, who, while they might not have been able to enter the meeting rooms of the state councils, could easily enter the private homes, gardens, and convents frequented by the monarch.[5] It was a relatively common practice for Empress María to leave the Descalzas to meet with Philip III and Margaret of Austria, for example.[6] This contact provided prime opportunities for his female relatives (and for individuals other than councillors of state) to influence the monarch.

In order to study the world in which Philip III and his closest advisers moved and in which decisions concerning the Spanish kingdoms were made, one has to look beyond the royal palace to include those convents and private homes that the monarch visited.[7] The royal palace in Madrid had covered passageways (*pasadizos*) to many of the adjoining buildings, such as the royal convent of the Encarnación and the church of San Gil, so these buildings could be considered physical extensions of the palace.[8] It is essential, therefore, to reconstruct the world in which the monarch moved and develop a picture of an expanded early modern Spanish court.

Politics, family, and religious devotion intersected at the court of Philip III. The Spanish monarch, known in his day for his piety, combined his political duties with confession, private communion, and attendance at religious services at a variety of convents and churches.[9] When performing these religious acts, the monarch was usually accompanied by his wife, Margaret of Austria, who followed an equally strenuous schedule of devotional practices.[10] The king and queen had a daily routine from which they rarely departed. In the mornings, they would attend private mass, usually individually in their own private chapels (*oratorios*). On some mornings, the monarchs attended early mass together in the queen's oratory. For example, during June and July 1609, Philip and Margaret heard morning mass together frequently. Joint attendance at the same morning mass during these months may have corresponded to the Duke of Lerma's absence from the royal palace; for this reason the king had even greater freedom to spend time with the queen.[11] The royal confessors normally said this early mass, although on occasion the royal almoner would substitute for the confessors.[12] Afterwards, the king and queen left the palace to attend mass elsewhere in a more public fashion. Although they usually attended their second mass at the same convent, they went separately, each attended by his or her own servants.

Philip III often attended this second mass at one of many cloistered convents located in Madrid, usually the royal convent of the Descalzas, where his grandmother, Empress María, and his aunt, Margaret of the Cross, lived. The queen also went to the Descalzas Reales to attend her second mass; she had papal dispensation to enter the cloistered section of convents, and one of her most frequent activities was to pray and speak with nuns in cloistered convents.[13] The Descalzas Reales was her preferred convent in Madrid until 1610, when she began the arrangements to found a new convent (the Encarnación) in the city.[14]

When the monarchs were not in Madrid (as happened from 1601 until 1606, when the court moved to Valladolid, and on the many occasions when Philip and Margaret went to their palaces at Aranjuez or El Pardo), they attended mass at a cloistered convent in the area.[15] The monarchs almost always entered a female convent for religious observances. Even for public religious festivities—such as the processions of the Virgin of Atocha or Corpus Christi—the monarchs went to convents. Thus, they both had almost daily contact with nuns.

Philip III has often been dismissed as merely a pious king uninterested in political events. Perhaps for this reason, historians have in large part failed to analyze his religious observances. Yet religious acts had definite political significance. These acts or rituals were inherently expressions of power relationships.[16] In a world in which the chief activity of the monarchs was to engage in religious rituals, a principal mark of royal favor was the privilege of accompanying the monarchs during these rituals or, if one were a nun, of having the monarchs visit one's convent. Moreover, one of the principal ways to reach the

monarch and influence his opinion or political decision was through participation in these pious activities.

The Duke of Lerma knew how to use religious occasions to enhance his
prestige as well. In 1610, on the feast of Christ's Incarnation, a procession began
in Madrid at the royal monastery of Santa Isabel and ended at the Descalzas
(the two convents the monarchs preferred). The queen, who was the major
sponsor for the procession and was in the process of founding a convent dedicated to the Incarnation, watched the procession from a window in the Duke
of Lerma's house, which was opposite the Descalzas monastery.[17] Lerma calculated that his honor and prestige would be enhanced when most of Madrid
saw the queen at his window. The event also highlighted the favored status of
the convents of Santa Isabel and the Descalzas. It was a mark of royal preference that the procession began and ended at these two convents, so this royal
favor enhanced the reputation of the women in them. This was the case every
time that the king and queen visited one of the convents. Their visits were public in the sense that the monarchs ostentatiously left the royal apartments and
entered a specific convent or church. Philip's and Margaret's regular visits to
the convents of the Descalzas and Santa Isabel brought continued prestige and
recognition to the nuns there. The regular visits also provided the opportunity
for nuns of both convents to present their needs and petitions to the king and
queen.

Philip III and Margaret of Austria rarely visited convents on their own.
Courtiers regularly accompanied the monarchs to important religious celebrations, and their rank was evidenced by their physical proximity to the king and
queen and by the role they played in the elaborate rituals. Philip III's mayordomo mayor, the Duke of Infantado, the papal nuncio, and the Venetian ambassador usually accompanied the king every morning for his second mass.[18]
They would leave the royal palace publicly with Philip and would sit with him
during the mass. These were clear signs of preference as well as opportunities
for these individuals to converse with the monarch. Councillors and ambassadors greatly valued these occasions because Philip III did not give audiences
easily.

Royal favor was also evident through active participation in the king's religious ceremonies. On Holy Thursday (the Thursday preceding Easter Sunday,
during which the king reenacted Christ's washing of the feet by washing the
feet of thirteen poor subjects) the king selected three individuals to help him in

the ceremony. These three assistants were singled out in part because of their religious office and also because of the trust the king placed in them. Philip III chose the papal nuncio, the royal almoner, and the Duke of Lerma to play major roles in this religious service.[19] During the ritualistic washing of the feet, the Duke of Lerma held the basin to catch the water that the nuncio poured over the individuals' feet. Philip III washed the feet with towels, which the royal almoner handed him. These acts were performed publicly in a church. Onlookers clearly interpreted the participation of the nuncio, the royal almoner, and the Duke of Lerma as signs of royal preference.

Because Philip III regularly went to the Descalzas convent, it was crucial for those who wanted to have access to the monarch to accompany him on these visits. For this reason, the Duke of Lerma sometimes visited the Descalzas convent with Philip III. The monarch's privado often participated in the processions and other religious celebrations that took place in the convent, but he did not usually accompany the monarch on his daily visits to the Descalzas. Within the convent, Philip III and Margaret of Austria almost always encountered the imperial ambassador, Hans Khevenhüller, who visited Empress María daily and acted as her private attendant.[20] They also saw Juan de Borja, Empress María's mayordomo mayor. These were choice opportunities for Khevenhüller and Borja to speak with the king about pressing matters. In fact, Hans Khevenhüller noted that he often discussed political affairs with Philip III when the monarch visited the Descalzas monastery.[21] These were also occasions for the monarchs to interact with Empress María and Margaret of the Cross. Philip III often used these opportunities to visit his grandmother and his aunt and have private conversations with them.[22] The queen also visited with Empress María and Margaret of the Cross on her daily outings to the Descalzas; she, unlike Philip III, was able to enter the cloistered section of the convent and communicate with all the nuns. Her visits alone with the other two Habsburg women tended to be more frequent and of longer duration than those in which she was accompanied by Philip III.[23]

Lerma was aware of the power that Philip III's relatives could exercise in these private moments. When the privado was trying to convince Philip to leave Madrid for an extended period, he thought that the empress might try to dissuade the monarch from leaving. For this reason, Lerma was anxious when the monarchs went to the Descalzas to celebrate the feast of the Purification with Empress María. On this occasion, Lerma approached Philip III as the monarch descended from his coach at the Descalzas convent and urged him to remain resolved to leave Madrid despite what the empress might say to him.[24] In this case, Lerma was successful in influencing Philip III, and Juan Carrillo, Empress María's secretary, was correct in using this incident to show the power of Lerma's *privanza*. However, this incident also clearly demonstrates Lerma's recognition of how Philip III's female relatives could influence him during private moments together.[25]

The pious activities of the monarch, his affinity for his female relatives, and the fluidity of Philip III's court gave special advantages to religious figures and allowed them opportunities to affect political decisions. Our understanding of the Spanish court would be incomplete without taking into account various individuals whose religious function gave them access to and influence with the king and queen. This was certainly true of the royal almoner, who was a key figure in this world of religious symbolism. He attended the king and queen at their private chapels in the mornings. While Philip III was at his chapel, the royal almoner was the only person allowed to speak to him.[26] The royal almoner was appointed by the king to dispense alms, but he was always in attendance at the court and had close contact with the king, the queen, and the councillors of state. The Spanish kings often appointed their almoner to the Council of State: García de Loaysa Girón, royal almoner under Philip II, was a councillor of state from 1598 until his death in 1599. Diego de Guzmán, Philip III's royal almoner from 1608 until 1621, also attended Council of State meetings,[27] and he was present at many of the audiences given by Philip III after the midday meal.[28] Royal almoners often served as tutors to the royal children; García de Loaysa Girón was Philip III's tutor while he was still prince, and Diego de Guzmán tutored the Infanta Anne, Philip III and Margaret of Austria's eldest child.[29] The royal almoner therefore had direct influence over the upbringing of the royal children.

Diego de Guzmán exercised an important say in Philip's court and had contact with the queen long before he was appointed royal almoner in December 1608. Through Empress María's intercession with Philip III, Guzmán had been appointed chaplain of the Descalzas Reales in 1602.[30] As chaplain of the Descalzas, Guzmán met daily with Empress María and the nuns of the convent, including the empress's daughter, Margaret of the Cross. Moreover, as chaplain, he was responsible for saying the daily masses at the convent, the same masses that Philip III and Margaret of Austria attended regularly, and he presided over any religious ceremonies the monarchs attended at the convent. Although he was appointed royal almoner in 1608, Guzmán continued to serve as royal chaplain of the Descalzas until April 1609.[31]

Guzmán undoubtedly served as a conduit for information and requests from the Descalzas to the royal palace, and vice versa. His close association with the monastery—even after 1609 he continued to celebrate masses and plan religious festivities at the convent—ensured that the needs of the cloistered nuns of the Descalzas would receive royal attention. Guzmán was also closely associated with the queen and was often present at audiences she gave.[32] He worked with her in the reformation of the royal convent of Santa Isabel and in the foundation of the Encarnación convent.[33] Together they arranged for Mariana de San José, a nun whom the queen had befriended in Palencia, to become the prioress of both these monasteries. As royal almoner, Guzmán consulted with the queen when she wanted to dispense alms. He thereby oversaw the queen's charitable deeds and was privy to her secret expenses. In his biography of the queen, Guzmán wrote that he had knowledge of her secret charitable acts and donations.[34] His appointment as tutor to the Infanta Anne only increased his contact with the queen because the infanta's rooms were adjacent to those of the queen and their households overlapped. In his memoirs, Guzmán recorded visiting Margaret of Austria in her oratorio almost every morning.

Guzmán served as the queen's connection with the Descalzas monastery, as one of the queen's direct contacts to Philip III, and as an instrumental link in her network of individuals at the Spanish court. The rituals surrounding Philip's daily religious devotions gave the royal almoner regular access to the monarch, access that Guzmán used to press for an agenda corresponding to Margaret of Austria's interests. Diego de Guzmán cooperated in this task with the queen's Jesuit confessor, Richard Haller. Guzmán, also a Jesuit, often met Richard Haller in the society's residence in Madrid. For example, after having been appointed tutor to the Infanta Anne, an office he apparently did not desire, Guzmán went to the Jesuit residence and discussed the matter with Richard Haller.[35] As the queen's personal confessor, Haller had intimate knowledge of her thoughts and actions. Haller undoubtedly shared some of this knowledge with Guzmán, and in turn, the royal almoner informed Haller of political negotiations that could affect the Austrian Habsburgs. Guzmán's case illustrates how religious office could provide an avenue to access and information, key ways to gain leverage at the court.

The king's piety and devotional practices ensured that the royal confessors would gain influence at the Spanish court. Philip III's confessors, like those of other European monarchs, had no clearly defined position at the court;[36] nevertheless, they often found official political roles there. Three of Philip III's confessors were members of the Council of State and were free to comment on political actions. Confessors received this governmental appointment because of Philip's high regard for their advice, because of the monarch's piety, and because of the individual confessor's personal influence over the king. However, appointment as confessor did not necessarily bring appointment as councillor of state. For example, Diego de Mardones, Philip III's confessor from 1604 to 1606, was never appointed councillor of state, probably because of his disagreements with the Duke of Lerma.[37] Luis de Aliaga became Philip III's confessor in 1608 but had to wait until 1611 to become a councillor of state. This latter appointment also demonstrated the Duke of Lerma's waning power. A strong rivalry had developed between Lerma and Aliaga, and Lerma was able to prevent Aliaga from joining the Council of State until 1611. The queen's death that year and the subsequent implication of Lerma's close associate, Rodrigo Calderón, in Margaret's death, caused Philip to begin relying less on his favorite's advice.

The political role played by royal confessors in Spain was in keeping with the religious nature of Spanish kingship. Spanish kings valued their title, given to them by the pope, of "defender of the faith," and this faith dictated that their political decisions be in accordance with divine law. Spanish kings traditionally sought the advice not only of secular councillors but also of theologians.[38] Charles V consulted with theologians about the rights of the New World inhabitants;[39] Philip II asked for the advice of theologians on his religious policy in the Netherlands;[40] and Philip III asked Cardinal Gabriel Trejo y Paniagua to comment on the monarch's supposed rights to the Bohemian and Hungarian thrones.[41] On a daily basis, Spanish monarchs relied on the advice of their confessors: as Jacobo Sobieski, a Polish prince who visited the Spanish court in 1611, remarked, "the confessors of the kings of Spain enjoy the highest authority."[42]

Once given political influence, the confessors' office allowed for myriad opportunities to voice their opinions on policy formation. Spanish kings met daily with their confessors and made their confession about once a week. Confession provided the perfect opportunity for royal confessors to voice opinions under the guise of moral guidance and divine plans. Given the personal piety of Philip III, it is no wonder that his confessors exercised important sway at his court. The Venetian ambassador Ottaviano Bon reported that the power of Gaspar de Córdoba, Philip III's confessor from 1598 to 1604, was second only to that of the Duke of Lerma. Bon commented that while the Duke of Lerma monopolized Philip III's affection, Gaspar de Córdoba controlled the monarch's conscience. Bon also noted that Córdoba was highly respected for having the king's ear whenever he wished, for being close to the Duke of Lerma, and for taking part in the informal negotiations of *juntas* (ad-hoc committees).[43]

Not all observers favored the powerful voice of royal confessors. In 1609, Juan de Ribera, Archbishop of Valencia, wrote to Philip III concerning the duties of royal confessors. Ribera advised the monarch to limit the power of his confessor by appointing two theologians to assist the confessor when he needed to give important moral advice to Philip III. As Ribera argued: "One can only marvel that for all the governmental ministries and the royal house, there are so many major and minor ministers and yet for the ministry of the royal conscience—the most worthy and important—there is only one minister."[44] Ribera recommended that the royal confessor and the two theologians be prohibited from holding any other office so that they could exercise their duties in a disinterested and objective fashion. These individuals, in Ribera's opinion, should never take part in juntas or become councillors of state because such offices would distract them from their principal duty, which was to advise the monarch in important ethical issues. Ribera undoubtedly thought that Philip III's royal confessor at the time, Luis de Aliaga, was too involved in political negotiations, and he believed that Aliaga pursued his own advancement at Philip's expense. Yet Ribera's advice clearly shows that some individuals worried about a royal confessor's power and recognized that the confessor's religious and moral duties often spilled over into political and economic issues, to the possible detriment of the monarch and the Spanish kingdoms.

Spanish royal confessors, who were always members of the Dominican order, often served as the king's messenger and the direct connection between king and councillors. They also often functioned as primary links between ministers and women at court. This was certainly the case with Gaspar de Córdoba, who regularly commented on policy (his opinions are recorded in the minutes of the meetings of the Council of State). Córdoba carried difficult messages from the king to individuals at the court. In December 1599, Gaspar de Córdoba informed the Duchess of Gandía, the queen's chief lady-in-waiting, that she was to leave the court.[45] Córdoba also had the unpleasant task of telling Empress María that the court had been transferred from Madrid to Valladolid.[46] In addition, the royal confessor's tasks often entailed advice about and involvement in the financial matters of the Spanish kingdoms. In 1600, for example, Gaspar de Córdoba intervened in the Council of Finance for Juan de Borja.[47] Luis de Aliaga, royal confessor from 1608 to 1621, played an enormous role within the Spanish government. He was widely criticized for using his religious office to gain greater access to the monarch and influence Philip III's political decisions. Aliaga allied himself with the Duke of Uceda, son of the Duke of Lerma, and together they helped bring Lerma's *privanza* to an end.[48]

The dual role of confessors such as Gaspar de Córdoba and Luis de Aliaga exemplifies the convergence of political and religious issues at the court of Philip III. As the king's confessors, they had access to his private thoughts; as councillors of state, they remained informed of the key political, military, and economic issues and were free to comment in the public forum of the Council of State meetings. Certainly these confessors often merged their dual roles and discussed political issues privately with the king. They therefore constituted potential threats to individuals such as the Duke of Lerma. Gaspar de Córdoba remained on amicable terms with Lerma until 1603, when the confessor criticized Lerma's policy regarding the arrest of the Infanta Anne's governess, the Marquesa del Valle. Córdoba then found himself suddenly out of favor with the royal favorite, and the confessor's subsequent death in 1604 was attributed by some to his fall from grace with Philip's *privado*. Jacobo Sobieski was probably referring to Gaspar de Córdoba when he wrote that the Duke of Lerma had one of Philip III's confessors drowned because he dared to speak privately with the king about political matters.[49]

Lerma clearly recognized the power royal confessors held. While Philip III searched for Gaspar de Córdoba's replacement, the Duke of Lerma arranged for his own confessor, Diego de Mardones, to become Philip III's interim confessor.[50] Mardones was subsequently appointed the monarch's official confessor, a post he held until 1606. Lerma believed that by having Mardones named Philip III's confessor, the priest would be grateful to him, and, therefore, dependent upon him. Lerma hoped both to circumvent the tremendous personal power of the royal confessor as well as to use the office to his own advantage. Yet Mardones did not prove to be the pliant and docile person that Lerma expected; instead he used his position to bring his own influence to bear on Philip III.[51] The privado and the confessor were often at odds, and, probably for this reason, Mardones failed to become a councillor of state. In 1606, when Mardones spoke out against Lerma's closest associate at the Spanish court, Rodrigo Calderón, Lerma arranged for the former to be named bishop of Córdoba and thus leave the court.[52] Lerma, however, did not learn from his mistake with Mardones. In 1608, at the death of Philip's third confessor, Jerónimo Javierre, Lerma once again engineered a plan for his personal confessor, Luis de Aliaga, to become the king's confessor. Aliaga quickly used his role as confessor to discuss political matters with the monarch, and especially to challenge the Duke of Lerma's authority.

The queen's confessor, Richard Haller, played a lesser role at the Spanish court than did Philip's confessors. Unlike the king's confessor, Haller had no official political role at the court; he certainly did not occupy a seat in the Council of State. Nevertheless, the association between Margaret of Austria and Richard Haller clearly shows the extent to which spiritual guidance could readily be translated into political advice.[53] Confessors such as Haller often acted as negotiators for and representatives of the queen in the male political world. Men at the court attempted to limit female action to domestic and religious realms; in order to use these realms to further their political ends, women consciously worked through confessors to voice their political concerns.

Far from acting independently at the Spanish court, Haller served as Margaret of Austria's representative and worked for the queen; she certainly did not work for him. The confessor was responsible for saying daily mass within the queen's chamber and for listening to her confession.[54] Although Haller's position was strictly defined as a spiritual office, as the queen's confessor he had daily, private access to Margaret of Austria, access that allowed her to discuss political matters with him and to work with him to further the interests of the Austrian Habsburgs. In this way, Haller's office paralleled that of the king's confessor, who, as we have seen, also had frequent access to Philip III.

According to tradition, Spanish queens' confessors were supposed to be Franciscans. For this reason, Mateo de Burgos, head of the Franciscan order, was appointed Margaret of Austria's confessor in 1598.[55] The queen, however, followed the Austrian Habsburg tradition of having a Jesuit confessor. Haller, a Jesuit, accompanied her from Graz to Madrid.[56] Once Margaret of Austria arrived in Spain, Lerma attempted to substitute Mateo de Burgos and have

Haller return to Central Europe. The queen refused to give up her Jesuit confessor and successfully pleaded with Philip III to allow her to retain Haller, arguing, among other things, that her Castilian was not good enough for her to communicate with a Spanish confessor.[57] Despite Lerma's disapproval, Philip III acquiesced to his wife's wishes and Richard Haller remained Margaret's confessor and confidant until her death, in 1611. Mateo de Burgos was instead named Bishop of Pamplona.[58] This victory is strong evidence of the young queen's determination and her influence with Philip III, especially because the Duke of Lerma and Richard Haller remained at odds until Haller's death, in 1612.

Haller's influence with the queen and his criticism of Lerma's policies caused much friction between him and the king's privado. Lerma tried to limit Haller's contact with the king, but through the queen Haller had indirect access to Philip III. In this way, Haller served as an Austrian Habsburg spokesman at the Spanish court. He regularly wrote and reported political events to the Austrian Habsburgs, particularly to Archduke Ferdinand, the queen's brother. He also pleaded the case for the Austrian Habsburgs to ministers and councillors. The Council of State minutes record that Haller brought particular concerns to the council—especially that of giving aid to Archduke Ferdinand against the Venetians and Turks.[59] Haller also delivered messages from the queen's brother Archduke Leopold to Philip III and Spanish councillors of state; for example, he reported Leopold's desire to succeed Rudolf II as emperor.[60] Haller frequently represented the interests of the Bavarian Wittelsbach family as well at the Spanish court. The relative success of Austrian Habsburg demands in Spain from 1598 to 1612 was in large part dependent upon the careful maneuverings of the queen and Richard Haller (who may be considered the male voice of Margaret of Austria) in conjunction with Empress María, Margaret of the Cross, and Hans Khevenhüller.

Along with the king's and queen's confessors, royal preachers also exercised a significant voice in Madrid and were, therefore, members of an expanded Spanish court. They, too, had important connections to the three Habsburg women. The preachers at Philip III's court were prominent figures in court politics and regularly gave sermons at private masses, major religious celebrations, and public events. Philip III employed at least eight royal preachers at one time. These preachers came from various religious orders (Dominican, Franciscan, or Jesuit) and in general were expected to deliver sermons with the proper

rhetorical content and clarity.[61] They were not free to express political sentiments openly, but their interest in politics and criticism of court figures were
well known. Preachers used their positions at the court to convey messages to
the king and queen about proper political policy. They had the freedom to comment on religious matters and could insert subtle political messages into their
sermons.[62] In this way, sermons on the feast of the Immaculate Conception
could become sermons on a king's duty to his people. Funeral sermons were
particularly appropriate occasions for commenting on court behavior and the
duties of kings, queens, and royal advisers.[63]

Principal among these preachers at Philip III's court was Jerónimo de Florencia, a Jesuit priest who won much favor with the queen and who was critical of the Duke of Lerma's influence at the court.[64] Florencia delivered the
funeral orations at the deaths of Empress María, Margaret of Austria, the Count
of Lemos, the Duke of Monteleon, and Philip III. He was one of Margaret of
Austria's favorite preachers; Diego de Guzmán regularly noted that Florencia
often gave sermons at the queen's masses.[65] Florencia's sermons at the queen's
death, particularly the one dedicated to the Duke of Lerma, show that he was
critical of the duke and saw the queen as a chief proponent of an anti-Lerma
court policy.[66] Florencia's sermons ultimately had a strong impact on Philip III.
In 1618, the king claimed that one of Florencia's sermons had inspired him to
dismiss the Duke of Lerma.[67] With the accession to the throne of Philip IV,
Jerónimo de Florencia maintained his court position (unlike other ministers,
such as Luis de Aliaga and Fernando de Borja, who were both expelled from
the court). Florencia continued to use sermons to reach the monarch. Shortly
after Philip IV assumed the throne, Florencia preached a sermon praising the
monarch for the effective manner in which the kingdoms were being governed,
praise that reflected well on the Count of Olivares. After hearing Florencia's
sermon, the monarch named the Count of Olivares a grandee. During Philip
IV's reign, Florencia served as confessor to the monarch's brothers and was appointed a member of the ten-man junta Philip IV had created to "restore moral-
ity to Castile."[68] Considering all these instances, it is clear Jerónimo de
Florencia's influence was profound in early modern Spain.

The monarchs' devotional habits also provided opportunities for nuns to exercise a political voice. This was particularly true of Mariana de San José, an Augustinian nun whom the monarchs met in Palencia. The queen was so
impressed by her that she decided to ask the nun to go to Madrid when the

court returned there in 1606. The queen had in mind the foundation of a royal convent in honor of the Incarnation. She also thought to reform the royal convent of Santa Isabel in Madrid and put it under the direct control of the royal almoner. In particular, the queen wanted the nuns of Santa Isabel to live more restricted lives, lives that were more in keeping with the reforms instituted in convents by such individuals as Teresa of Ávila.[69] Mariana de San José arrived at the court in Madrid in January 1611, and from that time until the queen's death, in October 1611, the queen had direct contact with her. After Margaret's death, Philip III continued to visit Mariana de San José and ask her opinion on both political and spiritual matters.

Philip III's friendship with and trust in religious figures such as royal almoners, confessors, preachers, and nuns caused observers to criticize his judgment. In particular, Philip III's secretary and court chronicler, Matías de Novoa, condemned the influence that priests and nuns had over Philip III, an influence he believed ultimately led to Lerma's and Rodrigo Calderón's loss of favor with Philip III. As Novoa wrote in his chronicle of Philip III's reign:

> Finally, they [priests and nuns] told her [the queen] that the king, liberal and generous as he was, gave [Calderón and others] too many gifts and they [Philip III and Margaret of Austria] had many children and it was necessary to curb them [these gifts] and to set some aside for them [their children]; that they [Calderón and others] should not be given such a big role in governing, because that would be going beyond royal generosity and converting lord to servant. . . . The queen, because she had a wonderful disposition and was so docile of character, accepted this rationale because she said that they [priests and nuns] counseled her with truly religious zeal. . . . She spoke with the king about what religious individuals had convinced her and because she truly loved him above all else . . . she wanted the king's will to follow only hers.[70]

Novoa in fact blamed Margaret of Austria for Philip III's reliance on religious individuals. Although he refrained from verbally attacking the queen and implied that she was acting out of good will, he depicted her as a credulous woman who was blind to the devious deeds of nuns and priests. Novoa also condemned Margaret's influence over Philip III, an influence that, in Novoa's estimation, lasted long after the queen's death, in 1611. Novoa ultimately believed that Philip III's trust in religious individuals during the later years of his reign was Margaret of Austria's legacy. Novoa was undoubtedly also reacting to Philip III's trust in Fray Juan de Santa María, confessor to the Infanta Doña María and author of the political treatise *Tratado de República y Policía Christiana*, which criticized the power and influence of privados. Novoa ascribed the fall of Lerma's close associate, Rodrigo Calderón, to Santa María and Mariana de San José's hold over the king.

Individuals around Philip III clearly recognized the monarch's piety and witnessed his frequent attendance at religious events. They believed that the king's devotional practices gave special influence to religious figures, in as much as Philip III's participation in religious activities brought him into the company of priests and nuns, who could then use this opportunity to speak to him and to voice their opinions on given matters. Ministers and councillors such as the Duke of Lerma realized that in order to reach the king, they needed to participate in the processions and visits to churches and convents. The Duke of Lerma even went so far as to found his own convents and take nuns from convents in Madrid to his newly founded institutions in the town of Lerma.[71] In so doing, Lerma followed a devotional practice of Spanish royalty and performed an act designed to make him appear grand.[72] The founding of convents also won attention for the duke and granted him extra favor with a pious monarch such as Philip III. In these ways, the monarch's piety had very definite repercussions on the making of political policy during his reign.

In addition to religious ceremonies, the rituals surrounding the midday meals of the monarchs also gave individuals the opportunity to gain an informal audience and curry favor with Philip III and Margaret of Austria. These midday meals formed an essential part of court ritual and political negotiations. On most occasions, Spanish monarchs ate privately. Philip and Margaret almost always ate separately; the queen usually remained in a convent to eat the midday meal with the nuns. Philip III, on the other hand, ate lunch either at the palace or at the home of councillors such as Juan de Borja or the Duke of Lerma.[73] The monarch ate alone, attended by a few servants and in the company of select individuals, often the Duke of Lerma and the royal almoner. John Elliott has described the private nature of these meals: "Apart from a few special occasions, by the seventeenth century, the King of Spain dined alone, except for the twenty or so officials who waited upon him, carrying and removing plates with the ritual precision required of a corps de ballet. The meal was taken in complete silence, and on the rare occasions when the queen dined with the king, she had her own separate service and no words were exchanged."[74]

After the meal, however, the king gave royal audiences during which he would meet with several individuals at the same time. Moreover, the time after the midday meal and after royal audiences was often reserved for decisions concerning alms. For instance, Diego de Guzmán recorded speaking with Philip III regularly after lunch, at which time the king would decide on dispensing alms to the poor, the needy, and the deserving.[75]

The Duke of Lerma realized that access to the monarch during the midday meal afforded an individual special attention and privileges. Because royal audiences often followed the king's midday meal, attendance at this meal could make one privy to matters discussed at these audiences. For these reasons, Lerma arranged for the monarch to eat regularly at his house. When the court moved back to Madrid in 1606, Lerma purchased several houses across the street from the Descalzas convent, knowing that the monarchs regularly attended morning mass at the convent and that the queen stayed there to eat.[76] Lerma understood that from the Descalzas Philip III could easily proceed to his house to eat and give audiences while still remaining close to the queen and the Descalzas, where the king often returned in the afternoons and early evenings. Lerma's calculations were correct: from 1606 until 1610, Philip III made it a practice to eat at Lerma's house by the Descalzas while the queen ate within the convent.[77] By arranging this, Lerma hoped to use to his advantage the system of etiquette governing a monarch's meal. This system allowed Lerma direct personal contact with the king and emphasized to others the degree of personal influence the Duke of Lerma had over the monarch. In this way, Lerma attempted to remain informed of all negotiations and personal requests brought to the monarch. In short, the Duke of Lerma's power over Philip III was grounded in this sort of personal contact, as well as in information about the monarch, his relatives, and members of the court. Housing him for the midday meal was only one of numerous ways in which Lerma attempted to control Philip III.

In contrast to her husband, Margaret of Austria rarely ate at the Duke of Lerma's house. The queen preferred to eat with the nuns; but she also purposely refused to honor the Duke of Lerma with her royal presence except on isolated occasions.[78] The direct link between the Descalzas convent and the king's midday meals at Lerma's house was the royal almoner; through Diego de Guzmán's attendance at the king's midday meals and at the royal audiences, Margaret of Austria remained informed of court matters.

This polarity between the Descalzas convent, where the queen ate, and Lerma's house, where the king ate, demonstrates the rivalry that existed at the court. It shows that Lerma felt threatened by the king's frequent visits to the convent and that he felt it necessary to provide an alternative space for the king to go. Lerma obviously recognized the importance of the Descalzas and the danger of the female community (including the queen) within the convent occupying the monarch's attention. Lerma purchased the house across from the Descalzas convent precisely because he realized that the king would frequently visit there. The king often went back and forth from Lerma's house to the Descalzas; he attended mass at the convent, ate at Lerma's house, then returned to the convent in the evening to be with the queen and their children. This interplay between the convent and Lerma's house was a physical representation of the two powerful influences in Philip III's life; he was torn between his female relatives and his privado.

Ultimately, however, Lerma lost. By 1610, the queen was in the process of taking over the royal convent of Santa Isabel as a preliminary to founding the royal convent of the Encarnación. Instead of going so often to the Descalzas, she then began to go to Santa Isabel. The king also changed his habit, and instead of eating at Lerma's house he began to eat more often at the palace. By founding her own convent where she and the king would go for religious activities, where she would eat, and where she would be recognized as the patroness, Margaret of Austria proclaimed her will and her influence over Philip III. She could not have founded and supported this convent without her husband's permission and financial support. In doing so, the queen pulled Philip III away from Lerma's house. Although it would seem that by favoring Santa Isabel the queen diminished the importance of the Descalzas, this was not necessarily the case. The monarchs continued to visit the Descalzas frequently, even if the queen no longer ate her midday meals there as often as before. The founding of this new convent was a sign of the growing power of the queen and of the Duke of Lerma's waning influence over the monarch.

After the midday meal, the queen remained at the Descalzas (or other convents), praying and speaking with the nuns. The king would either return to the palace for meetings with his councillors or join the queen to attend evening religious services at one of the convents. The king's passion for hunting pro-

vided breaks from this elaborate schedule of religious observance. He regularly
hunted in the afternoons and often went on hunting trips to the forests of El
Pardo or to Ventosilla, trips that would absent him from the royal palace for
several days. Like most Castilian monarchs before him, Philip III also regularly
traveled through his kingdoms, particularly in Old Castile. Historians have argued that the Duke of Lerma encouraged Philip to travel so as to remove him
from the influence of his wife.[79] These trips were perhaps also designed to give
Lerma exclusive time with the monarch and allow him to exert power and influence over Philip III. Margaret's frequent pregnancies supposedly made it impossible for her to accompany Philip III.[80]

An examination of the monarchs' itinerary throughout the years 1599–1611
does not fully confirm this picture.[81] Philip III certainly did go hunting often.
Margaret, who liked to hunt, accompanied him at times.[82] More often than
not, however, during the first few years of their marriage, the king went hunting without his wife although he continued to keep her in mind. He sent wild
boars, deer, and other animals as gifts from the monarch to the queen and as
signs of his affection and respect for her.[83] He also received messages about
how his wife was doing. At times these messages caused him to cut short his
trip and return to the palace earlier than expected.[84]

After Margaret had given birth to an heir in April 1605, her relationship with
Philip III changed. Certainly during the period from 1606 to 1611, the monarchs spent most of their time together. Philip III left the queen alone only for
short periods of time—an afternoon to a few days. Cabrera de Córdoba's reports for 1608–11 show that the monarchs were constantly together. Margaret
accompanied her husband on many of his hunting trips; even the birth of a
child did not always stop her. On 8 September 1606 the queen gave birth to a
daughter; as early as mid-October the queen left her newborn daughter in
Madrid so that she could accompany Philip III on his travels.[85] Pregnancy usually prevented the queen from traveling long distances, but she sometimes still
managed to go out, as long as she was taken in a chair.[86] Although Philip went
traveling alone for short periods of time during the early stages of her pregnancies, he was usually very reluctant to leave the queen when she approached
the final stages. Margaret's frequent pregnancies thus ensured that Philip III
would often be by her side. In fact, after 1606, the monarch rarely left the queen
alone for extended periods. These are clear signs of the affectionate, loving marriage that Philip III and Margaret of Austria enjoyed.

The queen clearly used these times to influence the monarch in both small and large ways. For example, Philip III had a celebration for the son of Margaret's lady-in-waiting and closest friend, Maria Sidonia Riderer,[87] and also appointed Sidonia's brother-in-law as viceroy of New Spain. The king humored Margaret, allowing her to choose where they would spend time, and he postponed taking long trips until the queen could accompany him.[88] The monarchs' close personal relationship flourished during those years (1606–8) when the Duke of Lerma was experiencing the first serious challenge to his power, namely, the discrediting of the *Junta de Desempeño* (Committee for Financial Solvency).

On those occasions when the king traveled for an extended period of time without the queen, Margaret stayed in the Descalzas convent with her children in the rooms that had housed Empress María until her death, in 1603. The queen stayed at the Descalzas even when the court was in Valladolid; when Philip III went to Valencia in December of 1603, Margaret of Austria and the Infanta Anne stayed at the Descalzas. This was one of Philip's longest absences from his wife, and she was not happy to be left behind. The queen stayed in the rooms that Juan de Borja had used when he was Empress María's mayordomo, and the infanta stayed in the room that had belonged to Empress María.[89] On such occasions, Margaret of the Cross helped care for the children. In fact, the royal children often went by themselves to the Descalzas and were allowed to enter the cloistered section of the convent.[90] These visits cemented the bond between the queen, Margaret of the Cross, and the other nuns of the Descalzas. Within the convent, Margaret of Austria found a network of women whom she could trust and with whom she undoubtedly discussed her problems and concerns. After the queen's death, in 1611, Philip III regularly left his children in the convent with Margaret of the Cross when he left Madrid.[91] The familial and religious connections between the monarchs and the Descalzas convent were very strong throughout his reign. The network of nuns within the Descalzas was a powerful female counterbalance to the male-oriented royal palace, which served as the meeting place for the councillors of state.

The king met about once a week with his councillors of state to discuss important issues. The meetings usually took place in the afternoon or early evening, once Philip III had finished his midday meal and given audiences. The Council of State's influence at the Spanish court had declined during the last years of the reign of Philip II,[92] who had relied more on juntas, which he created for particular matters. Composed of a few trusted advisers who reported directly to the monarch, these juntas tended to undermine the authority of the Council of State.[93] Philip III reversed the Council of State's decline. Shortly after assuming the throne in 1598, he did away with his father's powerful three-man committee, known as the *Junta de Noche*, and reorganized the Council of State. He increased the number of its members from fifteen to nineteen, in part to accommodate nobles that the Duke of Lerma wished to placate. Most of Philip II's councillors were removed from their important positions. The only councillors to make the transition from Philip II's to Philip III's Council of State were Juan de Idiáquez and the Marquis of Velada, both of whom the Duke of Lerma trusted. In this way, the Council of State emerged as the most influential of the royal councils during Philip III's reign.[94] It served as the chief advisory body to the monarch and in large part controlled the activities of other royal councils.[95]

The reorganization of the Council of State was lauded by many as a return to a more balanced form of government and an energetic political action on the part of the young monarch. However, observers such as the Venetian ambassador, Simon de Contarini, argued that the restructuring of the Council of State was merely cosmetic and that the Council was still subordinate to the wishes of Philip III's royal favorite. Contarini reported that the Duke of Lerma and his allies, Pedro Franqueza and Rodrigo Calderón, decided which matters would go to the Council of State. So, according to Contarini, the reinstatement of the Council of State was merely a facade for the Duke of Lerma's authoritarian practices.[96]

Although Contarini's negative assessment of the Duke of Lerma's intentions is debatable, Lerma certainly saw the benefit in relying on the advice and assistance of a select group of advisers on key issues of policy. For this reason, he encouraged the monarch to organize juntas again to discuss particular issues, and from 1600 to 1608, juntas once again were the rule within the Spanish political system. Lerma's closest advisers—individuals such as Juan de Borja, the Count of Miranda, and Rodrigo Calderón—regularly formed part of these juntas, which were instrumental in advising Philip III on domestic and foreign policy.[97] This system was not simply based on personal association with the Duke of Lerma, nor did it consist strictly of a clientage network. Lerma designed the system of juntas to deal with Spain's increasing economic and political problems and restore the financial health of the Spanish kingdoms.[98]

Ministers such as Count Juan de Idiáquez and the Duke of Infantado were chosen to join the juntas discussing Italian and Central European affairs, not because of their personal relationship to the Duke of Lerma, but because both ministers had personal expertise in those territorial regions.[99] Philip III and the Duke of Lerma created juntas to treat specific issues, such as the expulsion of the *Moriscos* or the financial recovery (*desempeño*) of the Spanish kingdoms, and once their work was done the juntas were dissolved. So while the juntas did play a major role in advising the monarch, they did not negate the power of the Council of State.

The use of juntas as informal committees for policymaking began to decline in the latter half of Philip III's reign. This decline roughly paralleled the gradual decline of the Duke of Lerma's influence and was connected to the king's gradual willingness to listen to voices other than Lerma's, principally that of the queen. The Duke of Lerma's influence began to decline in 1608, the year in which his close associate, Pedro Franqueza (who was also the queen's secretary), was investigated and tried for corrupt practices. Franqueza's trial threatened to bring down the Duke of Lerma because it concentrated on the abuse of power at the Spanish court. It was widely rumored that Margaret of Austria was instrumental in the campaign against Franqueza because, among other things, he acted as Lerma's spy within the queen's household. Lerma did not fall with Franqueza, but he did lose some of his hold over the king, who increasingly paid greater attention to Margaret of Austria.[100]

The Council of State had its rooms on the floor above the royal apartments in Philip III's palace, and the weekly meetings were usually held there.[101] The physical layout of the palace in Madrid—with royal apartments on the upper level and governmental offices on the lower—emphasizes the dual nature (personal and bureaucratic) of Spanish kingship (see figs. 12 and 13).[102] The juntas met in private settings rather than in the rooms designated for the Council of State. The individuals who composed the juntas met informally in Juan de Borja's summer house (*huerta*), or in Lerma's house, or in one of Philip III's hunting lodges.[103] Lerma and his closest associates often met in these private settings not only to discuss particular courses of action but also to confer with ambassadors such as Hans Khevenhüller about policy decisions. Women, too, had access to these locations and could be present when informal negotiations took place there. Empress María, for example, visited Juan de Borja's summer house frequently.[104] Although she did not record being at a meeting of a junta, she did meet with the king and queen at the house and could easily have discussed political matters with them. In ways such as these, the negotiations preceding political actions often occurred in locations outside the royal palace and involved royal women.

Because of their role in juntas and because of the trust Lerma placed in them, several other individuals figured prominently in political decisions at the Spanish court and must be included in any complete account. The Duke of Lerma elevated Pedro Franqueza and Rodrigo Calderón to power: two men of mediocre background and talents who then became Lerma's own favorites and did his bidding. Pedro Franqueza began serving on the Council of Aragón in the 1570s, and in the 1580s he was appointed secretary of this council in matters dealing with Valencia.[105] Franqueza occupied this secretarial post while the Duke of Lerma served as viceroy of Valencia (1595–97), and these years marked the beginning of close cooperation between the two men. Shortly after Lerma became Philip III's privado in 1598, he had Franqueza appointed secretary of state in Italian matters. In 1601, Franqueza was appointed secretary of the Inquisition, and in the following year he became secretary to the queen.[106] The Venetian ambassador Ottaviano Bon, referring to Franqueza's social rank as well as his character, described him as a man of "the lowest origins."[107] Another, more famous Venetian ambassador, Simon de Contarini, noted that despite Franqueza's low origins (*baxa calidad*), the secretary was intelligent (*de buena cabeza*) and very skilled at negotiations. According to Contarini, Franqueza's tremendous greed required that one negotiate with him through bribes, not skillful arguments.[108]

Lerma valued Franqueza's familiarity with the administrative side of the Spanish government and rewarded Franqueza with numerous governmental appointments.[109] Franqueza quickly became the Duke of Lerma's privado and an important instrument for monitoring the activities of courtiers and governmental councils. Franqueza also used his office as Margaret of Austria's secretary to keep an eye on the queen's actions. Franqueza's influence with Lerma won him honors with the king, who named him Count of Villalonga.[110] Franqueza worked closely with the Duke of Lerma and with Alonso Ramírez de Prado, a councillor of finance, in attempting to solve the financial problems of the Spanish monarchy. He also exercised a major role in the Junta de Desempeño, which was formed in 1603 to deal with royal finances.[111] This junta proposed a three-year plan for the financial solvency of the monarchy; ironically, its members were later implicated in siphoning funds from the royal treasury.[112] In January 1607, Franqueza was arrested, imprisoned, and his goods confiscated for his role in the financial misdeeds of the Junta de Desempeño. After being tried and found guilty of financial crimes against the state, Franqueza had to pay 1,400,000 ducats and was condemned to permanent seclusion and deprived of his title.

Margaret of Austria was undoubtedly behind Franqueza's investigation. The queen disliked the influence Franqueza had on the king through Lerma, and both she and the royal confessor had warned Philip III that the Junta de Desempeño had worsened, not improved, the monarchy's financial situation.[113] The trials against Pedro Franqueza and other members of the junta were the first serious challenges to the Duke of Lerma's power; these trials also marked the queen's growing influence over her husband, to the detriment of Lerma. His close association with Franqueza and other members of the Junta de Desempeño caused Lerma to be implicated in the financial misdeeds. In fact, Lerma claimed that his enemies (among them, Margaret of Austria) had engineered the trial against Franqueza in order to strike at him indirectly. In the end, however, Lerma had little choice but to abandon Franqueza and allow him to take responsibility for his actions. The duke survived the storm but his power over Philip III was never again as strong as it had been before Franqueza's fall.[114]

Rodrigo Calderón was another close associate and privado of the Duke of Lerma. He began his career as one of the duke's servants (*paje*), but through Lerma's influence he became assistant to the king's chamber (*ayuda de cámara del rey*) in 1599, and in the following year he became secretary of the king's chamber. Calderón held numerous other smaller offices and also received the titles of Count de la Oliva and Marquis de Sieteiglesias.[115] In 1606, the royal confessor, Diego de Mardones (a friend of the queen's), criticized Calderón's financial dealings—a move that caused the Duke of Lerma to have Mardones removed as royal confessor.[116] The following year, a former secretary of Calderón gave the Admiral of Aragón a list of Calderón's misdeeds. The admiral gave this list to the new royal confessor, Luis de Aliaga, but once Calderón found this out he arranged for the admiral to be arrested on charges of treason. Despite much criticism of his activities, Calderón fared well using such tactics at the Spanish court, until he was implicated in Queen Margaret of Austria's death, in 1611.

The problems between Calderón and Margaret of Austria were longstanding, and it was well known that the queen distrusted Calderón and encouraged her husband to investigate Calderón's financial dealings. When the queen died, in October 1611, the royal confessor, Luis de Aliaga, among others, accused Calderón of poisoning the queen. Although Philip III did not pursue legal action against Calderón, he did send him out of Spain, first as ambassador to Venice and then in 1612 as extraordinary ambassador to Flanders. After his temporary stay in Flanders, Calderón received permission to return to Madrid, but he never regained his former power at the Spanish court. Moreover, the outspoken criticism of Calderón at the Spanish court increasingly shifted to the Duke of Lerma, and, after 1611, Lerma's power over Philip III progressively declined. Calderón survived the last years of Philip III's reign relatively unscathed, but he ultimately paid dearly for his collaboration with Lerma. With Philip III's death, in 1621, and the initiation of a new reign, a widespread legal inquiry was made into the activities of Lerma and his associates, most of whom lost their offices and were fined or imprisoned. This investigation finally satisfied Calderón's longtime critics: Calderón was investigated, his goods were seized, and he was executed for crimes against the state. The charges that he had poisoned the queen were investigated but dismissed.[117]

At the Spanish court during Philip III's reign, there was no clear separation between the political and the religious, the public and the private, the governmental and the familial. The monarch certainly spent the majority of his day in religious, familial, and private activities—activities that necessarily brought him into contact with relatives, priests, and nuns. Yet this is not to say that Philip III did not concern himself with political deeds. In fact, these activities were in and of themselves political. As a symbol of this interpenetration of the private and public, the political and the religious realms, stands the Real Alcázar in Madrid, where the royal chapel literally divided the queen's half of the floor from the king's half (see figure 12). In this way, the chapel functioned as the physical meeting place between the king and the queen—which was very appropriate given that devotional practices tended to unite the monarchs and religious worship served as one of the principal means through which Margaret of Austria influenced Philip III.[118]

Even strictly public events afforded opportunities for exchanges between the monarch and his relatives. When Philip III's uncle, Archduke Maximilian, visited Valladolid in 1600, the king held numerous public celebrations for him and met Maximilian publicly with several coaches as he approached the city.[119] The archduke then entered the king's carriage along with Hans Khevenhüller, the Duke of Lerma, and the Marquis of Velada (a councillor of state). Once in the palace, however, the king and the archduke went to see the queen by themselves and stayed with her a long while. During a night of public mascarades (*mascaradas*) and street lighting (*luminarias*), Philip III, Margaret of Austria, and Archduke Maximilian sat alone together in a carriage, where they watched the festivities well into the night. In the midst of a public event, the monarchs remained both present and yet isolated from the public. In turn, this event provided an opportunity for private conversation between Maximilian and the king and queen, conversation that undoubtedly included talk of the needs of the Austrian Habsburgs in Central Europe.[120]

The fluid nature of Philip III's court benefited the Austrian Habsburgs. It allowed for their informal diplomatic representatives—in particular, their female relatives—to reach the monarch frequently and communicate their petitions. The fact that the Duke of Lerma tried to participate regularly in the rituals surrounding Philip III, that he took up religious patronage, that he purchased the house across from the Descalzas, and that he tried to prevent physical contact between Philip III and his female relatives, proves that access to the monarch was a principal way of gaining his attention and support, and that this access came primarily through participation in the monarch's daily religious and private routine.

Philip III and the policy decisions of his reign have to be analyzed in the complex context of his court, which incorporated confessors, preachers, councillors of state, ambassadors, nuns, and family members. This pious king readily listened to the voices of religious individuals, and he particularly listened to the voices of his female relatives, who were quick to remind Philip III of his duties to the Austrian Habsburgs. Although historians have emphasized Philip III's complete reliance on the Duke of Lerma, the king in fact looked to a wide range of individuals when negotiating policy and making decisions. The Spanish court was by no means a monolithic body presenting the king with only one course of action. Instead, the court consisted of several factions, which were often in opposition to one another and operated far beyond the official rooms of the Council of State. Their negotiations and maneuvering had a major impact on the making of policy during Philip III's reign.

2

Court Factions and Personal Networks

Historians of Philip III's reign usually emphasize the Duke of Lerma's power and influence over the monarch. They have often painted a picture of a court subordinated to the desires and demands of one individual.[1] Lerma's power, however, did not go unchallenged. From the beginning of Philip III's reign, certain individuals defied the Duke of Lerma and worked to limit his power at the court.[2] Recently, Antonio Feros, Patrick Williams, and R. A. Stradling have recognized that there was strong opposition to Lerma's influence.[3] In examining this opposition, these historians have followed the line developed by the nineteenth-century historian Edouard Rott, who identified three factions operating at the court of Philip III: that of Lerma and his associates, another centered on Margaret of Austria and the imperial ambassadors, and a third with the Duke of Uceda, Lerma's son, and Luis de Aliaga, the royal confessor, at its core.[4]

In examining the place that Empress María, Margaret of Austria, and Margaret of the Cross occupied at the court of Philip III, it is necessary to consider these three factions and to discuss them briefly, especially because the queen headed one of the principal groups in opposition to the Duke of Lerma. Moreover, an examination of these factions lays the groundwork for understanding Philip III's court and for establishing that the Duke of Lerma did not hold a monopoly over Philip's attention for the duration of his reign.

The opposition to Lerma was often quite organized. Nevertheless, by categorizing this opposition into factions, historians have presented it too neatly. In fact, individuals regularly crossed so-called factional lines. Individuals such as Magdalena de Guzmán, whom Lerma employed to monitor the queen's activities, actually became a friend and associate of Margaret of Austria. As a result, the Duke of Lerma had her arrested and imprisoned. Lerma's uncle and close associate, Juan de Borja, also served as Empress María's mayordomo and clearly negotiated for her vis-à-vis the Duke of Lerma. These two cases, among others, show that the boundaries between court factions were rather porous. The composition of any court faction was not static, but rather changed over time, depending on the given situation. In trying to separate court figures into distinct factions, historians have created artificial categories, categories that contemporaries did not themselves recognize.

Furthermore, historians have often ascribed overall agendas to the separate factions. Lerma's faction was concerned with the Iberian peninsula and with safeguarding the monarchy's coasts. The privado's faction supposedly also consisted of individuals who favored a rapprochement with France and who urged Philip III to pursue pacifistic policies.[5] Margaret of Austria's faction argued for assistance to the Austrian Habsburgs in Central Europe. Historians have completely overlooked the queen's support of Bavarian interests at the Spanish court.[6] Undoubtedly the queen helped the Bavarian Wittelsbachs; her mother was a Wittelsbach, and Margaret retained close ties to her mother's family. Richard Haller, Margaret's confessor, was from Bavaria and had represented Bavarian interests at the court in Graz. In Spain, Haller continued to negotiate matters for the Wittelsbachs.[7] Margaret and Richard Haller worked closely together on most issues, including those dealing with the Wittelsbachs. The queen's faction is often combined with that of the so-called Austrian Party. This party was represented by Spanish ministers in Italy, for example, the Count of Bedmar and the Count of Fuentes, and ambassadors such as Guillén de San Clemente and Baltasar de Zúñiga, who favored resolute defense of Spanish reputation abroad and closer cooperation with the Austrian Habsburgs.[8]

The last faction—that of the Duke of Uceda and Luis de Aliaga—is said to have had only personal and financial gain in mind. Their object was to discredit and then usurp the place and power of the Duke of Lerma. Historians have not analyzed whether these individuals had a coherent domestic or foreign policy that transcended the desire for financial profit.

Obviously, not every individual classified as part of a faction always agreed with the overall goals ascribed to that faction. At times much more immediate goals—personal or familial prestige, financial benefit, or revenge—determined an individual's association with a given court circle. So, for example, Margaret of Austria actually supported the marriage of her daughter Anne to the French prince Louis.[9] The queen seems to have recognized the growing importance of France and saw this union as a smart political move for one of her children. Yet most of the Austrian Habsburgs did not favor this Spanish-French tie and would have preferred Anne to marry an Austrian archduke. As this case illustrates, it is not always useful to study Philip III's court in terms of factions because this language at times actually obstructs our understanding of how the court functioned.

Factions certainly existed at the court, but they were supplemented by personal networks, which involved persons' functions, their access to those in power, and their familial or affectionate ties to the monarchs. Factions and personal networks were not mutually exclusive, and the lines between them were not always carefully drawn. In considering the different political networks operating within Philip III's court, I employ the language of factions when it seems appropriate, but I use *political network* more often than *faction*. The term *network* better captures the political climate of Philip III's court. Factions imply clearly delineated groups with hardened political agendas, whereas networks are more fluid, personal, and function based. The language of networks also better reflects how individuals, particularly women, negotiated and operated at Philip III's court.

An examination of the ways in which individuals negotiated at court allows for a comparison between the networks employed by men and those employed by women. There was, in fact, no inherent difference between "male" or "female" networks at the Spanish court; the avenues for negotiation were not gender-specific. Lerma knew to employ women when it was convenient to do so (particularly when he wished to control Margaret of Austria). Likewise, when Empress María, Margaret of Austria, and Margaret of the Cross wished to convey a message that was obviously political in nature, or when that message had to be conveyed to a councillor or minister, they relied almost exclusively on men to be their messengers. These men tended to be servants of the women—mayordomos, confessors, almoners, secretaries, or lesser servants. The royal women relied on these men because they trusted them; this trust was based on the regular and personal contact the women had with them owing to the offices the men held. Thus, one cannot say that the Habsburg women relied primarily on priests and nuns to convey messages because these individuals were particularly pious. Rather, it was because the women had frequent contact with religious figures that the latter were in a position to win the trust and respect of the women they served.

On the other hand, the Habsburg women often relied on women to convey messages to other women. So, for example, the queen asked her lady-in-waiting, Maria Sidonia, to give messages to Empress María and the nuns of the Descalzas. Nevertheless, gender was not the key to choosing to negotiate through a particular individual; an individual's function, acquired through the privileges of his or her office, was much more important than gender. This is not to say that gender differences were not apparent in these networks. Because women were not allowed to be present at the official meetings of the Council of State, or because it was considered unseemly for the Habsburg women to meet in private with men other than their relatives, these women often had to communicate with men through other men. Overall, however, one cannot divide these networks into neat factions based simply on gender; function within the court was at least as important.

The most influential political network in the early years of Philip III's reign was that led and dominated by the Duke of Lerma. Lerma's network consisted of individuals who, through Lerma's influence, were appointed to important state offices or secured high positions within the king's and queen's households. Those individuals who received posts in the royal households served as sources of information for the privado; their appointment was supposed to ensure that the king and queen were surrounded by individuals who were loyal to and dependent upon the Duke of Lerma. This was not always the case. Several individuals used their favor with Lerma to gain an important office, but once they had gained the office they followed an independent course contrary to Lerma's. Magdalena de Guzmán (the Marquesa del Valle) and the royal confessor Luis de Aliaga are examples of this type of individual.

Lerma made certain that men who cooperated closely with him received important state offices. Pedro Franqueza, the Count of Villalonga, who had collaborated with Lerma while the latter was in Valencia and who was one of Lerma's privados, was appointed secretary of state (in Italian matters) in 1598 and later formed part of the committee to consider Spain's financial resources (the Junta de Desempeño). Lerma relied on a select group of ministers to consider matters of state.[10] In the early years of Philip III's reign, this group, or junta, was composed of Fray Gaspar de Córdoba (Philip III's confessor), the Marquis of Velada (Philip's mayordomo mayor), Juan de Zúñiga y Avellaneda (the Count of Miranda), Pedro Franqueza, Rodrigo Calderón, Juan de Borja, and Juan de Idiáquez.[11] After Juan de Borja's death, in 1606, Franqueza's fall from grace, and the Count of Miranda's death, in 1608, Lerma incorporated Juan de Acuña (who served successively as president of the Council of Castile, the Council of Finance, and the Council of the Indies) and Francisco de Borja (Juan de Borja's son and heir) into his select council of advisers.[12] Because he had access to the highest state offices and because he could influence the election of individuals to the councils, Lerma was able to surround himself with men who depended upon him for their position and power, or men who had agendas similar to his own. Lerma could thus influence policymaking directly through his associates who held public office.

Lerma constructed his network of influence on the basis of court appointments and marriage agreements. One of his first actions as royal favorite was to place his relatives and confidants in key positions throughout the court.[13] This included positions on the various governmental councils as well as offices in the king's and queen's households. Lerma's brother, Juan de Sandoval, was appointed *Primer Caballerizo* to Philip III; Lerma's eldest son, Cristóbal Gómez de Sandoval (First Duke of Uceda), was named *Gentilhombre de la Cámara* to Philip III, as was Lerma's nephew and son-in-law, Pedro Fernández de Castro (Seventh Count of Lemos), and Lerma's cousin, the aforementioned Francisco de Borja, Prince of Esquilache.[14] All of these appointments placed Lerma's relatives physically close to the daily activities of the monarchs and afforded them personal access to the king. Lerma himself assumed the offices of *Sumiller de Corps*, which empowered him to attend the king in his most intimate activities, such as dressing and eating, and *Caballerizo Mayor*, an office that allowed him to accompany Philip whenever he went out and that gave him authority over all individuals in the royal stable (*caballeriza*).[15] These appointments gave the Duke of Lerma personal access to Philip III at all times, and access to the Spanish monarch was both a principal sign of favor and prerequisite to gaining influence with the king. Lerma's appointments as *Capitán General de la Caballería de España* (1603) and *Capitán General de la Caballería de Aragón* (1605) further extended his power over the Spanish kingdoms and their military might.

Lerma recognized the importance of securing his position by allying himself with other aristocratic families, something he did through marriage agreements.[16] In 1601, the Duke of Lerma arranged for one of his daughters to marry the eldest son (who was only four years old at the time of the marriage agreement) of the new Admiral of Castile and Duke of Medina de Rioseco. This marriage ensured a future bond with the powerful Enríquez family. In 1603, Lerma's second son, Diego Gómez de Sandoval, married Luisa de Mendoza, Countess of Saldaña and heir to the house of Infantado, a powerful, old Castilian family with numerous territories in Italy.[17] Quite appropriately, the Duke of Infantado, father of Luisa de Mendoza, was appointed Gentilhombre de la Cámara of Philip III the same day that the marriage contract between his daughter and Lerma's son was signed.[18] Infantado was subsequently appointed councillor of state. Other marriage alliances connected Lerma to the house of Medina Sidonia and solidified the already existing bonds between the Sandoval house and those of the Counts of Lemos and Miranda.[19]

These marriage arrangements, however, could not ensure that the individuals with whom Lerma allied himself would necessarily support his interests. The Duke of Infantado, although he received court offices through Lerma's support, still exercised an independent voice within the council and primarily favored Spanish interests in Italy, in large part because of his family's extensive possessions there. Infantado also had an important say on Central European matters, particularly from 1613 until 1618, and tended to agree more with the opinions of Baltasar de Zúñiga than with those of the Duke of Lerma.[20] Infantado's relationship with the Duke of Lerma soured after 1610, when Lerma and Rodrigo Calderón arranged for the arrest of Infantado's brother, Francisco de Mendoza, Admiral of Aragón. Calderón pursued the admiral because the latter had criticized him and had even gone so far as to give Luis de Aliaga a paper (*memorial*) detailing Calderón's misdemeanors and crimes.[21] Infantado, therefore, cannot really be considered part of Lerma's "faction"; his case once again points out the shifting nature of court circles in the early modern period.

As a man in the political world of the Spanish court, Lerma was able to use official state mechanisms to wield his influence. He could ensure that his male dependents were appointed to conciliar offices or court positions and that his female relatives found places within the queen's household. Lerma's network was different from other networks because it operated in large part through officially sanctioned offices, which his relatives and dependents received with the king's approval. Because his network had a base of public offices, Lerma and his associates could influence policymaking directly—even if they did not always leave a clear record of their meetings and decisions. Lerma relied heavily on the private reports of his relatives and dependents, who were instructed to comment on the activities of individuals whom Lerma wished to monitor and control. Those who reported to Lerma included Juan de Borja, who was expected to keep an eye on Empress María's activities, and Magdalena de Guzmán, Marquesa del Valle, who was supposed to monitor the queen's actions. Both Borja and Magdalena de Guzmán held formal court appointments: Borja was mayordomo to the empress and then to the queen, and Magdalena de Guzmán was the guardian (*aya*) of the royal princess. Juan de Borja and Magdalena de Guzmán exercised important influence within their court appointments, but their unofficial purpose of "spying" for Lerma remained unwritten and therefore largely undocumented.[22]

Despite the trust Lerma placed in them, Juan de Borja and Magdalena de Guzmán were not mere pawns in Lerma's game of chess; they developed great loyalty to the women they served, and this loyalty tended to neutralize their usefulness as informants for Philip III's privado. Juan de Borja and Magdalena de Guzmán illustrate the limitations of Lerma's network system: despite his promoting relatives and dependents, Lerma was unable to destroy the traditional bonds of loyalty and affection those individuals felt for royalty. Moreover, his system overlooked the fact that direct access to royalty (of the kind enjoyed by Borja and Magdalena de Guzmán) gave individuals power and prestige, and thus afforded them a certain degree of independence from powerbrokers such as the Duke of Lerma. This was also true for Lerma's own son, the Duke of Uceda. Uceda clearly took advantage of the access to Philip III which his court appointment brought him, an appointment Lerma had secured for him. Uceda then used this access successfully to challenge his father's predominance at the court. In this respect, Lerma's method of operation had inherent weaknesses. So, because the privado was not royalty and was always dependent upon the king's favor, he could never match the advantages enjoyed by the Habsburg women because of their lineage.

Lerma, because he often operated through political offices, usually relied on other men to give him advice in matters of state and finance. When he wanted to circumscribe the queen's activities, however, he relied in large part on a counternetwork of women, consisting of Magdalena de Guzmán, Catalina de la Cerda (his wife), and his two sisters, Catalina de Sandoval, Countess of Lemos, and Leonor de Sandoval, Countess of Altamira. By so doing, Lerma recognized the strength of a network of women, something also clearly evident in Lerma's attempt to reorganize the queen's household and purge numerous women from the queen's company.[23]

Lerma's prodding might very well have been what led Philip III, in 1603, to issue a new set of etiquette rules to govern the queen's household. These new rules were issued directly after the arrest of Magdalena de Guzmán, who had been accused of abusing the power of her office as governess to the princess. The most notable difference in the etiquette rules of 1603 was a detailed description and expansion of the role of the mayordomo mayor: the new rules emphasized his role as watchdog in the queen's household. Certainly the Duke of Lerma also surrounded the queen with male individuals, such as the Count of Altamira (Caballerizo Mayor), Juan de Borja (mayordomo mayor), Fernando Carrillo (*asesor del Bureo*), and Pedro Franqueza (secretary), but these individuals were not allowed into the privacy of the queen's inner apartments. Given the etiquette of the Spanish court, only women could serve the queen in these inner rooms, so Lerma surrounded the queen with his female relatives and dependents. This was the case with the office of camarera mayor, for which Lerma first appointed his wife, Catalina de la Cerda, and then later his sister Catalina de Sandoval. The camarera mayor was responsible for regulating the queen's domestic life, accompanying her at all hours, and sleeping in her room when the king was not present (and in an adjacent room when he was).[24]

By ensuring that his relatives had access to the queen in her most private moments, Lerma tried to monitor all of Margaret of Austria's activities. Yet his reliance on a group of women for this task demonstrates that women could operate very well in the private and political networks of the Spanish court. Through their court offices, women gained access to the queen which they could then use to acquire power at the court. Both Lerma's wife, Catalina de la Cerda, and Magdalena de Guzmán were eventually integrated into the queen's own network of influence; placed close to the queen so that they could supervise her activities and report them to the privado, both women grew to have more loyalty for the queen than for Lerma.[25] Women often found greater comfort and acceptance in networks composed of and dominated by other women than they did in networks controlled by men.

The political savvy of the queen, of Catalina de la Cerda, and of Magdalena de Guzmán was also evident in their ability to circumvent Lerma's network. Far from being ignorant of how to maneuver in court circles, these women used the power available to them to their own advantage. Lerma's sister, Catalina de Sandoval, Countess of Lemos, tried to get a court appointment for her son, Pedro Fernández de Castro, Count of Lemos. In this case, Catalina de Sandoval was more interested in using her office to further the career of her son than in helping the Duke of Lerma maintain his power.[26] Lerma reacted to the growing influence of individuals like Magdalena de Guzmán by emphasizing the role of the queen's mayordomo mayor as the head of the queen's household. The privado turned to a fellow man, Juan de Borja (who was also his relative), to attempt to rein in what he thought was an unmanageable female network at the Spanish court, a network that had grown to include his own wife.

In winning court appointments for his relatives, Lerma was surrounding himself with individuals he thought to be trustworthy. He was also attempting to promote his own Sandoval family and to benefit financially and territorially from Philip III's favor. Throughout the years that he enjoyed the monarch's support, Lerma amassed a personal fortune that allowed him to patronize the arts, found convents and monasteries, and develop his own town of Lerma.[27] Whereas in 1597 his estimated annual income totaled a thousand ducats, by 1616 this figure had jumped to 150 thousand ducats.[28] Lerma's personal associates also benefited financially from the privado's patronage. Rodrigo Calderón and Pedro Franqueza gained titles, offices, territory, and enormous wealth because of their association with Lerma. Juan de Borja, Lerma's uncle, became Count of Ficallo, a small town in Portugal.[29] He also held important positions in the Councils of Finance and Portugal. In these and other ways, Lerma amply rewarded individuals who cooperated with him. He relied on his personal influence with the monarch to secure positions and financial rewards for his own dependents, and, by providing for these dependents in turn, Lerma tried to assure himself a network of loyal individuals.

Lerma's efforts to build up a strong network of allies through whom he could control the monarch and the court were ultimately shaken by the financial mismanagement that characterized his and his associates' careers. Pedro Franqueza and Alonso Ramírez de Prado, the very individuals selected to head the junta examining the monarchy's financial recovery, were accused and convicted of embezzling funds. Lerma's emphasis on financial recovery (*desempeño*) then seemed preposterous to observers in light of the personal fortune he himself had amassed. Corruption was not the only factor that began to erode the strength of Lerma's network of influence. The deaths of key individuals upon whom Lerma had relied—Juan de Borja (1606), the Count of Miranda (1608), and the Count of Idiáquez (1614) — also gradually weakened the network. They were replaced by others, but the network never regained the strength it had possessed in the first years of Philip III's reign.

In selecting replacements for men such as Franqueza and Calderón, Lerma did not exercise the caution he had once used. The choice of his German Jesuit confessor, Hans Friedrich Helder, and the very young and inexperienced García de Pareja proved to be a liability. Helder betrayed Lerma's confidence to the king, and with his promotion of García de Pareja in 1616, Lerma was even suspected of homoerotic affection for the attractive young man. The privado at this point had become somewhat of a laughingstock at the court. Although Philip accepted Lerma's right to have close personal contact with these men, he adamantly refused to give them any political office.[30] These developments left Lerma open to increasing attacks and allowed his power to be challenged by that of Margaret of the Cross and her circle, as well as by that of his son, the Duke of Uceda, and Philip's confessor, Luis de Aliaga.

In 1612 Philip III issued a decree reaffirming the power of the Duke of Lerma and his right to sign royal documents. This decree actually demonstrates Lerma's diminishing influence at the court; Philip had to proclaim Lerma's power because it was under attack from so many sides.[31] An incident from 1613 is indicative of Lerma's dwindling influence at the court. The Countess of Porcia, who had been one of Margaret of Austria's ladies-in-waiting, was able to ask Philip III directly to favor her husband for a court appointment.[32] Because Lerma had ignored all of her husband's requests for assistance, the countess went straight to the king. As a result, Philip III made her husband a marquis, gave him title to a fief, and awarded him and his son several other privileges.[33] This incident was one sign that by 1613 Lerma no longer had the king's unwavering support. The competing factions and personal networks at Philip III's court were able to emphasize the corruption that characterized Lerma's administration and used that corruption to discredit Lerma and his policies. They could also cite the privado's lack of judgment and failing health as grounds to demand his removal from the court.[34]

※ ※ ※

The second principal political network at Philip III's court was that of the Habsburg women, not just of the queen. Although Margaret of Austria was indeed one of the chief sources of opposition to the Duke of Lerma, she worked with Empress María and Margaret of the Cross, and therefore all three women and their associates constituted an important network for negotiating policy at the Spanish court.[35] In fact, Empress María was at least as important as the queen in terms of negotiating with Philip III and Lerma during the first few years of the reign. When Margaret of Austria arrived in Madrid, the empress moved quickly to incorporate her into the strong female community within the Descalzas convent. María requested papal permission for Margaret to enter the cloistered section of the Descalzas monastery whenever she wished.[36] With the empress and Margaret of the Cross, the queen found acceptance and friendship, and she found individuals with whom she could converse in German.[37] The empress visited Margaret of Austria at the royal palace weekly, and Margaret went to the Descalzas on a daily basis. Empress María expressed her affection for the queen through gifts: on Margaret's first visit to the empress in November 1599, Empress María gave her a jewel decorated with the two-headed eagle (symbolic of the Habsburg dynasty) and with numerous precious stones. This jewel, which was valued at 34,000 ducats and considered to be the empress's most valuable piece of jewelry, remained in the queen's possession until her death, in 1611.[38] The gift of the two-headed eagle also symbolized the empress's acceptance of the queen into her inner circle and the women's devotion to the House of Austria.

The Habsburg women's lineage and their familial ties to the monarch gave them special status at the court, status that allowed them to negotiate directly with the king. All three women consciously used these powerful ties to influence Philip III's decisions and to transcend the networks of the Spanish court. Their main way of influencing policy was to meet with Philip himself. In practice, however, familial bonds did not always ensure that the Habsburg women's requests would be heard by the Spanish monarch, especially when the Duke of Lerma tried to limit their personal contact with the king. This was also true during the years when the court moved to Valladolid, and personal contact between Philip III and his relatives at the Descalzas was limited to those occasions on which the monarch visited Madrid.

Moreover, the Habsburg women at times had to reach Lerma and other ministers, and their familial relationship to the monarch did not necessarily help them in this matter. All three women gave audiences and would occasionally meet directly with Philip III's ministers or with foreign ambassadors. For example, Empress María met with Pedro Franqueza in the Descalzas to discuss Spanish assistance for Flanders.[39] Margaret of Austria gave audiences to

Lorenzo de Brindisi and Alfonso Carrillo, priests sent by Archduke Leopold and Maximilian of Bavaria respectively, to negotiate for Spanish assistance to the Catholic League in Central Europe.[40] The queen also gave audiences to Hans Khevenhüller, Dario Nomi (Rudolf II's ambassador, sent to negotiate with Philip III over the imperial fief of Finale), and to the Prince of Castiglione (an imperial ambassador, sent in 1610 to request Spanish financial assistance for Rudolf II).[41] Nevertheless, the Habsburg women at times had to rely on networks of individuals to put pressure on Philip III, the Duke of Lerma, and Spanish ministers. Empress María, Margaret of Austria, and Margaret of the Cross knew how to negotiate at the Spanish court; they knew how to reach Lerma and how to work through him and through individuals around them (even those placed by Lerma to monitor the women) in order to obtain what they desired. The Habsburg women were politically savvy and could turn a situation on its head when necessary.

All three women worked principally through the individuals who surrounded and served them. Empress María employed her mayordomo, Juan de Borja, to give messages to the Duke of Lerma and councillors of state. Juan de Borja obviously had great affection for Empress María. He accompanied her on the trip from Central Europe to Castile in 1581 as her mayordomo, and he served in that capacity until her death, in February 1603. He and his wife, Francisca de Aragón, cared greatly for the aging empress and served her faithfully. From 1599 until the empress's death, Juan de Borja corresponded regularly with his nephew, the Duke of Lerma, who instructed Borja to write him often and regularly.[42] Lerma sought to keep abreast of Borja's opinions and decisions in conciliar matters (Borja served on the Councils of Portugal and Finance), but he also wanted to monitor the empress's activities. Through Borja, Lerma hoped to watch the empress closely and prevent her from interfering in royal matters. Borja was caught between his duty and loyalty to Empress María and his familial connection to Lerma—a connection that brought Borja material benefits.

Nevertheless, Juan de Borja continued to serve the empress and present her requests to the Duke of Lerma. Empress María certainly took advantage of Borja's regular correspondence with and access to Lerma: she frequently sent messages to Lerma through Borja. Her letters to Philip III often went by way of Borja, who gave them to Lerma to deliver directly to the monarch.[43] When she wanted to protest one of Lerma's actions or petition him on behalf of one of her servants, she did so through Juan de Borja. In this way, Empress María made the most of a situation that Lerma had hoped to use to his own advantage. This was certainly true of her former servant, Pedro de Ledesma. In 1599, she petitioned on his behalf for the office of Secretary of the Council of Finance (*Secretario de Hazienda*). Borja grew tired of Empress María's demands and continuously reminded Lerma of the need to see to her request.[44] Eventually, Ledesma was granted the office that she had requested. Undoubtedly, Empress María had also asked the monarch directly. In fact, Borja noted that she wanted him to remind Lerma to give Ledesma the office, because Philip III had already assured her that he could have it.[45] The empress still knew that it was best to work through Lerma as well and to pester him until her demand had been met.

Empress María knew that Borja was supposed to write Lerma and detail her activities. She therefore used this opportunity to present her requests to Lerma, to ask him to talk to Philip III on her behalf, or simply to ask him of news of the monarchs and the court.[46] Empress María usually had Borja assure Lerma of her affection and regard for him.[47] This correspondence was a way for the empress to try to control Lerma. In January 1602, having heard of Spanish financial assistance to Flanders, Empress María thanked Lerma heartily and claimed that she would always be "most obligated to do all that would give pleasure and contentment" to him.[48] She (and Borja) recognized that Lerma needed constant reassurance and that her expressions of affection could only serve to win the privado over to her side.[49]

Although Empress María did not stop having direct contact with the monarch, she still recognized that it was important to appease Lerma and curry favor with him. Lerma was a principal way for Empress María to reach the monarch when Philip III was outside Madrid. But more than anything, Empress María knew that she could pressure Juan de Borja, and he in turn would have little choice but to press Lerma for her requests. Empress María was very successful in both employing Juan de Borja and winning Lerma's attention and assistance. Juan de Borja was a principal member of Empress María's network of individuals, and he subsequently served as the queen's mayordomo, thereby becoming part of the queen's network as well.

Empress María also relied on her secretary, Juan Carrillo, who served as the diplomatic representative of Archduke Albert at the Spanish court. Carrillo served Empress María for the last years of her life, not only reporting her activities to her son, Archduke Albert, but also helping her communicate with members of the Spanish court. Carrillo regularly visited the court when it moved to Valladolid, and Empress María was able to use him to take her messages there. In return, Empress María secured important offices for him. Through her petitions, Juan Carrillo became a secretary of the Inquisition, an office that brought him income and prestige.

The empress also employed the imperial ambassador Hans Khevenhüller to help her negotiate at the Spanish court. Khevenhüller took her requests to Lerma and other Spanish ministers, and, like Carrillo, he went to the court in Valladolid to convey messages from Empress María and from the Austrian Habsburgs. As the imperial ambassador to Spain, Khevenhüller had occasion to meet regularly with Philip III, Lerma, councillors of state, and other ambassadors. Empress María made sure that when Khevenhüller met with these individuals, he took messages from her. Khevenhüller reported the contents of these meetings to the empress and kept her abreast of political developments. Khevenhüller also met frequently with Margaret of Austria and was able to help the queen remain in touch with Empress María and Margaret of the Cross. By performing these functions, Khevenhüller was an essential link in the network of the Habsburg women.

Queen Margaret of Austria relied on a similar network of individuals for personal support and companionship and for influencing policy at the Spanish court. She could use her affectionate relationship with Philip III, her private access to him, and their blood ties to sway his opinion on given matters. Her power and influence were not direct; in large part she had a voice in political matters only because Philip III trusted her and listened to her advice. In this way, Margaret of Austria followed the pattern of other royal and aristocratic women, who wielded public power because they had private and personal influence with a powerful man.[50] Yet Margaret of Austria had to contend with the Duke of Lerma and with his efforts to limit her access to Philip. Lerma often encouraged the king to travel without his wife, whose frequent pregnancies gave the privado a legitimate reason for encouraging these separations.[51] The queen therefore developed her own ways of reaching the monarch, of gaining information about policy decisions, and of exercising a political voice. Moreover, she used her time away from Philip III to associate with other women, most of whom were nuns, and to strengthen her private network of influence. She regularly stayed at the Descalzas monastery when Philip III left Madrid, and she also visited nuns in cloistered convents. Through these activities, the queen gained a reputation for piety and even sanctity. The nuns would sing the queen's praises even when Margaret of Austria was not there. Because Philip III often visited convents with or without the queen, Margaret's networks of women within these convents helped remind the king of his wife and constituted an informal means for the queen to pressure Philip III on behalf of her own agenda.

Margaret of Austria worked primarily through her confessor, Richard Haller. Haller was often entrusted with communicating the queen's messages to councillors of state. Margaret would at times meet with these ministers at special audiences, but she relied on Haller to meet with them on a more regular basis. So, for example, in 1602 Haller gave a petition to Cristobal de Ipeñarieta, the secretary of the Council of Finance, asking for 100 ducats for Juan Ox, one of the queen's servants who regularly took her mail to Central Europe.[52] In this case, the money was given to Haller, who then used it to buy a chain (*cadena*) for Ox as a form of repayment. Thus, Haller not only delivered the petition but he was then entrusted with receiving and using the money. It is therefore fully understandable that Margaret of Austria eventually made Richard Haller one of the principal executors of her will. But Haller's central role as confessor to and messenger of the queen aroused Lerma's suspicion. Haller was forced to defend himself and the Jesuit order against charges that Jesuit confessors revealed the secrets of the confessional to their superiors.[53] In his letter of defense, however, Haller noted that a Jesuit priest could negotiate secular matters as long as he had the approval of his superior.

When the queen's two brothers, Archdukes Ferdinand and Leopold, requested financial assistance from Philip III for the struggle against the Protestants in Central Europe, Richard Haller gave a petition to the Council of State in which he suggested a way of giving the archdukes money through rents in Italy.[54] Although Lerma did not mention it on this occasion, Haller was undoubtedly acting in the queen's name. Haller's request followed a letter from Archduke Ferdinand to the queen asking her to plead with Philip III to help their cause. Ferdinand petitioned in his name, that of his wife, his sons, and the entire House of Austria.[55] In this case, as in others, the queen had Haller communicate the political message to the Council of State.

Haller also often communicated the queen's messages to others through writing. In 1606, for example, Haller wrote Duke Maximilian of Bavaria in the queen's name, telling him that the queen had met with Alfonso Carrillo, the representative for the Catholic League, and had promised to do all she could to assist him and the League.[56] In this case, the queen could show support for a cause such as the Catholic League without committing to it in writing. She could always claim that Haller had misunderstood her. Margaret of Austria was therefore able to take advantage of being a woman, who was not supposed to be directly involved in negotiating political matters. She could work through Haller, but working through an intermediary ultimately made her words less binding.

The other principal figure in the queen's network was Diego de Guzmán. As royal almoner, Guzmán had regular access to the king. He was able to speak to Philip III after lunch, he was present at the king's audiences, and he often attended the meetings of the Council of State. With such contact, Guzmán could report political matters to the queen and also bring her petitions to the attention of the councillors of state and of Philip III. The queen also worked very closely with Guzmán in matters that brought her fame and a reputation for piety: giving alms, feeding the poor, reforming the convent of Santa Isabel, and founding the royal convent of the Encarnación. The royal almoner cooperated closely with Richard Haller, and together they formed the core of the queen's network of influence at the Spanish court.

Diego de Guzmán has often been considered a part of the Duke of Uceda's network. In the last years of Philip III's reign, after the queen's death, Guzmán probably did seek the protection of the Duke of Uceda. He remained royal almoner until the end of Philip III's reign and seems to have fared well during the years of Uceda's privanza (1618–21). However, this should not hide the fact that he was one of the queen's closest associates, that he was also a direct link between the Descalzas and the court, and that he probably also worked in conjunction with Margaret of the Cross after the queen's death. The career of Diego de Guzmán shows the difficulties in separating court players too neatly into distinct factions.

The queen also worked successfully with the women around her. Her principal female associate throughout her years at the Spanish court was her Austrian lady-in-waiting, Maria Sidonia. Sidonia carried messages for the queen to the Descalzas and accompanied her in most of her activities.[57] The queen rewarded Sidonia financially throughout her lifetime and bequeathed her a large sum in her will.[58] As previously mentioned, the Duke of Lerma placed the Marquesa del Valle, Magdalena de Guzmán, in the queen's entourage in order to monitor her activities. The queen was successful, however, in incorporating the Marquesa del Valle into her personal network. The cooperation between the two women seems to have begun shortly after the queen's arrival in Spain. Empress María's secretary, Juan Carrillo, claimed that the Marquesa del Valle's support had allowed Haller to remain as the queen's confessor. This association between Haller and Magdalena de Guzmán may have helped the marquesa to cooperate and identify more with the queen than with Lerma.[59] Margaret of Austria was also successful in winning Lerma's wife, Catalina de la Cerda, to her side. When Lerma tried to remove his wife from her position as camarera mayor to the queen, Margaret tried to prevent him from doing so.[60] Through these women, the queen managed to subvert the very network Lerma had set up to control her. She also organized a powerful group of women through whom she could operate at the court and who would provide her with companionship. By acting as a benefactor for these women and winning financial benefits for them, the queen also displayed the influence she wielded with Philip.[61]

Until Empress María's death, Margaret of the Cross was not a major player in the game of politics at the Spanish court. When the empress died, however, Margaret assumed many of her mother's diplomatic responsibilities. To make this transition, Empress María left provisions ensuring her daughter received a mayordomo, was provided with servants and a regular income, and was granted the authority to give audiences.[62] Although Margaret of the Cross's biographer claimed that the nun did not welcome these new responsibilities, Margaret assumed them nonetheless. She worked primarily through her mayordomo, Rodrigo de Aguila, who took messages from the nun to the Spanish court. She often wrote directly to the Duke of Lerma and met with him at the Descalzas. She knew how to win his affection by appealing to his sense of power: in her letters, she always told Lerma that she trusted him, that she was sure he would assist her, and that she had great affection for him.[63] Margaret of the Cross certainly recognized the influence Lerma had at the Spanish court and realized that a good way of being successful with her petitions was to work directly through him.

Margaret of the Cross also regularly wrote to the Archduke and Archduchess in Flanders (Archduke Albert and Isabel Clara Eugenia), who she knew corresponded with Lerma and had a good relationship with him. She always reminded them to speak well of her to Lerma and ask him to meet her requests and those of her brothers in Central Europe. Archduke Albert and Isabel Clara Eugenia did indeed write to the Duke of Lerma and ask him to see to Margaret's needs and requests. In addition, Margaret of the Cross worked closely with Hans Khevenhüller and the ambassadors who succeeded him. She worked well with his nephew, Franz Christoph Khevenhüller, the imperial ambassador who arrived at the Spanish court in 1617 and remained throughout the reign of Philip IV. She also became involved in the scramble for power that followed Lerma's dismissal from the court, in 1618. Margaret favored her distant relative Prince Filiberto of Savoy, who also had the support of Juan de Santa María.[64] Although Filiberto did not succeed in becoming Philip III's privado, Margaret's support of his pretensions shows her active involvement in court politics—especially on behalf of her relatives. It also demonstrates her allegiance to such critics of Lerma's privanza as Juan de Santa María.

The agenda of the three Habsburg women often matched that of councillors of state such as the Duke of Infantado and Spanish ambassadors in Central Europe such as Guillén de San Clemente and Baltasar de Zúñiga. All of these men stressed the importance of Spanish assistance to the Austrian Habsburgs in Central Europe (including Flanders) and continued Spanish financial involvement in the area. However, there does not seem to have been regular correspondence between the women and Spanish ambassadors to the imperial court. That is, there was no organized faction incorporating all of these people.[65] Nonetheless, taken together, they constituted a strong voice at the Spanish court, one that continuously reminded Philip III of his duties to his relatives in Central Europe.

The three women differed slightly in their support for the Austrian Habsburgs. Empress María was primarily concerned with assisting her sons, Emperor Rudolf II and Archdukes Matthias, Maximilian and Albert. She helped Archduke Albert in particular (he was clearly her favorite) and was especially concerned with getting Philip III to assist him in Flanders.[66] Margaret of the Cross also petitioned specifically for her brothers Rudolf, Matthias, Maximilian, and Albert. Even though Margaret of Austria petitioned for these men (her cousins) as well, she was more concerned with helping her own brothers, Archdukes Ferdinand, Leopold, and Maximilian. She was also very interested in arranging suitable marriages for her sisters and was very successful in getting Lerma to help her negotiate matches. Lerma consistently pressed Rudolf II to assist in negotiating marriages, and eventually Archduchess Maria Magdalena, one of Margaret's sisters, married the son of the Grand Duke of Florence. In this way, the queen successfully used Lerma's power and influence at the court to advance her own agenda. The difference in focus among the three women clearly shows that aristocratic women were supposed to work for the benefit of their own family, and that family was often narrowly defined. For whatever purposes, the Habsburg women were quite successful in negotiating at the Spanish court and working in concert with the individuals who surrounded them.

As members of the royal family, Empress María, Margaret of Austria, and Margaret of the Cross followed the Spanish royal tradition of protecting their privacy and remaining inaccessible to the public. They were even more isolated than the king because, as women, they needed male permission or male escort to be seen in public.[67] Their daily contact was with those relatives, servants, nuns, and priests who made up their support network. As women, Empress María, Margaret of Austria, and Margaret of the Cross could not hold public office or attend meetings of governmental councils. Their open participation in the political world was further curtailed by a society that emphasized women's maternal and pious roles and tended to see women as domestic creatures. The focus of such women was supposed to be on issues dealing with relatives, religion, servants, and patronage.

Aristocratic women had a strong network of servants who relied on them for pensions, offices, and other types of financial support. For the Habsburg women, these included Juan de Borja, Pedro de Ledesma, Maria Sidonia, Richard Haller, and the nuns of the Descalzas (who regularly had Empress María and Margaret of the Cross ask the monarch to provide them with necessities such as wood).[68] It was important for the Habsburg women to petition successfully on behalf of these individuals, because doing so was a sign of their power as well as their influence with Philip III. Moreover, if they failed to provide for their network of friends, clients, and servants, then they would not have fulfilled the duties expected of aristocratic women.

The third principal political network at the court of Philip III was that led by Cristóbal Gómez de Sandoval, Duke of Uceda and eldest son of the Duke of Lerma, and Luis de Aliaga, the royal confessor. The Duke of Uceda benefited from his father's privanza: as mentioned earlier, Lerma had Uceda appointed Gentilhombre de la Cámara to Philip III, an appointment that allowed

Uceda access to the king's private chambers. For the first years of Philip III's reign, Uceda cooperated with his father in promoting the interests of the Sandoval family. Although he had gained power through his father, Uceda became conscious of his own ability to win influence and favor at the Spanish court. As his father came to be embroiled in court politics and the problems surrounding the arrest of Alonso Ramírez de Prado and Pedro Franqueza in 1607, Uceda began to court Philip III and Margaret of Austria for his own interests.

Lerma indirectly assisted his son in these political aspirations by delegating greater authority to him. This was particularly true during Lerma's periodic bouts of melancholy, which often occurred at times of personal crisis; he experienced this malaise in 1608, after Franqueza's arrest, and again in 1612, when Rodrigo Calderón was accused of having poisoned the queen.[69] The Duke of Lerma also reacted to the criticism he was experiencing by directing his efforts to becoming a cardinal.[70] This desire to hold one of the highest religious offices caused Lerma to hand over the court offices of Caballerizo Mayor and Sumillers de Corps to his son. In fact, by 1615 Lerma had left most of the day-to-day activities of his palace appointments and official correspondence (*despachos*) to Uceda.[71]

Although Uceda did not immediately challenge his father directly or openly, he profited from the greater access to Philip III these court offices brought him.[72] Uceda gradually began to usurp the very networks Lerma had set up. By 1615, Lerma's continued support of Rodrigo Calderón, who had by then been discredited at the Spanish court, caused the privado's influence to diminish greatly and, in turn, caused Uceda to break with his father openly and side with Luis de Aliaga, Philip III's confessor.[73] Uceda acted in part to protect the interests and reputation of the Sandoval family, a reputation that was being spoiled by Lerma's continued association with Calderón. Yet the break with his father and the association with Luis de Aliaga allowed the Duke of Uceda to usurp his father's position at the Spanish court, and with it came greater personal power and prestige.

One sign of Uceda's increasing influence at the Spanish court and his greater means of winning favor with the king and queen was the lavish way that he waited upon the Spanish monarchs. In 1611, Uceda hosted the king and queen and their entourage at his home in Madrid. Diego de Guzmán reported that more than six hundred dishes were served at the afternoon meal (*merienda*). Afterward, Uceda gave the king a desk whose drawers were filled with pieces of crystal, gold, and silver. The queen received a silver perfume dispenser, the Infanta Anne an agate rosary, the Countess of Lemos a *bunquillo* of diamonds, and all the ladies-in-waiting amber gloves and perfumed water (*agua de olor*) in silver flasks.[74] The striking difference between the gifts for the king and queen indicates that Uceda aimed to win the king's favor and not necessarily the queen's. Moreover, the value of his gift to the Countess of Lemos, the queen's camarera mayor and Uceda's aunt, at least equaled that of the queen's. Uceda clearly did not see the queen as a prime candidate for his favor; the disparity among the gifts undoubtedly also reflects the animosity and rivalry between Margaret of Austria and the Duke of Uceda. Nevertheless, because entertaining the monarchs was a privilege enjoyed by very few individuals, Uceda's ability to invite the king and queen to dine at his home was a clear sign of his growing influence at the court. On the other hand, Uceda's faltering relationship with Philip III can be seen in an incident from 1620. Philip III and his children were visiting Uceda's new house on Corpus Christi and Uceda presented them with an impressive banquet, and yet the king refused to touch any of the food.[75]

On the whole, the Duke of Uceda was interested in securing court offices only because these offices gave him access to the monarch. He also tried to get individuals favorable to him appointed to important positions: for instance, when the presidency of Castile became vacant in 1610, Uceda and Aliaga pressured Philip III to choose Juan de Acuña, a relative of Uceda's wife.[76] Uceda had clearly learned his tactics from his father. The case of Juan de Acuña particularly tested the relative powers of Uceda and Lerma with Philip III. Lerma presented his own candidate for the position, but the king ultimately awarded it to Acuña.[77] Like his father, Uceda refrained from seeking an appointment to the Council of State, even when the death of the Count of Idiáquez in 1614 brought about a vacancy in the council. Uceda seems to have had no clear foreign policy agenda or even a consistent political policy to urge on Philip III. Instead, Uceda was motivated strictly by his own personal gain and that of his family.

Uceda's collaborator from 1615 until 1621 was Luis de Aliaga, a Dominican priest. In 1608, when Philip III's confessor was removed because he openly criticized the Duke of Lerma, Aliaga was appointed as royal confessor. Lerma believed that by so doing, he could control the confessor and gain access to the king's most private thoughts. However, Aliaga was a personally ambitious man who used his new position to enhance his own power and eventually to work against his patron, the Duke of Lerma. It was Aliaga who worked against Rodrigo Calderón and began the rumor that Calderón had poisoned the queen. Yet Calderón's return to the Spanish court in 1612 did not signify a loss of influence for Luis de Aliaga.

Aliaga's appointment to the Council of State in 1611 was one of the clear indications of Lerma's diminishing favor. Lerma felt so threatened by Aliaga that in 1615 he went so far as to send his Jesuit confessor, Hans Friedrich Helder, to urge Philip III to dismiss Aliaga. Philip III refused to do so and Aliaga remained Philip's confessor up until the monarch's death, in 1621.[78] Thus, Philip's support of Aliaga rivaled Lerma's influence, and it was clear that by 1615 the king was not listening exclusively to his *privado*. Together Aliaga and Uceda worked to limit Lerma's power and take advantage of his physical weakness and waning influence with the monarch.

Uceda and Aliaga retained much influence at the Spanish court until the end of Philip's reign; however, their influence never reached the level Lerma's had. For example, Philip III issued a decree in 1618 that he alone would sign royal orders. This decree effectively ended the Duke of Lerma's ability to sign royal decrees, but it also meant that no one else—including Uceda and Aliaga— would receive this right. This decree implied a change in the style of government and meant that Philip III would not give anyone the *privanza* he had accorded to the Duke of Lerma.[79] Moreover, Philip III continued to seek the advice of other individuals even as he relied on Uceda and Aliaga. From 1618 until 1621, court observers wondered if the Duke of Lerma would return, especially once it became clear that neither Uceda nor Aliaga had great political talents.[80] This was particularly a problem when the situation in Central Europe became tense in 1618.

Observers speculated about who would assume Lerma's place with Philip III. Among those supposedly favored by Philip III were Prince Filiberto of Savoy and Juan de Santa María.[81] The court preacher Jerónimo de Florencia was also thought to have much influence over Philip III.[82] The king began to follow the advice of Baltasar de Zúñiga, who had returned to Madrid in 1617. His expert opinion about Central Europe proved especially valuable to the monarch from 1618 to 1621. Zúñiga also used his position as tutor (*ayo*) to Prince Philip (the future Philip IV) in order to influence the successor to the throne. In this way, Zúñiga worked against Uceda and Aliaga. Nevertheless, none of these men was able to gain the power at court Lerma had once held.

That people wondered which of these individuals would gain full power at the court, however, is a clear sign that Philip III did not listen to any one single person in the last few years of his reign. The monarch might even have been consciously playing these competitors off each other in order to ensure that no one person became too powerful. At Philip IV's accession to the throne, Uceda, Aliaga, and most of their associates were quickly discredited. Aliaga was stripped of all his offices and exiled to a little town in Aragón. Uceda was permanently dismissed from court and died in Alcalá de Henares in 1624.[83] With Zúñiga's influence at the Spanish court, the group who had supported the cause of the Austrian Habsburgs won prominence at the court, and after Philip III's death, the Habsburg women's cause finally won out.

Lerma's gradual loss of favor with Philip III created a vacuum at the court, a vacuum in which many individuals scrambled for power. In particular, the Sandoval family, which had profited so much from the Duke of Lerma's privanza, struggled among themselves to retain their influence. The jockeying for power between the Duke of Lerma and the Duke of Uceda, the attempts by the Count of Lemos to gain court appointments and his mother's frustration with the Duke of Lerma for not supporting him, were part of a larger conflict within the Sandoval family to recover power at Philip III's court. This breakdown of family unity and the disorder their quarrels brought to the court caused Philip III to give prominent court offices to another family: that of the Zúñigas and Guzmáns. Individuals such as Baltasar de Zúñiga and his uncle, the future Count-Duke of Olivares, received appointments to the household of Prince Philip, appointments that in earlier days would have gone to the Sandovals. These offices allowed them to gain influence with Prince Philip and paved the way for the Zúñigas and Guzmáns to take over the court, displacing the Sandovals.[84]

※ ※ ※

The Habsburg kings were private monarchs who emphasized their majesty by restricting their contact with most individuals, a tendency the Duke of Lerma encouraged in Philip III. Lerma knew that his favor with the monarch would gain him private access to Philip and that the king would refrain from seeing other individuals. To this end, Lerma attempted to control access to the monarch. Lerma's efforts to limit access did not cause courtiers to give up trying to reach the monarch. Instead, courtiers sought access to Philip III through other means. In particular, they tried to use the Habsburg women to reach the king.

Empress María, Margaret of Austria, and Margaret of the Cross had the right to meet with Philip III privately because of their familial connections to the monarch. Moreover, the devotional practices of the Habsburg family ensured that Philip III would regularly join the Habsburg women in religious activities. When these religious activities occurred in places such as the Descalzas Reales, the monarch often stayed afterward to visit his grandmother and his aunt. On account of this contact, the Habsburg women served as alternate routes for individuals to reach the monarch. These routes transcended the power of Philip III's privado; the Duke of Lerma was unable to destroy or to usurp these familial paths.

The Duke of Uceda and Luis de Aliaga provided still other alternate routes to Philip III. Uceda took advantage of the offices his father had won for him, offices Lerma thought would secure his own power at the court. Uceda increasingly bypassed his father, thereby becoming a rival path to Philip III. Luis de Aliaga followed a similar strategy, having acquired influence through Lerma; and yet the office he gained—that of royal confessor—in essence gave him power over Philip III that Lerma could never fully enjoy. His appointment as royal confessor allowed Aliaga to win the monarch's confidence (by all accounts, Philip III was very pleased with Aliaga as his confessor), and in turn meant that Aliaga no longer had to rely on the Duke of Lerma to gain access to the king. Aliaga could then serve as a conduit for other individuals to reach the monarch without having to go through the Duke of Lerma.

Even as the Duke of Lerma set out to create a network that would afford him exclusive access to Philip III, his network carried the seeds of its own destruction. Lerma thought he could rely on his own family and his own clients (*hechuras*) to cement his privanza. However, these proved to be some of his most dangerous enemies. Moreover, his familial network also held an inherent disadvantage. Although Lerma could promote his own Sandoval family, he still could not destroy the familial bonds that linked Philip III to his Austrian Habsburg relatives. Lerma was unable to remove the privileges that familial ties afforded the Austrian Habsburgs, so Empress María, Margaret of Austria, and Margaret of the Cross were able to find the means to circumvent the privado's authority. Lerma's system dictated the type of maneuvering that individuals would pursue at the court; that is, people seeking access to the monarch would have to win court office, work through royal confessors, or have influence with the Habsburg women. Lerma's system was not new; many before him had gained power with monarchs in similar ways. What was new was the particular family in power and the extent of Lerma's influence at the court. Nevertheless, Lerma never had exclusive control over the monarch, and various individuals challenged his authority consistently throughout the reign. The Habsburg women were some of Lerma's most powerful opponents and were certainly a major part of the factional conflict at the court.

3

Fashioning Female Models
from Royal Women

Posthumous Accounts

THE HISTORICAL IMAGE OF Empress María, Margaret of Austria, and
Margaret of the Cross has in large part been shaped by men whose purpose was to create a devotional and idealized picture of these Habsburg
women. This picture, presented in eulogies and biographies written after the
women's deaths, set up the Habsburg women as examples of feminine virtue
and proper behavior for aristocratic women. Such an account of these royal
women does not correspond to the reality of their lives; that is, the authors portrayed only select facets of their lives, facets that corresponded to the picture
those men wished to portray—and even then, these details were cast in a biased
light. In these documents, there was little or no mention of the political side of
the Habsburg women's lives. This devotional literature was at root pedagogi-
cal because the authors aimed not only to eulogize and praise the women but
also to present them as models for other generations of royal women. Moreover, male relatives usually commissioned the authors to write the laudatory
works.

Empress María, Margaret of Austria, and Margaret of the Cross clearly transcended the roles prescribed for them by men. Despite the attempts of their biographers to depict and define them in strictly pious terms, the comments of
individuals around the women demonstrate that all three concerned themselves
with political issues. Although they followed seventeenth-century notions of
piety and, like many Spanish aristocratic women, patronized religious institu-

tions, their piety did not preclude a concern for political issues, particularly those matters that affected their relatives. These women often used religious devotion and familial duties as a means of expressing their political concerns; that is, they consciously couched their political demands in the language of family and piety. Furthermore, the reports of their piety come to us from male observers, who no doubt thought this religious devotion was appropriate for royal women.

The picture presented in biographies and eulogies, however, cannot be completely dismissed because of its overt bias. Men perpetuated this image of royal women, which served to tell later generations that royal women had no political role and were supposed to spend their lives in prayer and charitable deeds. This portrayal corresponded to early modern notions that women should speak only through prayer and examples. Therefore, by examining this picture, we can begin to understand how men wanted to perceive royal women, how they tried to use the printed word to restrict female action and power, and how, as an unfortunate result, historians have written the history of politics without considering the role played by royal women. By describing women in strictly devotional terms, men attempted to marginalize them and to obscure their political importance. We can then turn to an evaluation of the political roles these women actually did play and compare them to these male-created images.

Empress María of Austria was the eldest daughter of Charles V, and in 1548 she married her cousin, Maximilian of Austria. In the same year, Charles V, Holy Roman Emperor and King of Spain, appointed the married couple regents of Spain: Maximilian served as regent until 1550, and María until 1551. In 1551, Maximilian and María went to Central Europe, where Maximilian served first as King of Bohemia and then, from 1564 until his death, in 1576, as Holy Roman Emperor. María remained in Central Europe until 1581, when Philip II gave her license to return to Madrid and enter the convent of the Descalzas Reales. This convent, established by the Infanta Juana, (also a daughter of Charles V), housed many noblewomen, including several women of the Habsburg family.[1] When the empress left Central Europe for Madrid, she was accompanied by her daughter Margaret (who was to take the name Margaret of the Cross), her mayordomo, Juan de Borja (who had served as Philip II's ambassador in Prague), and a large retinue of servants.

The court-sanctioned picture of Empress María, of her life and accomplishments, appeared in 1603 in the funeral sermon delivered by Jerónimo de Florencia, court preacher to Philip III and a member of the Jesuit order. Fray Jerónimo gave the sermon at the funeral service offered by the Jesuit school in Madrid (to which the empress left a large sum in her will), and the sermon was subsequently published in a book commemorating the event.[2] Jerónimo de Florencia's funerary sermon later formed the core of the biography of Empress María which Rodrigo Mendes Silva wrote in 1655.[3] Mendes Silva, who was court chronicler to Philip IV, was most probably commissioned by the king to write the work.

Jerónimo de Florencia and Mendes Silva depicted Empress María strictly as a pious widow who had retired to the monastery in order to live a life of prayer. Nevertheless, Fray Jerónimo emphasized the political, and even masculine, ramifications of that prayer. He argued that Empress María chose a life in a monastery in order to pray and work incessantly for the defense of the Catholic faith. In sixteenth- and seventeenth-century terms, the defense of the Catholic faith meant primarily a defense of western Europe from the advances of the Turks into the lands of the Austrian Habsburgs. A defense of the faith also meant a support of the struggle against Protestants in Central Europe and in Flanders, territories controlled by Austrian Habsburgs. Fray Jerónimo argued that Empress María had chosen a female way—that is, prayer—to fight for the interests of her family. While her sons in Central Europe struggled to defend the Catholic church against the Protestants and the Turks, Empress María struggled spiritually in the Descalzas. The honor and respect she gained by living in a monastery lent her pleas concerning her Austrian relatives more weight with Philip II and Philip III, particularly because she could claim to be closer to God and more able to interpret his wishes.

Through prayer, Empress María supposedly fought as hard for the faith as did her sons on the battlefield. Jerónimo de Florencia argued that, in fighting for the defense of Catholicism, Empress María fought like a male warrior. "She fought in a manly fashion [*varonilmente*] from the monastery, from the choir, with squadrons of heroic virtues."[4] When emphasizing the strength of the empress's prayer and her fight to defend the faith, Fray Jerónimo chose masculine terms because physical strength and battle skills were thought to be exclusively male attributes. Widows like Empress María were thought to take on masculine characteristics when forced to assume greater responsibility after their husbands' death.[5] In fact, the moralist Juan de la Cerda implied that a good widow had to be masculine: "The masculine and good widow has to be both father and mother. [She] has to have the rod and discipline of the father, and the breasts of the mother: the breasts of gentleness [*mansedumbre*] and good teaching and the rod of strict punishment and discipline."[6]

It was also common to describe nuns who were especially fervent in their prayers as masculine. So, for example, Mariana de San José, prioress of the Monastery of the Encarnación in Madrid from 1612 to 1638, was described by her nuns as virile (*varonil*). Madre Aldonza, who succeeded Mariana de San José as prioress, described her predecessor as "a prudent, manly woman who can be called a prudent and wise woman."[7] Madre Aldonza also said that Mariana de San José's tears were those of a man, not of a woman. These comments, found in testimonies taken from nuns who knew her, were the first part of a process to beatify the prioress. The masculine qualities attributed to Mariana de San José were used to make her more legitimate to a masculine audience. Thus, when female piety had direct implications for the political, military, and intellectual world, or when an author wished to characterize female piety as a positive attribute, it was usually described in masculine terms.

Jerónimo de Florencia's descriptions illustrate the inability of seventeenth-century men to accept that women (even those of imperial lineage) could, by nature, be strong, constant, and wise.[8] Women who exhibited these characteristics were said to have superseded the expectations of their gender. Men cast women as pious creatures, content to retreat into monasteries and convents to pray for the success of their male relatives; yet, to lend importance to that piety, its effects had to be described in masculine terms. Fray Jerónimo depicted Empress María in a way that her contemporaries could understand her—as a woman following accepted notions of proper behavior for widows and for Habsburgs. After all, her father, Charles V, and her sister, the Infanta Juana of Portugal, had also spent the last years of their lives in religious institutions. Because Jerónimo de Florencia wanted to emphasize that Empress María could be a role model for other aristocratic women, he stressed female characteristics and actions that the male world found appropriate while also emphasizing that if women succeeded in following this model, they could show the strength of men and gain acceptance in a male world.

In his sermon, Jerónimo de Florencia also wished to show that Empress María continued to aid her relatives in Central Europe even as she lived in a monastery in Madrid. Because María's prayers had political significance and because men considered the political world to be their domain, Jerónimo de Florencia had to describe the effectiveness of her prayers in masculine terms. In his account, however, he implied that Empress María's political action was limited to prayers and did not involve any direct pressure on the male hierarchy of the Spanish court. In this way, Florencia upheld the early modern notion that a woman should remain silent whenever possible and should voice her concerns only privately, through prayer. As the influential Castilian humanist Juan Luis Vives explained, speaking did not become a woman: a husband should teach his wife to be silent because silence was the "most pleasing attire of her sex."[9]

Empress María was usually described solely in terms of her relationship to male members of the Habsburg dynasty and her place within a patriarchal family. Her importance was measured according to her conjugal and maternal connection to rulers. Rodrigo Mendes Silva's *Amirable vida y heroicas virtudes de aquel glorioso blasón de España* examined the life of Empress María from infancy to death.[10] In the biographer's estimation, María's particular distinction lay in her roles of wife and mother. God had given the empress the supreme happiness of "august earthly sons."[11] Mendes Silva also emphasized Empress María's renowned lineage, forged through blood and marriage ties to three emperors: she was the daughter of Charles V, the daughter-in-law of Ferdinand I, and the wife of Maximilian II. The empress was said to have had all of those qualities perfectly suited to women: "She sparkled in the Catholic world of the faith, [she was] rare in her discretion, admirable in her prudence, great in her mildness (*benignidad*), marvelous in her zeal, superior in justice, singular in modesty, and inimitable in her spirit and fervor."[12]

The picture of Empress María created by Mendes Silva posed no threat to existing male notions of royal women; María was a pious woman who knew her place within a patriarchal dynasty. As members of a dynastic house, royal women were expected to foster the interests of that house through marriage alliances and by providing heirs.[13] Undoubtedly, Empress María and the other Habsburg women identified with the needs of this patriarchal dynasty because their familial associations provided them with status, honor, and prestige.[14] Nevertheless, an examination of the lives of Empress María, Margaret of Austria, and Margaret of the Cross demonstrates that their political functions were not confined to serving the patriarchal dynasty.

Because a principal function of royal women in the early modern period was to serve as an example of upright conduct and familial devotion for other women, Mendes Silva emphasized the empress's proper role as mother and protectress of her family and of all her subjects. The good wife maintained order within her household because this household was a reflection of the family and of the father's authority. As the Franciscan priest Juan de la Cerda explained: "It is a known fact that when the wife tends to her duty, the husband loves her, the family functions well [*anda en concierto*] and the children learn virtue, and peace reigns, and one's wealth [*hazienda*] grows."[15] Cerda implied that the household was an essential part of the court. A good queen or empress was supposed to satisfy the requirements for a good wife, and she should also carefully supervise her retinue of servants to make her husband's court the model for a peaceful and orderly realm. In this conception, the feminine sphere of household management served as a parallel for the masculine sphere of the political realm. The line between the political and the familial was not clearly delineated in the early modern period. There was no exact division between private and public, between personal and political; the separation was largely for rhetorical purposes.

Uncontrollable servants signified poor management, which in turn implied that the wife was not fulfilling her duties.[16] This could not be said of Empress María, who, according to Mendes Silva, was personally responsible for her peaceful court because she embodied tranquility and benevolence. Mendes Silva noted that Empress María had a large entourage of servants from diverse territories, as was common in the multifaceted Central European empire of the Austrian Habsburgs. But the size and diversity of her personal court did not prevent the empress from imposing order, and her servants "never caused any scandal."[17] In the biographer's estimation, Empress María's great affection for her people contributed to this tranquil court. Mendes Silva reported that the empress told her confessor, in highly maternal language: "I truly love my subjects as children, and I would like to give each one blood from my veins."[18] Judging from such accounts, the empress seemed to fit the contemporary notion of royal women as benevolent mothers to their subjects, lovers of peace and tranquility who brought order to their homes and to their kingdoms.

Mendes Silva did not note, however, that Maximilian II's reign was anything but tranquil; during this period the Protestants in Central Europe gained religious concessions and the emperor himself began to have Protestant leanings.[19] Empress María attempted to instill orthodox Catholicism in her husband and her sons but was not completely successful. Afraid that they might imbibe the Protestant airs of Central Europe, María sent her sons Rudolf and Ernst to the Catholic court of Philip II from 1563 to 1571, so that they might learn Tridentine Catholicism and Spanish etiquette. Nevertheless, Rudolf and another son, Matthias, both future emperors, made major confessional concessions to the Protestants in their struggles against each other and in attempts to retain the imperial crown.[20] Mendes Silva wrote his biography of Empress María in 1655, after the Thirty Years' War and when the effects of Rudolf's and Matthias's religious concessions to the Protestants had become well known. But to mention María's inability to instill religious orthodoxy in her sons would have been a radical departure from the idealized picture of her as protectress of the Catholic faith, a picture that Mendes Silva and his patron, Philip IV, wished to project.

A good wife while her husband lived, according to observers Empress María also embodied the good widow after Maximilian's death, in 1576. As such, she was expected to retire from life, pray, and not burden her family.[21] Thus, Mendes Silva recorded that at Maximilian's death the empress shut herself up with her husband's corpse and prayed for his soul—an activity moralists had prescribed for widows. Juan de Sota recommended that widows remain close to their husbands' sepulchers and ensure that sacrifices were offered for the repose of their souls.[22] As her biographer noted, Empress María "had been an example of a perfect spouse; now she was a true example for widows."[23] The widowed empress, reported Mendes Silva, continued to be a proper mother, looking after the welfare of her children; after Maximilian's death she supposedly decided to devote her life completely to prayer, but she remained in Central Europe "settling imperial matters, to leave them in good order for her eldest son Rudolf."[24] The empress left for Spain only after she was sure that Rudolf could reign peacefully. Mendes Silva's portrayal overlooked the fact that Rudolf II refused at first to allow his mother to return to Spain.[25] The emperor was famous for his uncontrollable anger and ever-changing moods; his reluctance to allow his mother to leave for Castile was probably motivated more by ongoing political disagreements with Philip II than by filial affection.[26] Only after much pleading by Empress María and complicated diplomatic negotiations with Philip II did Rudolf consent to his mother's leaving Central Europe.

Empress María eventually followed her own inclination to return to the Spanish kingdoms and live within the Descalzas monastery. The empress's move to Castile signified much more than a retreat into a life of prayer; it was an act guaranteed to bring greater freedom and independence to a woman who was accustomed to having political influence. In the Descalzas convent, Empress María did not live the life of a cloistered nun. She had her own servants and a large court, complete with several poets and musicians who were well known in her day. She was free to leave the Descalzas—she regularly visited the royal family and conferred with Philip II and later with Philip III. She also received visitors at the monastery, including the king and queen, their royal children (all of whom visited the empress weekly or even daily during some periods), foreign ambassadors, and the papal nuncio.[27] Finally, she bequeathed a significant collection of art and religious objects that she had acquired both in Central Europe and in Spain to the Descalzas.[28]

The empress's decision to return to Castile should also be understood in light of her ongoing difficulties with her son Rudolf II. María did not enjoy a good relationship with Rudolf: the empress disapproved of her son's erratic behavior, and Rudolf II did not welcome his mother's political assistance. The emperor increasingly retreated from family, ministers, and courtiers and even moved the capital from Vienna to Prague to escape frequent contact with people.[29] Given such a situation, the empress's desire to move to Castile can be seen as a realization that she was unable to work closely with her son and that she might gain greater freedom and authority in the Spanish kingdoms. Rather than interpret Empress María's eventual trip to Spain as a sign of her independence and determination to pursue a life of her own choosing, Mendes Silva preferred to describe these years in terms of María's motherly and pious concerns. Although he emphasized that the empress devoted her life to prayer, Mendes Silva failed to mention that she continued to concern herself with political matters up until her death.

Humility was also a characteristically feminine virtue, particularly in a widow. As Juan de la Cerda explained, "a widow should be humble in spirit and should consider herself below all others."[30] Mendes Silva painted a portrait of Empress María as the humblest of women, whose humility emulated that of Christ himself. Although she could command respect as an empress, she chose instead to live the life of a nun. Mendes Silva recorded: "The perseverence which she always had in spiritual exercises seemed more those of a discalced religious than of an august empress."[31] Jerónimo de Florencia had also noted that María lived more like a nun than an empress. On the one hand, these comments emphasized the empress's humility; on the other, they implied that the humble life of a nun was more in character for a woman than that of a noble empress. It was almost formulaic to say that royal women lived more like nuns than royalty and that they preferred the life of the convent to that of the court. Mendes Silva wrote that Empress María refused to exercise authority over servants, preferring to request rather than demand their assistance, and she would not allow the nuns to call her "Majesty."[32] Authority and power were more in keeping with the male character, so it was fitting for royal women to show more deference, and less authority, toward others.

This mother of emperors and archdukes supposedly subordinated even her motherly instincts to her religious life. Both Jerónimo de Florencia and Mendes Silva reported that when letters from her children arrived, letters that the empress expected anxiously, they were not delivered until after she had finished her religious exercises.[33] Likewise, when her son Archduke Maximilian arrived at the Descalzas unexpectedly in 1601, the empress refused to see him until she had received communion. Maximilian waited the entire day before he was able to see his mother—a particularly noteworthy delay if it is true that Maximilian arrived incognito in Madrid after having secretly left Innsbruck. According to several reports, Maximilian's relatives feared that the archduke had died and were tremendously relieved when he appeared in Madrid. Nonetheless, his mother kept him waiting on account of her religious practices.[34]

The empress's choice of a solitary life corresponded to contemporary attitudes about widows. As Francisco de Osuna wrote, a widow was supposed "to be ashamed to walk around [*andar*], her house should be closed like a monastery, and she should not go out to visit, unless it is out to a hospital, or [to visit] the sick, and she should be ashamed of company; [she should only be with] widows and virgins."[35] Empress María's decision to live among the cloistered Franciscan nuns was thoroughly in keeping with such prescriptions, so Mendes Silva could claim that the empress set an example of virtue and displayed appropriate behavior for grieving widows. In describing her life, Mendes Silva used the accepted motif of aristocratic women giving up the secular world in exchange for a life of prayer and retirement in a monastery.

Yet, while men may have found the life of a convent an acceptable refuge for unmarried or widowed women, this way of life undoubtedly afforded women a certain amount of independence from the male world and allowed them to function within a community of women with similar backgrounds and outlooks.[36] For Empress María, moving into the Descalzas allowed her to retain her servants, attendants, and court, to accept visits from foreign ambassadors, and to act as the spokesperson for a group of aristocratic nuns. Although Empress María received many visitors at her rooms in the Descalzas, she was also able to leave the monastery whenever she desired and to negotiate informally for the Austrian Habsburgs at the Spanish court.

Empress María had served, with her husband Maximilian, as regent of the Spanish kingdoms from 1548 to 1551, while Charles V was in Brussels and Central Europe. Mendes Silva could not easily overlook the empress's political role,[37] and he noted that in Central Europe the empress "worked on reports and advice given to rulers in councils [*consultas*], grew weary [seeing to] governance . . . awarded prizes, weighed punishments, and as many actions as were performed because of her counsel, were then praised as right [*acertados*]."[38] This picture of María's political role, while probably glorified and exaggerated, at least acknowledged that, as the wife of Maximilian II, she had exercised a considerable political say. In fact, in Mendes Silva's description of the empress's political activities, she appeared sovereign, with little mention of her having a subordinate role to Maximilian II. Nevertheless, the political side of Empress María's life was not what her biographer ultimately wished to stress; his overall portrait was that of a devout wife and mother, and later of a good, pious widow.

Jerónimo de Florencia, unlike Mendes Silva, reported numerous breaks in the empress's religious schedule, which allowed her to give audiences and to speak with her daughter, Margaret of the Cross, and with the abbess and nuns at the Descalzas. Juan Carrillo, María's secretary and Archduke Albert's representative at Philip III's court, also noted these breaks in the empress's schedule in his history of the Descalzas Reales.[39] In his letters to the archduke, Carrillo stated that Empress María gave audiences,[40] but he failed to elaborate on their content, asserting only that at her meetings with her daughter and other nuns Empress María discussed strictly religious subjects. Jerónimo de Florencia, however, did not comment on the content of these meetings, although he implied that they were religious in nature. Nevertheless, by noting these occasions for conversation and, especially, the official audiences, Jerónimo de Florencia and Juan Carrillo acknowledged the empress's important voice both inside and outside the convent walls.

A pious widow living within a monastery of cloistered nuns and devoting her life to prayer for the success of her male relatives and the defense of the faith: this was the picture of Empress María that Jerónimo de Florencia and Rodrigo Mendes Silva presented. In every way possible, these authors stressed Empress María's embodiment of the standard set for women by men and created an image that did not challenge existing Spanish notions of proper female behavior. In fact, for the most part, Jerónimo de Florencia and Rodrigo Mendes Silva fit Empress María into preexisting male categories for discussing female activities; when she rejected or deviated from these stereotypes, her actions were reinterpreted in male categories so as to still allow the empress to conform to male notions of appropriate female behavior.

Margaret of Austria, Philip III's queen from 1599 until her death, in 1611, and an influential critic of the Duke of Lerma, came from the Styrian branch of the Austrian Habsburgs. Her biographer, Diego de Guzmán, noted that her daily activities as a young girl included attending mass, studying grammar, physical exercise, visiting the sick, and feeding the poor.[41] Book-learning blended regularly with charitable activities. Her mother, Archduchess Maria of Bavaria, was a formative influence in Margaret's education.[42] Although we know little of Margaret's schooling, we know that, like her sisters, she studied Latin. Margaret's older sister, Anna, began to study Latin at the age of six with a private tutor and also received extensive training in the German language.[43] Given Archduchess Maria's piety, it is not surprising that she chose a tutor for Margaret of Austria who specialized in theology.[44]

Archduchess Maria insisted that her children follow a daily schedule of charitable activities. From an early age, Margaret was trained to consider charitable deeds a central part of her life and of her education. These deeds were supposed to inculcate the virtues of piety, humility, and charity as well as ensure that the young girl stayed busy. Along with these qualities, Margaret's mother trained her to think about death and the afterlife rather than dedicate herself to the pursuit of material possessions.[45] These virtues were highly prized in noblewomen, and when Philip II chose Margaret as the bride for his son, Philip III, the Spanish king took into consideration her piety and education in Tridentine Catholicism.[46] Margaret had supposedly chosen the life of a nun before her betrothal to Philip III.[47] When she arrived in Spain in 1599, she was only fifteen years old, but her youth did not prevent her from stating her opinions and from defending the interests of her Austrian Habsburg relatives at the

Spanish court. The queen had eight children between 1601 and 1611, and she gained particular honor from giving birth to four sons, among them the future Philip IV.

When Margaret of Austria died at the age of twenty-six, rumors abounded that she had been bewitched and poisoned by the Duke of Lerma's close associate, Rodrigo Calderón (whom the queen had criticized openly).[48] As discussed earlier, this accusation eventually led to a criminal investigation, but Calderón, although he was convicted of other charges, was acquitted of murder. Numerous Spaniards bemoaned the great loss Margaret's death meant for the Spanish kingdoms; there were even those who claimed that Margaret had died a martyr.[49] This image of the saintly queen, sacrificed for her subjects and for her rejection of dishonest practices at the Spanish court, was established, however, only at the queen's death. It was perhaps the most powerful image created of Margaret of Austria and one that eulogists and her biographer perpetuated not only to use her as an example of a virtuous wife, mother, and queen but also to voice their criticism of the Spanish court during the reign of Philip III.

The predominant image of Margaret of Austria fostered by male observers was that of a devout and humble queen who was submissive to the men around her. In this way, the queen served as a "mirror for queens."[50] Diego de Guzmán, Philip III's royal almoner, wrote the queen's biography, most probably following Philip III's instructions. The king wanted the book to serve as a model for his daughter Anne, who married Louis XIII of France. Guzmán's goal, therefore, was to depict the perfect queen. Philip III instructed his daughter to read this account of her mother's life and to follow its example.[51] Guzmán noted Margaret's complete obedience to her confessor, Richard Haller, a Jesuit like Guzmán: "To her confessor she was so submissive and obedient that she could tell him what she felt with complete liberty, as if she were a novice in the faith. And on certain occasions she said to him, 'Father tell me . . . what I am in conscience obliged to do, and I will do it, even if it costs me my life.' . . . On another occasion she said that she would not be able to retain a confessor who did not tell her the simple, clear truth."[52]

Jerónimo de Florencia, the Jesuit priest and court preacher who delivered several of Margaret's eulogies, also emphasized the queen's submissiveness to her confessor.[53] According to Fray Jerónimo and Diego de Guzmán, Margaret of Austria treated Richard Haller (and all priests) with tremendous deference,

something which a queen was not commanded to do but which was manda-
tory for a religious novice.[54] In this way, she exemplified the saintly, pure queen
who modeled herself after a nun and thus confirmed and even surpassed the established social norms for royal women.[55] As Florencia stated, "in her person
she had the purple of a queen but in her soul lay the inclination and love of
the virginal state of nuns."[56]

Margaret of Austria seemed to fit the mold of obedient wife, acting under
her husband's orders and spending time in prayer when she could not be with
him. She was supposed to follow the advice given to wives of all social classes,
to stay in the house when ordered to do so by her husband, without attending any social functions and without speaking to anyone.[57] She also followed
her mother's instructions to obey, respect, and love Philip III (in that order).[58]
Diego de Guzmán recorded that when Philip went to Valencia to attend a
meeting of its parliamentary body (*corts*), he left Margaret in Madrid at the
Descalzas monastery with instructions to remain there until he returned.
Guzmán noted that the queen hated to be left behind, but she agreed to follow
her husband's orders. "Never did a wife . . . with the great love she had for her
husband, suffer so much to be away from him . . . no other [wife] was so re-
signed in this and in everything which he ordered her. She was certainly a rare
example in both things."[59]

While at the Descalzas, according to Diego de Guzmán, the queen did not
leave the convent except with the express consent of her husband. Guzmán indicated two such occasions: one to attend a mass presided over by Guzmán
himself at the Jesuit residence in Madrid, and the other to visit orphans.[60] Because an aristocratic woman was expected to concern herself with piety and
charitable deeds, it was acceptable for the queen to leave the convent on those
two occasions. Guzmán's glowing description of the queen was intended to
project an image of wifely deference and compliance; this language hid the fact
that the Descalzas was actually one of the political centers in Madrid.

According to Jerónimo de Florencia, Margaret of Austria was a "brave and
strong" (*valerosa y fuerte*) woman.[61] Fray Jerónimo claimed that the queen
thought always of her salvation and in so doing demonstrated masculine
strength and a rational mind. In order to concentrate on salvation, Florencia
reported, one needed a manly heart (*pecho varonil*), something the queen clearly
possessed. As in his description of Empress María, Fray Jerónimo compared
Margaret's strength, described in masculine terms, to that of military squad-

rons. "The queen showed this [manly strength] in the ease with which she conquered her desires and preferences, always giving in to reason, for which more strength is needed than that to conquer squadrons."[62]

Jerónimo de Florencia undoubtedly held the common early modern notion that women lacked rational minds and their actions were subject to ever-changing humors and emotions. His description of Margaret of Austria and the strength necessary to deal with matters on a rational basis reflected the assumption that reason was a masculine characteristic, and by demonstrating rational thought, Margaret of Austria had acted like a man.[63] The queen's ability to overcome her female nature, that is, a nature dominated by passion and uncontrollable emotions, was extraordinary in Fray Jerónimo's opinion, and he described this ability as masculine because only men were thought capable of conquering their emotions. By describing Margaret this way, Jerónimo de Florencia paid her the ultimate compliment.

The image of Margaret of Austria as a strong, manly woman also appeared in the eulogy given by Fray Andrés de Espinosa in the funeral honors for the queen at the University of Salamanca.[64] Espinosa characterized Margaret of Austria as a brave woman who possessed all possible virtues. Espinosa explained that in saying that the queen was a strong woman (*mujer fuerte*), he meant that she was "adorned with all virtues." A virtuous woman, in Espinosa's description, should be saintly, chaste, charitable, and pious. But a virtuous woman who was truly brave and strong should be married and should be loyal to her husband, as well as demonstrate strength and justice on all occasions.[65] Espinosa succeeded in defining Margaret of Austria strictly in her position as a wife: she could be virtuous and strong because she was subordinate to a man. Following Espinosa's reasoning, an unmarried woman who was not under male authority could not be strong and completely virtuous. Association with a man strengthened a woman, because, by nature, women lacked moral and physical strength.[66] Margaret of Austria, in Espinosa's eulogy, was mostly an appendage to Philip III. The queen was a "joy to our king . . . and crowned and adorned his regal head."[67] Yet Espinosa claimed that a queen gained status from her marriage to a king; as a king was supposed to be a shepherd to his people, so a queen, as the king's wife, could also be considered a shepherdess to his subjects.[68]

These observations about the queen should obviously not be taken at face value. They come to us from male observers, several of whom were Jesuit priests who enjoyed close personal contact with Margaret. It was customary for men to praise women for their passive, obedient behavior, and for priests to hold the celibate life of a nun as the highest calling for all women. Certainly Margaret of Austria was pious by early modern standards, and she relied on the advice and counsel of several Jesuit priests. These same priests subsequently praised the young, "submissive" queen, who patronized them and the Jesuit order. Their praise tells us more about male standards for female behavior than about Margaret of Austria's conduct. Moreover, both Diego de Guzmán and Jerónimo de Florencia emphasized the queen's virtue, piety, and honesty in part to contrast her conduct with that of Philip III's ministers, including the Duke of Lerma and Rodrigo Calderón. They set the queen up as a standard for proper behavior and then proceeded to use this impossible standard to judge the behavior of other members of Philip's court. These male writers consciously used a supposedly apolitical woman for decidedly political purposes.

Guzmán and Florencia recorded Margaret of Austria's respect for honesty and truth,[69] stating that the queen was unable to deceive—something, according to Guzmán, that was "completely different from the ways of the world, and especially in a prince's court, where some political figures [*políticos*] wrongly claim that good government lies . . . in pretense and dissimulation."[70] Both Guzmán and Jerónimo de Florencia recorded an incident in which the queen desired a particular course of action, but an "honest councillor" advised her that it was not best for the monarchy. According to both authors, the queen accepted the councillor's advice and subsequently praised and respected him for his honesty. They added that the queen asked the king to reward the minister's honesty because she thought that "ministers who have the courage to speak the truth in similar occasions are rare."[71] Diego de Guzmán also wrote that the queen wished that ministers would be honest with Philip III, "contrary to that [manner] which is used in many princes' houses."[72]

On another occasion, the queen requested a bishopric for one of her brothers. When Philip III's councillors told her that another person with qualifications greater than her brother's was being considered for the office, the queen urged Philip to give the office to the most deserving person. Her biographer added that Margaret "was so adamant about this that it seemed to several people that Her Majesty spoke against familial laws, and she responded that she would act against herself in order to fulfill [the laws] of justice and reason, and that no one, not even a relative, would get more from her than that which corresponded to justice and reason."[73] Guzmán and Fray Jerónimo wanted to emphasize that the queen, unlike so many of Philip's ministers, prized honesty and upright conduct and did not merely pursue those goals that benefited her family.

However, these accounts also show that Margaret of Austria did attempt to influence political policy, particularly decisions affecting her relatives. Although in Guzmán's account the queen denied placing her family above just and reasonable concerns, the aforementioned incident indicates that the queen was certainly negotiating for her family.[74] Both Diego de Guzmán and Jerónimo de Florencia tacitly recorded the queen's dissatisfaction with court politics and with the dishonest nature of courtiers. Although neither author explicitly stated that dishonest councillors characterized Philip's court, they implied as much. In their accounts, the queen played much more than a religious role; she acted as an intermediary whose virtue and honesty set an example for political advisers to follow.

Jerónimo de Florencia ended his first sermon at the queen's funeral by stating that Margaret of Austria gave inspired counsel even from the grave. She advised Philip III to govern in a manner that would bring him eternal salvation and provide "good laws . . . rewards [*mercedes*] for service, rewards to those who deserve them, punishment to the delinquent, open audiences, efficient government [*los despachos de negocios*]."[75] Philip III should concern himself with the welfare of the commonwealth (*la republica*), which was like a second wife to a king. Margaret told privados to use their great power to help the powerless; and she urged presidents of councils to pursue just causes unselfishly. The advice that the dead queen provided obviously came from Jerónimo de Florencia, but the preacher undoubtedly thought the queen's reputation, particularly in death, could influence the highest political officers. Now dead, she could be made to counsel them openly, something that she was not supposed to do in life. Moreover, Fray Jerónimo made the queen represent good government and love of the republic. In his sermon, he insisted that the queen would disapprove of the current politics at the Spanish court and that she had the same sound political judgment in death as she had had in life. The queen's eulogy provided an opportunity for the preacher himself to criticize court politics safely, albeit through the voice of the deceased queen.

Margaret of Austria's legacy to Spain, in Jerónimo de Florencia's opinion, was twofold. On the one hand, she provided a model for female conduct. By exercising her hands instead of her mouth and by controlling her emotions, she set an example for women of all social classes. On the other hand, her legacy applied to men as well as women. Her eulogist reminded all Spaniards that Margaret had gone to heaven and would thereafter act as an intercessor with God for her subjects. Her death should remind everyone of their own mortality, and they should pray to the queen for her assistance as well as follow her example of a life spent in prayer and in charitable deeds. Fray Jerónimo thus clearly stated the place of women, particularly royal women, in the secular and the divine hierarchies: on earth they were silent and industrious, and behaved as pious, good wives, mothers, and queens; in heaven they interceded on behalf of others.[76] On earth, women played roles subordinate to men and constantly had to sacrifice themselves and their own goals for those of others. In heaven, however, women had greater authority. Jerónimo de Florencia certainly idealized the queen at her death and held her up as an example of purity and feminine virtue. Nevertheless, this idealization, like the Catholic idealization of the Virgin Mary, gave the impression that few women ever reached the heights set for them by males and that when they did, it was by subordinating themselves to the will and goals of men.

Jerónimo de Florencia's and Diego de Guzmán's writings were certainly rhetorical pieces that employed the literary conventions of their genres—eulogy and biography, respectively. Nevertheless, their accounts of the queen were meant to be read by other generations of royal women and men and were designed to serve as a model for a queen. Although royal women might not live up to the ideal, this model remained the standard for acceptable female behavior. A royal woman's political activities were rarely if ever mentioned in funeral sermons or biographies, and these pieces often entered other women's collections and were meant to inspire similar behavior in the recipients. Margaret of Austria, for example, owned a copy of the eulogy given by Jerónimo de Florencia at Empress María's funeral in 1603. Ideally, the queen was to model herself after the image Fray Jerónimo presented of María, an image that accentuated only her piety and familial devotion despite her having exercised important political roles as joint regent of Castile and Holy Roman Empress.[77]

🙚🙠 🙚🙠 🙚🙠

Whereas Empress María and Queen Margaret of Austria were often compared to nuns, Margaret of the Cross actually took the vows of a cloistered Franciscan nun and lived under the rules of the order in the Descalzas Reales in Madrid. Margaret of the Cross, born on 25 January 1567, was the youngest daughter of Empress María and Emperor Maximilian II, and she accompanied the empress when she left Central Europe for Castile, in 1581. Upon arriving in the Spanish capital, both women resided in the Descalzas Reales; Empress María's sister had founded this monastery, and because it was under royal patronage it had become customary for women of the family to stay there when the monarch was absent from Madrid. In February of 1582, when Empress María and Margaret reached Madrid, Philip II was in Lisbon making his first visit there as King of Portugal. The monarch requested that his sister and his niece join him, and so in March the two women traveled to Portugal.

Rumors circulated that the monarch wished to marry his niece Margaret, because his fourth wife had recently died.[78] Empress María and Margaret's trip to Lisbon was thus seen as the first step toward negotiating a marriage agreement between Philip and Margaret. But the marriage did not come to pass. When Philip II, Empress María, and Margaret returned to Madrid, the two women immediately took up residence in the Descalzas monastery, and three years later Margaret took the vows of a cloistered nun and spent the rest of her years within the cloistered section of the monastery.

Juan de la Palma, a Franciscan priest and confessor to Margaret of the Cross during the last years of her life, wrote the official biography of the Franciscan nun.[79] Palma carefully detailed Margaret's piety, her commitment to the life of a nun, and her spiritual marriage to Christ. According to Palma, Margaret knew she wanted to enter the Descalzas monastery and take formal vows when she left Central Europe in 1581. In his account, María and Margaret had gone to Castile to fulfill Margaret's desire to join the cloistered Franciscan order.[80] Hans Khevenhüller also reported that Empress María had arrived in Castile with the specific intention of placing her daughter in the Descalzas convent.[81] Philip II directly challenged Margaret's intention when he developed an interest in marrying her.

Central to the biographical picture of Margaret of the Cross was her rejection of the king's marriage proposal. This rejection formed a crucial part of the lore about the woman's strength, character, and piety. Whereas biographers of Empress María and Margaret of Austria had to emphasize the women's piety and motherly duties, for Margaret of the Cross they had to explain why she chose not to marry and produce heirs. Juan de la Palma described the long process by which Margaret struggled over Philip's offer and whether God wanted her to become a queen or a nun. In this description, the incident was the first serious challenge to Margaret's personal resolve to become a nun. Palma chronicled the attempts by Empress María, Juan de Borja, and Margaret's confessor, Juan de Espinosa, to persuade Margaret to marry Philip. While Empress María did not pressure her daughter excessively and eventually accepted Margaret's rejection of the marriage offer, Juan de Borja and Espinosa exerted much greater force. The two men urged Margaret to marry the king and reminded her of her duty to the House of Austria and to the continuation of the Habsburg dynasty.[82]

Borja's arguments, as recorded by Palma, exemplify the male view of a dynastic marriage. Borja told Margaret that it was no challenge for her to become a cloistered nun; instead he reminded her that to "be a religious in the palace, and an example of how queens are to be saints . . . that is the ultimate virtue." He further told Margaret that "your mother desires it, your house needs it, the king proposes it, ministers advise it, the kingdoms request it."[83] Borja expected Margaret to put aside her own personal goals and submit to the higher duties of family and state; however, as Palma wrote in his biography, Margaret remained firm in her plans and Philip II finally desisted in his intention to marry her.

The issue of Margaret of the Cross's proposed marriage to Philip II is not corroborated by the historical documents,[84] so it is unclear whether Philip II ever considered or proposed marriage to his niece. Perhaps Hans Khevenhüller was referring to the possible marriage when he wrote that the empress should not rush to place Margaret in the cloistered convent. Khevenhüller argued that "persons of this rank serve God more in their [secular] occupations than by retiring [to a convent]."[85] Biographers and eulogists certainly seized the rumor of the marriage and perpetuated it in order to emphasize that Margaret of the Cross was an extraordinary woman who had chosen the life of a nun even though she had been offered the life of a queen.

Although this picture reinforced the common notion that women should be chaste, pious, and enclosed, Palma's account clearly reflected the dilemma that many aristocratic women faced: should they follow their own wishes or subordinate those wishes to the needs of their family? Palma clearly recognized that the life of a nun was not always an easy choice for women, but he also realized that, for some women, life within a convent was preferable to marriage. Palma had to justify to his readers Margaret's rejection of marriage to a monarch in order to follow her own calling. He did so by calling attention to her long-standing desire to devote herself to God and by using the accepted argument that the chaste life of a nun or religious figure was a higher calling than that of a queen or king, and that Christ was a better bridegroom than any man. Margaret's decision could not be adequately explained in human terms, that is, that she shied away from marrying her old, infirm uncle, who had previously been married to her sister (who herself had only recently died). Margaret's biographer recognized the magnitude of her decision, especially because few royal women would have rejected a proposal that would have made them queen of Spain. Margaret's independence was never mentioned. Instead, Palma explained her decision in the only way acceptable to an early modern audience: as submission to a male authority higher than Philip II—namely, God.

Margaret's personal struggle over Philip II's supposed marriage proposal was also recounted by a well-known preacher, Fray Hortensio Paravicino, who delivered the eulogy at the nun's funeral.[86] Paravicino described Margaret's long prayer to Jesus Christ, during which she asked for a sign to guide her in her decision and questioned whether Christ had rejected her love. The issue, in Paravicino's rendering, was settled when the sign that Margaret had prayed for appeared: the image of Christ on the cross to which Margaret prayed bent his head and nodded, signaling that indeed she should be his bride and not marry Philip II.[87] Paravicino also argued that an imperial or a royal marriage would have stained Margaret's virginal soul, and that by rejecting Philip II's proposal, Margaret had retained her purity (*pureza*).[88] Paravicino wrote his account during Philip IV's reign, right after Margaret's death. His task was an attempt to praise the life of a chaste nun and single out a royal woman who had spent the better part of her life in a convent. In Paravicino's eulogy, Margaret was able to communicate directly with Christ by meditating on the crucified Christ figure.[89]

Paravicino described in great detail Margaret's piety and saintly behavior, and listed her many virtues—in particular her self-mortification. According to Paravicino, Margaret avoided pleasure and comfort; she actually welcomed unpleasant things. She tried to forget and even scorned her high birth (*grandeza*) and did not allow other nuns in the Descalzas to treat her as royalty. She derived much pleasure from serving common people, and even cared for reprehensible individuals.[90] She also reportedly mortified her flesh as much as her health allowed and thus was "an excellent religious."[91] Paravicino praised Margaret because she suffered in silence; for example, she let no one know that she wore a hair shirt (although somehow Paravicino knew of its existence). This silence also applied to Margaret's many illnesses, which she accepted as a personal cross to bear. Paravicino recounted two times when Margaret of the Cross cut her chest with a knife in order to do penance and to show her love for Christ. He stated clearly, however, that others should not follow her example, but rather should merely marvel at these saintly acts. Thus Paravicino depicted Margaret of the Cross as the perfect nun, whose example others should admire but not necessarily imitate.[92]

According to Paravicino, Margaret signed a pact with Christ in blood, and she served him for her entire life. Her story accords with those of Empress María and Margaret of Austria as presented by biographers and eulogists. In these narratives, royal women had to renounce the privileges that their lineage afforded them and live humble and pious lives. These writers recognized implicitly that royal birth gave aristocratic women the means to challenge the gender restrictions society placed upon them. Piety, humility, and enclosure, however, were thought to keep women submissive and subordinate.

In his description of Margaret of the Cross, Paravicino emphasized the essential qualities of a nun: self-inflicted pain, suffering in silence, humility, and total submission to her confessor and to God. These were qualities that Juan de la Cerda also listed in his *Vida política de todos los estados de mujeres*, a book he dedicated to Margaret of the Cross.[93] Cerda counseled female novices to submit to the will and the wisdom of their confessor and their abbess or superior and to continue to do so throughout their lives as nuns.[94] A nun should meet with her confessor once a week and report her thoughts, good or bad, to him. Cerda also noted that a novice would be forced to endure verbal attacks, some of which would be unfair. Cerda argued that these attacks were designed to try a novice's patience and humility, so a nun should never defend herself against them. Instead, she should submit to these attacks and humbly declare her guilt by kneeling, bowing her head, and accepting the charges against her.[95] Humility and self-abnegation were the preeminent signs of a good nun, and Margaret of the Cross, in the opinion of Palma, Paravicino, and Cerda, exemplified this religious perfection.

Juan de la Palma also noted Margaret's obedience to the abbess of the Descalzas and to her confessor. "She told them [her confessors] everything with admirable subjection and submissiveness. Her Highness [Margaret] would tell her female companions: 'When he speaks as he performs his ministry, I do not hear the words of a confessor as his own words but the words of God, and thus my heart embraces them and my soul receives tremendous relief.'"[96] According to Palma, Margaret of the Cross always conferred with the abbess of the monastery and with her confessor before making a decision about anything, including very private matters. In this way, according to Palma, she presented a model of absolute virtue; her subjection and submissiveness were proper qualities for a cloistered nun and for all women.[97]

Even though she had chosen the life of a nun, Margaret still had to fulfil familial duties. In this respect, Palma depicted her as the ideal daughter and aunt. She cared for her mother daily, especially as the empress grew older and required more attention, and she also looked after the children of Philip II (and later of Philip III) at the Descalzas when the monarch left Madrid. However, as a good nun, she subordinated her love for her mother and relatives to her religious life. Palma recounted that when plague besieged the city of Madrid in 1598, Empress María asked for papal permission to take Margaret out of the monastery temporarily in order to seek refuge in the countryside.[98] Margaret refused to comply with her mother's wishes because to do so would have violated the vows of a cloistered nun. Palma also noted that when Empress María lay dying in her room, Margaret still insisted on continuing her daily religious exercises and did not allow herself to remain at her mother's bedside. In these instances, she placed her religious duties above her filial devotion and her private suffering at her mother's approaching death. Her religious vows were more important to her than her personal comfort or her emotional needs.

Even as he stressed her commitment to the life of a nun, Juan de la Palma noted that Margaret remained in touch with the secular world of the court. Palma admitted that she interfered in politics when church matters were concerned: she received petitions from the pope, she met with papal nuncios, and she forwarded their requests to Philip III. Palma claimed that Margaret of the Cross held audiences to press foreign dignitaries to strive for peace, and in this way she allegedly played an instrumental role in the peace that the Spanish kingdoms enjoyed throughout most of Philip III's reign.[99]

Palma's association of Margaret of the Cross with pacifistic policies forms an interesting parallel to Jerónimo de Florencia's account of Queen Margaret of Austria. Fray Jerónimo attributed Philip III's pursuit of peace to Margaret of Austria's influence and claimed that peace resulted from the Spanish monarchy's longstanding defense of Christianity, a cause Margaret of Austria held particularly dear throughout her life. Florencia stated that God had granted peace to the Spanish kingdoms because of the queen's virtuous qualities. This was a bold claim, given that the Duke of Lerma had worked consistently throughout that period to encourage Philip III to adopt pacifistic policies, and Fray Jerónimo even made this claim in the sermon that he dedicated to the Duke of Lerma. Although the topic of peace might have appealed to Lerma, Jerónimo de Florencia certainly realized that the duke could not have been pleased to have his rival, the queen, credited with bringing peace to the Spanish monarchy.[100]

It is not surprising, however, that Juan de la Palma and Jerónimo de Florencia associated Margaret of the Cross and Margaret of Austria with peace. In the early modern period, women were often identified with peace and tranquility.[101] As mentioned above, moralists wrote that if a wife fulfilled her duties properly, peace would reign in the family. Likewise, when a queen governed herself and her household appropriately, peace would reign in the kingdom.[102] As Jerónimo de Florencia wrote about Margaret of Austria: "The husband of a valorous woman will have no need of plunder [*despojos*], nor of going to battle in order to get it [plunder], because God will give peace and tranquility to his [a king's] kingdoms on account of her merits."[103] A queen's bravery and piety brought her close to God, who in turn rewarded a kingdom with peace; in this way such a queen was a valuable asset to a king. However, by emphasizing that Queen Margaret of Austria and Margaret of the Cross both desired peace, Jerónimo de Florencia and Juan de la Palma implied that when these women intervened in state matters, their influence was beneficial to the kingdoms.

Margaret of the Cross also helped Spain in another way: Palma claimed that she was instrumental in Philip II's choosing Margaret of Austria as the bride of his son and heir. In this fashion, Margaret of the Cross indirectly provided the Spanish kingdoms with a fertile queen, who in time gave birth to Philip IV. A chaste, virginal nun helped Philip III to have male heirs who would serve as kings and thereby upheld the idea that the ultimate purpose of an aristocratic woman was to produce heirs.

Palma indicated that in all these ways, Margaret of the Cross served the Spanish monarchy despite her physical isolation in the Descalzas convent. She was the perfect example for women because while she devoted her life to God and to prayer, she still exercised her duties as daughter, aunt, and member of the Habsburg dynasty. She renounced the honor and prestige that her high birth afforded her, but she did not renounce her obligation to tend to the needs of her relatives and to the advancement of the House of Austria. Even if early modern aristocratic women were able to avoid marriage and childbirth, they were unable to escape the pressures of family and lineage. Palma's narrative highlights the fact that royal women who lived in convents were far from isolated from the secular world. Their lineage and their familial connections made them important channels for influencing policymaking, and they were often called upon by their relatives, by foreign rulers, or by their servants to make use of these connections.

⁂ ⁂ ⁂

Rodrigo Mendes Silva, Diego de Guzmán, Jerónimo de Florencia, Juan de la Palma, and Hortensio Paravicino all created portraits of virtuous Habsburg women, committed to their family and to their religion. Yet these portraits also hint at some of the incongruities and conflicts within these women's lives, and perhaps unknowingly, their biographers showed that these women participated in the world of politics in their own fashion. Because these authors all had the express purpose of writing commemorative works that could serve as models for other women, they did not choose to highlight the women's political capacities or to note any conflict between the women and the male hierarchy. The model that biographers followed was that of the funeral oration; their writings show an indebtedness to Florencia's and Paravicino's eulogies. This model emphasized the virtues, and particularly the piety, of these royal women; this was the picture presented for posterity.

Yet royal women, and certainly the Habsburg women, did not always conform to these devotional models. The women often exploited the female image presented by men in order to further their own goals. They knew to employ such stereotypes as the emotionally unstable woman and the good mother or wife to sanction their political voice. They also readily defined their concerns as pious or familial and in this way justified intervention in terms that the male world found acceptable for aristocratic women. While the devotional and stereotypical pictures of the Habsburg women were intended to marginalize them and limit their political activities, these same portraits, though not allowing women to challenge the male hierarchy directly, gave them the means to subvert this hierarchy from within. Ironically, then, royal women could use male views and prejudices to empower themselves.

4

Correcting the Image
Contemporary Male Accounts

BIOGRAPHERS AND EULOGISTS chose to portray the Habsburg women as pious and saintly figures, but not everyone described Empress María, Margaret of Austria, and Margaret of the Cross in such laudatory terms. Court chroniclers, ambassadors, and personal attendants depicted the three women in a less devotional light. These authors were able to note the women's foibles, personalities, political voices, and personal interests because they knew the women personally. In so doing, these male observers commented on the role royal women actually played at the Spanish court of Philip III and gave a male opinion on how the female relatives of a monarch should act. This more balanced, hardheaded view serves as a sharp contrast to the devotional view discussed in the previous chapter.

In the Descalzas monastery, Empress María did not live the life of a cloistered nun, and, for her, life in a monastery did not signify an abandonment of any political functions or a full religious retreat to the contemplative life.[1] Empress María was free to leave the Descalzas, and during Philip II's reign she often went to the palace and to the Escorial to be with the monarch and his children.[2] She spent the summer of 1584 at the Escorial to escape the heat of Madrid,[3] and during Philip III's reign, the empress made weekly visits to Queen Margaret of Austria at the royal palace until the court moved to Valladolid. Empress María also occasionally visited the king and queen when they were on the outskirts of Madrid, at the hunting lodge of El Pardo, or at the summer house of Juan de Borja.[4] She used these numerous opportunities to discuss political matters with the monarchs. At the Descalzas, the empress received regular visits from the king and queen, ambassadors, nuncios, and other political figures. She remained abreast of political developments in Central Europe, Flanders, Italy, and the Low Countries through her correspondence with relatives and through the daily reports of Hans Khevenhüller, who discussed all political matters with her.[5]

The empress never forgot her imperial background and the power she had exercised as the wife of Emperor Maximilian II. María's official portrait in the Descalzas monastery, attributed to Pantoja de la Cruz, provides an interesting contrast to Florencia's and Mendes Silva's accounts of the empress's life.[6] In Pantoja's portrait, Empress María wears a widow's simple garb and holds a rosary in her left hand; next to her, prominently displayed on a table, is the imperial crown (see figure 1).[7] Despite the empress's decision to live in the monastery, she never relinquished her imperial title and the honor it brought her. The religious symbols in the portrait are tempered, if not overshadowed, by the dominant symbol of imperial political might. This portrait clearly suggests that while Jerónimo de Florencia and Rodrigo Mendes Silva preferred to depict the empress strictly as a pious, passive woman, the Habsburg family and María herself continued to emphasize her political role and her imperial might.

A balanced portrait of Empress María emerges from the letters of her mayordomo, Juan de Borja; from the diary and correspondence of Hans Khevenhüller; and from the correspondence of her secretary and Archduke Albert of Flanders's representative at the Spanish court, Juan Carrillo. These three men had daily access to Empress María as well as regular contact with Philip III's court. The ties of affection and service bound them to the aging empress, but they were not blind to her many faults. Borja, Khevenhüller, and Carrillo found their political duties hampered by the amount of time they needed to spend with Empress María and the demands she made on them. When the court moved to Valladolid in 1601, Borja, Khevenhüller, and Carrillo stayed in Madrid with her. To do so, Borja gave up the presidency of the Council of Portugal, an appointment he valued greatly because he had territorial holdings and familial connections in Portugal, through the family of his wife, Francisca de Aragón. Likewise, Khevenhüller and Carrillo found it difficult to perform their diplomatic duties so far from the Spanish court. To travel to Valladolid for a royal audience, they needed not only Philip III's invitation but also Empress María's permission, which she granted sparingly and reluctantly.

Borja, Khevenhüller, and Carrillo knew the multifaceted nature of the empress's daily life. Their letters clearly record her interest in political issues and her ability to maneuver through situations in order to get her own way. Borja, Khevenhüller, and Carrillo often wrote letters to other men, so they tailored their depiction of Empress María to the prejudices and assumptions of a male audience. However, their letters also show how the empress continued to influence political policy at the Spanish court.

Unlike Jerónimo de Florencia and Rodrigo Mendes Silva, Juan de Borja scarcely ever mentioned Empress María's religious activities. His comments on her health, her moods, her requests, and her complaints depict an infirm empress given to frequent bouts of melancholy but unwilling to relinquish her political role. Juan de Borja often emphasized the empress's age and physical weakness in order to urge Lerma and Philip III to make allowances for her behavior. Borja also minimized the extent of the empress's complaints by claiming that they revolved around seemingly trivial matters that had little significance beyond María's personal satisfaction. In effect, however, these complaints were significant; they centered on Lerma's interference with María's ability to petition directly for her servants, with the makeup of her household, and with her ability to reach Philip III. These were not minor issues, since they were crucial to María's independence and power.

Borja's letters depict a headstrong, willful empress whose age and infirmities did not prevent her from fighting for her interests. This was the case with the empress's petition for a court appointment for a former servant, Pedro de Ledesma. María had petitioned in Ledesma's favor, but in discussing his case the Count of Miranda, President of the Cámara de Castilla and a close associate of the Duke of Lerma, discovered some irregularities in Ledesma's past service. For this reason, Ledesma came under investigation. Empress María took this investigation as a personal affront because she had interceded on Ledesma's behalf. Borja reported the empress's anger to the Duke of Lerma: "What hurts the empress is that instead of rewarding him because of her intercession, it [her petition] has been a way to resurrect his faults and to punish him."[8] Borja feared Lerma's reaction to these comments and excused himself by saying, "[I write only] to fulfill the empress's order and very much against my will because of my obligation to the Count [of Miranda] and the great desire I have to serve him."[9] The Ledesma issue formed a regular part of Borja's correspondence over subsequent months. Borja even reported that "the empress kills me every day" about settling this issue, and Borja begged Lerma for a resolution.[10] Eventually the case was settled in Ledesma's and the empress's favor, and then Borja continued to remind Lerma to give Ledesma the office of secretary which Philip III had awarded him.

The empress's seemingly erratic behavior helped her to win concessions from the Duke of Lerma and the notoriously slow Spanish government. This account of a stubborn, manipulative woman contradicts the image, presented by Mendes Silva and Jerónimo de Florencia, of a humble widow dedicated solely to a life of prayer. Empress María clearly used emotional outbursts—thought to be natural to women—as a means of having her demands heard and met. It was also in Borja's own interest to portray Empress María as a headstrong woman whose bad health caused her to criticize powerful (and usually male) persons. In this way, Borja could pressure Lerma on specific issues but always avoid ultimate responsibility for such pressure.

Empress María depended upon letters from the archdukes in Flanders, Rudolf II in Prague, and Archduke Matthias in Vienna to find out about political and familial developments in Central Europe. When she failed to receive letters, she became moody, melancholic, and depressed. In June 1602, Empress María began to believe that the Duke of Lerma had intercepted several letters written to her from Flanders, and Borja's correspondence with Lerma records the empress's frustration and her constant insistence that the letters be found. Borja wrote to Lerma, telling him that "the letters from Flanders for the empress have not arrived here and I beg Your Excellency to make sure to send them to Her Majesty because of the sudden fear [*sobresalto*] she feels when she knows there is mail and her letters are not given to her."[11] While this may have been behavior expected of a seventy-four-year-old woman, it also shows that the empress did not easily put up with Lerma's attempts to control her correspondence. Letters cemented the familial relationship among the Habsburgs and were central to communicating political and dynastic issues. Correspondence was also a key way in which aristocratic women built up patronage and affectionate networks. Thus, María's complaints when she believed that Lerma was interfering with such matters were very understandable. Borja refrained from saying who the empress thought was keeping her letters, but the implication was that she blamed the Duke of Lerma. (Eventually the letters were discovered among Juan Carrillo's mail—a logical place, given that Carrillo was Archduke Albert's representative in Spain—but it is quite possible that Lerma had arranged for them to be found there.) Far from being the passive, devout woman described by Florencia and Mendes Silva—both of whom claimed that the empress refused to read her relatives' letters before finishing her spiritual exercises—Empress María voiced her opinion even to criticize powerful figures such as the Duke of Lerma. Her piety did not preclude a defense of her independence and power.

Empress María often used the bonds of affection and family to vent dissatisfaction with Philip III and his ministers. When the Duke of Lerma began to restructure the queen's household in order to surround Margaret of Austria with his own relatives and trusted associates, Empress María was among those most directly affected. The restructuring threatened the empress's regular contact with the queen, as María would now have to work through Lerma and his associates in order to reach Margaret. Moreover, as we have seen, Lerma's relatives occupied high positions within the queen's household, positions that allowed them to be present at meetings between the empress and the queen. In February 1600 the king, through Lerma, requested that Beatriz de Cardona and Isabel Mexia, two of the queen's ladies-in-waiting who had had trouble at the court with Lerma, be allowed to stay with the empress at the Descalzas. In effect, the two women were being dismissed from court. As early as August 1599, the Duke of Lerma expressed his frustration with Beatriz de Cardona to Juan de Borja: "I assure you that the other day I was ready to put her in a carriage [*litera*] and send her to her mother's house and it would have been done if not for [my] respect for the empress."[12] In the same letter, Lerma remarked that Beatriz de Cardona annoyed the queen and her German attendants. Lerma was undoubtedly paving the way toward Cardona's dismissal, with little concern for the queen.

The empress was clearly displeased with the incident, particularly because Beatriz de Cardona was the daughter of one of her closest ladies-in-waiting, Margarita de Cardona, who had accompanied María from Central Europe to Castile. Nevertheless, Borja reported that "the empress will do everything which His Majesty desires because in nothing can the empress take [greater pleasure] than in giving [pleasure] to his Majesty."[13] Lerma interpreted this response to mean that Empress María would allow the two women to enter the Descalzas. However, when Lerma sent the two women to the empress on 13 February 1600, Borja reported that María claimed never to have given her consent. Yet the women arrived nine days after Borja had written to Lerma to say that the empress would follow Philip III's wishes. Apparently, either Empress María conveniently forgot that she had given her consent, or Lerma mistook the empress's willingness to do Philip III's bidding as a sign that she would accept the women into the Descalzas. In this case, as in others, the empress used formulaic expressions of affection toward Philip III to register frustration and annoyance with his and Lerma's demands, and then, in whatever way she could, displayed her disapproval of Philip III and Lerma. The empress apparently feigned forgetfulness regarding Beatriz de Cardona and Isabel Mexia as a form of protest against Lerma's interference with Margaret of Austria's household.

The Duke of Lerma and other members of Philip III's Council of State made it a point to inform Empress María of political developments that concerned her sons. So, for example, in August 1599, Borja noted that the Marquis of Poza, President of the Council of Finance, had asked him to tell the empress that 200,000 ducats were being sent to Archduke Albert to help put down the rebellion in Flanders.[14] In this instance, Empress María went so far as to tell Lerma how she thought the money should be distributed.[15] Hans Khevenhüller informed Empress María when Archduke Albert faced military defeat in 1600.[16] Lerma himself often kept Empress María abreast of Spanish assistance to the archdukes in Flanders;[17] María regularly petitioned for this assistance through Juan de Borja and so Lerma knew to keep her informed. Otherwise, the empress would not let the matter rest and would continue to ask Borja to petition Lerma and Philip III on the archdukes' behalf. In addition, by informing the empress of such assistance, Lerma sought to maintain good relations with her. The duke needed to be careful with the empress because Philip III had such great affection for her and because she had much influence over her sons.

Empress María also negotiated for her sons' ministers and servants. In 1600, through Juan de Borja and Lerma, she asked Philip III to pay a pension that had been promised to Rudolf II's mayordomo, Wolfgang Rumpf. María reminded the monarch of Rumpf's service to the Spanish kingdoms, and, as so often, the importance of her petition transcended the level of service and patronage. Wolfgang Rumpf was one of Rudolf II's closest advisers. During those periods when Rudolf isolated himself in his castle, Rumpf saw to the daily administration of imperial matters and was one of the few individuals who continued to have access to Rudolf.[18] Empress María petitioned on Rumpf's behalf because it was politically expedient to keep Rumpf loyal to the Habsburg dynasty and to the Spanish king. When Rudolf II suddenly dismissed Rumpf and another trusted councillor, Paul Sixt Trautson, Borja made sure to inform Empress María.[19]

On another occasion, Empress María reminded Lerma to see to the petition of Fernando Spinola, one of Archduke Albert's servants. The empress told Lerma that Archduke Albert had a shortage of servants and that Lerma should quickly see to Spinola's request.[20] Empress María's daily concern for news of Central Europe and Flanders, her petitions for her sons and their ministers, and the regular updates she received from Borja, Lerma, and Khevenhüller clearly show that the empress was far from isolated within the Descalzas and that she successfully and continually influenced political matters.

The clearest picture of Empress María as a political player, however, emerges from the letters and the diary of Hans Khevenhüller. The imperial ambassador met daily with Empress María, and in his diary and letters he commented extensively on the empress. When she first arrived in Madrid, the empress took up most of Khevenhüller's time.[21] The ambassador noted the many times they met and indicated that on almost all those occasions he discussed political matters with her. This was true during the reigns of both Philip II and Philip III. Khevenhüller reported to Empress María the contents of letters received and sent to Central Europe as well as the substance of meetings with the king and his ministers.[22] The empress was a channel for the Austrian Habsburgs in negotiations with the Spanish monarch; she oversaw Khevenhüller's dealings with Philip II and Philip III and even his correspondence with Emperor Rudolf II.

Khevenhüller's writings reveal that he enjoyed a reciprocal relationship with the empress. He informed her of political affairs; she advised him. She shared personal worries; he consoled her. On 12 December 1582, Khevenhüller found the empress in low spirits. He tried to cheer her by reminding her of her imperial lineage. He noted that she was the descendant of empresses, had married an emperor, and was the sister of the king of Spain. He also reassured her that many of her decisions affected all of Christendom.[23] The ambassador, who knew the empress so well, clearly believed that these arguments would carry great weight with her.

The ambassador also acted as a conduit between Philip II and Empress María. Khevenhüller often met separately with the monarch and then with the empress. He would convey messages and information between Philip II and Empress María, so the two did not necessarily have to meet personally to discuss and settle important matters. For example, on the evening of 1 February 1584, Khevenhüller met with the empress to discuss matters concerning her. The following day he met with Philip and that evening met again with the empress, to whom he gave a detailed report on his talk with the king. The ambassador did not record the content of his meetings but did say that he discussed "important matters."[24]

Empress María had frequent contact with Philip III before and after he became king. While he was prince, Philip often stayed at the Descalzas with his sister, Isabel Clara Eugenia, and the empress. Once he assumed the throne, in 1598, he turned to the empress for political counsel and personal support. Khevenhüller noted in his diary that the new king visited the empress often, and these visits became daily ones during the month of October 1598. In 1599, however, the king met with the empress twelve times; all but one of these meetings occurred during the last three months of the year because Philip was away from Madrid from April until October, to meet and marry his bride. Since Khevenhüller went to see María daily, he often met the king there. On such visits, Khevenhüller was able to bring imperial matters to the attention of the king. Once the court moved to Valladolid in 1601, Philip III was unable to visit Empress María regularly at the Descalzas; however, the empress did communicate with him indirectly through the Duke of Lerma. The monarch also returned to Madrid several times in order to visit her.

Besides commenting on Empress María's piety, eulogists and biographers also emphasized Empress María's charitable contributions. Contrary to these reports were those of Venetian ambassadors, who noted that Empress María was famous for her prodigality.[25] The Venetian ambassador Francesco Soranzo reported that Philip II refrained from giving his sister any authority, particularly in financial matters, because she immediately spent what was given her, and more.[26] Although Soranzo may have been voicing a current stereotypical view of women's extravagance, Empress María did accumulate a large number of debts throughout her life, and at her death debts remained that her inheritance did not cover completely.[27] The empress's ability to spend money did not, however, limit her influence or cause Philip II to avoid giving her authority, as Soranzo claimed. In fact, Philip II consulted with her consistently during the last two decades of his reign.[28] Some observers even believed that Philip II planned to have the empress govern Portugal for him.[29]

For Empress María, as for many other aristocratic widows, independent financial resources gained from her inheritance afforded her great power, and the use of such resources to finance charitable institutions and pious works was in itself a mark of independence and an enhancement of personal prestige. Moreover, by purposely spending money without regard to financial concerns, women could show disregard for the male world that surrounded them. This was certainly a habit of Empress María, who consistently incurred new debts before she was able to settle old ones. However, this was not a strictly female behavior; the men of the Habsburg family borrowed enormous sums that they were ultimately unable to repay. Charles V's and Philip II's large expenses are well documented and were well known even in the sixteenth century.[30] The ability to dispose of money was a sign of power, power that royal women craved as much as men did.

Although Khevenhüller and the Venetian ambassadors noted the empress's interest in matters of state, her regular consultation with the imperial ambassador, and her discussions with Philip III, the papers of state (*consultas*) never mention María's role in advising the monarch. The absence of Empress María from the official political records suggests that royal women influenced policy in an indirect fashion. They could counsel the king in meetings occasioned by familial contact, meetings that often took place in religious settings (such as the Descalzas) or for religious functions (for example, processions of the Virgin of Atocha). Women could also exert influence through individuals beyond the Council of State—as María worked through Juan de Borja, Juan Carrillo, and Hans Khevenhüller. The king, in deciding state matters, did not give a full account of who had influenced his decision. He certainly would have made no mention of royal women, because they were not expected to have any say in the making of political policy. Yet, indirect references clearly show that these royal women had real political power and at times were alternately critical or supportive of the king's actions.

Empress María did not hesitate to tell Philip III when she disagreed with his decisions. Hans Khevenhüller discussed an occasion when María warned Philip III against changing too many of his councillors and giving too much influence to Magdalena de Guzmán, the Marquesa del Valle, a close associate of the Duke of Lerma. The ambassador noted that Empress María had told Philip III that it was because of her affection and familial ties that she dared to warn him about these political matters.[31] According to Khevenhüller, Philip III did not appreciate the empress's advice on this issue; he subsequently told the Duke of Lerma about his meeting with the empress, and, in Khevenhüller's opinion, Lerma encouraged Philip III to transfer the court to Valladolid in order to curtail such interference.[32] The empress, who knew that Philip III had disapproved of her advice, recounted the incident to Khevenhüller, who assured her that she had acted as a good grandmother.

The empress also asked Khevenhüller if he thought the Austrian Habsburgs should use money to gain a say among Philip III's ministers, because in her opinion that was the way to gain the ministers' support. Khevenhüller responded that the Austrian Habsburgs should not lower themselves to use what he thought were pernicious tactics.[33] Again, Khevenhüller recorded Empress María's keen political sense and her concern for political matters both in Spain and in Central Europe. Particularly in Khevenhüller's letters, the empress emerges as a strong woman, knowledgeable about political affairs and the workings of the Spanish political system.

Empress María clearly pursued both personal and familial agendas throughout her time in Madrid. As an aristocratic woman with a large retinue of servants, she considered it her duty to see to the needs of her attendants and regularly petitioned Philip II and Philip III on their behalf.[34] She usually requested pensions or other types of financial assistance. Because María lived in the Descalzas convent and had direct ties to the Spanish monarch, the nuns of the Descalzas used her as their link to the king.[35] A principal concern of the nuns was choosing the priests and confessors assigned to the Descalzas. So, for example, in July 1601, when Don Pedro de Luna, capellan mayor of the Descalzas, asked permission to leave this post, Empress María voiced her disapproval and asked Lerma to offer him or his son a gift (*merced*) to entice Luna to stay.[36]

Empress María's reputation as a devout, pious woman led her to intercede frequently on behalf of nuns and priests.[37] She represented the interests of these and other individuals whenever she visited with the king and queen in the monastery or in the royal palace. Even if Jerónimo de Florencia and Juan Carrillo were correct in saying that Empress María talked about religious issues with the nuns at the Descalzas, it is important to understand that the boundary between religious and political concerns was quite permeable in the late sixteenth and the early seventeenth centuries. In fact, Empress María wielded power at the Spanish court by bringing to the attention of the Spanish government such "pious" and familial concerns as financial assistance to the Austrian Habsburgs in their struggle against the Turks as well as to the archdukes in Flanders against the Dutch Calvinists.

❦ ❦ ❦

Like Empress María, Queen Margaret of Austria had specific political demands. These demands centered on assistance to her brothers, Archdukes Ferdinand and Leopold of Styria; to her sisters, Maria Christina, Eleanora, Maria Magdalena, and Constantia; and to several convents and religious orders that she patronized.[38] Margaret of Austria also encouraged Philip to rely less on the Duke of Lerma and to listen more often to her advice and that of his relatives. The queen operated with a notion of the Spanish monarchy similar to that of Empress María. That is, the Spanish kingdoms were part of a larger collection of Habsburg territories, and Philip III, as a Habsburg prince, had financial obligations to his Austrian Habsburg relatives. Thus, the queen's loyalty to the House of Austria and to the interests of her relatives pitted her against the Duke of Lerma in his designs to curtail Spanish involvement in Central Europe and Flanders.

Whereas Diego de Guzmán and Jerónimo de Florencia did not mention Margaret's political agenda, court chroniclers and foreign ambassadors noted the queen's concern with political matters and commented that she pressured the king to meet her relatives' needs. These same chroniclers and ambassadors discussed the queen's connection to palace intrigues and to the Duke of Lerma's opposition. These reports confirm the queen's interest and participation in the political developments at court. From these documents, Margaret of Austria emerges as one of the major political players at the court.

The Venetian ambassador, Ottaviano Bon, reported in 1602 that Queen Margaret of Austria was "capable of great things, so much so that she would govern if she could in a manner different from that of the king."[39] In fact, Bon implied that the queen's political intuition was sounder than her husband's. Francesco Soranzo, Venetian ambassador in Spain from 1598 to 1600, reported that Philip III loved his queen very dearly. According to the ambassador, Margaret of Austria was "astute and very skillful [*grandemente artificiosa*] in securing the king's love . . . she wants to be respected and known as queen." Although Soranzo implied that Margaret of Austria was an intelligent and resourceful queen, he added that she "likes to have others think that she has great authority with the king, but she does not have it except in petitions of little importance."[40] According to Soranzo, Lerma watched the queen and ensured that she had little influence with the king.

Ottaviano Bon, who noted Margaret's political acumen, also reported that the queen was "circumscribed [*circondata*] by the Duchess of Lerma and the Duke her husband . . . and the king has greater estimation of them than of her in many things, which makes her withdrawn, melancholic, and without any authority."[41] In this way, Bon indirectly criticized the king for not following the intelligent counsel of his wife and preferring the counsel of individuals who were obviously motivated by self-interest. The ambassador also made the connection between disapproval of the ways of the Spanish court and the rise of melancholic humors in a female. Francesco Priuli, writing in 1608, described the queen in much the same terms. Priuli reported that the queen had no influence whatsoever in the government and that no one could obtain favors through her intercession because the queen had too much reverence (*riverenza*) for the king and because Lerma kept the queen isolated.[42]

Girolamo Soranzo, Venetian ambassador to Madrid from 1607 to 1611, claimed that Margaret of Austria had learned not to intervene in political matters.[43] Lerma had threatened to keep Philip III traveling alone outside Madrid if the queen continued to speak to the king about political affairs. According to Soranzo, the queen decided to refrain from expressing her political opinions because she feared frequent solitude. Soranzo went so far as to argue that Margaret needed Lerma's help in order to secure financial assistance for her brothers in Central Europe.[44] In Soranzo's account, rather than oppose the Duke of Lerma, Margaret cooperated with him in the last years of her life.

Venetian ambassadors were certainly correct to note that the queen had political concerns and tried to negotiate for her relatives in Central Europe. However, Margaret did not stop trying to influence political decisions, as Girolamo Soranzo believed. Faced with opposition from Lerma, the queen adopted a different strategy in order to express her political voice. In particular, she continued to work through others, such as Diego de Guzmán and the royal confessors. These men communicated her opinions and desires to Philip when the queen was unable to do so herself. Certainly Margaret expressed her opinion very clearly in 1607, when she and Philip III's confessor, Diego de Mardones, criticized the activities of the Junta de Desempeño. Philip listened to her criticism, and as a result, Pedro Franqueza and Alonso Ramírez de Prado, key members of the junta, were arrested and prosecuted for fraud.[45] Venetian ambassadors argued that the queen had retreated into a life of religious devotion, a life devoid of any political activity. However, the queen's pious activities made powerful political statements. The queen used her frequent visits to convents and churches to strengthen her network of influence. These visits also allowed her time with the king and opportunities for political discussions with him.

Matías de Novoa, court chronicler, secretary to Philip III, and close supporter of Rodrigo Calderón and the Duke of Lerma, certainly saw the political ramifications of the queen's pious activities. Novoa depicted Margaret of Austria as the perfect royal wife: "a strong mother, prudent, religious, and wise. . . . Her palace is a house of prayer, her ladies-in-waiting and servants live in imitation of her example. . . . She frees republics from vices; she desires and procures the best and the most useful [things] for the government."[46] In his description of the queen, however, Novoa hinted at her interest in governing—although he presented this interest as that of a devout mother for her child. Yet Novoa criticized the queen for what he considered extreme and naive piety. This piety, according to Novoa, at times clouded Margaret's vision and made her overly susceptible to the dangerous counsel of priests and nuns.

In particular, Novoa criticized the prioress of the convent of the Encarnación, Mariana de San José, and Juan de Santa María, a Franciscan priest who was one of Philip III's chaplains. Novoa also wrote that in founding the royal convent of the Encarnación, the queen and Mariana de San José consciously intended to rival the convent of the Descalzas. Novoa, however, blamed San José for this development; he refrained from implicating the queen.[47] Novoa claimed that religious figures at court were motivated by personal greed and political designs.[48] The chronicler detailed the declining fortunes of Lerma's close associate Rodrigo Calderón. After Philip III's death, Calderón was arrested, prosecuted, and executed for his financial misdeeds during Lerma's privanza. Calderón's demise seems to have wounded Novoa personally, and he ascribed it to the influence religious figures exercised over Philip III. This influence, according to Novoa, began with Margaret of Austria. When discussing Calderón's loss of power in 1611, Novoa noted the queen's "secret entreaties" (*secretas persuasiones*) with Philip III. In this way, Novoa explicitly connected the queen's piety and devotional practices to political developments at court. Novoa implicitly blamed the queen for Calderón's, and eventually Lerma's, fall from royal grace.

The Duke of Lerma also clearly believed that Margaret of Austria had great influence with Philip III, an influence that could be used for political purposes. When Lerma and Juan de Borja discussed the issue concerning Beatriz de Cardona, the servant of the queen who had supposedly caused problems at the court and was therefore sent to the Descalzas monastery, Lerma noted the queen's leverage with Philip III. Borja reported to Lerma that Empress María knew the details of Beatriz de Cardona's problems at the court even before he had spoken to her. Borja claimed not to know how Empress María had learned these details,[49] but Lerma responded that the matter had been discussed, and "the queen is intelligent and prudent to answer His Majesty directly."[50] The Duke's comment implied that Margaret of Austria had communicated directly with Empress María to explain the situation to her and had subsequently defended herself directly to Philip. Lerma's comments about the queen's intelligence were not words of praise; they were words that judged the strength of a potential rival. Lerma's remarks also indicate that the queen, having direct access to Philip, had been able to discuss these matters in private with him.

In December 1599, the Duke of Lerma wrote to invite Juan de Borja and his wife, Francisca de Aragón, to dinner. The privado commented that he and his wife were not busy because his wife was not serving in her usual capacity as the queen's camarera mayor, an office that normally required her constant presence at the queen's side. The queen had asked Philip to send Lerma's wife home for the evening. Lerma commented that "the queen asked this of her husband in such a way that we did not delay one hour."[51] With this comment, the Duke of Lerma clearly noted the queen's influence with Philip III in internal court matters and also documented the power he felt Margaret had with the king. This incident and the matter surrounding Beatriz de Cardona were relatively minor occurrences and did not have obvious political ramifications. However, both incidents show Lerma's awareness of the queen's independence and her influence over Philip III, and they could be seen as warning signs of how the queen might react to issues of greater consequence. In fact, because of incidents such as these, the Duke of Lerma took further steps to try to limit Margaret's contact with Philip III.

The more frequent references to Margaret of Austria center on her unhappiness at the court, an unhappiness brought on by Lerma's influence with Philip III. So, for example, Hans Khevenhüller wrote a scathing commentary on a conversation he had had with the queen. He reported that the queen was so unhappy that she had told him that she would "much rather be a nun in a convent in Goricia [Styria] than Queen of Spain."[52] Khevenhüller attributed this unhappiness to Lerma's attempts to isolate the queen from Philip. According to Khevenhüller, Lerma had gone so far as to interfere in the private moments the king and queen shared by instructing Margaret not to speak about political matters with the king at any time, and especially not during their time alone together at night. To ensure the queen's compliance, Lerma threatened to arrange royal excursions that would leave Margaret alone in Madrid. He also threatened to remove Maria Sidonia, the queen's lady-in-waiting and closest friend, from the court.[53] These were potent threats to a young queen, who initially had difficulty speaking Castilian and who was far away from much of her family.

Two women close to the queen's inner circle also noted her discontent. Beatriz Ramírez de Mendoza, Countess of Castellar, a holy woman (*beata*) who had much contact with the court in Madrid, recorded an interview she had with the king. Because the countess was considered to be a visionary and was highly respected by many persons at court, the king asked her to visit him. They met at the monastery of the Descalzas, and the countess told Philip III that Margaret was unhappy and that he should listen more often to Margaret's counsel because the queen loved him greatly. The countess noted that, after having met with the king, she spoke to Margaret of Austria, who cried and told the countess that Philip III did not love her and would not listen to her.[54] The countess assured Margaret that this was not the case.

The countess's letter presents a woman's interpretation of events at the Spanish court in the early years of Philip's reign. Her fascinating account of her meetings with the king and queen highlights many of those factors that are central to an understanding of Philip III's court. The countess's meeting with Philip, which lasted several hours, took place at the Descalzas, not at the royal palace. Philip III sought, and listened to, her advice precisely because she was known as a pious, virtuous woman. Thus, the countess's piety gave her access to royalty and allowed her the opportunity to comment on the most serious political matters—in this case, Philip III's reliance on the Duke of Lerma. She advised the monarch to listen to his wife, whom the countess praised because of the queen's virtue and love for Philip. Thus, a pious woman defended a pious and devout wife.

Like Khevenhüller, the Countess of Castellar noticed Margaret's unhappiness and attributed it to Lerma's attempts to limit the queen's access to and influence upon her husband. Lerma felt so threatened by the countess's advice to Philip III that he ultimately looked for an opportunity to prosecute her. In

Lerma's estimation, the countess was involved in one of the first major crises of Philip III's reign: the Marquesa del Valle's abuse of her office as governess to the Infanta Anne.[55]

The Countess of Castellar was implicated in this issue because of her friendship with the Marquesa del Valle.[56] Lerma attempted to have her arrested, but the countess was able to find refuge within a convent in Madrid. She arrived late at night in the convent of the Concepción Jerónima in Madrid, where the nuns allowed her to take religious vows immediately. This colorful and possibly apocryphal story has the nuns waking up and putting on their habits at midnight to allow the countess to take religious vows. When royal officials arrived in the morning to arrest the countess, they were unable to do so because she was protected by ecclesiastical law.[57] This incident clearly shows the close relationship between the opposition to Lerma and the world of convents and churches. It also lends weight to Novoa's statement that the queen placed much trust in religious individuals. But, whereas Novoa believed that this interaction was problematic for the monarchy, in this case Margaret of Austria's religious connections actually constituted a source of organized opposition to Lerma and provided a way for critics of the privado to find protection. Finally, Castellar's retreat into a cloistered convent demonstrates that convents could be political spaces and that cloistered nuns were often well aware of political developments.

The event that gave Lerma this opportunity to pursue the countess was the prosecution of Magdalena de Guzmán, Marquesa del Valle, who served as Lerma's most immediate spy over the queen from 1601 until 1603. Lerma had promoted her and assured her a high court office, and he regularly communicated with her so as to be informed of events in the queen's household. The marquesa readily agreed to tell Lerma when the queen was annoyed with him and to report any complaints the queen had about him.[58] Until 1601, the marquesa was one of Margaret of Austria's ladies-in-waiting (*dueñas de honor*). In that same year, the marquesa became the governess of the Infanta Anne. As governess, she remained in the palace, and on at least one occasion when the queen's camarera mayor, the Duchess of Gandía, became ill, the marquesa assumed her responsibilities.[59] The office of camarera mayor required that she sleep in the queen's bedroom. The governess was supposed to sleep with the infanta, but because of her influence with Lerma, the marquesa was exempted from this responsibility.[60]

Through her office, the marquesa del Valle won great power and developed her own network, separate from that of the Duke of Lerma, for influencing court policy. At first, individuals wrote to the Marquesa del Valle so she would channel their petitions to the Duke of Lerma. Soon the Marquesa was in such demand that, according to Juan Carrillo, she gave official audiences, which were scheduled in advance.[61] Juan Carrillo frequently referred to the marquesa's power at the court and with the queen, power she had apparently exercised as early as 1599. Far from reporting to Lerma about the queen, the Marquesa del Valle won the queen's favor and together they directly petitioned the king for requests. For example, the Marquis of Montesclaros, who, in 1603, was sent as a royal official to Mexico, wrote to the marquesa thanking her and the queen for getting him his appointment.[62]

As the Marquesa del Valle gained influence, and particularly as she won the queen's favor, she became less useful to the Duke of Lerma and actually began to constitute a political threat. So, in October 1603, the Marquesa del Valle was ordered out of the court and was taken to the fortress at Simancas, where she was tried for abuse of her office. Ana de Mendoza, the Marquesa del Valle's niece and secretary, was also imprisoned. Both were sentenced to house arrest in Logroño. In 1608 they were freed, although neither woman was allowed to visit the court. Their release signaled Lerma's waning influence at the court; after Philip III's death, the marquesa was allowed to return to court, where she died, in 1621.

In her declaration to the judges sent to question her, the Marquesa del Valle mentioned the queen's unhappiness, noting that the queen had confided in her.[63] The marquesa never stated that this unhappiness was due to Lerma's actions, but the implication was clear. Rumors of Margaret's displeasure with Lerma and with the court reached such a level that the men sent to question the marquesa asked her if there was truth to the story that the queen had asked the pope to annul her marriage to Philip III.[64] The marquesa's comments and the questions asked of her also indicate the level of intrigue that characterized Philip's court; the marquesa certainly placed Margaret of Austria at the center of this intrigue. According to the marquesa, Margaret told her that if she wished to write to her, she should do so through Richard Haller or through another priest by the name of Ballester.[65] By no means should the marquesa send written messages to the queen through Lerma. While Lerma would get information about the queen from the Marquesa del Valle, the queen also used the marquesa to communicate her dissatisfaction or annoyance to Lerma. In this way, Margaret of Austria consciously took advantage of means that Lerma had set up to try to monitor her. The queen used the marquesa to control the privado's information and to determine what he knew about her.

The case of the Marquesa del Valle ultimately led to changes within the queen's household. In 1603, the same year as the Marquesa del Valle's exit from the court, the king published new rules governing the house of the queen. These rules (*etiquetas*) particularly specified that none of the queen's ladies-in-waiting (*damas*) were to become involved in private negotiations or accept petitions (*memoriales*) from individuals; instead they should be concerned strictly with serving the queen. This activity—accepting petitions from individuals and then submitting them to the queen to take directly to Philip III—was in fact exactly what the Marquesa del Valle had done. Because the women were able to circumvent the Duke of Lerma, this system threatened the privado's power. In response, Lerma may very well have encouraged Philip III to issue these new rules governing the queen's household.

Although the Duke of Lerma recognized the queen as one of his strongest rivals, he and those around him did not believe that she was fully responsible for her actions. Instead, they attributed some of the queen's ideas to her confessor, Richard Haller. They certainly knew that Haller criticized Lerma and Rodrigo Calderón and believed that he was largely responsible for the queen's negative opinion of them. In a letter from 1610, one of Calderón's men commented that Haller had criticized Calderón to the queen and that he was to blame for the queen's dissatisfaction with Calderón and Lerma.[66] This connection between Haller's influence and the queen's discontent shows once again that observers thought that Margaret relied too heavily on religious advisors, and that these priests and nuns were responsible for creating problems at the Spanish court. These accounts also indicate that even as the queen was praised for her piety and virtue, others at court (most of them men) felt threatened by this piety because it indirectly empowered persons who, because of their religious functions, were more difficult for Lerma to control. Lerma and his associates might have thought Margaret of Austria incapable of such strong opinions because of her youth. However, it is more likely that they blamed Haller because it was easier for them to criticize a priest than to criticize a queen who enjoyed her husband's affection.

Richard Haller certainly did not like the Duke of Lerma or his associates. Haller wanted the queen to assume her proper place at the court. In a letter written by the Duke of Poli, the Duke of Parma's representative at the Spanish court, Poli related a conversation he had had with Haller. Poli commented that the queen's numerous familial connections in Central Europe, Italy, and Spain made her the principal woman in Europe. As Poli said, "in little time she will become the patroness of this empire." Haller, according to Poli, replied that this would certainly be true if God would allow two people to die. Poli believed that Haller was referring to the Duke of Lerma and his sister, the Countess of Lemos, both of whom constantly kept watch over the queen.[67] So Lerma and Calderón were correct when they assumed Haller's hostility toward them. Although he certainly influenced the queen and shared her negative assessment of Lerma and his associates, Haller did not determine her opinions. Like other royal women sent by their relatives to a foreign court, Margaret of Austria arrived in Spain already determined to further an agenda favorable to her family. Lerma attempted to prevent the queen from pursuing this agenda. From the beginning of Philip III's reign, Margaret opposed Lerma's policies and formed a circle of supporters dedicated to pressuring the king for policies that would favor the Austrian Habsburgs. Haller was central to this circle, but he was only one of many individuals with whom Margaret of Austria worked.

In the same way that Jerónimo de Florencia, in his eulogy, argued that Margaret of Austria represented good government, court observers noted that the queen's ways differed greatly from those of others at court. The queen was known for seeking the truth and for despising lies, and she rewarded those who spoke honestly to her. These traits, uncommon at the Spanish court, gave the queen a reputation of wisdom.[68] Her approach seemed to be a way to change the course that the Spanish monarchy had taken under Philip III. The Prince of Castiglione, the imperial ambassador to Spain, argued that the queen was very much loved and respected throughout the Spanish kingdoms. Writing in 1611, Castiglione believed that Spain was in somewhat of a crisis. The ambassador claimed that if the king were to die, the unity of kingdoms would fall apart. However, had the queen lived, this would not happen because all of the kingdoms would gladly have had her as governess, and she would have been able to maintain peace and unity throughout the Spanish kingdoms.[69]

Despite the attempts of biographers and eulogists to deny that Margaret of Austria exercised a political voice at her husband's court, and, despite chroniclers' negative assessment of the impact of the queen's advice, Margaret did succeed in voicing her opinions and winning the ear and the support of Philip III. The queen consistently sought to negotiate favorable marriages for her sisters and successfully arranged for one of them to marry an Italian prince. In order to do this, Margaret negotiated with Rudolf II for his assistance, and Rudolf

regularly wrote to her asking her for help in negotiating two of the major con-
flicts between him and Philip: Spanish assistance in the war against the Turks
and Spanish restitution of imperial fiefs in Italy (particularly the fief of Finale).[70]
Hans Khevenhüller also visited the queen regularly to convey messages from
Rudolf II and to ask her to intervene with Philip III in these important issues.
Margaret always assured Khevenhüller that she would do her best and that she
always had Rudolf's best interests in mind. In turn, however, she expected
Rudolf to meet her demands and help arrange favorable marriages for her sis-
ters.[71]

The negotiation of marriages was an area in which women were allowed—
and even expected—to intervene.[72] Therefore it is not surprising that Philip
supported Margaret's wishes and even got the Duke of Lerma to speak to
Khevenhüller and remind the ambassador of the need to press for these favorable marriages.[73] Yet the queen's forceful pursuit of the issue and her ability to
make her intervention with Philip III contingent upon Rudolf's cooperation
shows Margaret's political astuteness and her skills as a negotiator. The Austrian Habsburgs certainly considered Margaret to be an essential and strong
lobbyist at the Spanish court, and they consistently directed their requests to
her. Moreover, when they requested the queen's support, the Austrian Habsburgs did not confine themselves to minor issues or spheres traditionally
thought to be feminine.

Margaret was particularly successful in getting Spanish aid for her brother,
Archduke Ferdinand. In October 1600, the queen persuaded Philip III to give
Ferdinand a monthly stipend of 5,000 ducats.[74] Ferdinand valued his sister's influence, and even after Margaret's death, in 1611, Ferdinand continued to use
her memory to negotiate matters at court. In his instructions to an ambassador
he was sending to the Spanish court in 1613, Ferdinand listed individuals at the
court on whom the ambassador could count because they had had great affection for Margaret.[75]

It is noteworthy that Philip III's pursuit of his claims to the Bohemian and
Hungarian thrones—claims that brought him into direct competition and conflict with Archduke Ferdinand—did not begin in earnest until after Margaret's
death. Although the issue had been brought up as early as 1603 by Guillén de
San Clemente, the Spanish ambassador in Central Europe, and again in 1611 by
his successor, Baltasar de Zúñiga, it did not receive serious attention until
1612.[76] Philip III did not want to offend the queen by pursuing claims that
would pit him against her brother.

Margaret's influence with Philip III was personal and familial; they had an affectionate, close relationship, particularly after Margaret had borne a son in 1605. The king listened to her requests and to her comments; for example, in 1610 he followed her advice and that of Margaret of the Cross to consider Rudolf II's request to have princes treated the same as Spanish grandees at the court.[77] Philip III also listened to his wife's criticism of the Junta de Desempeño and her disapproval of the Duke of Lerma. Before her death, Margaret even told the king that Lerma had tried to poison her.[78] Although Venetian ambassadors claimed that the queen was unable to circumvent Lerma's influence and that she remained frustrated in her attempts to have a political say, Margaret nonetheless did reach her husband, and, because of this contact, she consistently proved a threat to the Duke of Lerma and his network of power and influence.

Philip III did not comment upon his wife's role in politics; or at least none of these comments has survived. However, in his advice to his daughter Anne when she married Louis XIII of France, Philip did note what he thought to be a queen's proper role. His comments provide an interesting perspective on his own wife's court function. Philip first of all advised his daughter to guard her faith and devotion to God, "from whose hand we receive the crown which we have."[79] After her trust in God, she was to "have faithful and true love for her husband." Philip knew that his young daughter would need councillors to advise her. He therefore recommended that she take advice from "wise, prudent, and experienced men," but he also advised her that "in no way should you interfere in matters of government or justice, because this does not concern you. [Concern yourself with these matters] only if the king, your husband, orders you to do so, and then show preference for mercy and clemency [*misericordia y clemencia*]."[80]

In this advice to his daughter, Philip III clearly argued that a queen should not interfere in political matters. A queen was to be primarily a wife, obedient to her husband and devoted to God. Her public acts revolved around charity and piety, the accepted public domain for women. Philip III obviously believed that his own wife had fulfilled these roles, because he advised his daughter to follow her mother's example and to study the biography of Margaret of Austria which Diego de Guzmán was writing.[81] At least the monarch knew that Guzmán's biography would present the proper image of a queen, if not a completely accurate representation of Margaret of Austria. In these instructions, Philip III also warned Anne against people who gossip (*parlerais*) and advised her to investigate matters secretly before believing everything that was told her.[82] The Spanish monarch knew well the ways of the court, but his advice also demonstrates that he accepted the stereotype of women being too credulous and easily manipulated; he clearly subscribed to the notion that gossip and idle talk plagued women in particular.

Finally, in his letters to Anne after she married Louis XIII, Philip consistently referred to the need to produce an heir. He questioned his daughter on how often her husband slept with her; he asked her to tell him "if the king, when he feels well, always sleeps in your rooms or [only] sometimes."[83] Philip complained that Anne did not answer him and wrote her: "I confess to you even if you blush that I wish that since the king spends much time during the day in your rooms, that he also spend some [time] during the night."[84] In a letter of April 1617, Philip acknowledged that his daughter thought his advice malicious, but he sincerely wished that Louis XIII would move beyond friendship to a more intimate relationship with Anne.[85] After all, Philip thought that in order for his daughter to become a woman, she had to become a mother. As he wrote in November 1616, "I am anxious that you become a woman; I could benefit from that and . . . from you giving me a grandson soon."[86] On this occasion, as on many others, Philip encouraged his daughter to become more intimate with her husband. The king wanted his grandson to become king of France and therefore he pressed his daughter to produce an heir.

To Philip, the roles of queen, wife, and mother were intimately connected, and all three were subsumed under the category of "royal woman." The monarch certainly recognized, however, that by providing a king with an heir, a woman strengthened her own position and that of her family at court. In Anne's case, Philip III looked forward to better relations with France. Philip had his own wife's case in mind; from personal experience, he knew how Margaret of Austria had gained power and strength by ensuring the continuation of his line and by cultivating an image of piety and virtue.

❦ ❦ ❦

Even more so than Empress María and Margaret of Austria, Margaret of the Cross has been described strictly in terms of her piety and religious devotion. Because of her religious vocation, she does not appear as often as Empress María or Margaret of Austria in the chroniclers' and ambassadorial reports of the period. Historians have assumed that because she lived in a cloistered convent she was concerned only with spiritual matters. However, throughout

Philip III's reign and until her death, in 1633, Margaret of the Cross was one of the principal representatives of the Austrian Habsburgs in Madrid. She met regularly with Philip III and Margaret of Austria, as well as with their children. She also corresponded and met with the Duke of Lerma. Imperial ambassadors such as Hans Khevenhüller, Dario Nomi, and Franz Christoph Khevenhüller visited the cloistered nun and discussed political matters with her. Hans Khevenhüller in particular noted visiting with Margaret at the Descalzas and discussing numerous matters with her, including such issues as her own household, Empress María's final will, and assistance to Flanders and Central Europe. The ambassador also regularly commented on Margaret's illnesses, annual occurrences that lasted for weeks, according to Khevenhüller.[87]

Margaret of the Cross's activities and her involvement in many of the central issues of Philip III's reign demonstrate that the walls of a cloistered convent were permeable. One of the primary ways in which Margaret crossed these walls was through her correspondence. She maintained regular contact with many of her relatives, but in particular with Archduke Albert in Flanders. She also wrote to and received letters from Philip III and the Duke of Lerma.[88] These letters complemented the visits of the monarch and his privado to Margaret in the Descalzas. Through this correspondence, Margaret remained informed of developments in Spain, Flanders, and Central Europe, as well as of such personal concerns as the health of her relatives. Margaret also received written petitions from many other individuals, including her servants and those of her mother or brothers. She then would write to Philip III or to other royal figures, such as Archduke Albert, on behalf of these people. Margaret's letters in support of these petitions show that the nun took her role as intermediary seriously; she considered it her duty to transmit petitions to influential people. In turn, such intervention undoubtedly brought the nun a sense of importance and power in the secular world.

Margaret of the Cross had detailed information about events in Central Europe and about matters concerning her brothers, Emperor Rudolf II and Archdukes Matthias, Maximilian, and Albert. In her letters to Rudolf II, she mentioned the meeting of Habsburg princes which took place in 1610 and told Rudolf that she was very happy such a conciliatory meeting had occurred.[89] From 1600 until 1612, Rudolf II and Archduke Matthias were often at odds over who would succeed Rudolf II as emperor; Rudolf had refused to nominate a successor to the throne. Frustrated with the emperor's vacillation, especially because he was the next in line to the throne, Matthias engaged in numerous political and military intrigues designed to increase his authority and to improve his bargaining power with the emperor.

In 1606, for example, Matthias asked his brother Maximilian and his cousins Ferdinand and Maximilian Ernst, Archdukes of Styria, to help persuade Rudolf to appoint him commander-in-chief of the army to be sent to crush a revolt in Hungary. Surprisingly, Rudolf agreed to this appointment, and Matthias wasted no time using this command to increase his own power. After signing a peace treaty with the Hungarian rebels in 1608, he quickly consolidated his power, becoming the de facto ruler of Hungary. He subsequently threatened to besiege Bohemia unless the emperor officially ceded Hungary and the Austrian hereditary lands (*Erbländer*) to him. This tactic worked, and in 1608 Rudolf officially proclaimed Matthias king of Hungary.

In 1610, Rudolf and Matthias reached a preliminary agreement. Once she heard this news, Margaret wrote to Rudolf and told him that she was very happy about the agreement (*concordia*), and she urged him to do his best to maintain the peace with his brother.[90] Margaret was also informed of the pensions and any financial assistance given to her brothers. In the case of the pension given to Matthias, Margaret knew the precise amounts and even knew exactly from which funds the monies would come.[91] The nun went so far as to write Lerma to give her opinion about how Philip III could come up with the specific amounts Matthias needed.[92] On several occasions, the Duke of Lerma informed Margaret of the assistance that would be given to the emperor or to the Habsburg archdukes.[93] These instances clearly show that Margaret was involved in negotiations between the Austrian and the Spanish Habsburgs; both sides informed her of their petitions and demands. Her relatives on both sides expected her to negotiate with the other branch for them.

The Austrian Habsburgs wrote Margaret of the Cross frequently and asked for her assistance in negotiating some of their most pressing concerns. For example, in 1618 the imperial ambassador Franz Christoph Khevenhüller asked Margaret to speak to the Count of Lemos about Spanish occupation of the imperial fief, Finale. Throughout Philip III's reign, the Austrian Habsburgs had requested Margaret's assistance in mediating this thorny issue. Rudolf II regularly wrote Margaret about this and other matters, such as assistance in fighting the Turks. He asked her to plead his case with Philip III, something that Margaret certainly did. The Spanish king visited his aunt frequently at the Descalzas convent; Khevenhüller recorded many of these meetings, as did Luis Cabrera de Córdoba.[94]

Philip III clearly spoke to Margaret about a wide range of issues, including political matters. The Council of State disapproved of and feared Philip's candid talks with his aunt. The Council advised the king to be more careful about what he discussed with Margaret because "she is a saint and with this intention she writes what she hears and this is inconvenient."[95] This conciliar warning proves that Philip III did speak about political matters openly with his aunt and that she in turn communicated these matters to others. The statement is also interesting not only because it shows that the Council disapproved of Margaret's actions but also because the councillors thought that her piety prevented her from being sufficiently circumspect about state matters. The Council preferred to suggest that Margaret was not fully responsible for her actions, but the councillors might have communicated their concern in this way because they feared telling the king that Margaret was actually taking advantage of his confidence and affection. The Council certainly thought Margaret a sufficient threat that they warned Philip III to be more guarded in his conversations with her.

Margaret expressed her political opinions to Philip III and even seems to have been involved in a plot against the Duke of Uceda, Lerma's eldest son, who gained great favor with the king in the last years of his reign. Margaret cooperated with Prince Filiberto, son of the Duke of Savoy, in an effort to discredit Uceda with Philip. Filiberto hoped to replace Uceda in Philip's favor. Another chief conspirator was Juan de Santa María, one of Philip's chaplains. The plot did not succeed, but numerous witnesses noted Margaret's important role.[96] They also noted that Margaret allied herself with another religious who had political pretensions, Lope Díaz de Paniagua.[97] These reports once again point out that Margaret was at the center of political discussions and was willing and able to involve herself in political developments at court. Margaret's influence with Philip III was such that some observers believed that Uceda had encouraged Philip to travel to Portugal in 1621 in order to remove him from Margaret's influence.[98] Such rumors circulated about all three Habsburg women. So, too, Lerma had supposedly wanted Philip to move the court to Valladolid, to remove the monarch from Empress María's influence, and he had also threatened to have Philip travel frequently, thereby preventing Margaret of Austria from regularly speaking to him about political matters.

Margaret of the Cross, with the assistance of Margaret of Austria, went to the extreme of helping in the publication of a book that was indirectly critical of Lerma's privanza. The author, Cristóbal Pérez de Herrera, detailed the problems facing the Spanish kingdoms and was criticized for presenting the state of the monarchy in too negative a fashion. When questioned about how he received permission for the book, Pérez de Herrera explained that Margaret of the Cross had given the manuscript to the king.[99] Pérez de Herrera had asked Margaret of the Cross and Margaret of Austria for an audience with Lerma in order to give Lerma the book. Instead, Margaret of the Cross and the nuns at the Descalzas read the book and then sent it directly to Philip III via his royal almoner, Diego de Guzmán.[100] According to the author, then, there could be nothing questionable about the book if it had received the support of such pious and virtuous women.[101] Margaret of the Cross and Margaret of Austria must have realized that by claiming the Spanish kingdoms to be in a very sorry state, Pérez de Herrera was indirectly criticizing Lerma's power. The two women, however, agreed with this viewpoint and sought a way to remind Philip III that his reliance on Lerma could have pernicious effects on the Spanish kingdoms. This case proves that Margaret of the Cross could bypass Lerma in order to reach Philip and also emphasizes that Diego de Guzmán served as an intermediary between the nuns of the Descalzas and the king. Margaret of the Cross certainly intervened in this political matter, but she did so purportedly because of her piety and virtue—characteristics that led her to be concerned with the fate of the Spanish kingdoms.

⚜ ⚜ ⚜

Although biographers and eulogists chose to depict the three Habsburg women in a strictly devotional light, all three women were important political players at the Spanish court. Chroniclers and ambassadors reported the women's interest and involvement in political matters; their reports present the Habsburg women in a more realistic light than do the accounts of biographers and eulogists. Moreover, conciliar reports and letters written by the women themselves help to sharpen this image of the politically active and knowledgeable Habsburg women. All three women were involved in challenging the Duke of Lerma's power, and all three were implicated in some of the major court intrigues of Philip III's reign. The Habsburg women clearly thought that they were acting in the best interest of their family when they intervened in politics; indeed, their relatives expected them to intervene and to mediate between the two Habsburg branches. Nevertheless, they did so in ways that would not provoke much hostility and that seemed acceptable to the men around them, in particular, to Philip III.

5

Family, Affection, and Politics

THE THREE HABSBURG WOMEN who are at the center of this study were defined primarily by their familial connections. Biographers and eulogists referred to them as the daughters, wives, and mothers of emperors and princes. Rodrigo Mendes Silva, Empress María's biographer, noted that she was the mother of two emperors, two queens, twelve archdukes, and the mother-in-law of two emperors and wife of another.[1] The title of Mendes Silva's biography of Empress María also referred to her as "daughter of the ever unconquerable Emperor Charles V."[2] An inscription dedicated to the empress in the church of the Descalzas convent called her "daughter of Emperor Charles V, wife of Maximilian II, Emperor of Germany, mother of Rudolf II, of Matilde and Anna, Queen of Spain, and of Isabel of France."[3] Likewise, Margaret of the Cross's biographer, Juan de la Palma, consistently reminded his readers that the nun was also the daughter, aunt, and sister of the most important individuals in the world.[4] Fray Hortensio Paravicino, Margaret of the Cross's eulogist, mentioned first in the title of his funeral sermon that Margaret was an imperial princess, then that she was the daughter, sister, cousin, and aunt of emperors and kings, and only lastly did he say that she was the "bride of Jesus Christ."[5] Margaret of Austria's eulogist also described her as the daughter of Archduke Karl and Maria, granddaughter of Emperor Ferdinand, niece of Charles V and Maximilian II, cousin of Rudolf II, Matthias I, and Archdukes Maximilian and Albert, sister of Archdukes Ferdinand, Maximilian, Karl, and Leopold, and sister of the queen of Poland. Only at the end did Margaret's eulogist mention that she was the "great queen" of Spain.[6]

Rather than limiting their activities, familial connections gave women status, leverage, and power. Biographers and eulogists mentioned these familial ties in order to remind their audience of the importance of the Habsburg women. For male writers and observers, all three women deserved recognition precisely because of their relationship to men and because of the degree to which the royal women served and aided their dynasty. However, familial connections also empowered the Habsburg women; through their family ties, Habsburg women often gained political assignments and played active roles at court in promoting the interests of their family. As informal diplomats, these women actually had great room to maneuver as long as they were seen to be acting for the benefit of their family. In most cases, they were doing what many aristocratic women did: promoting the interests of their children or their paternal family.[7] However, in the case of the Habsburgs, the dynasty's political power and territorial holdings allowed female members of the family to play an important political role even while performing the familial duties expected of aristocratic women. Because the Habsburg family was a political unit, within the dynasty the line between the familial and the political was permeable.

The frequent mention of the lineage of Empress María, Margaret of Austria, and Margaret of the Cross highlights the importance of family for the Habsburgs. The Habsburg dynasty—or the House of Austria, as it was called in the early modern period—saw itself as a family unit governing diverse territories throughout Europe.[8] Although this dynasty was split into two branches, one Austrian and the other Spanish, the members of the dynasty saw themselves bound together by ties of family, affection, and religion. If one branch of the family was attacked, this was thought to be an attack on the other branch as well.[9] Thus, for example, the Spanish Habsburgs expected the Austrian Habsburgs to assist them in suppressing the revolt in Flanders, and in turn, the Austrian Habsburgs expected Spanish assistance in fighting the German Protestants and the Turks. These expectations, that familial ties translate into financial and military assistance, were not always met, and they were the focus of much conflict between the Spanish and the Austrian Habsburgs during the sixteenth and seventeenth centuries.[10] Nevertheless, both branches argued that their familial connections should indeed result in closer cooperation.[11]

The political ramifications of familial ties is clearly evident in the marriage negotiations of the Habsburgs. During the reign of Philip III (and certainly during the reigns of Charles V and Philip II), the Spanish and Austrian Habsburgs were closely bound through marriage.[12] Philip III's wife, Margaret of Austria, was from the Austrian Habsburg hereditary land of Styria. Philip III's sister, Isabel Clara Eugenia, married Archduke Albert, brother of Emperor Rudolf II; this marriage was a preliminary step toward the couple's joint rule of Flanders. One of Philip III and Margaret of Austria's daughters, María, married her cousin, Emperor Ferdinand III. Marriages in the early modern period were clearly seen as a means of developing, furthering, or cementing political and economic alliances, and they played an enormous role in the diplomatic relations between countries.[13] The Habsburgs' propensity to intermarry in the early modern period shows that the two branches saw the need to work together and to foster the familial ties between the Austrian lands and the Spanish monarchy.

Women played crucial roles in these marital strategies and in promoting the interests of a dynastic clan. The female members of a family were expected to form marriages that would further strengthen the paternal family. They were also expected to produce children to continue the dynastic line. Within marriage, a woman was supposed to ensure that her husband was favorably disposed toward her relatives. This was particularly true for female members of a royal family who married foreign royalty. In these instances, women were expected to negotiate for the needs and interests of their natal family and act as informal ambassadors and even spies. Philip III, for example, expected his daughter Anne to protect Spanish interests when she married the king of France, Louis XIII. He particularly wanted her to fight against heresy in France and to make sure that her husband did not aid any rebellions against Spain.[14] In these ways, royal women functioned as diplomatic representatives of their male relatives and tried to influence political policy.

Women also often took care of negotiating marriages for their male and female relatives; this function, which men often turned over to their female relatives, afforded women a great deal of influence over the future of the dynastic line.[15] In the case of the Habsburgs, women also occupied important political positions. Habsburg women were politically active notably in the Low Countries. Margaret of Austria, Charles V's aunt, governed the Netherlands from 1507 to 1515; Maria of Hungary then took over until 1555; and Isabel Clara Eugenia governed jointly with Archduke Albert from 1599 to 1621 and by herself until 1633.[16]

Women were able to exercise greater influence within a system in which domestic and political spheres overlapped than in a system in which these spheres were carefully separated. Louise Lamphere has argued that women within systems with no clear separation between domestic and political functions usually cooperated with each other and with men. Joan Kelly-Gadol has also stressed that women in societies with no clear distinction between private and public realms were better able to enjoy positions of equality with men.[17] On the other hand, in systems in which the political world is controlled by men and in which women are relegated to domestic duties, one finds more conflict between women. In the latter case, women influence politics only by working through men and trying to influence their decisions. The early modern Spanish court does not necessarily follow Lamphere's model. The overlap between the public and private realms meant that women (in particular, royal and court women) could more readily have access to the political world. However, a male hierarchy did attempt to control this political world, and women often did have to work through men in order to influence political policy. In addition, even though the line between domestic and political spheres was fluid, there was substantial conflict between women at the Spanish court.[18]

In the early modern period, there was no clear division between the private and the public worlds, so royal and aristocratic women were often able to influence political policy through their contact with kings and ministers or through the status they held because of their lineage, their offspring, or their wealth. This was particularly true for the female members of the Habsburg dynasty. The strong emphasis the Habsburgs placed on family meant that the female members of that family also had accepted and respected roles to play, roles that often took on political overtones. The male leaders of the Habsburg family were certainly used to their female relatives' occupying political posts and thereby exercising a political voice. This voice, however, was always thought to be in keeping with the larger concerns and interests of the Habsburg dynasty, rather than the personal benefit of the woman in power.

The female ruler was merely a representative of the House of Austria and was usually appointed by a male emperor or king to represent his interests. She received the right to rule because of her familial connection to a male Habsburg, and she was performing a duty for a male relative and for her house. It was natural, therefore, for the Habsburgs to expect female members of the dynasty to have opinions on political matters and to influence political policy even when these women were not technically in a position of authority at a court.

A familial system like that of the Habsburgs rested upon the premise that all family members would be committed to the protection and promotion of the family. Women were expected to meet the needs of their dynastic house in numerous ways: through marriage, through holding political office, and through applying informal pressure to influence policymaking at a court. In these and other ways, Habsburg women played a vital role in promoting the interests of their family.

Empress María, Margaret of Austria, and Margaret of the Cross all assumed the task of pressuring Philip III to aid their relatives. In so doing, these Habsburg women were taking on roles that many other aristocratic women embraced and that many other Habsburg women before and after them held. However, their task was made more difficult by the financial constraints that the Spanish monarchy faced and by the influence of the Duke of Lerma, who encouraged Philip III to see to the needs of the Iberian peninsula before those of the House of Austria.

Lerma encouraged Philip to pursue a foreign policy of moderation. This entailed avoiding warfare and its expenses and seeking peace with England, France, and the Netherlands. Such a policy would have allowed Philip to conserve and restore the monarchy's resources and reputation. In the case of the Twelve Years' Truce (1609–21) with the Netherlands, it might well be that Philip and Lerma fully expected to resume fighting eventually. They believed that a truce would weaken the Dutch, break the coalition among the provinces, and ultimately favor Spain.[19] Nevertheless, the truce still provided the Spanish monarchy with a respite, during which the king could see to pressing needs such as the expulsion of the Moriscos and the defense of the Mediterranean. In fact, the truce did allow Philip III to divert some funds to the Mediterranean.[20]

Lerma and other ministers urged the king to make decisions based on the financial requirements of the Spanish kingdoms and not on the demands of his relatives.[21] In this way, Lerma attempted to separate familial affection and devotion from political decision making: Lerma was actually claiming that the Spanish kingdoms were distinct from the House of Austria and deserved primary attention. He was also following the arguments of political theorists who stated that a monarch had to place the interests of his state above those of family and religion.[22]

Part of Lerma's plan was for Philip to forge closer and more peaceful ties with Spain's traditional enemies: France and England. In order to do so, the

Spanish government negotiated a joint marriage between the French prince Louis XIII and the Spanish princess Anne, as well as between the future Philip IV and the French princess Isabel.[23] These French marriages were in large part negotiated by the Duke of Lerma, but Queen Margaret also supported the arrangement because she understood the need for a rapprochement with France.[24] The Spanish government considered arranging a marriage between the Infanta María of Spain and the heir to the English throne.[25] This marriage did not occur, however, owing in part to pressure from Margaret of the Cross and the Austrian Habsburgs, and the Infanta María subsequently married the son of Emperor Ferdinand II.

The Austrian Habsburgs did not look favorably upon these marriages because they saw the unions as symptomatic of the weakening of familial ties during Philip III's reign. They also recognized that without marriage ties, there might be less incentive for the Spanish Habsburgs to continue to provide financial assistance to the Austrian Habsburgs. Moreover, throughout this period the Austrian Habsburgs believed that they were under attack and that their enemies were conspiring against them. During such times, they felt that the two branches of the Habsburg family should work even more closely together. Marriages were a good sign of dynastic unity and were meant to ensure cooperation between the two branches.

It was within this new framework of strained Spanish-Austrian relations that Empress María, Margaret of Austria, and Margaret of the Cross had to operate. They had to find a way to argue against Lerma and in favor of the Habsburg family. This was a consistent problem throughout Philip III's reign, but one that was eventually settled in the Habsburgs' favor. After all, when the Bohemian estates revolted in 1618, Philip III intervened on the side of his Austrian Habsburg relatives.[26] Spain then cooperated closely with the Austrian Habsburgs, at least until the end of the Thirty Years' War, in 1648.

Empress María, Margaret of Austria, and Margaret of the Cross were quite conscious of their place within the House of Austria, and they were determined to protect and further the interests of their male relatives and those of the Habsburg dynasty as a whole. They knew what was expected of them by their relatives, and their success in winning financial support for the Austrian Habsburgs shows that they were adept at performing their duties. The three Habsburg women accepted their prescribed roles because these roles afforded them power and influence both at the Spanish court and within the Habsburg dynasty.[27] As female members of the dynasty, they were recognized as key political players. Foreign ambassadors visited them, and many people requested their mediation because it was known that the women's familial connections gave them access to the king, who would listen to their requests.

One of the principal expectations of women in such a family was that they produce heirs. By perpetuating the family line, women satisfied one of the essential needs of any dynasty. Empress María and Margaret of Austria certainly fulfilled this duty. The empress gave birth to fifteen children; Queen Margaret, eight. Empress María had five girls and ten boys. Two of her sons, Rudolf II and Matthias I, went on to become Holy Roman Emperors; one son, Archduke Albert, served as governor of the Low Countries. Her daughter Anna became queen of Spain and Philip II's fourth wife; she gave birth to Philip III. Another of Empress María's daughters, Isabel, married Charles IX of France. Hence, by giving birth to numerous children, María provided individuals to serve as the political leaders of the House of Austria. Her biographer stressed this fact because it increased Empress María's worth, particularly in the eyes of male observers. The ability to produce heirs was at the core of early modern society's judgment of an aristocratic woman; her reputation improved even further if those children went on to assume important political offices or if they contracted advantageous marriages.[28]

Margaret of Austria gave birth to eight children and died from complications resulting from the birth of her last child, a son. Her eldest son became King Philip IV; her daughter Anne married Louis XIII and became queen of France. Her daughter María married Ferdinand III and became Holy Roman Empress. Margaret of Austria fulfilled her responsibilities as wife and mother by producing these children and even giving up her life in childbirth. These were the duties expected of a wife in the early modern period, duties that supposedly brought happiness to women. As the moralist Juan de Mora wrote, a married woman desired to be loved and to have children.[29] Commentators noted that by giving birth to children, Margaret of Austria had left "jewels" for the Spanish monarchy which would make Spain the envy of all other nations.[30] Certainly the queen's ability to produce heirs for Philip III gave her greater worth in the king's eyes, increased the affection between the two monarchs, and made Philip III more inclined to listen to her advice. Philip himself believed that one of the principal duties of a queen was to produce heirs; his wife clearly fulfilled this duty.[31]

Margaret of the Cross, because she chose to be a cloistered nun, did not bear any children. However, she fulfilled a maternal role by caring for the children of Philip III and Margaret of Austria. The monarchs left their children with Margaret of the Cross on numerous occasions, and when the king traveled alone for extended periods of time, he insisted that his wife and their children remain at the Descalzas convent. Margaret of the Cross often tended to the children during these times. After the queen's death, in 1611, Philip III continued to leave his children at the Descalzas with Margaret of the Cross. The cloistered nun therefore exercised a formative influence on the royal children and performed a duty that was expected of her. From her letters, it is clear that Margaret loved the royal children and welcomed the chance to spend time with them. She commented fondly on their health, their appearance, and their actions.[32] She acted as a surrogate mother, which helps to explain Philip IV's great attachment to and respect for the Franciscan nun.[33]

Another primary purpose of marriage was to further the interests of the paternal family.[34] In their marriages, Empress María and Margaret of Austria certainly fulfilled this role as well. Empress María began the task long before she entered the convent of the Descalzas Reales and long before Philip III's reign. She proved to be an invaluable ally for her brother, Philip II, while she was in Central Europe. One of Philip II's principal concerns during his reign was to strengthen the Catholic faith throughout Europe. During her years as Maximilian II's wife, Empress María attempted to strengthen orthodox Tridentine Catholicism both in her husband's lands and within her own family.

Maximilian II had Protestant leanings and was inclined to make compromises with the Protestants in Central Europe.[35] For this reason, Empress María tried to ensure that he did not make religious or territorial concessions to Protestants, and she cooperated with Philip II to send two of her sons, Rudolf and Ernst, to the Spanish court, where they would receive daily education in the Catholic faith.[36] The empress even tried to wed Rudolf to Philip II's daughter, Isabel Clara Eugenia, in order to ensure that Rudolf would continue to have someone close by who was educated in Tridentine Catholicism. Philip II disapproved of Empress María's plan, however, because of the age difference between Rudolf and Isabel Clara Eugenia. The Spanish king argued that Rudolf should be told that if he defended orthodox Catholicism in Central Europe, he would be assured of Spain's continued support. Philip believed this would be sufficient motivation for Rudolf to avoid making concessions to the

Protestants.[37] In these attempts to strengthen orthodox Catholicism in the empire, Empress María clearly acted as a representative of the Spanish Habsburgs in Central Europe and used her position at the imperial court to press for an agenda that was agreeable to her own religious tendencies and to those of her brother, Philip II.

While in Central Europe, Empress María also worked closely with the Spanish ambassadors to ensure that their petitions and requests received the attention of Maximilian II. This was true with the Count of Monteagudo, Spanish ambassador to Central Europe from 1570 to 1577. Empress María regularly invited Monteagudo to take his evening meal with the emperor, at which time the ambassador could discuss political developments with Maximilian.[38] Philip II valued his sister's assistance in negotiating issues enough to instruct his ambassadors to discuss questions with her before taking them to the emperor.[39] The monarch wrote his ambassador, the Count of Monteagudo, "in all matters you should always rely on her [the empress's] favor and intercession and follow her command and advice before speaking to the emperor because she will tell you the way and the time to discuss them so that they will be successful. In the end, you should be careful to proceed and to follow the path which my sister commands you to take."[40]

Empress María's family connection to the emperor, her familiarity with him, and her knowledge of political matters all made her an important tool for Spanish negotiations at the imperial court. Monteagudo followed Philip II's advice; his letters to the Spanish monarch demonstrate that he consulted with the empress before speaking to Maximilian about any concern.[41] The ambassador relied on the empress's advice, and in turn, Empress María gave the ambassador regular access to Emperor Maximilian. In 1571, when Maximilian became ill and was bedridden for weeks, other ambassadors and ministers were unable to consult with the emperor, but the Count of Monteagudo continued to visit Maximilian and discuss political issues with him.[42] From these examples, it is clear Empress María fulfilled one of the principal duties of a female member of a royal family: to further the interests of the paternal side and to act as informal negotiator for her male relatives.

The empress obviously welcomed this task and did her utmost to promote Spanish interests. She was frequently present at the audiences Maximilian gave or at his meetings with councillors;[43] this allowed her to keep abreast of political developments and to have the knowledge with which to negotiate for

Philip II. The Count of Monteagudo's reliance on Empress María also demonstrates the degree to which the empress was informed about political affairs and wanted to influence the making of policy at the imperial court. In general, the empress seems to have been primarily concerned with religious matters (in particular, with stopping the spread of Protestantism in Habsburg lands), but she had opinions on a wide variety of issues, opinions she readily shared with the Count of Monteagudo. For example, she discussed the attempts of Catherine de Medici to interfere with Isabel's household. The empress also expressed her ideas about how to keep certain imperial ministers well disposed toward Spain.[44]

Monteagudo pinpointed the root of Empress María's influence at the imperial court: the affectionate relationship and personal contact she enjoyed with her husband. Because of the strength and duration of her marriage to Maximilian, the empress could manipulate him (*torcer al Emperador*) and could be a "most valuable means and instrument for influencing and guiding the emperor."[45] This is a clear demonstration of the way in which familial connections could translate into political influence and allow royal women to exercise a political voice. By taking advantage of their affectionate relationships and of the access to political figures which their familial connections afforded them, royal women could influence the making of political policy at an early modern court.

This type of influence was also recognized by the women's male relatives, who often tried to use a woman's influence to their own advantage. This method was employed by Philip II, who knew that Empress María could affect Maximilian's decisions. He encouraged his sister to use her influence with the emperor in order to have him make decisions that were in accordance with Philip II's desires. Philip urged Empress María to ensure that Maximilian make no concessions to the Protestants, that he accept Spanish interference in the imperial fief of Finale, and that he cooperate with the pope.[46]

When Empress María moved from Central Europe to Madrid, she took up the causes of her sons more directly. Her primary concern while residing in the Descalzas convent during the last two decades of her life was to further the interests of her sons in Central Europe and in Flanders and to win Spanish support for Austrian Habsburg needs. She used the same skills she had acquired at the imperial court to negotiate policies at the Spanish court. Once again, her influence was directly connected to her familial and affectionate relationship with the Spanish monarchs. Her relationship with Philip II and Philip III ensured that she would have regular access to the monarchs and could speak with them about matters concerning the Austrian Habsburgs. In this way, Empress María was fulfilling the role of the "good mother," who looked out for the interests of her children (in particular, her sons).

As a widow, María was no longer attempting to further the agenda of her paternal line but rather that of her own offspring. Her position as a widow gave her a certain degree of independence, which freed her to press for the needs of her sons. Widows were supposed to care for their family and ensure that their husband's will was carried out. They were expected to have primary loyalty to their children and to fill the role of father as well as that of mother.[47] Moreover, by seeing to the needs of her sons, Empress María was able to assume a position of power at the Spanish court and continue to serve as an informal diplomatic representative. María was used to exercising influence at a court and voicing her political opinions; by negotiating matters with Philip II and later with Philip III, the empress retained her political functions. This gave her a sense of power, which she had been accustomed to wielding at the imperial court and which she was reluctant to relinquish despite retiring to the convent.

In a similar fashion, Margaret of Austria used her marriage to Philip III to further the interests of her relatives. Throughout her time at the Spanish court, Margaret consistently reminded Philip III of the needs of her family and pressured him for assistance of all types for her relatives. So, for example, she convinced Philip to give her brother Archduke Ferdinand a monthly stipend of 5,000 ducats.[48] She also ensured that the king regularly assisted Ferdinand financially in his wars against the Turks. The Venetian ambassador Ottaviano Bon reported that because Margaret was Ferdinand's sister, Philip provided the archduke with soldiers and 6,000 *escudos* for the fighting in Croatia.[49]

Margaret's other brother, Archduke Leopold, also regularly wrote the queen to inform her of developments in Central Europe and ask for her assistance in negotiating matters at the Spanish court. On one occasion, Leopold notified Margaret of Matthias's agreement with the Hungarian Protestants, an agreement that allowed the Protestants religious freedom. Leopold emphasized the damage this pact had caused him and Archduke Ferdinand. He wanted the queen to ask Philip III not to support Matthias's actions and to continue to assist him and Ferdinand in fighting the Hungarian Protestants (or "heretics," as he called them).[50] The queen took this and other requests to her husband, who was usually inclined to grant them because of Leopold's familial ties to

Margaret. When the Spanish government began to criticize Archduke Maximilian, Margaret's brother, the queen tried to improve the archduke's reputation at the Spanish court and went so far as to complain to the Spanish ambassador in Prague, Guillén de San Clemente, that he was spreading false stories about the archduke.[51]

Observers recognized the queen's intercessory powers for her relatives. As the Venetian ambassador Francesco Soranzo pointed out in 1600, "the queen's intercessions always have great strength in this matter [assistance to Archduke Ferdinand]."[52] Another Venetian ambassador, Girolamo Soranzo, reported in 1611 that because of the queen, Philip III greatly loved Archduke Ferdinand and the other Styrian archdukes. According to Soranzo, Philip gave Ferdinand 5,000 escudos a month; Ferdinand and his brothers could always count on much assistance from Philip because Margaret of Austria never ceased interceding for them.[53]

The Austrian Habsburgs knew to take advantage of the familial and marriage bonds they had with the Spanish Habsburgs. Whenever the Austrian Habsburgs requested something from Philip III, they wrote to their female relatives in Spain asking them to petition the king in their favor. For instance, Rudolf II asked Margaret of Austria to speak to Philip about returning the fief of Finale to him.[54] Rudolf also wrote his ambassador, Hans Khevenhüller, and Philip directly about this concern; but he relied on the queen to help negotiate the matter. When Archduke Ferdinand lost the city of Canisia to the Turks in 1601, Rudolf wrote the queen and the empress asking them to speak to Philip about providing Ferdinand with further financial and military assistance.[55] Ferdinand in turn relied on his mother, Archduchess Maria of Bavaria, to write to Philip III about the loss of Canisia. On this same occasion, Archduchess Maria also wrote to Richard Haller, Queen Margaret's confessor, and asked him to bring the matter to Philip's attention.[56] The Austrian Habsburgs' female relatives living in Spain and in Central Europe served as the conduits for information and appeals on these and other occasions.

Rudolf II clearly recognized the important role played by his female relatives. In a letter to Khevenhüller about negotiating at the Spanish court, the emperor instructed his ambassador to inform Empress María of all developments and work through her at the court.[57] The emperor also wrote his mother asking for her assistance in winning Spanish aid for his wars against the Turks.[58]

Margaret of the Cross received regular letters and petitions from the Austrian Habsburgs as well, asking her for assistance in negotiating issues with Philip III and with the Duke of Lerma. The Franciscan nun was very well informed about political negotiations, although in her letters she assumed an attitude of humility and piety. For example, she knew the particulars of Spanish financial assistance to Archduke Matthias; she knew the exact amount of his pension from Philip III, the amount that had already been paid and the amount that still needed to be paid.[59] The nun served as an essential link between the two branches of the family and continued to fill the role traditionally played by aristocratic women within a dynasty. Her choice of a life as a cloistered nun did not free her from such duties to her male relatives; she continued to see to the needs of the Austrian Habsburgs despite her religious obligations.

The diplomatic role played by all three Habsburg women certainly shows that the Austrian Habsburgs thought familial ties should translate into political assistance. There was nothing unusual or unexpected about the Austrian Habsburgs writing their female relatives and believing that the women's intercession with Philip III and the Duke of Lerma would be decisive. The Austrian Habsburgs assumed that their female relatives would play a political role at the Spanish court. This did not entail expressing an independent voice in political matters; it meant representing the concerns of their male relatives and putting pressure on the Spanish government concerning issues that benefited the House of Austria. Nevertheless, this was a political (and diplomatic) role that the women were expected to play; women did have a political voice, even though that voice often promoted the interests of a patriarchal dynasty and of male concerns within that dynasty.

As mentioned above, another key area in which women intervened was in the negotiation of marriages for their male and female relatives and, in particular, for their children. All three Habsburg women at the Spanish court fulfilled this function. Empress María was instrumental in arranging the marriage of her daughter Anna to Philip II. Anna was originally supposed to marry Philip II's only son and heir, Carlos, but after Carlos's death Philip sought to marry Anna himself. With Empress María's assistance, this arrangement was concluded, and Anna married Philip in 1570. In dynastic terms, this proved to be a successful marriage. Philip II had married his niece in the hopes of producing a male heir to the Spanish throne, and Anna indeed gave birth to the future king, Philip III. Empress María also negotiated the marriage of her daughter Isabel to Charles IX of France. The empress saw Isabel as a crucial diplomatic link to

France and was very annoyed when Catherine de Medici removed all of Isabel's Austrian attendants, including her confessor. Empress María's continued part in the negotiations concerning Isabel's attendants shows that she was expected to involve herself in this matter; this was an acceptable role for royal women.

Empress María also attempted to arrange a marriage for her eldest son, Emperor Rudolf II. She sought to have him marry either Isabel Clara Eugenia, Philip III's sister, or one of the daughters of Archduke Karl of Styria. The empress and Hans Khevenhüller negotiated the issue with Rudolf II repeatedly during the last years of Philip II's reign. The matter, however, was never resolved, in large part because of Rudolf's inability to make up his mind about choosing a wife.[60] The empress's active role in the process can be inferred from the portraits of Archduke Karl's four daughters (including Margaret of Austria) which she had sent to her from Central Europe so that she could determine who would be an appropriate match for her son.[61] Rudolf II never married, but the failure of these marriage negotiations is indicative more of Rudolf's stubbornness and eccentricities than of Empress María's failure as a negotiator.

Margaret of Austria took it upon herself to find suitable matches for her two younger sisters. She sought to have them married to prominent princes, and she won the support of Philip III and the Duke of Lerma in this task. She also regularly wrote Rudolf II and petitioned Hans Khevenhüller to remind the emperor of the need to marry these women to appropriate spouses. She was very successful: her sister Maria Magdalena married the son of the Grand Duke of Florence, and her sister Constantia became the second wife of Sigismund, King of Poland (Sigismund's first wife had been another sister of Margaret of Austria). Margaret was also instrumental in arranging the marriage of her daughter, Anne, to Louis XIII of France.[62] Although this marriage broke the tradition of Spanish-Austrian connections, the queen recognized the need for Spain to have an alliance with France, its chief rival in the seventeenth century. At least in this instance, Margaret of Austria placed the interests of Spain and of her own children above those of the Habsburg family. Certainly she recognized, as did Philip III and the Duke of Lerma, that the Spanish princess would be marrying one of the most powerful European monarchs. The marriage was designed not only to win the good graces of France but also to increase the prestige of Spain's ruling family.

Margaret of the Cross was also a key participant in marriage negotiations. She urged Philip II to choose Margaret of Austria as the bride for Philip III and was ultimately successful in this pursuit.[63] She also dissuaded Philip III from arranging to have his daughter María marry an English prince; instead, Margaret of the Cross persuaded the king to marry María to Archduke Ferdinand's son.[64] In the marriages of both Philip III to Margaret and the Infanta María to the future Ferdinand III, Margaret of the Cross helped to strengthen the ties between the Spanish and the Austrian Habsburgs.

Aristocratic women also exercised power through the control of their inheritance. Royal women were able to dispose of sizeable fortunes and thereby greatly affect the lives of their relatives. Empress María, by her marriage agreement, had the right to dispose of half of her dowry and half of the 40,000 florins Maximilian had given her in jewels.[65] The other half of her dowry was to go to her children, and Maximilian would retain half of the jewels. The stipulation that a substantial portion of her dowry be reserved for her children seems to have been an attempt to ensure that, regardless of what became of Empress María, her children would be provided for financially. The empress was actually able to bequeath more than this stipulated amount because Emperor Maximilian II gave her his half of the 40,000 florins to dispose of as she saw fit. Like many early modern aristocratic women, much of Empress María's wealth was in jewels. As Sharon Kettering has written, "the jewels of noble wives were a reserve account and a source of ready cash in times of emergency."[66]

Margaret of Austria was able to bequeath 200,000 ducats given to her by Philip III as part of their marriage contract. Her dowry from her father was quite small, and therefore she only bequeathed the amount given to her by Philip III. Margaret made her will in 1601, before she gave birth to her first child. The queen seems to have feared dying in childbirth and wanted to leave a will in case she did not survive. Because he recognized the importance of her will and knew that it would reveal the queen's predilections and favorites, Lerma attempted to have this will opened.[67] When Margaret died in 1611, her will was contested because she favored her close friend and lady-in-waiting, Maria Sidonia, over her children. There were those who contended that since the will was written before Margaret gave birth to her children, she would have therefore wanted it amended. Nevertheless, her will was valid, and Philip III had little choice but to have its provisions carried out. The concerns surrounding the queen's will clearly show the threat that women could pose and the power they could wield by being able to dispose of wealth and property.

It also shows that women did not necessarily always put their family first when making a will.

Margaret of the Cross received 200 ducats a month from her mother, Empress María. She received another 200 ducats a month left to her by her sister Isabel. Because Margaret had never married, she did not have a dowry to dispose of, but she was able to bequeath the amounts left to her by her mother and sister.

Empress María, Margaret of Austria, and Margaret of the Cross, when bequeathing part or all of their inheritance, left most of it for religious purposes such as saying masses or establishing chapels; for charitable causes such as clothing the poor or providing dowries for orphaned girls;[68] for Jesuit colleges;[69] or for female relatives and friends. Margaret of the Cross left much of her material possessions, such as silver plates and kitchenware, to her niece, Sor Ana Dorotea, the illegitimate daughter of Rudolf II and a fellow nun in the Descalzas convent.[70] Margaret of the Cross also left much of her inheritance to the abbess of the Descalzas so that the abbess would perform certain pious acts in her name. Margaret of Austria bequeathed much of her money, clothes, and jewels to her good friend and lady-in-waiting, Maria Sidonia. Cabrera de Córdoba reported that Margaret left Maria Sidonia 40,000 ducats as well as the jewels and the silver that she had brought with her from Central Europe.[71] She also left generous amounts to Maria Sidonia's siblings.[72] Empress María left money to her servants, such as her mayordomo, Juan de Borja, and his wife, Francisca de Aragón. She also left money to the imperial ambassador in Madrid, Hans Khevenhüller. Most of the servants María remembered in her will, however, were women.

Through their wills, the three Habsburg women continued the pious activities they had undertaken while alive, activities that won them a reputation for religious devotion and even sanctity. It is fitting that the inscription in honor of Empress María in the Descalzas noted that she had lived her life performing pious deeds and that she had died with the odor of sanctity.[73] The wills of the three Habsburg women show that they prized piety, service, devotion, and friendship. Neither Margaret of the Cross nor Margaret of Austria stipulated any amount in their wills for their male relatives, and the only female relative mentioned in either of the two wills was Ana Dorotea. Empress María did leave half of her dowry to her children, but this was part of her marriage agreement and therefore not necessarily of her own choosing.

The wills of these three women, then, provided them with an opportunity to act independently. They allowed the women to finance deeds they found appropriate, deeds that usually helped to immortalize them. In general, the women did not use their wills to help their families; if they did, it was because a male relative had dictated this course to them (as was the case for Empress María). The money and wealth these women had was acquired through men, except for Margaret of the Cross, who received her inheritance from her mother and sister (and partially from money given to her by Philip III). But these women did not, in general, use their wealth to benefit men.[74] Instead, they left their wealth to other women, to devoted servants, to religious institutions, and for pious and charitable deeds. Moreover, Empress María, like many other aristocratic women, even preferred to be buried in a convent of nuns rather than among her relatives.[75] This surely indicates that the empress greatly valued the company and friendship of nuns, perhaps even more than that of her family.

Whereas the three women were defined in terms of their familial connections and had significant political responsibilities because of their lineage, they did not necessarily think of their family as their only or even primary concern. Perhaps with the Habsburg women we have an example of what Stanley Chojnacki has observed about Venetian women. Chojnacki argues that early modern women, because they had both natal and marital families, were not tied closely to either family. As a result, women were less bound to family than were men.[76] Empress María, Margaret of Austria, and Margaret of the Cross certainly saw pious and charitable deeds as their lasting contribution. They also valued and rewarded the friendship, loyalty, and service of their attendants. Empress María and Margaret of Austria probably expected that their male relatives would see to the needs of their children. The only one who left part of her dowry to her children was Empress María, a widow. Because her husband was dead, the empress had a greater obligation to provide for their children.

The empress's will also clearly shows that of all her children, she was primarily concerned with the fate of her daughter Margaret of the Cross. Empress María worried that Margaret would suffer financial difficulties and would live too harsh a life. For this reason, the empress left her daughter a monthly stipend and asked Philip III to ensure that Margaret have servants to help her within the Descalzas.[77] The empress seems to have been concerned that after her death, her daughter might be forgotten by her male relatives. Thus, when providing for her children, the empress put the needs of the daughter with whom she had spent the last two decades of her life before the needs of her sons. Here Empress María was acting like other aristocratic women, who often were more concerned for their daughters and younger sons than for their firstborn son. The empress and her eldest son, Rudolf II, actually argued over Margaret of the Cross. A letter from the empress to Hans Khevenhüller instructed him to write Rudolf and say that María would provide for Margaret out of her dowry. The empress, however, did not write Rudolf II directly.[78]

While the testaments of the Habsburg women show the women's preferences and indicate that they did not always share the same priorities as their male relatives, the correspondence among the family members indicates that the Habsburgs felt a need to mention their common lineage. Both the Spanish and the Austrian Habsburgs regularly referred to the familial bonds between them when corresponding with one another and when discussing political matters. This language was supposed to remind the recipient of the ties that bound the Habsburgs together, ties that should ensure cooperation and assistance.

Philip III often mentioned his kinship with the Austrian Habsburgs. He particularly made these references when Spanish-Austrian relations were strained or when he needed Austrian assistance. From 1599 to 1612, Philip and Rudolf II argued over the future of Finale, an imperial fief in northwestern Italy which the Spanish monarch desired for strategic reasons.[79] Finale offered Spain the possibility of constructing a port to be used as the point of disembarkation for men and supplies meant for Flanders. In 1599, Philip III wrote to Hans Khevenhüller about Finale and urged him to remind Rudolf of the familial connections between them. In the letter, Philip III used the language of affection, telling Khevenhüller that Rudolf II should demonstrate love for his nephew (Philip III) and that Rudolf II should act in such a way that "blood and all other respects oblige him to [act]."[80] The Spanish monarch was in fact arguing that, because of their familial ties, the emperor should allow Spain to take over the fief of Finale.

The issue of Finale continued to sour Spanish-Austrian relations and to elicit the language of familial duties and devotion. The Spanish Council of State, when advising Philip III about Finale, also referred to the nature of Spanish-Austrian ties. In October 1600, the Council of State criticized Rudolf II for failing to reach a decision about whether to award Finale to Philip. Rudolf, according to the Council, was delaying any action until he received a payment of 300,000 ducats, which Philip had promised him for the war against the

Turks. The Council advised Philip to instruct his ambassador in Prague, Guillén de San Clemente, to "show disappointment that His Imperial Majesty re-
frains from granting His Majesty [Philip III] the investiture to Finale, especially
after Your Majesty [Philip III] has aided him with such a large sum of money
at a time of great difficulties. Moreover, Your Majesty's affairs are like the emperor's own as is required by the kinship, the friendship, and the union which
should exist between both Majesties."[81]

Rudolf II did not grant Finale to Philip III, and as a result, the Spanish governor of Milan, the Count of Fuentes, took matters into his own hands. He in-
vaded the fief in January 1602, ostensibly to safeguard the territory for the
emperor. When Rudolf II condemned Spanish seizure of the fief, the Council
of State advised Philip that the emperor's anger might be alleviated if Philip
wrote a letter expressing love and respect for Rudolf. The Council suggested
that Hans Khevenhüller inform Rudolf that Philip III

> is especially deserving of his uncle's love, affection . . . and trust be-
> cause of their ties of blood and friendship, and when the electors con-
> demn what the Count [of Fuentes] did and attempt to impede it, His
> Imperial Majesty should not allow it since . . . it is of such importance
> for the conservation and the augmentation of the House of Austria,
> not only to conserve the union and good reciprocity [*correspondencia*]
> which until now has existed between the emperor and Your Majesty,
> but also to extend it with reciprocal actions which will foil the evil in-
> tention of those who wish to sow discord between Your Majesties. It
> would be undignified and alien to the love and affection which His
> Imperial Majesty owes Your Majesty for the emperor to be offended
> instead of being grateful for the service rendered him.[82]

Despite Spain's attempt to appease the emperor, Rudolf was infuriated by the
Count of Fuentes's seizure of Finale. He was not at all pacified by the count's
explanation that he had occupied Finale in order to protect imperial soil from
those who wished to usurp it. San Clemente, who was afraid that Rudolf might
denounce Philip III at an Imperial Diet, invoked the language of familial devotion in order to pacify the emperor. As he told Philip III in a dispatch of 1603,
"If he [the emperor] does not wish to take my word that Your Majesty loves
and respects him, he should at least be certain that . . . Your Majesty has an interest in the conservation of his [Rudolf's] house . . . and that there is enough

[reason] for Your Majesty to see to his [the emperor's] affairs even if there were no love between you."[83] Given the Spanish seizure of Finale, Rudolf had reason to doubt Philip III's affection. However, the Spanish-Austrian negotiations about Finale show that the Habsburgs expected kinship ties to translate into political and military cooperation. When they did not, there was annoyance and bad blood on both sides.

Rudolf II used the language of familial affection and devotion when negotiating with Philip III and especially when requesting financial assistance from Spain. In a letter to Philip from 1602, Rudolf asked the Spanish monarch to aid him financially for his wars against the Turks "first of all because if you do not, grave ruin threatens our House of Austria and all the Christian religion . . . and so we ask you because of our common religion and because of our kinship [*parentesco*], and we offer to reward this friendly goodwill."[84] On this same occasion, Rudolf also wrote to Margaret of Austria asking her to intercede for him with Philip III. Once again the emperor used the language of familial duty and affection: "We hope that His Most Serene Majesty, our nephew and our beloved grandson and your husband will favor us abundantly by giving us greater support than [he gives] to others. That [support] is worthy of a great king and of a relative with such close kinship [to us]. In order to attain this more quickly we send this special mail with certain hope that Your Serenity will persuade the Most Serene king, your husband."[85]

In this instance, Rudolf knew enough to remind the Spanish monarchs of their kinship ties to him, ties that should cause them to help him. Rudolf also knew to use the familial network—namely, Margaret of Austria—to pressure Philip for assistance. Rudolf's letter to the king clearly indicates that Rudolf had no illusions about what might motivate Philip to assist him. The emperor promised to reciprocate Philip's assistance with "goodwill"—a vague term that implied financial and military reciprocity. This reciprocity was also understood as part and parcel of familial relations.

When responding to Rudolf's many requests for Spanish assistance to fight the Turks, the Spanish Council of State also referred to the kinship ties between the Spanish and the Austrian Habsburgs, even if the Council did not always believe that these ties should translate into financial assistance. "Your Majesty and your kingdoms profit from having them [the Turks] occupied. . . . This is sufficient reason to say that the 300,000 ducats are well spent, even if there were no considerations (as there are) of kinship [*deudo*] and friendship, [or] the convenience of keeping the emperor satisfied."[86] In this case, although the councillors noted the blood ties between the Spanish and the Austrian Habsburgs, they argued that aid to Rudolf was necessary not only because of these ties but also because it made good, pragmatic sense for Philip III and his kingdoms.

The language of family and affection was often used by both branches to pressure the other into complying with a given request or to lessen the blow of a hostile action. In the instructions he gave to his ambassador to Spain in 1613, Archduke Ferdinand said:

> What I primarily desire is that in all the occasions that seem appropriate to you, do not fail to remind the king of the obligation that this house has to serve His Majesty [Philip III] . . . with much love and we will honor this [obligation] as often as His Majesty wishes to avail himself of it. Throughout all my life I will consider myself very devoted to his royal service and will not stray one bit from His Majesty's goodwill and pleasure. In whatever occasion that occurs, I will run to his royal aid with the same trust that I desire. I ask His Majesty to consider as his my person, brother, children, finances, estates, and everything else in this house, as is required by our close kinship.[87]

At this time, Archduke Ferdinand was attempting to convince Philip to renounce his claims to the Bohemian and Hungarian crowns and to recognize Ferdinand as the legitimate heir to these thrones.[88] The language of affection, duty, and devotion was meant to remind Philip of the need to cooperate with Archduke Ferdinand and give in to his wishes. In turn, Ferdinand promised to reciprocate with support for Philip.

During Philip III's reign, the Spanish government emphasized the need for reciprocity in Habsburg relations. Philip and his ministers believed that the Spanish monarchy's relationship with the Austrian Habsburgs was too one-sided and that Spain consistently gave financial assistance to the Austrian Habsburgs and received nothing in return. The Spanish government therefore attempted to win territorial concessions from the Austrian Habsburgs in return for Spanish financial assistance.[89] When Philip finally ceded his claims to the Bohemian and Hungarian thrones in return for territorial compensation in Alsace and in Italy and also agreed to aid Ferdinand's struggle against the Venetians, Ferdinand responded with the language of family and affection. In a letter from 1618, Ferdinand wrote Philip that he remained "perpetually and infinitely obliged for the care and solicitude shown in the peace negotiations [between Ferdinand and Venice] as well as for the brotherly and fatherly care shown to me and to my troops during the war."[90] The Spanish and the Austrian Habsburgs obviously used this affectionate language in a rhetorical fashion; it was designed to elicit a specific, positive response from their relatives, if not a feeling of guilt and obligation as well. Nevertheless, its frequent use demonstrates that such familial language was a powerful and well-understood tool in Habsburg negotiations and that the Habsburgs placed great importance on kinship ties.

In their correspondence with one another, the Spanish and the Austrian Habsburgs usually stated the familial relationship between the writer and the recipient of the letter, as well as the ties between them and other named Habsburg family members. So, for example, in his letters to the Duke of Lerma, Archduke Albert usually referred to Margaret of the Cross as his sister and not by her given name.[91] Albert's wife and co-ruler, Isabel Clara Eugenia, also always referred to Margaret of the Cross as her aunt.[92] Archduchess Maria of Bavaria, Margaret of Austria's mother, wrote to Philip III and referred to him as "Most Serene King, loved from the heart, lord, son."[93] In a letter to Emperor Matthias after the Bohemian Revolt in 1618, Philip III addressed Matthias as "the Emperor my uncle and cousin" and signed the letter "Good nephew and cousin of Your Majesty."[94] Philip referred to Archduke Ferdinand as "my very dear and very loved brother" in a letter from 20 March 1619.[95] Philip informed Ferdinand that he was sending the Duke of Alburquerque to Rome and had given him instructions to see to Ferdinand's matters as if they were his (Philip III's).

This practice of stating the actual familial bonds between individual Habsburgs served to emphasize the blood ties that united them, especially in cases in which the relatives did not have daily or frequent contact with one another. Yet the familial references served a further purpose. The Habsburgs regularly stated their familial ties when they were asking for favors or assistance or when they anticipated that given actions would be deemed hostile by other family members. The language used in these instances worked to soften the impact of petitions, requests, or actions. Both male and female Habsburgs used such familial language; it was by no means an exclusively male or female strategy. Nevertheless, it was a political language often used in letters discussing political actions.

Men such as Hans Khevenhüller, Juan Carrillo, and Juan de Borja used the language of family to convey the messages of the Habsburg women to their male relatives; it served to make the petitions, requests, or opinions of the women acceptable to their male relatives. The frequent references to affection and devotion worked to soften the opinions that the women were expressing and to reassure male relatives that the women were merely speaking out because of affection and familial concern. When Empress María and Rudolf II wrangled over the issue of his marriage, Hans Khevenhüller wrote the emperor that although the empress was "so holy and such a good woman and mother as Your Majesty knows, I have found her very altered and affected" by the negotiations. The ambassador had assured the empress that Rudolf "did not fail to respect and love her as a good son."[96] In 1599, in a letter from Khevenhüller to Rudolf, the ambassador reported that the empress as "woman and mother" cared for the matters concerning Rudolf II.[97] When the court moved to Valladolid in 1601, Khevenhüller told Rudolf that Empress María, "in motherly trust," had asked him to tell the emperor the news.[98] On this same occasion, the empress had expressed her fear that Khevenhüller would accompany the court to Valladolid. The ambassador assured her that he would do whatever Rudolf wanted and that, in turn, Rudolf would certainly act like the "very good son" that he was.[99]

In a similar fashion, Khevenhüller referred to Rudolf's need to see to the marriage of Margaret of Austria's sister with "fatherly" help.[100] On many occasions, Khevenhüller referred to Rudolf II's fatherly concern and affection for both Margaret of the Cross and Margaret of Austria.[101] Khevenhüller also wrote that Margaret of the Cross understood that Rudolf acted with "fatherly and brotherly love";[102] the nun was using the language of family to elicit a specific response from Rudolf II. When Empress María was concerned about Archduke Albert's health, Juan Carrillo wrote that her concern was that of a mother and a saint.[103]

The empress also used the language of affection to excuse expressing her opinions to Philip III. According to Khevenhüller, when the empress warned Philip III not to give so much power to Magdalena de Guzmán, Marquesa del Valle, María first told him that no one else had the affection for him that she had because of their "shared kinship" (*obligaciones que hay de por medio*).[104] She said that because of this affection and devotion, she felt obligated to speak. In this case, the empress's reference to familial affection was intended to alleviate her criticisms of Philip's conduct and his reliance upon Lerma and the Marquesa del Valle. The court chronicler, Jerónimo de Sepúlveda, recounted another meeting between Empress María and Philip, during which the empress urged the king not to move the court to Valladolid. She reminded him that she was his "grandmother, aunt, and mother and was impartial about everything and did not seek any personal gain but only the good of his kingdoms and vassals."[105] By invoking her familial connection to Philip, Empress María was reassuring him that she was acting only out of affection for and goodwill toward him. This familial language was supposed to help condone the empress's comments, which certainly were political in nature.

Empress María was often concerned about Spanish provisions to Flanders. She always wanted to know when the Spanish government had approved aid for the archdukes in Flanders, and she regularly petitioned Philip III for this assistance. In order to justify her concern and her frequent petitions, Empress María referred to her maternal duties. As Borja explained to Lerma in 1601,

> although the empress understands very well that you take care to supply the archduke with provisions and [although] one tells her of the [financial] constraints that impede these provisions, she still cares so deeply about Flanders that the necessities suffered there are amplified. Her Majesty thinks that she would not fulfill her obligations if she did not ask her grandson and remind Your Excellency [Lerma] that the mail be sent quickly with the letters from February and March.[106]

These letters presumably informed Archduke Albert that he would receive financial assistance shortly. Like Empress María, Isabel Clara Eugenia, wife of Archduke Albert, also used the language of family. When she wrote to Matthias in 1600 commending him for his improved relations with Emperor Rudolf II, she said that he had acted as a good brother.[107]

The use of this familial language in their correspondence shows that the women believed their familial connections should translate into particular duties and specific behavior. In 1592, Empress María wrote her son Archduke Matthias to ask him to see to the execution of his sister Isabel's will. In the letter, Empress María commented on Matthias's health (she had heard that he was too thin) and reminded him that he had to have strength to see to the service of God and of his brother, Rudolf II. The empress ended the letter by telling Matthias that she would try to help him in all matters—big and small—so as to demonstrate how much she loved him, "a good son, who will respond by being a good Christian."[108] Likewise, when María asked Rudolf II to reward her mayordomo, Juan de Borja, by giving him the title of marquis, she couched her request in the language of a mother asking her son for a favor.[109] In this case, as in others, Empress María used affectionate terms to assure her relatives of her support for them and to excuse all political actions she might take. She also coupled her requests with promises of comparable political favors.

Margaret of Austria referred to familial ties in her letters to Italian princes to whom she was related. In 1608, she wrote to the Prince of Tuscany, who was to marry Margaret's sister, Maria Magdalena. She told him that she had demonstrated the great esteem that she had for him by giving him for a wife "that jewel which [she] love[s] so much." She went on to say, "I do not doubt that you will demonstrate your recognition of this [gift] on all occasions and I desire many [occasions] to give you pleasure and satisfaction."[110] Margaret also wrote to the prince's father, the Grand Duke of Tuscany, and once again used the language of familial affection. The queen expressed her pleasure at the marriage that had been concluded and assured the grandduke that she would make these new familial ties profitable for him.[111] In these instances, Margaret of Austria was clearly promising special treatment and favors because of the marital ties between the Tuscan and the Spanish ruling families.

In return, the queen used the familial links between Spain and Tuscany to petition the Grandduke of Tuscany for assistance. When Father Lorenzo de Brindisi arrived at the Spanish court asking for assistance for Rudolf's struggle against the German Protestants, the queen, through her confessor, asked the Tuscan ambassador to request 300,000 *scudi* from the grandduke for this cause.[112] The queen certainly believed that kinship ties should bring about greater cooperation on all types of issues, and she was not afraid to use these ties to further matters that were especially dear to her.

In her letters to Philip III, Margaret of the Cross also used a language of assurance, based on her familial connection to and affection for the Spanish king. She often thanked Philip for his generous gifts and his letters, and she assured him that she had great trust in him. She also noted the "love and desire" she had to serve Philip.[113] On one occasion, Margaret asked for a favor for a former servant and said that she was sure that Philip would not deny it to her.[114] On another occasion, she asked the king to assist a representative of Rudolf and Matthias. Margaret commented that she had made the request only because she knew that she was "performing a service for [her] brothers" and was very certain that Philip would listen to her. She added that she hoped her "intercession was worth something[,] although I know that when it concerns my brothers, nothing else is needed."[115] Margaret also stressed her unworthiness and the inherent lowliness of any request that she made. However, this apparent humility on Margaret's part also served to excuse her speaking out on a political matter. In her request, she clearly stated that Philip saw to her brothers' needs and implied that he did so out of familial affection for her and for Matthias and Rudolf.

Philip's devotion to his aunt also allowed her to petition for the needs of the nuns in the Descalzas. In 1605, Margaret wrote to Philip III about a relatively minor issue: the specific clothing that the nuns in the Descalzas would wear. She noted that Philip had already given instructions in the matter, but these instructions did not correspond to what the nuns wanted. For this reason, Margaret wrote to ask him to change his instructions. He should do this "only to favor her," and everyone would understand that he had changed his mind because she asked him to do so.[116] Margaret always claimed to be certain that Philip would listen to her requests. This certainty was based upon his love for her and his sense of familial duty—a duty that allowed her to gain the monarch's ear and his assistance in a wide range of issues.

As Margaret's petition for the nuns of the Descalzas indicates, familial connections made the Habsburg women intercessors both for family members and for third parties. Empress María, Margaret of Austria, and Margaret of the Cross received letters, petitions, and requests from many people, including their relatives, which they took to Philip III—proving that familial connections indeed translated into key political roles for all three Habsburg women.

The Habsburg family was an affectionate and a political unit. Within this unit, there was little division between the public and the private, between the political and the personal. In the early part of the seventeenth century, the Habsburgs believed that they were being assaulted on all sides. For this reason, they were even more adamant than usual about the need to work together. This was especially true of the Austrian Habsburgs, who felt financially and militarily dependent upon the Spanish monarch. Because they occupied important roles within a family, because their familial roles placed them strategically close to Philip III, and because the line between private and political was still permeable in the early seventeenth century, Empress María, Margaret of Austria, and Margaret of the Cross were all able to play crucial political roles. All three women took advantage of their familial and affectionate ties to Philip to press for an agenda that was favorable to the Austrian Habsburgs. As members of the Habsburg dynasty, they had many familial duties and responsibilities that often prompted them to work for the benefit of their male relatives. However, these familial duties also offered the three women a vehicle for expressing their political voices and wielding political power.

Fig. 1. *Empress María of Austria*, by Juan Pantoja de la Cruz (Convent
of the Descalzas Reales, Madrid, n.d., copyright Patrimonio Nacional).
The empress is dressed in the garb of a Franciscan nun; however, she
never took the vows of a nun. In fact, this attire was typical for Habsburg widows. In the painting the empress holds the rosary, but beside
her is the imperial crown, an obvious symbol of royal might that un-
derscores the empress's important political functions.

Fig. 2. *Queen Margaret of Austria*, by Bartolomé González (Kunsthistorisches Museum, Vienna, 1603). Margaret of Austria gave birth to eight children in eleven years. This portrait shows a pregnant queen and thus accurately depicts Margaret of Austria's years in Spain. The girl beside her is the Infanta Anne. Pregnancy often brought greater affection, respect, leverage, and power to the queen.

Fig. 3. *The Annunciation*, by Juan Pantoja de la Cruz (Kunsthistorisches Museum, Vienna, 1605). The Virgin Mary in this portrait is Margaret of Austria, while the angel Gabriel is the Infanta Anne. The portrait emphasizes the piety and even sanctity of the queen and the divine right of the Habsburg line to rule.

Fig. 4. *The Birth of the Virgin*, by Juan Pantoja de la Cruz (Kunsthistorisches Museum, Vienna, 1603). The figure in the right foreground washing the baby is a portrait of Archduchess Maria of Bavaria, Margaret of Austria's mother. The other two women at the right looking at the viewer are Margaret of Austria's sisters. Although the face of Saint Anne, mother of the Virgin Mary, is not recognizable in the painting, the presence and roles of Archduchess Maria and the Styrian princesses might indicate that the woman giving birth is supposed to be Margaret of Austria. Once again, Pantoja de la Cruz emphasized the divine origins of the queen's family.

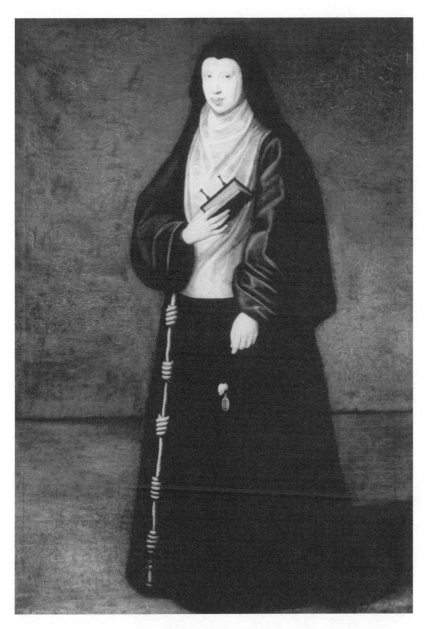

Fig. 5. *Sor Margaret of the Cross*, by Antonio Rizi (Convent of the Descalzas Reales, Madrid, 1603, copyright Patrimonio Nacional). This portrait shows Margaret of the Cross at age thirty-six, in the garb of a cloistered Franciscan nun. She holds the symbols of religious devotion—the rosary and the prayer book. Margaret spent the last forty-eight years of her life as a Franciscan nun in the Descalzas convent.

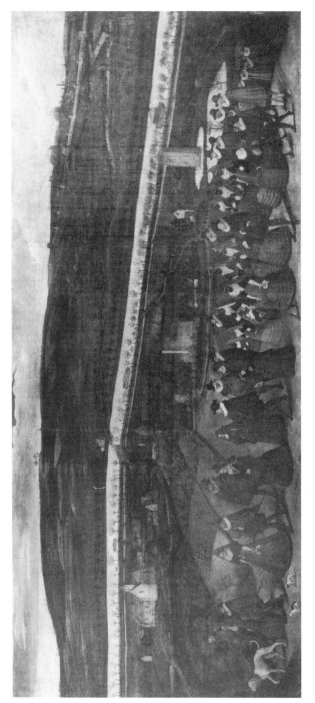

Fig. 6. *Trip of Empress María from Prague to Madrid*, by Hans van der Beken (Convent of the Descalzas Reales, Madrid, 1601, copyright Patrimonio Nacional). Empress María left Central Europe for Spain in 1581. She was accompanied by her daughter, the Spanish ambassador, Juan de Borja, and a retinue of servants and attendants.

PRECIOSA IN CONSPECTV DOMINI MORS SANCTORVM EIVS.

Fig. 7. *Death of Empress María*, by Pedro Perret (from Juan de la Palma, *Vida de la sereníssima Infanta Sor Margarita de la Cruz, religiosa Descalza de Santa Clara*, Seville, 1653). The empress is attended by her daughter, Margaret of the Cross, and other Franciscan nuns. Beside the bed is the crown, the symbol of imperial power. Thus, even as Perret depicted the empress's humble death, he emphasized the power that she had wielded in life.

Fig. 8. *Philip III*, by Juan Pantoja de la Cruz (Prado Museum, Madrid, 1606). Pantoja de la Cruz depicted Philip III in a standard fashion for rulers of the late sixteenth century. The monarch carries the baton of royal power; his left hand is on his sword, as if he were ready for battle. This is an interesting depiction given that Philip III is known as a king who favored peace over war.

Fig. 9. Portrait of the Duke of Lerma, by Peter Paul Rubens (Prado Museum, Madrid, 1603). This painting is a detail of the equestrian portrait of the Duke of Lerma and emphasizes his prowess and strength. Lerma is depicted in a fashion similar to that of a king who is ready to lead his troops into battle.

D FELIPE III R DE SPAÑA · · D! MARGARITA R DE SPAÑA

Fig. 10. *Marriage of Philip III and Margaret of Austria*, attributed to Pedro Perret (Biblioteca Nacional, Madrid, n.d.). The marriage of Philip and Margaret took place in April 1599 in Valencia. Philip was twenty-one years old and Margaret was fourteen and a half.

Fig. 11. Portrait of Hans Khevenhüller von Aichelberg, in Georg Mohs-
hamer, *Khevenhüller-Familienchronik* (1638) (Österreichisches Museum für
Angewandte Kunst, Vienna, n.d.). Khevenhüller is shown with his territorial possessions in Spain, Arganda. The imperial ambassador retired to these
lands regularly and invited the monarchs and the empress to visit him at his
home in Arganda. At Khevenhüller's death, the house was sold to the Duke
of Lerma, reportedly for twelve thousand escudos (although the estate was
valued at forty thousand).

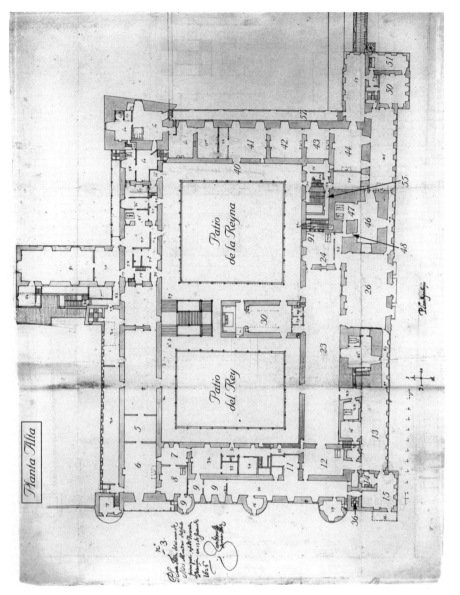

Fig. 12. Floor Plan for the Upper Floor (*Planta Alta*) of the Real Alcázar in Madrid, designed by Juan Gómez de Mora, 1626 (Foto Biblioteca Vaticana).

5. *Saleta del cuarto del rey*, the king's drawing room.

6. Antechamber in which there was a throne; the king would celebrate certain public acts here.

7. Antechamber for ambassadors, where they waited to accompany the king on his public outings.

8. Room where the king gave audiences and received ambassadors on their first visit.

9. Rooms where the king ate midday meals and gave private audiences to ambassadors.

11. Room where the king ate the evening meal.

12. Room where the king sometimes slept and gave audiences, especially to the presidents of the various councils.

13. *Galería del mediodía del Rey*, where the king was normally to be found.

14. The king's private oratory.

15. *Despacho*, the king's office.

23. *Salón Grande*, room where monarchs attended performances and ate in public.

24. *Salón de las Furias*, the king's bedroom.

26. *Salón nuevo*, meeting place between the king's and queen's apartments; monarchs watched public festivities from this room. It also functioned as a private space for the royal family.

30. Royal chapel.

36. Secret stairwell leading outside.

40. Official entrance to the queen's apartments.

41. The queen's drawing room.

42. The queen's antechamber.

43. Room where the queen ate in public.

44. Room where the queen received visitors.

46. Room where the queen dressed.

47. Alcove where the queen slept.

48. Passageway from the king's room to that of the queen.

50. The new tower, where the queen had her desks.

51. The queen's private oratory.

55. Stairway from which the ladies-in-waiting entered the queen's apartments from their rooms upstairs.

57. Private passageway between the queen's apartments and those of the royal princess.

91. Door to the passageway that went to the House of the Treasury (*Casa del Tesoro*) and to the royal monastery of the Encarnación. From this passageway the king had windows overlooking the rooms where the Councils of the Indies, Military Orders, and Finance met.

From José Manuel Barbeito, *El Alcázar de Madrid* (Madrid: Colegio Oficial de Arquitectos de Madrid, Comisión de Cultura, 1992), 127–31, 136–40; *Juan Gómez de Mora (1586–1648): Arquitecto y trazador del rey y maestro mayor de obras de la villa de Madrid* (Madrid: Ayuntamiento de Madrid, 1996), 381–83.

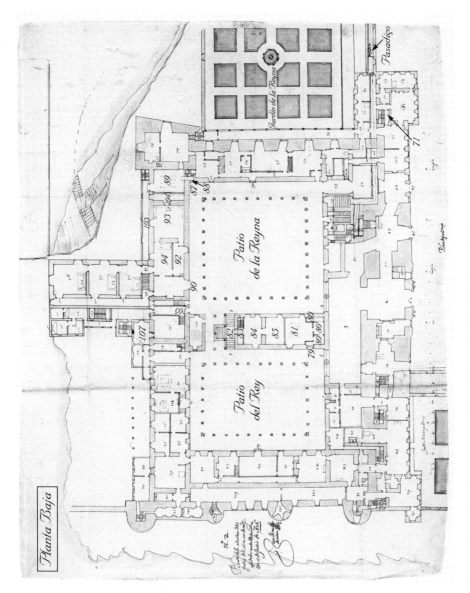

Fig. 13. Floor Plan for the Lower Floor (*Planta Baja*) of the Real Alcázar in Madrid, designed by Juan Gómez de Mora, 1626 (Foto Biblioteca Vaticana).

71. Stairway that went from the queen's rooms to the garden. Above this room was the passageway that connected the Alcázar to the House of the Treasury (*Casa del Tesoro*).

79. Entrance to the meeting room of the Council of Portugal.

80. Service rooms for the Council of Portugal.

81. Room where the Council of Portugal deliberated (*tribunal*).

82. Entrance to the sacristy of the Royal chapel.

83. Room for the sacristy.

84. Room for the sacristy.

85. Room for the sacristy.

87. Doorway from the queen's courtyard (*Patio de la Reyna*) to the meeting room of the Council of State.

88. Entrance to the meeting room of the Council of State.

89. Room where the Council of State deliberated (*tribunal*). On some days, the Council of War would use this room.

90. Entrance from the queen's courtyard to the meeting room of the Royal Council.

92. Passageway to the main hall.

93. *Sala mayor*, the main hall of the Royal Council.

94. Room for the secretaries and the scribes.

103. Passageway used by the king to reach the meeting rooms of the various councils.

104. Room with windows for the king to see into the room of the Council of State and the main hall of the Royal Council.

105. Entrance to the meeting room of the Council of Aragón.

107. Room where the Council of Aragón deliberated.

From *Juan Gómez de Mora (1586–1648): Arquitecto y trazador del rey y maestro mayor de obras de la villa de Madrid* (Madrid: Ayuntamiento de Madrid, 1996), 384–85.

6

Pious Women and Court Politics

EMPRESS MARÍA, Margaret of Austria, and Margaret of the Cross had reputations for being extremely devout women who spent most of their days in spiritual contemplation and prayer. Biographers and eulogists emphasized that Empress María left Central Europe for Madrid in order to retire to a convent and devote herself to a life of prayer and isolation.[1] Biographical accounts of Margaret of the Cross's life note that she gave up the chance to become Philip II's fifth wife and queen of the vast Spanish empire in order to put on the robes of a cloistered nun.[2] Biographers and eulogists even claimed that Margaret of Austria, although she became queen of the Spanish kingdoms, would have preferred the life of a nun to that of a queen, and so she spent most of her days within convent walls visiting and praying with nuns.[3]

The appeal of a life in the cloister or of a life devoted to pious and charitable activities was strong for many early modern women. The three Habsburg women seem to have chosen such lives because they afforded the women a world in which they could command authority and respect. Indeed, because of their reputation for moral rectitude, the women gained fame and attention from their contemporaries. Margaret of Austria's reputation for holiness even caused some people to wonder if she had died a martyr to the faith.[4] The women's expressions of piety were also public manifestations of the Habsburgs' religious devotion and their commitment to orthodox Catholicism.[5]

Piety could have political ramifications for women, and through their pious activities women could exercise power and influence at court. Therefore, the pious deeds of these three women merit study because these activities demonstrate precisely how royal women became politically active. Instead of isolating a woman within a convent, spiritual devotion could actually increase her reputation and bring her into greater contact with the male world around her. That is, religious life could afford a woman a type of public role. Certainly this was true of the numerous beatas, or spiritual women, of early modern Spain whose reputation for holiness gained them male—and public—attention.[6] This was also true of the female prophets in England during the Interregnum period, women whose irrationality and susceptibility supposedly allowed them to become possessed with God's will and who were therefore allowed by the male religious and political hierarchies to preach publicly.[7]

There are several issues to consider when examining the pious practices of these Habsburg women. First of all, what were these practices? Second, did their pious activities truly remove them physically from the Spanish court and leave them little opportunity to influence policy formation at the court (as historians have assumed)? Third, why did they engage in these pious activities? What benefits, if any, did the women gain from their piety? And last of all, what connection was there between a woman's piety and her political influence at the Spanish court?

Margaret of the Cross and Empress María had direct connections to convents—in particular, to the convent of the Descalzas Reales in Madrid. Margaret, as a cloistered Franciscan nun, lived by the strict rules of the Franciscan order and did not leave the Descalzas convent from the day she professed, in 1585, until her death, in 1633. She had a chance to leave the convent in 1599, when Madrid was threatened by an outbreak of the plague. Empress María had requested and received papal permission to allow her daughter Margaret to leave Madrid and seek refuge in the countryside around the city. However, even with this permission, Margaret refused to leave.[8] Empress María lived in rooms adjacent to the convent, and on a daily basis she entered the cloistered areas and joined the nuns for prayers, mass, and occasional meals. She resided there from 1583 until her death, in 1603. But María never took the vows of a nun and was always free to leave the convent, which she did regularly.

Margaret of Austria visited convents on an almost daily basis no matter where she was. This was a habit she must have acquired while growing up in Central Europe; her mother, Archduchess Maria of Bavaria, had also visited convents and churches several times a week. The archduchess may even have taken her children with her on these visits.[9] Reports from the trip Margaret and her mother made from Graz to Spain, in order for Margaret to marry Philip III, show that they visited convents all along the way, particularly in Italy and Valencia.[10] Margaret requested and received papal permission to enter cloistered convents on this trip as well.

As queen, Margaret heard daily mass in her private oratory in the morning and then attended mass at a convent in the late morning.[11] After mass at the convent, she usually stayed to have the midday meal with the nuns and did not return to the palace until the early evening. Juan de la Palma, Margaret of the Cross's biographer, reported that when the queen was in Madrid, she visited Margaret of the Cross at the Descalzas on a weekly basis.[12] When the court moved to Valladolid from 1601 to 1606, the queen attended masses at several other convents there. Moreover, whenever Philip III had to leave Madrid (or Valladolid) for an extended period of time, he left Margaret and their children at the Descalzas convent.[13] (The monarch must have believed it inappropriate for the queen to remain alone in the royal palace; a married woman, after all, had to be under some type of supervision.)[14]

The queen's connection to convents does not end there. She was instrumental in moving a convent of Augustinian nuns, the Convent of the Visitation, to the royal school of Santa Isabel founded by Philip II.[15] The convent then received royal patronage and was known as the Royal Convent of Santa Isabel. Margaret replaced the prioress of Santa Isabel with Mariana de San José, a nun she had befriended in Palencia (a town close to Valladolid) and whose purpose was to reform Santa Isabel. The queen claimed that because of poverty, the nuns were failing to comply with the constitution of their order.[16] The Augustinian nuns had lived next to a theater where comedies were performed; Margaret maintained that this made it difficult for the nuns to keep to their religious schedule and vows. The nuns even suggested to the queen that they might construct windows from their convent to the theater in order to sell seats to wealthy individuals and use the money to buy another convent in a quieter area of the city.[17] This proposal persuaded the queen to relocate the nuns to the royal school of Santa Isabel.[18] Margaret also put them under the authority of the royal almoner, Diego de Guzmán, a personal associate and friend of the queen. However, the nuns did not welcome the new prioress and her reforms, nor did they welcome being placed under the royal almoner's authority. Nine of the twenty-eight women refused to go along with the changes and asked to be transferred to another convent.

Finally, Margaret of Austria decided to found another royal convent, the convent of the Encarnación, which would be adjacent to the royal palace and would be connected to it by a passageway.[19] The queen desired a passageway to the convent because she planned for her daughters to be educated there, and she also wanted to be able to withdraw to the convent to spend time with the nuns as often as possible.[20] The founding of this convent was supposed to be an act of thanksgiving to God for the "peaceful" expulsion of the Moriscos from Spain during the years 1609 to 1611.[21] The queen again designated Mariana de San José as the convent's prioress. When Mariana became prioress of the Encarnación, she left the convent of Santa Isabel along with the three nuns who had accompanied her from Palencia to Madrid and a novice. With the founding of the Encarnación, Margaret of Austria in fact abandoned Santa Isabel. She allowed the Augustinian nuns to remain there but did not allow them to accept any new members. Nevertheless, after 1619, the convent was allowed to accept novices again.[22]

The queen's founding of the convent of the Encarnación and her sponsorship of the convent of Santa Isabel gained her a type of immortality; she would forever be remembered as their patroness. Margaret's involvement in the reform of Santa Isabel also clearly shows that this was an area in which she was allowed to exercise independence and power. Philip III gave her free rein to reorganize the convent, despite the protests of the nuns.[23] The king also followed Margaret's wishes after her death and did not allow the convent of Santa Isabel to take new novices after 1612. He changed his mind by 1615, but only after Diego de Guzmán, a friend and associate of the queen, persuaded him to do so.[24] Moreover, by undertaking the reform of a female religious community, Margaret was following in the footsteps of such famous women as Teresa of Ávila.[25] Certainly the queen made the connection between her actions and those that had gained Teresa not only fame but also beatification.[26] These were all powerful motivations for a queen to devote a great deal of her efforts to charitable and religious causes.

Both Margaret of Austria and Empress María demonstrated particular interest in contact and friendship with nuns and beatas. This is quite evident in the queen's friendship with Mariana de San José and in her close relationship with and sponsorship of a beata in Madrid, Mariana de Jesús.[27] Empress María, while in Portugal in 1582, made it a point to visit Sor María de la Visitación, the famous "Nun of Lisbon."[28] Empress María also met daily with the nuns in the Descalzas.

For the Habsburg women, association with nuns and beatas provided the possibility of friendship on a level that would have been impossible with men. Margaret of Austria undoubtedly visited and ate with cloistered nuns because she found a community of women with whom she could converse and to whom she could relate—if only on a spiritual level. Such friendship was often denied women at a male-dominated court, and queens such as Margaret were forced to find female companionship in convents.[29] In fact, when Margaret of the Cross professed her religious vocation in 1586, three Austrian aristocratic women who had accompanied her from Central Europe to Madrid took their religious vows as well. All three women had served the empress and were the daughters of prominent nobles. They would probably not have entered the convent had Margaret of the Cross not done so. Juan de la Palma, Margaret of the Cross's biographer, wrote that it seemed "convenient" that the three women professed before Margaret.[30] They entered the Descalzas convent where they could provide companionship, friendship, and assistance for her.

The three Habsburg women sought each other out for companionship as well. The queen, who was not fluent in Castilian when she arrived in Spain in 1599, was able to speak German with Empress María and Margaret of the Cross at the Descalzas, and all three shared a common interest in the fortunes of the Austrian Habsburgs. Juan de la Palma noted that the queen met frequently with Margaret of the Cross, and the two always spoke in German.[31] Hans Khevenhüller stressed that the queen insisted that he speak only German with her.[32] German served as a private means of communication for the women because most of the people at the Spanish court could not understand the language. By speaking German, the women thwarted the Duke of Lerma's efforts to monitor their conversations. The meetings of the three women allowed them to develop methods and strategies for furthering an Austrian Habsburg agenda at the Spanish court.

The queen's need for female companionship is also clearly seen in her determination to retain her Austrian lady-in-waiting, Maria Sidonia, who had accompanied her from Central Europe to Madrid. The Duke of Lerma attempted to remove Maria Sidonia from the queen's service by having her married to the Count of Barajas. By so doing, Lerma was following a practice common at early modern courts to dispense with the attendants of a foreign queen and replace them with people whom the king could trust.[33] Yet Lerma was ultimately unsuccessful because the queen was able to add the Count of Barajas to her list of supporters and thereby keep Maria Sidonia close by. Sidonia, in fact, was present at the queen's deathbed in 1611,[34] and in her will, Margaret left Maria Sidonia a large sum of money and all of the jewels she had brought from Central Europe. The queen also left money to Maria Sidonia's relatives both in Spain and in Central Europe. These are all clear signs of the value the young queen (she was twenty-seven at her death) placed on female companionship.

All three women left a good portion of their wealth for charitable and pious deeds. They stipulated that certain sums be distributed annually for such pious deeds as providing food and clothing for poor women and children (Margaret of the Cross's will specified that these women and children had to be honorable and too ashamed to beg—*pobres vergonzantes honrados*), as well as for poor beggars, for the sick, for hospitals, and for the release of a certain number of prisoners who were in jail for debt. In return, both Margaret of Austria and Empress María requested that these recipients of charity pray for their benefactors' souls. María and Margaret of Austria also left sums to help rescue Christians (in particular, children) who had been captured by Moslems. Margaret of Austria left 1,000 ducats for monasteries in financial difficulties and 1,000 ducats for both of the English colleges in Salamanca and Valladolid.[35] According to her biographer, Empress María gave financial assistance to more than six hundred institutions, and in some cases she even sold her jewels to be able to provide charity.[36] These charitable activities were not necessarily specifically feminine deeds; Philip III left similar provisions in his will.[37]

Margaret of the Cross also bequeathed amounts in order to sponsor celebrations on specific holy days. She stipulated an annual celebration for the crucified Christ on 14 July in order to compensate for the sacrilege committed by a Portuguese man who had been executed by the Inquisition for desecrating an image of the crucified Christ. Her will noted that this celebration should first take place in 1632 on the feast of the triumph of the cross at the Descalzas convent. In turn, all the churches, convents, and hospitals in Madrid followed her example and commemorated the feast.[38] The nun also left 100 ducats a year for the abbess of the Descalzas to use to commemorate the feast of the royal matins (*maitines de los reyes*).[39] Margaret of the Cross also left money so that the convent of the Descalzas would continue her practice of having special masses said on the feasts of particular saints. Of the thirteen saints she designated, eleven were male; she stipulated only two female saints, Saint Agueda and Saint Clare, both of whom were last on her list. Margaret's devotion to male saints corresponded to the belief that a virginal nun exhibited masculine strength.

Early modern nuns were indeed encouraged to have male role models.[40] Empress María left 100 ducats annually for masses to be said on the feasts of Mary's conception, Saint John the Evangelist, Saint Augustine, Saint Anthony of Padua, Saint Valerio, Saint Bicilao, Saint Leopold (patron saint of the Habsburgs), the 11,000 virgins, Saint Cecilia, Saint Elizabeth of Hungary, and Saint Catherine.[41]

Through their patronage of religious institutions and their charitable deeds, and by endowing convents and schools, all three Habsburg women won a name for themselves both in their own lifetime and for posterity.[42] Mendes Silva, Empress María's biographer, claimed that because of her charitable work, the empress was venerated by the faithful and respected even by Protestants (*los hereges*).[43] Veneration and fame were undoubtedly an important motivation for the Habsburg women to engage in pious activities. Empress María and Margaret of Austria chose to be remembered as patronesses of Jesuit schools: María left the bulk of her estate to the Jesuit school in Madrid and Margaret gave a large sum to a Jesuit school in Salamanca. The queen stipulated in her will that the Jesuits should then name her as their foundress and patroness. She claimed that she wanted to found this Jesuit college so as to leave "a living, never proud, but beneficial [*provechosa*] remembrance" of herself in Spain.[44] The queen clearly wanted to be remembered for her charitable contributions.

Margaret of Austria explained that she chose to be the Jesuits' patroness because of her family's devotion to the Society of Jesus and because of the many ways in which the Jesuits had helped her and her family.[45] The queen was also undoubtedly following in the footsteps of her mother, Archduchess Maria of Bavaria, who had founded three Jesuit schools.[46] The queen's actions might have been partially motivated by devotion to her confessor, Richard Haller, who was a Jesuit. Rather than interpret the queen's devotion to the Jesuits as a sign of Haller's influence over Margaret, I would argue that this loyalty was instead a continuation of the close cooperation between the queen and her confessor. Haller acted as Margaret's ally and confidant from 1598 until the queen's death, in 1611, and he helped her negotiate policies at the Spanish court. Haller and Margaret cooperated on political, personal, and charitable activities. In her will, Margaret stipulated that Haller be responsible for distributing certain monies that she had left for charitable purposes. The queen indicated that she chose Haller for this purpose because he would "faithfully execute this according to what he ha[d] heard orally from [her]."[47] Haller was also in charge of making sure that the masses Margaret had requested were celebrated, and he served as one of the executors of the queen's testament.[48] It was a relationship of "mutual dependence," but one in which Haller operated within Margaret's network of influence, and not vice versa.[49]

The Habsburg women's charitable deeds also included sponsoring processions, decorating altars, and saying numerous masses (Margaret of Austria's will called for 14,000 masses) for the repose of their soul and the souls of their relatives. Empress María requested that 10,000 masses be said to commemorate the wounds of Our Lady of the Angels (*de las llagas de nuestra señora de los angeles*).[50] Clearly, pious activities were a central facet of their lives, and the three Habsburg women believed that through these pious deeds they would long be remembered.

The pious activities of the Habsburg women in Spain differ significantly from those of their English counterparts. Barbara Harris has shown that very few medieval English aristocratic women entered convents. Convents played a "peripheral role in their spiritual and philanthropic lives."[51] In examining female piety in early modern England, Diane Willen shows that piety among English Protestant women consisted of reading the Scriptures daily, attending sermons, and spending time in private meditation.[52] Charity was a common feature of both Catholic and Protestant female piety, but this charity took on definite political overtones in Catholic Spain.[53]

Men around the Habsburg women did not always appreciate the women's acts of charity. Venetian ambassadors reported that Empress María spent all her money on charity and that Philip II refused to give her money because she wasted it very quickly.[54] Jerónimo de Florencia also claimed that the empress incurred numerous debts financing her charitable activities,[55] and Empress María certainly did not have much wealth at her death. Philip III held up the execution of María's will for years, in part because he insisted that he should have a share but also because he opposed giving a large sum to the Jesuit school in Madrid. He also tried unsuccessfully to prevent his wife's money from going to the Jesuit school in Salamanca.[56] Through pious deeds, therefore, Empress María and Margaret of Austria demonstrated their independence and their defiance of the male political network. Through their wills, aristocratic women could force men (and in this case, even the king) to fulfill their demands even when those demands did not seem financially appropriate to the men.

Did religious activities remove the women from the court and make it dif-

ficult for them to influence political policy? This certainly has been the interpretation of historians such as Patrick Williams, who discounts the claim that
the Duke of Lerma moved the court from Madrid to Valladolid in order to remove Philip III from the influence of Empress María. Williams writes that
"there seems little reason to believe that Lerma moved the Court to escape from
the hostile influence of Empress María in Madrid; he could easily circumvent
her—she was, after all, now a nun."[57]

Williams assumes that Empress María took the vows of a nun and that nuns
were unable to exert political influence because they were cloistered in a convent. First of all, Empress María did not take the vows of a nun, and she left
the convent on a weekly basis to visit the monarchs in the palace (at least until
the court moved to Valladolid).[58] Second, monarchs, councillors of state, papal
nuncios, and foreign ambassadors visited the Descalzas convent and conferred
with Empress María and Margaret of the Cross.[59] Empress María gave daily
audiences, and the king, when in Madrid, visited her at the convent several
times a week.[60] Moreover, the Austrian ambassador, Hans Khevenhüller, served
as the empress's personal attendant and was at the convent every day. Here one
sees a clear example of the overlap between the religious and the political
spheres at the Descalzas convent. The convent functioned as one of the centers
of the Austrian Habsburg diplomatic network in Madrid throughout the reign
of Philip III. After Empress María's death, Margaret of the Cross took up her
mother's political role and gave daily audiences.[61] Thus, Empress María and
Margaret of the Cross were well integrated into the political life of the court,
even if they spent most or all of their time in the convent.

By retiring to a convent, Empress María and Margaret of the Cross were also
following a Habsburg tradition. Charles V, Empress María's father, had retired
to a monastery in Yuste for the last few years of his life. His daughter, and Empress María's sister, Juana, founded the convent of the Descalzas Reales and retired there after her husband's death. Philip II's construction of the Escorial can
also be seen as a type of retirement into a monastic existence, and he spent the
last years of his reign in semiretirement there. Empress María's daughter Isabel,
after having served as queen of France, entered a cloistered convent in Vienna,
where she died, in 1592. And Margaret of Austria's older sister Eleanor also became a cloistered nun when she entered a convent in Hall in the Tyrol. She died
there on 28 January 1620. The Descalzas convent could also serve as a haven for
the illegitimate female offspring of the Habsburgs; for example, Ana Dorotea,

Rudolf II's illegitimate daughter, entered the Descalzas as a cloistered nun. Therefore, retirement into a convent was not necessarily an exclusively feminine form of piety, but it was certainly a relatively common practice among Habsburg royalty in the sixteenth century.

Life in a convent allowed women to escape from what was a predominantly male world, enter a female community, and create an alternate political network.[62] Surely Empress María benefited greatly from entering the Descalzas convent. Within the convent she was able to have her own apartment, filled with art treasures, where servants attended her every need and where musicians, playwrights, and poets entertained her.[63] I would argue that, within the Descalzas, the empress established her own independent court. Moreover, Empress María served as a type of sovereign to the nuns with whom she lived. They deferred to her opinion and treated her with the respect due a ruling monarch. Empress María certainly had greater power than the abbess of the convent, and the abbess and nuns used the empress as their connection to the monarch. Through her, they petitioned for financial support and for any other needs they had.[64] So, by retiring to the Descalzas convent, Empress María prolonged her life as a ruler—something she had been unable to do in Central Europe once her son Rudolf II became emperor, and something she undoubtedly would have found difficult to do at the court of Philip II or Philip III.

The empress's decision to enter the convent takes on added significance if one considers that Philip II might have had other plans for her. Rumor had it that her brother Philip had wanted her to serve as ruler of Portugal.[65] When María left Central Europe, observers commented that although she wanted to live a life of solitude in the Descalzas, it was unclear whether Philip II would allow her to do so. The monarch's needs and those of the Spanish kingdoms were supposed to come before her personal wishes.[66] In light of this pressure, the empress's ability to enter the Descalzas was a clear mark of her independence and personal strength.

By entering the convent as a cloistered nun, Margaret of the Cross avoided a marriage with Philip II—her uncle and forty years her senior. The convent provided her (and many other early modern women) with an escape from an undesirable marriage. During her years at the Descalzas convent, Margaret of the Cross gained a reputation for personal sanctity and spiritual perfection, especially because she had chosen to give up the privileged existence of a Habsburg princess for that of a cloistered nun. As her eulogist, Fray Hortensio

Paravicino, explained, God was especially pleased by a royal person's spiritual devotion and religious profession. Margaret supposedly also engaged in bodily mortification; she wore a hair shirt and performed deeds that others considered repugnant. She delighted in such tasks as washing dishes in the kitchen of the Descalzas, an act that would have been unacceptable for royalty under any other circumstances. Paravicino noted that, despite her work in the kitchen, the nun "smelled more of sanctity than of food."[67] Her eulogist also saw a mark of sanctity in Margaret's ability to withstand illnesses, especially progressive blindness, without complaint. Paravicino claimed that Margaret welcomed blindness as a punishment for her own weakness and concern with material things. The nun reportedly saw her condition as a further means of freeing herself from the secular world and concentrating on spiritual matters. Such patience and fortitude were particularly noteworthy in a woman, according to Paravicino, because women were by nature prone to complain. Margaret's biographer, Juan de la Palma, claimed that the nun had cut her breast in retribution after hearing that a man had sold his soul to the devil.[68] These acts of self-mortification and physical deprivation marked Margaret as a saintly woman, just as such acts had distinguished Saints Catherine of Siena and Catherine of Genoa.[69] In his eulogy commemorating Margaret of the Cross's death, Paravicino referred to the nun as that "great and saintly woman" and as God's "saintly wife."[70]

In a similar fashion, Empress María's biographer, Rodrigo Mendes Silva, also described his subject as a saintly woman. He referred to the empress as "that human deity" and claimed that in her lifetime, the faithful venerated her as a saint. Mendes Silva also wrote that even heretics respected Empress María as a prudent Zenobia. (Zenobia of Palmyra was a frequently cited model of a wise, married queen.) He did not note that Empress María engaged in self-mortification as her daughter did, but he did claim that the empress spent most of the night on her knees praying, "with tears and sighs that reached heaven."[71] At her death, a globe of light supposedly appeared over the room where her body lay; this miraculous sign was held to be proof of her sanctity.[72]

Empress María's and, especially, Margaret of the Cross's reputations for sanctity certainly spread from the convent to the male world of the court. This fame was a direct benefit that women derived from their pious activities; piety, virginity, and sanctity won respect for women in the male political world as well as the female world of convents. Men valued these activities and virtues in women and sought the opinion of women who devoted themselves to a life of prayer. This certainly was true for Empress María and, particularly, Margaret of the Cross. Ambassadors and papal nuncios consulted with them because they knew these women were powerful and could effectively petition the king in both religious and political matters. Piety gave women such as Margaret of the Cross a reputation for personal strength that, when applied to political goals, could prove formidable.

A reputation for piety is what allowed a woman such as Beatriz Ramírez de Mendoza, Countess of Castellar, to express her opinion on political matters. Philip III wanted to speak with this beata specifically because she was known to be a devout, spiritual woman. Her piety gave her the ability to speak out, and she was not limited to speaking only about religious matters. During her audience with Philip III, the countess warned the monarch that his kingdom was going to ruin. She also added that the king was to blame for his kingdom's problems because he had handed the reins of governance to the Duke of Lerma.[73] Philip conferred with the Countess of Castellar for several hours. The length of this meeting in itself is proof that the monarch valued her opinion and thought that she could discern God's wishes. The countess's piety also won her an audience with the queen, who freely confided in the countess during this meeting. Because of the Countess of Castellar's reputation for piety, the monarchs sought and valued her advice on both political and personal matters.

Philip continued to value the opinion of other holy women as well. In 1612, he visited a nun who was reputed for her sanctity (she supposedly survived only on the Eucharist) and was thought to have the gift of prophecy. The king spent an hour speaking with her, and he was particularly concerned to have her opinion about and her prayers for the expulsion of the Moriscos from the Spanish kingdoms.[74]

The reputed piety and virtue of Margaret of the Cross and the nuns of the Descalzas allowed them to sponsor the publication of a manuscript that was critical of the state of the Spanish kingdoms and indirectly critical of Lerma.[75] The author of the manuscript, Cristóbal Pérez de Herrera, knew that Margaret and the nuns of the Descalzas were a reliable channel to Philip III. Moreover, by gaining the support of devout women, Pérez de Herrera legitimized his criticisms, which then became the concerns of virtuous people who had in mind only the best interest of the monarch and the monarchy. A reputation for piety gave the nuns of the Descalzas a high moral ground from which they and others could criticize Lerma. In turn, the author of the political tract was also able to use the nuns' reputation to sanction political criticism. Finally, the nuns could appeal to Philip III's piety in order to get him to read the book. In effect, the pious activities of Margaret of the Cross and her fellow nuns gave them room to maneuver and to express their opinions about political issues that were central to the future of the Spanish monarchy.

Piety was also supposed to give a woman such as Empress María insight into political problems and the ability to comment objectively about state matters. When Jerónimo de Sepúlveda recounted Empress María's conversation with Philip about keeping the court in Madrid, Sepúlveda described the empress as a "very prudent woman and one who always got to the root of matters. . . . She knew so much from her great experience acquired from so many years of governing, and . . . [her] opinion had to be valued and taken into account because she was so saintly a person, as all the world knows." Sepúlveda went on to criticize Philip for not listening to the "saintly and pious admonitions" of Empress María.[76] In this way, Empress María's spiritual activities not only legitimized her as an able political commentator but also singled her out as one of the few people who could provide impartial advice to the monarch.

When considering if these women were isolated in the Descalzas convent, one also has to keep in mind the character of Philip III. By all accounts, the king was an extremely pious individual himself, who spent a good deal of his time attending mass and visiting convents with his wife. Therefore, Philip III had regular, and often daily, contact with nuns and other religious individuals, and particularly with Empress María and Margaret of the Cross. He was often accompanied by ambassadors or select councillors of state on these visits to convents, and political negotiations took place within the convent walls. Almost every time he visited the Descalzas from 1598 until 1603, Philip III saw the imperial ambassador, Hans Khevenhüller. (After Empress María's death in 1603, Khevenhüller moved to Valladolid to be at the court.) These visits were occasions for Khevenhüller to discuss political matters with the king.

What other benefits did the three Habsburg women derive from these pious activities? Pious and charitable deeds were traditionally considered to be the domain of women. Women were supposed to be merciful and devout and were thought to be the more pious sex. As Jo Ann McNamara has shown, kings in the Middle Ages tended to express a fierce, warrior image whereas their wives were supposed to represent the "merciful side" of power.[77] This image certainly applied to Philip III, who hoped to lead his army into battle in Northern Italy but had to be dissuaded from doing so by the Spanish Council of State.[78]

Margaret of Austria, on the other hand, was thought to have greatly aided the Spanish kingdoms with her virtue and benevolence. In an anonymous report written after her death which considered the possible grounds for declaring Margaret a martyr to the faith, the author listed the queen's service to Spain. The author commented that she had fought against court intrigues with "heroic virtue because it was for God's glory, and for justice, for love of neighbor and of the fatherland [*patria*], and benefit of the kingdoms, and hatred of evil."[79] The author also implied that Margaret had fought specifically against Rodrigo Calderón, who was rumored to have poisoned her. Margaret's virtue thus allowed her to voice her political opinions because she was apparently doing so only for the good of Spain. Altruistic activities were characteristic of a virtuous and devout woman. In fact, when the church of San Gerónimo was decorated for Margaret of Austria's funeral and the queen's virtues were allegorized, charity toward the people was listed as one of her principal virtues.[80]

Yet charity and almsgiving were also among the few activities that allowed women a type of "public role." The distribution of charity was indeed expected of Habsburg women. For this reason, Empress María left money in her will so that her daughter Margaret could help the poor. As Juan de la Palma noted, it would have been unseemly for the daughter of an emperor and the aunt of the king of Spain not to dispense charity when there were so many needy people. Margaret of the Cross regularly made charitable contributions. Among other things, she gave away all the gifts which the queen brought her.[81] It is therefore understandable that Margaret of the Cross had particular devotion to Saint Clare of Assisi, foundress of the Franciscan order for nuns and also well known for her charitable works.

Noblewomen such as Margaret of Austria commonly visited hospitals, orphanages, and schools and dispensed charity in these public places.[82] Legend had it that the future queen was making the beds of the poor in a hospital when she received word that she would be married to Philip III.[83] By performing these services, women gained honor and recognition, something that was usually denied them in the political world.[84] In fulfilling these duties, a queen such as Margaret exercised a political function; she represented her husband and helped to foster an image of a benevolent and caring monarch. She also created an image of herself as an essential counterpart to the king and as a royal figure who had the needs of the Spanish people in mind. As one of the queen's eulo-gists wrote, Margaret was a "shepherdess" to Philip III's subjects.[85]

By cultivating the virtues of virginity and chastity, a woman supposedly raised herself up to the moral level of a man. Theologians as far back as St. Augustine had argued that by choosing to live as a virgin, a woman showed virility and masculine strength.[86] Because women were thought to be more prone to sexual activities and sexual misdeeds, chastity was thought to require a strength not usually associated with women. It is not surprising, therefore, for male writers to note that Empress María exhibited masculine strength through her prayers; or for Jerónimo de Florencia, when delivering the sermon at Margaret of Austria's funeral, to argue that the queen demonstrated virility by being able to control and even conquer her natural desires and by having a rational mind.[87] By living in or frequenting convents, both women consciously culti-vated the appearance of a virginal nun. Empress María even had the court painter, Juan Pantoja de la Cruz, paint her in the garb of a Franciscan nun (see figure 1). This was a practice common among Habsburg women; Philip III's sister Isabel Clara Eugenia, who jointly ruled the Netherlands with her hus-band, Archduke Albert, also had herself depicted as a nun.[88] These Habsburg women undoubtedly portrayed themselves in this way because the role of a nun afforded them power and respect.

Men believed that devout women could indeed exercise power because of their piety. The Habsburg women's reputation for piety meant that they could petition God for assistance; and people therefore sought out these women as types of religious "intercessors." According to Jo Ann McNamara, when me-dieval women were deprived of the ability to dispense alms and minister to the poor, they found other ways of expressing their sanctity. Specifically, women claimed to be able to see souls in purgatory and save them through prayer and self-mortification.[89]

Margaret of the Cross was thought to have the ability to save souls in pur-gatory. According to Agustín de Castro, a Jesuit priest who gave a eulogy at Margaret's death, the nun's prayers succeeded in liberating the soul of a Fran-ciscan priest from purgatory.[90] Hortensio Paravicino, Margaret of the Cross's eulogist, claimed that Margaret's dead father, Emperor Maximilian, appeared to her and asked her to remind her mother, Empress María, to have masses said for the repose of his soul.[91] After Margaret had completed his request, a re-splendent Maximilian reappeared to her to thank her and also to ask her why she had neglected to say her usual prayer for the calm repose of his soul; these prayers were essential for his soul to leave purgatory.[92] Although Paravicino emphasized Margaret of the Cross's reputed power to intercede with the saints, he also hinted that Maximilian was still in purgatory because of the forgetfulness of his widow and his daughter. Thus, a text that was supposedly meant to sing the praises of a woman still contained subtle misogynistic elements.

Paravicino also related another incident in which a noblewoman, the Countess of Fuenteidueña, appeared to Margaret to tell her that she had died in childbirth. The countess asked Margaret to pray for her and to have masses said for her soul.[93] Perhaps Margaret of the Cross's prayers were deemed particularly powerful in this case because of her name: Saint Margaret is the patron saint of women in childbirth. Paravicino explained that Margaret had presaged the death of the Countess of Fuenteidueña, who had appeared to the nun and told her of her death several days before the news reached the Descalzas convent. Paravicino also claimed that Margaret of the Cross had special interest in those who had died because their cases were more desperate than those of the living and they were in greater need of her help.

Likewise, Margaret of Austria's eulogist reminded Spaniards that in heaven, the dead queen could petition God for the souls of her Spanish subjects, and that they should pray to her.[94] In their wills, Margaret of the Cross and Margaret of Austria requested that masses be said for the relief of souls in purgatory. Both women obviously believed that through their efforts they would succeed in helping these souls; in this belief they were following the long tradition of holy women who claimed to be able to provide such relief for souls suffering in purgatory.[95] In both cases, one is confronted with male accounts of the power of female sanctity, but women could certainly use this power for their own purposes.

Margaret of Austria undoubtedly took advantage of the fact that male artists represented her as the highest example of female sanctity: the Virgin Mary. In 1605, Juan Pantoja de la Cruz completed a painting of the Annunciation with Margaret of Austria as the Virgin Mary and her daughter Anne as the angel Gabriel (see fig. 3). In the painting, the Holy Spirit in the form of a dove hovers above the queen's head and blesses her. Pantoja de la Cruz also painted a scene of the birth of the Virgin in which the infant Mary is held by Archduchess Maria of Bavaria, Margaret of Austria's mother. Her mother's prominence suggests the artist wanted to imply Margaret was the woman giving birth to the

Virgin (see fig. 4).[96] Both of these paintings were designed for devotional purposes, so the viewer, while venerating the image of the Virgin Mary, was actually venerating Margaret of Austria. Because Pantoja de la Cruz was a court
painter to Philip III, these paintings were probably commissioned by the monarchs. The works were meant to emphasize the divine origins of the Habsburg
family and their divine right to rule.[97]

By depicting Margaret of Austria as the Virgin Mary, Pantoja de la Cruz set
the queen up as the most perfect example of female virtue. Divinity passed
through her line, and the corollary to this was that Margaret was responsible
for the divine nature of the Spanish monarchy. The queen was certainly aware
of Pantoja's allegorical representation and knew that she herself stood to gain
from such representation. Margaret's use of the image and the cult of the Virgin Mary was not as blatant as that of Queen Elizabeth, however, who clearly
usurped numerous Marian symbols in order to replace the cult of Mary with
that of the Virgin Queen.[98] Nevertheless, like Elizabeth, Margaret recognized
the power of Marian imagery and knew that it could be employed to increase
devotion and respect for her and for the Spanish monarchy. Depictions of Margaret as the Virgin Mary emphasized the moral and political power that Margaret wielded within the Spanish court.

All three Habsburg women used the respect, honor, and position they won
through pious activities in order to influence political policy at Philip III's
court. They consciously used their reputations to win the attention of Philip
III, who himself devoted much time to pious activities and was more likely to
listen to the opinion of women who also were known for their piety and spir-
ituality. Because Empress María, Margaret of the Cross, and Margaret of Austria represented the interests of the Austrian Habsburgs at the Spanish court,
it was essential for them to win the king's attention if they were to petition him
successfully for their needs and those of their relatives in Central Europe.

The goals of the Habsburg women were particularly problematic because
the Duke of Lerma sought to refocus Spanish attention, drawing it away from
Central Europe in order to be able to see to the specific needs of the Spanish
kingdoms. Lerma discouraged Philip from committing Spain's limited financial resources to Central Europe, and for this reason, his agenda clashed with
that of the Habsburg women. Lerma sought to distance Philip from all three
women because they posed a personal challenge to his influence over the monarch and a political challenge to his foreign policy. Lerma found the Habsburg

women especially threatening because, as the monarch's relatives, they could meet with him privately and did not necessarily have to go through the Duke of Lerma to gain an audience. Lerma recognized that access to the monarch meant power and influence, and therefore he tried to curtail the women's contact with the king. Yet, as we have seen, the three Habsburg women developed their own network of individuals to reach Philip III and their own schedule of pious activities, which won them the respect and attention of the monarch and which brought them into daily contact with him.

When the king attended mass or services at the Descalzas convent, he often remained afterward to converse privately with Empress María and Margaret of the Cross. These were choice moments for the Habsburg women to remind the monarch of the need to provide financial assistance to the Austrian Habsburgs.[99] And because the queen accompanied Philip on most of his religious outings, she also had frequent contact with the monarch. These opportunities were significant because the Duke of Lerma tried to control the private moments the monarchs shared. Religious activities allowed for interaction between the monarch and his female relatives, and this interaction provided opportunities for the Habsburg women to voice their concerns and their opinions to Philip III.

Finally, all three women knew to voice these concerns in the language of religious devotion. Since piety was an acceptable feminine realm, women could effectively speak out in matters of religion. When expressing opinions or when petitioning their male relatives, Empress María, Margaret of the Cross, and Margaret of Austria often claimed to be speaking as devout women who were primarily interested in the protection of the Christian faith as well as in the maintenance of the House of Austria. This was particularly true of Margaret of the Cross, who, as a nun, could surely claim to have the right to invoke the divine. When Margaret of the Cross wrote to Lerma asking him for financial assistance for Rudolf II, she added that this assistance was for the good of Christianity and was therefore an appropriate concern for Philip III.[100] On another occasion when she asked Philip for aid for her brothers, Margaret said that she did so "for the love of God."[101] She used this same phrase in another letter in which she freely combined familial and political matters. In the letter, Margaret mentioned how she had enjoyed the visit of Philip's children to the Descalzas and then spoke of a revolt that was under way in Flanders and of the need to assist Archduke Albert in suppressing this revolt. She explained, "I beg you for the love of God to order that the provisions be sent on time so that no other revolts occur."[102] Margaret also invoked her mother in the role of heavenly intercessor when writing to Philip. When thanking the monarch for helping her brothers in Central Europe, she wrote that Empress María in heaven would ask God to repay Philip for all he had done for the Habsburgs.[103] The nun then mentioned that she was sure that Philip III would help the archdukes in Flanders.

Because she couched her suggestions in this way, men could overlook the fact that Margaret of the Cross was voicing political opinions (and was thereby violating the accepted norm that virtuous women should remain silent). Furthermore, her reputation lent strength to her pleas for actions that would benefit Christianity. Margaret of the Cross, like her mother and Margaret of Austria, identified all assistance to the Austrian Habsburgs (for their struggle against the Turks and for their fight against the German and the Dutch Protestants) as actions that would benefit Christianity. Thus, piety freed these women to express themselves in matters that had obvious political ramifications; piety gave them a language to voice their concerns and gave these concerns great weight with men.

7

Melancholy and Infirmity

ILLNESS WAS A COMMON THEME in the lives of Empress María, Margaret of Austria, and Margaret of the Cross. Whether it was because of advanced age, childbirth, or physical sacrifice, all three women experienced periods of illness. This poor health was a natural and predictable part of life for early modern nobility. Because of their wealth and their lifestyle, aristocrats tended to eat meals that were poor in nutritional value, while they consumed rich foods in excess. Philip III and Margaret of Austria were no exception: they liked to eat.[1] Noblewomen had the added burden of childbearing, which endangered their lives and shortened their lifespan. Many early modern persons were concerned about their health, which is not surprising given the prevalence of plague, cholera, and other serious epidemics.[2] The Habsburgs always inquired about the health of their family members, and they often reported the state of their health when writing to relatives. It is not surprising to find that the Habsburgs and others commented frequently on the health of Empress María, Margaret of Austria, and Margaret of the Cross.[3]

Of the various infirmities that afflicted early modern people, melancholy was one of those most often mentioned. In fact, in the late sixteenth and early seventeenth centuries, melancholy was a "popular" disease among European elites. Excessive amounts of bile in the body, prolonged sadness, fear, and a desire to be isolated from others were all said to be symptoms of melancholy.[4] Melancholy tended to be a debilitating illness because it usually caused sufferers to retreat into isolation and rendered them unable to perform the most mundane of tasks. This ailment was also considered to afflict artistic, creative, and sensitive persons and, perhaps for this reason, was the preferred illness among many early modern nobles, many of whom even feigned the symptoms.[5] For early modern aristocrats, melancholy was an acceptable explanation for inactivity, lethargy, and boredom, as well as a culturally permissible means of expressing sorrow and loss. The political theorist Giovanni Botero claimed that Spanish men were particularly susceptible to the disease: he wrote in 1603 that the men in Spain "have more than a bit of melancholy, which makes them severe in manner, restrained and sluggish in their undertakings."[6] In fact, melancholy often characterized rulers, and the Spanish kings Charles V and Philip II supposedly regularly suffered from this malady.[7] Emperor Rudolf II, who isolated himself from his family and councillors in his castle in Prague, also demonstrated a melancholic temperament.[8]

Several prominent individuals at the court of Philip III were diagnosed as having melancholy. The Duke of Lerma suffered from periodic bouts,[9] as did his wife.[10] The Duke of Sessa, councillor of state, ambassador to Rome, and Queen Margaret's mayordomo mayor, also had problems with melancholy.[11] Philip and Margaret's daughter was thought to be melancholic even at the age of seven.[12] Empress María supposedly had an excess of melancholic humors which regularly interfered with her activities, and Margaret of Austria was said to have occasional problems with the ailment.

While these persons might have suffered from depression, and while their symptoms might have been "real," women and men alike could nevertheless use melancholy (and other illnesses) as a political ploy and a negotiating tool. Whether real, embellished, or imagined, melancholy could be an effective political device. Some early modern commentators clearly made the connection between political setbacks and melancholic humors. It was the uncertainty of whether melancholy was caused by actual health problems or by political forces (or a combination of both) which made it such an effective weapon in the early modern period.

"Illness" for some Spanish nobles provided a means of leaving the court and isolating themselves from their critics. This was true for the Duke of Lerma, who, as Philip III's royal favorite, was regularly the focus of gossip, criticism, and political schemes. Although it might have been more advantageous for Lerma to remain at court and defend himself against his critics, he often preferred to retreat into isolation. Early modern physicians believed that the intrigues and commotion at court actually brought on melancholy in individuals.

Therefore it made logical, medical sense for Lerma to retreat from court activities;[13] he invoked his melancholy as a reason to avoid political negotiations and serious conversations. In March 1604, for example, when the Cardinal of Toledo tried to visit Lerma, he was told not to come if he wanted to discuss political matters. When melancholic, the privado refused to grant audiences or to receive any petitions for assistance. In addition, his attendants made sure that music was played at his meals to distract him from any serious thought.[14] In this way, Lerma could blame his retreat and his neglect of state matters on his melancholy rather than admit it was owing to his inability to handle criticism or his need for rest.

For women, however, illness served further purposes. On the one hand, women could use illness to excuse their behavior, especially when that behavior contradicted what men expected of them. This tactic was used, for instance, when Spanish royal women expressed political views that differed from those of Philip III's councillors or those of the Duke of Lerma. Because the political realm was considered to be a male preserve and because men attempted to limit women to private, domestic, or religious realms, when women expressed political opinions they regularly couched them in the language of family or religion. In turn, men often excused these opinions by claiming that the women were ill (often melancholic) and therefore could not be held responsible for their words or actions. On the other hand, Spanish royal women could also use illness as a sign of protest against actions taken by Philip or his ministers; illness was in this case intended to attract attention to the afflicted woman and to pressure men to give in to her desires. The Habsburg women's various illnesses, especially their spells of melancholy, often reflected their discontent with Lerma's policies. Illness, therefore, could help or hinder women in maneuvering in the labyrinth that was Philip III's court.

Empress María regularly claimed to have melancholic humors, and those around her also reported her illness. The empress experienced many of the symptoms usually associated with a melancholic temperament: she had difficulty eating and sleeping; she was sorrowful, fearful, suspicious, and jealous; and she had fever and a weak pulse.[15] In 1598, the papal nuncio in Spain reported that the empress was suffering from melancholy, and so Philip III and his sister, Isabel Clara Eugenia, went to visit María as often as possible.[16] The empress's melancholy was probably connected to the recent death of her brother, Philip II, and to Philip III's impending departure for Valencia to meet and marry Margaret of Austria. Empress María regularly complained whenever her relatives failed to visit her. She undoubtedly knew that physicians thought excessive solitude caused a person to become melancholic; therefore, complaints of melancholy would naturally have motivated her relatives to think about and visit her. In fact, Philip III visited the empress on an almost daily basis during the last months of 1598, particularly because she was suffering from melancholy. Her illness might have been—at least, in part—a calculated ploy to get Philip to visit her during the busy first months of his reign. Empress María's bouts of melancholy often coincided with times when the empress wanted the king and queen to visit her—an activity that Lerma sought to curtail.

People around her recognized the connection between the empress's health and her desire for contact with her relatives. Empress María's secretary, Juan Carrillo, often mentioned the empress's state of health and commented particularly on her melancholy. Carrillo served as Archduke Albert's diplomatic representative in Spain. Albert asked Carrillo to inform him about his mother's health on a regular basis, and so Carrillo filled his letters with references to the empress's physical and mental condition. He noted the connection between Empress María's melancholy and her need to hear news of her relatives: when too many days went by without the empress receiving news, the melancholic humors in her body rose. For this reason, Carrillo encouraged Albert to write his mother often with news of his health and that of his wife, Isabel Clara Eugenia.[17]

Carrillo, however, did not hesitate to state that there were some nonmedical causes for the empress's ill health. In May 1600, Carrillo reported that the king and queen visited the empress at the Descalzas convent, where they found the empress in bed suffering from melancholy caused by her age and by "feelings of embarrassment" (*algunos bochornos*). Carrillo did not explain the cause of this embarrassment, but he did note that after the monarchs' visit the empress's health improved. Her doctors claimed that she was well and that the root of her melancholy had been her imagination.[18] Given that at this time the Duke of Lerma was trying to limit the monarchs' visits to the empress, Empress María's malady can be seen as a reaction to Lerma's plans and a conscious effort to escape Lerma's control. The improvement in her health would have been a direct result of having accomplished her goal.

In a similar vein, Archduke Albert wrote Lerma directly in November 1600 commenting on Empress María's ill health and attacks of melancholy. Albert added that Philip III's visits to the empress helped her greatly and improved her health.[19] Carrillo continued to report the empress's melancholy in June of 1600: "The empress is healthy although she has a bit of melancholic humor. This is of no concern and already Her Majesty gives several audiences."[20] Through reports of her ill health, Empress María succeeded in gaining the attention of Archduke Albert, who in turn pressured Lerma to allow the king and queen to visit her. The empress's melancholy also ensured that she would remain on the minds of the monarchs, thereby making it much harder for the Duke of Lerma to discourage their visits to the Descalzas. Because these visits allowed Empress María to converse privately with the monarchs about familial and political matters, her melancholy served as an effective tool for gaining power and voicing her opinions on policy decisions.

The connection between Empress María's health and events at the Spanish court is clearly evident in the correspondence of her mayordomo, Juan de Borja, with his nephew, the Duke of Lerma. In early June 1600, Empress María awaited the visit of Pedro Franqueza, secretary of state and one of Lerma's closest associates. Franqueza delayed his visit to the empress, and Borja reported that Empress María was consequently getting so upset that her melancholic humor was rising, and she did not fail to remind him and his wife every time she saw them of her need to see Franqueza.[21] Presumably, Empress María was concerned with matters in Flanders, and she felt that Franqueza's delay in seeing her meant a delay in Spanish assistance to her favorite son, Archduke Albert. In this instance, the empress put constant pressure on Juan de Borja to communicate her needs to Lerma. Her illness served both as a means of frightening Borja into complying with her demands and as a way for Borja to excuse his own actions to the Duke of Lerma.

In the same month, Empress María and the Duke of Lerma quarreled over one of the empress's doctors, Luis de Ávila. Lerma sought to remove Ávila from the empress's employ, ostensibly in order to place him in Philip III's household. Lerma's reasons are unclear, but Empress María resented his actions and tried to prevent Ávila's removal. Borja reported to Lerma that Ávila needed to bleed the empress because of her poor health and that the empress, because of her frequent illnesses, desired to keep Ávila as her doctor.[22] Empress María greatly resented meddling with her personal staff, and undoubtedly had instructed Borja to plead her case with Lerma. Lerma's actions interfered in a realm over which the empress had exercised great influence and power—her own household. Ávila, as the empress's doctor for many years, served as María's ally and was certainly aware that the empress's health complaints were often "symptoms" of discontent with court politics. His removal would have deprived María of a valuable associate in her political stratagems.

In July 1601, Borja reported the empress's poor health in order to defend her petition for the king to settle a dispute involving her lady-in-waiting and close friend, the Duchess of Villahermosa. According to Borja, the empress needed the duchess close by to assist her, but the dispute had forced the duchess to return to her territories in Aragón.[23] In this case, Borja's report of Empress María's illness was effective: Lerma used the same language to write to officials to request that they see to the duchess's case quickly.[24]

Empress María also used her health as a way to keep Borja near her. Borja was a member of the Council of Portugal and the Council of Finance, and he was one of Lerma's principal financial and political advisers. At times these responsibilities required Borja to travel to the court in Valladolid. The empress disliked Borja's absences, most probably because he went to Valladolid to see her rival, the Duke of Lerma. When Borja sought to go to Valladolid in November 1601, Empress María initially agreed. However, as the day for Borja's departure approached, she became extremely sad and did not want to let him leave the Descalzas. She cried continuously (an acceptable female ploy), she could hardly speak, and she became melancholic. Borja, however, tried to reason with the empress by reminding her that he would be going to the court to, among other things, see to the interests of her relatives, the Austrian Habsburgs. Borja also told the empress that it did no good for her to "blame her inconsistencies on her melancholy." Yet, as he wrote to Lerma, this melancholy had great power (*estas pueden más que todo*).[25] Clearly Borja recognized that María used her melancholy as a means of exerting control over him and others at the Spanish court.

Borja also told Lerma that if he really wanted him to go to Valladolid, Lerma should have Philip write Empress María requesting her permission. However, Borja explained that Lerma himself should not ask María directly because she was jealous of Lerma and believed that he wanted Borja to go to Valladolid permanently. Jealousy was one of the characteristic symptoms of a melancholic individual, and therefore Empress María's behavior was consistent with her recognized illness. Borja also reminded Lerma that one had to be careful and patient with the empress because of her age.[26] In this case, as in others, Borja cited old age and illness to excuse the empress's behavior and to explain why one had to be mindful of her needs. Empress María's outbreak of melancholy directly followed her discovery that Borja had informed Lerma of her complaints, namely, that Philip had not been generous enough with her servants.[27] The empress's poor health and unwillingness to allow Borja to go to Valladolid were clearly linked to Borja's actions. María felt betrayed by Borja's comments and she exploited her condition to punish him for his actions.

At approximately the same time, Empress María had been pressuring Philip to appoint a new chaplain at the Descalzas because she and the nuns were unhappy with the current one. Empress María wanted Diego de Guzmán, a Jesuit priest, to be chosen, but she needed the king's approval to have him appointed. Her melancholy and her reluctance to allow Borja to leave Madrid were bargaining tools to force Philip and Lerma to resolve the issue of Guzmán's appointment. Empress María's complaints and illness produced the desired result. On 12 December 1601, Borja (who was still unable to leave for Valladolid) wrote that Philip had agreed to appoint Diego de Guzmán as chaplain to the Descalzas.[28] He added that the empress was well, very happy, and calm. Several days later, Borja once again reported that the empress was very happy with the news, which, according to Borja, would make her healthy.[29] Hearing of Guzmán's appointment also finally persuaded Empress María to allow Juan de Borja to travel to the court in Valladolid.

Juan de Borja consistently depicted Empress María as an old, infirm, melancholic widow. Borja's characterization of the empress, while perhaps rooted in physical reality (Empress María was seventy-two years old in 1600), accomplished various purposes. Age and illness functioned to excuse Empress María's actions and to lessen the severity of her complaints about Philip's court. Borja was genuinely devoted to Empress María and served her well, despite his relationship to the Duke of Lerma and his occasional frustrations with the empress's tactics. Borja was a skilled statesman with an accomplished career of negotiating policy both in Prague and in Madrid. His frequent references to María's ill health served as a means of negotiating with the Duke of Lerma, who, as a fellow melancholic, would have understood the nature of her illness (and the rules of the game). Moreover, Borja also shifted any blame from himself to the empress, whose melancholy supposedly caused her to make irrational demands on Philip and Lerma. The Duke of Lerma could not then hold Borja responsible for the sentiments or the tactics of Empress María which he recorded in his letters. In this way, Borja was able to serve the empress and also protect his political future at the Spanish court.

Melancholy and illness could at times link individuals closer together and create a common bond, as happened with Empress María and Hans Khevenhüller. The inventory of Khevenhüller's possessions at his death includes a reference to a stone given to him by María to treat melancholy.[30] Among Khevenhüller's possessions were still other stones to treat melancholy and more medical stones that had belonged to the empress.[31] Empress María and Hans Khevenhüller developed a friendship and a partnership at the Spanish court over a period of approximately twenty years. Together they had attempted to win Spanish attention and financial resources for the needs of the Austrian Habsburgs, and they had also commiserated with each other when the Duke of Lerma brought changes to the court and persuaded Philip to move the court to Valladolid.[32] Undoubtedly the empress and the ambassador, both of whom were elderly individuals, shared medical complaints as well. As noted above, the empress even gave Khevenhüller stones that she thought would help his melancholy. Not only does this imply that the empress thought she could treat melancholy in herself and in others, but it also shows that illness could unite individuals.[33] For women in particular, illness could foster affectionate friendships that helped relieve the boredom and isolation royal women often experienced within the confines of an early modern court.

Empress María's melancholy followed her to her grave. In the posthumous report, her doctors stated that she died in part from an excess of choler (*cólera*), or bile.[34] In the early modern period, this condition was often thought to be associated, and even interchangeable, with an excess of melancholic humors.[35] Indeed, in her last days, doctors diagnosed the empress's condition as being wholly in keeping with that of a melancholic.

In a more limited fashion, Margaret of Austria also used illness to express her discontent with politics at the Spanish court. The Venetian ambassador Ottaviano Bon reported that Margaret desired to have political influence at the court but was frustrated in her attempts because her activities were circumscribed by the Duke and Duchess of Lerma. Bon reported that, consequently, the queen was "withdrawn, melancholic, and without any authority; she found herself completely alone in the company of few of the women from her country."[36] Bon connected the queen's melancholic humors to her supposed inability to reach her husband and to her isolation within the court. Although Bon exaggerated the queen's isolation and certainly failed to note the extent of Margaret's influence with her husband, his connection between political actions and melancholic humor clearly demonstrates that some early modern commentators saw political causes for the "illness" of melancholy.

The queen's ailments on other occasions were also connected to events at the court. In November 1601, Margaret of Austria became deathly ill almost immediately after Philip left her alone in Valladolid. The king had to cut short his trip to San Lorenzo and El Pardo, and he returned to find his wife unable to recognize him. The doctors struggled to find the cause for Margaret's illness until Philip's physician finally established that it was connected to her having recently given birth (*mal de madre*).[37] However, as the queen recovered, another explanation for her sickness emerged. The court chronicler Luis Cabrera de Córdoba reported that "this illness has been attributed to the sorrow she felt at His Majesty's departure, and for his not taking her with him, as he had had her understand many days before. [This illness has also been attributed to] certain displeasures which she experienced in not being allowed to be served by the female servants whom she brought with her from Germany, and in other [things] which go against her desires."[38] Another court chronicler, Fray Jerónimo de Sepúlveda, reported the same incident but attributed the queen's illness to the conflict that had arisen when Margaret wanted the sister of her closest friend, Maria Sidonia, to join her household; instead, Lerma had filled the vacancy with his niece. Sepúlveda reported that the queen became deathly ill (the doctors gave her only three days to live) because of the thought that even as queen she could not control who would be in her household.[39] In this instance, the queen's actions brought her some success: Philip cut short his trip and returned to Valladolid to be with her. Philip remained near his wife for several months after that. In doing this, Philip was following conventional wisdom that if he left Margaret, her illness would return, so any trips he took would have to be with the queen.[40]

Margaret was in fact able to use illness quite effectively to ensure that Philip did not travel much without her. On numerous occasions, reports of her illness forced the monarch to delay, cancel, or return early from a trip. In March 1600, Philip was supposed to go to Toledo, but the queen suddenly took ill and had to be bled. As a result, the king (who himself was not feeling well) postponed his trip.[41] In December 1603, the queen became sick immediately after Philip left her at the Descalzas while he went to Valencia. The illness was attributed to her having stayed earlier at Lerma's house, which was newly built and had many fountains and pools. The doctors thought she became ill because she had been exposed to too much humidity in the winter.[42] In this case, Margaret might not only have been expressing her dissatisfaction with her husband for leaving her behind, but she might also have wanted to blame her illness on Lerma, who had undoubtedly encouraged Philip III to travel alone.

Like illness, pregnancy also served as an effective way for Margaret of Austria to gain influence with Philip III. Margaret was often pregnant; in ten years she gave birth to eight children. The queen's pregnancies were discussed and reported in a very detailed manner. The court chronicler Luis Cabrera de Córdoba noted all the times that the court suspected the queen was pregnant. He related occurrences when the pregnancies were false, and he even reported on several occasions that the queen had begun to menstruate again (or that her menstruation was late and she was therefore thought to be pregnant).[43] Cabrera de Córdoba listed when the queen's pregnancies were confirmed and then noted the development of each pregnancy. The issue was clearly not a private matter, but rather a public, political event.

Pregnancy incapacitated the queen to a certain degree. She was no longer allowed to ride a horse but rather had to be taken around in a chair. She was also discouraged from taking long trips or traveling to locations that were considered unhealthy. This made it difficult for her to accompany her husband on his frequent travels. However, the queen also gained attention and influence through her pregnancies. She was allowed to determine where she would spend the last months of her pregnancy and where she would give birth. She could use this license to win more influence with Philip or to torment the Duke of Lerma.

Margaret certainly showed her power during the events leading up to the birth of her first child. The queen was supposed to give birth at Lerma's house, and she allowed Lerma and his wife to prepare the house completely. A few days before she gave birth, however, the queen decided that she wanted to give birth instead at the house of the Count of Benavente. The ostensible reasons the queen gave for this decision were that Lerma's house was still under construction and that one of Philip II's wives had died while giving birth in that same house.[44] With another pregnancy, in 1609, she persuaded Philip III to take her to San Lorenzo (the Escorial) because she wanted to give birth there.[45]

Because pregnancy was associated in the popular imagination with caprice and whims, Margaret was able to use her pregnancies effectively to get her way in diverse issues.

Philip stayed by his wife's side during the last stages of her pregnancies and was present at the birth of almost all his children. Rather than distance the queen from her husband, Margaret's frequent pregnancies gave her leverage with him and increased his attentiveness to her. Pregnancy and illness often overlapped, as Margaret sometimes took ill while she was with child. In these cases, she could use both pregnancy and illness to her advantage. In August 1602, while the queen was four months pregnant, she became sick en route to Burgos with the king. As a result, the king postponed his trip.[46]

The queen's illnesses mobilized Spain: the country prayed for her, there were processions attended by members of all the councils, and statues of Mary were publicly and solemnly brought to the palace.[47] This is not to say that Margaret of Austria regularly feigned illness; however, she must have been aware of the effect her illnesses had and the indirect and direct rewards that she gained from them. So, for example, when the queen became ill in 1599, Empress María went to visit her. Illness could serve as a way for Margaret to gain companionship: in this case, it also allowed her to maintain contact with the empress, contact that Lerma must have found threatening.[48] She therefore had incentive to emphasize or exaggerate sickness. Moreover, since illness was thought to be a reaction to external conditions, Margaret might have been conditioned to express her discontent in a physical fashion.

Female illness in general aroused suspicion among men in the early modern period. In 1606, a committee sent to examine the queen's household reported that Margaret of Austria's ladies-in-waiting asked for too many medications, which court doctors only too willingly provided.[49] This committee wanted to reform the queen's household in order to curtail the Spanish government's financial expenses. The committee's report shows that there was close cooperation between women and their doctors, a cooperation that men often feared. The report also suggests that the queen and her ladies-in-waiting might have been controlling their doctors and actually prescribing medications for themselves. Moreover, the report indicates that male councillors believed that women often feigned illnesses. These councillors sought to control female illness (and its expenses) within the queen's household by having the queen's mayordomo, a man, decide if and when a lady-in-waiting needed medication.[50]

In the committee's opinion, a lady-in-waiting should not receive medication unless she had a fever or other condition that forced her to remain in bed.

Throughout much of her life in the Descalzas, Margaret of the Cross suffered from periodic illnesses. Hans Khevenhüller reported that the nun had annual bouts of serious illness, and the ambassador seemed to fear each time that she would not survive.[51] Perhaps because of the nun's physical frailty, Khevenhüller and Juan Carrillo regularly commented on Margaret's health when they wrote the Austrian Habsburgs.[52] Margaret of the Cross also suffered from eye problems, which became so severe that she gradually lost her eyesight. Juan de la Palma, Margaret's biographer, explained that prior to her illness, Margaret had loved to gaze upon beautiful objects as a way to contemplate Christ's divinity. However, the nun became obsessed with these objects and asked God's assistance in ridding herself of this obsession. In answer to her prayers, according to Palma, God gradually took away her eyesight.[53] Thus, Palma rationalized Margaret's progressive blindness as a divine effort to help the nun become even more pious. Nevertheless, he blamed the blindness on Margaret's vanity and weakness.

Margaret of the Cross may also have accepted her affliction as divinely sent, and, like Palma, she seems to have accepted this blindness in a positive light: as a test from God and as one of the many ways that she could suffer to help others. Margaret does not seem to have paid much attention to her failing eyesight at first. In a letter to Archduke Albert, she commented that she had experienced discharge from her eyes but that she did not think it was noteworthy.[54] The growing blindness caused her doctors to discourage her from writing letters. Margaret then commented in letters that her secretary was writing or that she was writing in spite of her doctors' order. In 1617, for example, Margaret had her secretary write Archduke Albert and in a postscript asked Albert to forgive her for not writing the letter herself. She explained that she had been bled that day and that the doctors would not allow her to write.[55] The nun also cited her infirmity to excuse her brief letters and her bluntness when making petitions.

Margaret's infirmities certainly gained her attention. Her illnesses bound her to the numerous saints before her who had joyfully accepted their suffering as a way to join in Christ's pain on the cross.[56] It won her a reputation for sanctity which was quite advantageous for her. Her illness also brought her attention and occasioned visits from many of her relatives. Philip III, in particular, and Margaret of Austria went to see the nun when she was ill, and at times the

Duke of Lerma also went. These were all opportunities for Margaret to voice her numerous requests. As with the queen, Margaret of the Cross did not necessarily feign illness. Nevertheless, she could still take advantage of her infirmities to gain attention and to exercise power at the court. Although Teresa of Ávila believed that nuns were particularly prone to melancholy in order to draw attention to themselves, I have found no reference to Margaret of the Cross having suffered from this malady. Perhaps because her other ailments occupied her fully and gained her much notice, Margaret had no need to become melancholic.[57]

Melancholy was not an illness that was exclusive to women. In fact, early modern society tended to have much greater understanding of melancholy in men than in women.[58] While melancholy in women was often associated with irrational and uncontrollable characters, in men it was usually associated with artistic, creative personalities—even genius. In women, melancholy was also often related to childbirth, and women often described themselves as being melancholic during their pregnancies and after giving birth. Physicians believed that melancholy in virgins and widows, on the other hand, resulted from sexual abstinence.[59]

The Spanish physician Juan Huarte de San Juan distinguished between the humors of phlegm and blood, which weakened the flesh (and were especially prevalent in women and children), and those humors of choler and melancholy, which toughened the flesh. According to Huarte de San Juan, the latter two humors produced prudence and wisdom in men.[60] In this way, Huarte de San Juan implied that melancholy was not a positive female characteristic.[61] This corresponds to Juliana Schiesari's analysis of melancholy and loss in Renaissance literature; Schiesari argues that only male sorrow and loss were characterized as melancholic and thus heroic. According to Schiesari, such interpretations of melancholy were normally denied women; female sorrow and loss were devalued. Observers allowed that Empress María and Margaret of Austria suffered from melancholy, but this melancholy was regarded somewhat differently from that experienced by the men around them. Whereas, for Empress María and Margaret of Austria, melancholy supposedly reaffirmed female moral and physical weakness, for the Duke of Lerma, melancholy was an acceptable reaction to the pressures associated with his numerous responsibilities at the Spanish court.

Nevertheless, melancholy could be a powerful political tool for women and men alike. The Duke of Lerma's frequent melancholic spells served a purpose similar to those of Empress María and Margaret of Austria; like these women, Lerma used his illness as a political ploy. When the queen refused to give birth to her first child in Lerma's house, Lerma became melancholic. His melancholy clearly resulted from his ongoing battle with Margaret of Austria. The queen had written her will at that time in case she should die in childbirth, and Lerma was trying desperately to have the will opened.[62] Lerma may also have become melancholic in order to gain sympathy and support for his cause from Philip III. Nevertheless, the privado lost this battle.

From March until July 1604, Hans Khevenhüller reported Lerma's bouts with melancholy. In March, when Philip and Margaret traveled from Valladolid to Madrid, Lerma did not accompany them because of weakness caused by melancholy. At the end of the same month, Lerma was still sick and therefore handed over most of his court duties to his son, the Duke of Uceda. As late as June of the same year, Khevenhüller continued to report that Lerma was unwell and would not write or speak with anyone.[63]

In his letters to Rudolf II, Khevenhüller never tried to explain the cause of Lerma's melancholy. Nevertheless, at this time the ambassador reported events concerning the imprisonment and the legal process against Magdalena de Guzmán, the Marquesa del Valle,[64] an issue that was one of the first challenges to Lerma's control. Lerma sought to have the king and queen testify against Guzmán, but, on the advice of their respective confessors, Philip and Margaret refused to do so. The hostility at the court escalated when the king's confessor, Gaspar de Córdoba, an associate of the queen and an opponent of Lerma, died of an apparent heart attack. Court chroniclers commented that Lerma's verbal attacks on the confessor for advising the king not to testify had directly caused Gaspar de Córdoba's death. In Lerma's estimation, the case of Magdalena de Guzmán marked the first time that Philip III had not had complete confidence in him. It is not surprising, therefore, that Lerma should have been melancholic during this period. His melancholy allowed him to be absent from the court at a time when he was being criticized and was under attack. His illness was undoubtedly a reflection of his political woes.[65]

In 1606, Lerma found himself involved in a struggle with the queen and Philip's new confessor, Diego de Mardones. Both the queen and the royal confessor questioned the activities of the Junta de Desempeño, which had been set up in 1603 to look into the financial recovery of the Spanish monarchy. Margaret and Mardones accused the members of the committee of financial mismanagement and corruption. The queen went so far as to warn Philip that the Junta de Desempeño had only worsened Spain's economic problems.[66] Mardones also criticized Lerma's close associate Rodrigo Calderón.

During the course of this court struggle, Lerma once again became melancholic. The papal nuncio reported that Lerma was troubled with great melancholy and was considering retiring from the court and from secular life to become a monk.[67] Lerma's melancholy was an expression of his disappointment at being attacked, but it was also an acceptable way for him to remove himself from his critics and retire temporarily to his estate. In 1607, Pedro Franqueza and Alonso Ramírez de Prado, key members of the Junta de Desempeño and associates of Lerma, were prosecuted and convicted of misappropriating royal funds. This incident marked another serious challenge to Lerma's power at the Spanish court. Nevertheless, the privado did succeed in having Philip remove Diego de Mardones from his position as royal confessor; Mardones was appointed Bishop of Córdoba and had to leave the court to take up his new office. Melancholy for Lerma served as a socially acceptable way to distance himself from the unpleasant developments at court and take time to recover politically. Lerma's absence from Madrid was a type of self-enforced and well-calculated political exile.

In early modern Spain, illnesses such as melancholy could surprisingly bring financial rewards to their victims. When illness required bleeding a patient, as melancholy usually did, it was the custom among Spanish nobles to send gifts to the person being treated.[68] When the queen was bled in February 1600, she received many jewels.[69] Luis Cabrera de Córdoba reported that when Margaret of Austria was bled in October 1602, those who were present at the bleeding as well as some persons who were absent sent her gold objects (*piezas de oro*) and other small trinkets. Cabrera de Córdoba claimed that this was a habit newly introduced with the queen's arrival in Spain, and the objects were meant to be good luck tokens.[70] Juan de Borja, on the other hand, claimed that this was originally a German custom, which nobles such as Empress María adopted.[71] According to Tomé Pinheiro da Veiga, the Portuguese chronicler who visited the Spanish court in 1605, this was also a common practice among nuns.[72] The custom of sending jewels was probably connected to the curative powers associated with certain precious stones; diamonds, for example, were thought to help cure melancholy.[73]

Regardless of the origins of the practice, melancholics such as the Duke of Lerma clearly profited from such gifts. Lerma customarily received jewels when he was bled; Pinheiro da Veiga noted that Italian rulers sent jewels to Lerma when they heard he was sick. The Portuguese chronicler mentioned that on one occasion, Lerma's earnings from such presents amounted to as much as 200,000 cruzadas.[74] When Lerma became melancholic after the queen refused to give birth in his house, Philip consoled him by sending him pearls from the royal collection which were valued at 30,000 ducats.[75] Lerma, however, preferred cash to jewels.[76] In July 1600, when Lerma was bled, Empress María decided to send him two jewels made of gold, another element thought to have curative powers. She consulted with Juan de Borja, however, and he informed her that the duke preferred cash because he had great expenses and could use the money. Consequently, the empress sent Lerma 2,000 escudos: the monetary value of the two jewels.[77]

This method was perhaps a standard practice for the Duke of Lerma; Juan Carrillo commented that on another occasion Lerma was able to pay most of his debts to a given individual using the gifts he had received for being bled.[78] The amounts of such gifts depended upon one's standing at the court. While Lerma could command 2,000 escudos, his close associate and dependent Pedro Franqueza received only 1,000. The Duke of Infantado, councillor of state to Philip III, received only 400.[79]

Financial rewards from melancholy and bleeding do not seem to have been uppermost in the mind of Empress María, Margaret of Austria, or Margaret of the Cross. Instead, their crucial concerns seem to have been the political leverage and the personal attention they could derive from melancholic bouts. The three Habsburg women greatly resented Lerma's attempts to exclude them from political decisions at the Spanish court. As key figures in the diplomatic network of the Austrian Habsburgs in Spain, these women needed to find ways to bring the petitions of the Austrian Habsburgs to the attention of Philip and his ministers. For these women, illness often served as a means of drawing attention to themselves, protesting actions taken by Philip III and his ministers, and expressing their political opinions. Maladies such as melancholy might have been part of the women's strategy to exercise power in a predominantly male political world. Illness was an effective tool for these women, one that took advantage of male notions of the weak female constitution and inverted them in order to afford royal women greater power and control.

Conclusion

Women and Spanish Policy
at the Court of Philip III

M Y EXAMINATION OF Habsburg women at the court of Philip III forces us to modify some of our notions about politics in the early modern era. It was clear to the Habsburg women, as it was to their contemporaries, that politics and decision making were not solely a male pursuit. Ambassadors, special envoys, nuncios, archdukes, emperors, and kings readily recognized the crucial political power and positions of Empress María, Margaret of Austria, and Margaret of the Cross. They knew to employ these women as intermediaries for them at the Spanish court and as avenues to the Austrian Habsburgs. Although this was clear to contemporaries, it has been slightly less so to modern historians, who have tended to view the early modern Spanish court as a relatively closed institution within which only councillors, privados, and kings contemplated and enacted policy.

This traditional view of the early modern court is not incorrect, merely incomplete. The Council of State, the privado, and the king were only *some* of the players in early modern European politics. Confessors (whose political importance has long been understood), family associates, court attendants, and especially royal women were also important political actors.[1] Even as modern historians begin to incorporate women into the narrative of the past, they do not always appreciate precisely how politically active these women were.

In exercising a political voice, Empress María, Margaret of Austria, and Margaret of the Cross were following in the footsteps of a long line of politically active Habsburg women,[2] who had been educated and trained to serve the varied needs of the dynasty, which were often political in nature. Undoubtedly, the three women at Philip's court had been brought up to expect that they would spend their lives serving the greater goals of the House of Austria. For this very reason, observers such as Juan de Borja and Hans Khevenhüller hesitated to approve Margaret of the Cross's decision to enter the Descalzas convent. The dynasty's greater need during that time seemed to be a new wife for Philip II. Yet, even as she entered the cloistered convent, Margaret of the Cross knew that she was not relinquishing her obligation to the Habsburg family. She continued to work for her relatives, helping them negotiate issues and assisting them in settling thorny problems.

Habsburg women took their political roles as a given; they expected to have political influence and power and to use them to assist the dynasty in furthering its political, military, and territorial goals. Whenever that role was threatened (as when Lerma attempted to block access to Philip), the Habsburg women reacted strongly to protect their interests. In so doing, they were acting not only for the greater benefit of the House of Austria but also to safeguard the personal power that political influence accorded them. In fact, for these women, serving the House of Austria was in most cases indistinguishable from serving their own personal needs. As women, Empress María, Margaret of Austria, and Margaret of the Cross knew how to negotiate and work through informal and indirect means, as well as through formal avenues of power. They were able to use personal contacts to reach councillors and rulers, and they wrote or met directly with influential individuals. All of these methods served them well at the Spanish court.

My examination of political women during the reign of Philip III has also demonstrated the need for some revision of the historiographical view of the way early modern politics functioned. We have seen that in Spain, at least, the court was a highly flexible institution. Politics were often discussed and decisions apparently reached in gardens, private homes, hunting lodges, and convents, in addition to the more obvious sites of governmental deliberation such as the meeting rooms of the Council of State. This expanded court was a critical feature of Philip III's reign, and it was undoubtedly not unique to seventeenth-century Spain.

Perhaps what was occurring in the first two decades of the seventeenth century was the movement away from an earlier, "premodern" era of politics, in which informal contacts and quasi-official locations were just as important to the political decision making process as were regular Council of State meetings and the advice of privados to kings. The ascent of figures such as the Duke of Lerma and later the Count-Duke of Olivares, seen from this perspective, was an attempt to cut through some of this older political culture to create a more "rational," or "modern," political system. In the early seventeenth century these two political cultures contested with each other for dominance in the political process. It was not obvious to contemporaries what the outcome of that struggle would be. To us, it is clear that the system of "rational" policymaking gradually supplanted the more informal political culture represented by, among others, the Habsburg women. This process, however, had clearly not been completed by 1618 and the coming of the Thirty Years' War. Indeed, it was the contention in Spain between these two political cultures which made Spanish policy in the preceding two decades inconsistent with that of the Austrian Habsburgs and which made Spain's eventual entry into that fateful conflict all the more likely.

This expanded court, at which women played crucial roles, was not only spatially flexible, it also featured fluid alliance systems. Historians have sought in vain to reduce early modern Spanish politics (and those of other European countries) to easily discernible camps, cliques, or factions. My examination of Philip III's court has shown that all such efforts are bound to fail; alliances were not firm, nor were camps longstanding in the early seventeenth century. Although Empress María, Margaret of Austria, and Margaret of the Cross clearly represented Austrian interests in Madrid or Valladolid, they were willing to use a variety of persons and techniques to pursue those policies. Some allies, such as Hans Khevenhüller, were long-term associates of the women; others, such as Magdalena de Guzmán, started out as political appointees of Lerma only later to gravitate toward the political policies of the women. Still others, like Juan de Borja, straddled the line between the women's interests and Lerma's agenda.

What is clear is that although the alliances were fluid, policies generally were not. The women at the court, like Lerma himself, followed a relatively consistent policy: they coupled Spanish interests to Central European designs. The Habsburg women consistently defended the idea that Spain was part of a European—not an Iberian, a Mediterranean, or even a New World—empire. Thus, their influence, both in its direct and indirect instances, kept Spain heavily involved in European affairs, undoubtedly much to the consternation of a statesman such as Lerma.

In order to work within the fluid networks of the court and to make policy sympathetic to their position, these imperial women employed numerous strategies, many of which revolved around the use and manipulation of rhetoric and images of women—rhetoric and images that were quite strong in the early modern period. The concepts of piety, illness, and family could all be used to attempt to limit the influence of powerful women. Powerful women, in turn, could use these same concepts and images to subvert attempts to limit their influence. Empress María, Margaret of Austria, and Margaret of the Cross not only used piety and illness defensively to ward off the attempts to marginalize them politically; they also used piety and illness as offensive strategies to pursue political objectives and to put political men on the defensive. At times, the use of such tactics—as in the melancholic battles between Lerma and Empress María—reached the level of an elaborate linguistic game.

These rhetorical strategies are fascinating in themselves, but they are also crucial to our understanding of early modern Spanish political culture. Historians have fortunately become much more sensitive to language as an object of study in recent years. Clearly this discussion of the early modern court of Philip III, its political decision making process, and the essential roles played by women within both has been greatly enriched by an examination of the rhetorical strategies employed by Empress María, Margaret of Austria, and Margaret of the Cross. I do not side with those who claim that discursive strategies are everything, but clearly they formed an important part of early modern political culture and were central to the political roles played by women at the time.

My study of these three Habsburg women provides a means of analyzing exactly how women exercised political power. Historians have too often overlooked Empress María, Margaret of Austria, and Margaret of the Cross because these women are not regularly mentioned in the consultas of the Council of State, which record the decisions taken by this governmental institution. Historians have also been unable to look beyond the devotional representations of these women written by observers such as Rodrigo Mendes Silva, Jerónimo de Florencia, Diego de Guzmán, Juan de la Palma, and Hortensio Paravicino. The three women have been categorized as pious women who were more concerned with prayer than with politics. Yet, as historians have begun to recognize, piety often served as a means of empowerment, particularly for women.[3]

The Habsburg women used devotional practices as a way to gain a reputation for sanctity and thereby win secular and political influence in their own lifetime, as well as to attain immortality after their death. My study of these women shows, therefore, that we should not dismiss them as political players because of their attention to pious deeds. We should certainly not think of them as women who separated religious and political concerns. In fact, for the Habsburg women, no distinct lines separated religion, family, and politics. Empress María, Margaret of Austria, and Margaret of the Cross drew strength from religious, familial, marital, and political ties. Far from limiting the women, piety, family, and devotion gave them the means to find a voice and to gain personal and political influence. Margaret of Austria was hailed as a saint and martyr at her death.[4] The queen's reputation for sanctity helped sustain continued criticism of Rodrigo Calderón, Lerma's closest associate, during the last ten years of Philip's reign—long after Margaret's death. When Calderón faced prosecution for poisoning the queen and for other alleged charges, his crime seemed all the worse because he was suspected of having murdered a woman renowned for her piety and her pursuit of peace.

Historians should attach importance to the pious deeds of these women and to their representations as devout women precisely because the Habsburg women's contemporaries did so. These women were remembered and respected because they were known to be religious women. This recognition is a first step toward reexamining the documents of the time. Contemporaries did note the political influence of these women: ambassadors recorded visiting the Habsburg women, working through them, and discussing political decisions with them. Lerma and his associates certainly recognized the power exercised by these women and attempted to find ways to curb their influence. Venetian ambassadors found it necessary to add these women to their list of prominent people at the court whose favor needed to be won. The Austrian Habsburgs regularly directed their petitions to them.

My examination of the influence of Empress María, Margaret of Austria, and Margaret of the Cross more accurately reflects the political reality of Philip III's court than have previous studies, which have overlooked the roles played by these women. Historians such as Ciriaco Pérez Bustamante and María Jesús Pérez Martín recognized that Empress María and Margaret of Austria exercised influence at the court, but they never fully examined or analyzed this influence. Moreover, they argued that the Duke of Lerma successfully eliminated any influence that these women had. Furthermore, these and other historians never examined the influence of Margaret of the Cross. Her life as a cloistered nun seemed to ensure that she had no interest or role in politics. However, this assumption needs to be challenged, especially in view of the excellent studies done on the involvement of nuns in secular matters.[5] The pious activities of the three Habsburg women did not remove them from the center of political action. Philip III, the Duke of Lerma, councillors, and ambassadors all regularly followed a rigid schedule of devotional practices. The religious and the political world often overlapped in such a way that pious nuns and devout women could gain Philip III's ear.

In a similar fashion, the illnesses that characterized the lives of the Habsburg women could function as a path to political influence. Illness actually served to empower both men and women at the Spanish court. It served as a mechanism to gain attention, favor, and rewards. Through complaints of illness, Empress María received royal visits, Margaret of Austria kept her husband close by, and the Duke of Lerma paid his debts. In Margaret of the Cross's case, infirmity increased her reputation for sanctity, which in turn motivated influential individuals to visit her. Likewise, pregnancy also served as a means for Margaret of Austria to retain her husband's attention and increase his devotion to her. The queen certainly knew that when she was pregnant, Philip would more readily try to please her in numerous ways. We should not assume, therefore, that women were confined by biology. Rather, they clearly knew how to take advantage of its apparent limitations and convert it into a strength.

The ultimate impact of the Habsburg women's influence needs to be understood in light of the course that Spanish politics took in the last decade of Philip III's reign. During this period, Philip paid increasing attention to Central Europe, going so far as to consider pursuing the imperial crown.[6] Although there were clear instances of Spanish-Austrian rivalry and tension, on the whole one can detect growing cooperation between the Spanish and the Austrian Habsburgs. While these developments occurred after the death of Empress María and Margaret of Austria, they were nevertheless the culmination of these two women's efforts, along with the continued efforts of Margaret of the Cross.

This is not to say that the Habsburg women were solely responsible for focusing Philip's attention on Central Europe. This shift was also a sign of the decreasing influence of the Duke of Lerma, who had tried to focus Spanish resources on the Iberian peninsula. As Lerma's personal influence over Philip declined and as the Sandovals maneuvered against one another for power at the court, the monarch looked elsewhere for support and advice. Events in Central Europe, particularly in Bohemia, demanded attention.[7] The Spanish monarch began to listen to individuals such as Baltasar de Zúñiga, Philip's ambassador to the imperial court, who advised him that the future of the Spanish monarchy lay in Central Europe. As early as 1612, Zúñiga urged Philip III to have his sons educated in Bohemian and German because he believed that this would improve their chances of winning the Bohemian crown. Zúñiga argued that Bohemia was the key to Europe.[8] By 1618, when Spain intervened to help the Austrian Habsburgs put down the Bohemian revolt, Philip chose the agenda of the Habsburg women at his court and of individuals such as Zúñiga.[9] By that time, the king was convinced that the destiny of the Spanish monarchy was intimately tied to the fortunes of the Austrian Habsburgs.

Spain's focus on Central Europe also indicates that Philip was conscious of a need to work closely with the Austrian Habsburgs. In the period directly preceding the Thirty Years' War, the Habsburgs believed that their power was increasingly under attack. They thought that there was a concerted effort on the part of the English, the Dutch, the Venetians, and German Protestants to undermine Habsburg power. The perceived attack was seen to be against both the Austrian and the Spanish Habsburgs. Philip therefore progressively identified with the Austrian Habsburgs, at least insofar as Habsburg territory needed to be defended. For Philip, it was in the Spanish monarchy's best interest to cooperate with his Austrian relatives and to work together on common defense. In particular, Philip cooperated with his brother-in-law, Archduke Ferdinand. The future of the Austrian Habsburgs clearly lay with Ferdinand because, unlike the other Austrian Habsburgs, Ferdinand had several male (and female) heirs. Moreover, through Margaret of Austria's intervention, Philip had regularly favored and assisted Ferdinand. Margaret of the Cross's efforts furthered this cooperation during the period from 1611 to 1621; its most visible manifestation was in Spanish assistance to Archduke Ferdinand in suppressing the Bohemian revolt.

Ironically, for those who would romanticize the role of these imperial women, this European focus would prove disastrous for Spain. The Habsburg women thought primarily of the needs of the House of Austria and of their own power and reputation, not necessarily of the needs of the Spanish monarchy. By encouraging Philip to assist the Austrian Habsburgs financially, the women helped to involve the monarchy in a war that was ultimately devastating for Spain. This attention to Central Europe prevented Philip and his government from focusing attention on the Iberian peninsula. Instead, the Spanish government continued to spread itself thin over most of Europe and to mismanage its financial resources. Involvement in the Thirty Years' War may not have been the sole cause of the historic "decline" of Spain, but it was certainly injurious to the economic and political position of the Iberian peninsula in European power politics.[10]

Appendix

Key Individuals during the Reign of Philip III

ALBERT, ARCHDUKE OF AUSTRIA AND FLANDERS (1559–1621): son of Empress María and Maximilian II. Philip II appointed him governor of Portugal in 1583. He married Isabel Clara Eugenia, Philip II's daughter, and with her ruled the Netherlands until his death.

ALIAGA, FRAY LUIS DE (1565–1626): Dominican priest, served as Lerma's confessor before being appointed confessor to Philip III in 1608 and also served as councillor of state. He became one of Lerma's principal rivals at the court and retained the king's favor until Philip's death, in 1621. With Philip IV's ascent to power, Aliaga was dismissed from court and exiled to a small town in Aragón.

BORJA, JUAN DE (1533–1606): the Duke of Lerma's uncle, served as ambassador to Central Europe from 1578 until 1581, when he accompanied Empress María from Central Europe to Madrid. He then became Empress María's mayordomo mayor. He also served on the Council of Portugal and the Council of Finance. After the empress's death, he became Queen Margaret of Austria's mayordomo, a position he held until his own death.

CALDERÓN, RODRIGO (1570–1621): along with Franqueza, one of the Duke of Lerma's closest associates. Through Lerma's efforts, he received the titles of Count of Oliva and Marquis of Sieteiglesias. In 1611, Calderón was accused of poisoning the queen but was later acquitted of the charges. To escape criticism, Calderón left Spain to serve as ambassador first to Venice and then to Flanders. He never regained his former favor at the court. In 1621, he was arrested for his participation in the financial misdealings associated with the Duke of Lerma's circle. His goods were seized and he was eventually executed for crimes against the state.

CARRILLO, JUAN (d. 1616): Franciscan priest and representative of Archduke Albert at the Spanish court. He also served as Empress María's secretary at the Descalzas. With Empress María's assistance, he became a secretary of the Inquisition. In 1616, while serving as confessor to the nuns of the Descalzas, he wrote a history of the convent, entitled *Relación histórica de la real fundación del Monasterio de las Descalzas de Santa Clara de la villa de Madrid.*

FERDINAND II OF AUSTRIA (1578–1637): brother of Margaret of Austria, son of Archduchess Maria of Bavaria and Habsburg Archduke Karl of Styria. Ferdinand became King of Bohemia and Hungary in 1617 and Holy Roman Emperor in 1618. His implementation of Counter Reformation policies in Central Europe is considered to be a major factor behind the outbreak of the Thirty Years' War (1618–48).

FLORENCIA, JERÓNIMO DE (1565–1633): Jesuit priest and court preacher under Philip III. He wrote the eulogies commemorating the lives of Empress María and Margaret of Austria. One of Florencia's sermons allegedly inspired Philip III to dismiss the Duke of Lerma. Under Philip IV, Florencia served as confessor to the king's brothers and was appointed to a ten-man junta organized to see to the moral regeneration of the Spanish kingdoms.

FRANQUEZA, PEDRO (1573–1614): one of the Duke of Lerma's closest collaborators. He served on the Council of Aragón in the 1580s. In 1598, he was appointed secretary of state for Italian matters. He became secretary to Queen Margaret of Austria and later served as a secretary of the Inquisition and a principal member of the Junta de Desempeño. Through Lerma's patronage, Franqueza acquired the title of Count of Villalonga. In 1607, he was arrested on charges of financial corruption; he was imprisoned and his goods were seized. He died in prison.

GÓMEZ DE SANDOVAL Y ROJAS, FRANCISCO, FIRST DUKE OF LERMA (1552?–1625): Fifth Marquis of Denia, appointed viceroy of Valencia in 1595. He returned to court in 1597, where he gained great favor with Prince Philip (the future Philip III). Upon Philip III's accession, he quickly became the king's favorite (*privado*). In 1599, Philip III made him the first Duke of Lerma. He was appointed a cardinal in 1618, the same year that he was dismissed from court.

GUZMÁN, DIEGO DE (d. 1631): Jesuit priest and Archbishop of Seville, appointed chaplain of the Descalzas Reales in 1602. In 1608 he was named Philip III's royal almoner, and in 1610 he received the additional appointment of tutor to the Infanta Anne. He died in January 1631 while accompanying the Infanta Mariana to Central Europe for her marriage to the future Ferdinand III. He was buried in the Jesuit college in Ávila.

Guzmán, Magdalena de, Marquesa del Valle (d. 1621): With Lerma's
assistance, she became a lady-in-waiting to Margaret of Austria and then was appointed the guardian (*aya*) of the Infanta Anne. In October 1603, however, the
Marquesa del Valle was arrested for supposed abuse of her office. She was sentenced to house arrest in Logroño, and in 1608 she was freed, although she was
not allowed to visit the court. She finally returned to court after Philip III's
death, and she died there, in 1621.

Haller, Richard (1550–1612): born in Nuremberg, Haller entered the Jesuit
order in 1569. He served as rector of the Jesuit universities in Innsbruck and In-
golstadt (Bavaria) before becoming rector at the Jesuit university in Graz, where
he came to the attention of members of the Styrian branch of the Habsburgs,
who appointed him confessor to Margaret of Austria. In this position, he accompanied Margaret to Madrid, where he died, in 1612.

Isabel Clara Eugenia (1566–1633): sister of Philip III and daughter of Philip
II and his third wife, Isabel of Valois. She served as joint ruler, with Archduke
Albert, of the Netherlands and as sole ruler from 1621 until her death.

Khevenhüller, Johann (Hans) (1538–1606): imperial ambassador to the
Spanish court who served under Maximilian II and Rudolf II. Khevenhüller
originally went to Spain as a special envoy before being appointed resident am-
bassador in 1573. When Philip III moved the Spanish court to Valladolid,
Khevenhüller remained in Madrid to be close to Empress María. He died in
Spain.

Margaret of Austria (1584–1611): daughter of Archduchess Maria of Bavaria
and Karl of Styria. She married Philip III in 1599 and gave birth to eight children. Queen Margaret died from complications of childbirth.

Margaret of the Cross (1567–1633): youngest daughter of Empress María
and Maximilian II. She entered the Descalzas convent in Madrid and took the
vows of a cloistered Franciscan nun in 1585. She lived in the convent until her
death.

Maria of Bavaria, Archduchess (1553–1608): from the Wittelsbach family,
she married Karl of Styria and was the mother of Queen Margaret of Austria and
of Ferdinand II. She was instrumental in educating her daughter and in choosing Richard Haller as Margaret's confessor. She accompanied her daughter on
the trip from Central Europe to Spain.

MARÍA, EMPRESS (1528–1603): daughter of Charles V, she married Maximilian II and served with him as coregent of Castile from 1548 to 1551. After Maximilian's death, in 1581, María returned to Spain. She lived in the Descalzas convent in Madrid, where she died.

MATTHIAS I (1557–1619): son of Empress María and Maximilian II. Matthias became King of Hungary in 1608, King of Bohemia in 1611, and Holy Roman Emperor in 1612, a title he held until his death, in 1619.

PHILIP III (1578–1621): son of Philip II and his fourth wife, Anne (Empress María's daughter). As prince, he began to attend the meetings of the Junta de Gobierno, created by Philip II in 1593 as an intermediary body between the king and the councils. He assumed the throne in 1598, at the age of twenty.

RUDOLF II (1552–1612): eldest son of Empress María and Maximilian II, he succeeded his father as Holy Roman Emperor. Known as an eccentric, melancholic emperor, he never married and refused to declare an heir. It was only through open conflict that his brother, Matthias, was able to become King of Bohemia and Hungary before Rudolf's death.

SANDOVAL, ROYAS Y DE LA CERDA, CRISTÓBAL DE, FIRST DUKE OF UCEDA (1577–1624): eldest son of the Duke of Lerma, he became his father's chief rival. Philip IV dismissed him from the court and he died in disgrace in Alcalá de Henares.

SAN JOSÉ, SOR MARIANA DE (1568–1638): Augustinian nun whom Margaret of Austria met in Palencia. In 1611, she went to Madrid at the queen's insistence in order to reform the convent of Santa Isabel. She became the first prioress of the royal convent of the Encarnación, which the queen founded.

SIDONIA RIDERER, MARIA: accompanied Margaret of Austria from Central Europe to Madrid in 1599. Maria Sidonia served as Margaret's lady-in-waiting and closest friend. She was even referred to as the queen's *privada*. In 1603, Maria Sidonia married the Count of Barajas.

ZÚÑIGA, BALTASAR DE (1561–1622): served as ambassador to Flanders from 1599 to 1603 and ambassador at the French court in Paris from 1603 to 1606. In 1608, he became the Spanish ambassador at the imperial court. In 1617, he returned to Madrid, where he became a councillor of state. In 1619 he was appointed tutor to Prince Philip (the future Philip IV). Along with his nephew, the Count-Duke of Olivares, he gained great favor with Philip IV, and he was in effect Philip IV's first minister.

Abbreviations

Add. Ms.	Additional Manuscript
AGR	Archives Générales du Royaume, Brussels
AGS	Archivo General de Simancas
AHN	Archivo Histórico Nacional
AHP	Archivo Histórico de Protocoles
APR	Archivo del Palacio Real
ARMEN	Archivo del Real Monasterio de la Encarnación
ASV	Archivio Segreto Vaticano
BL	British Library
BN, Madrid	Biblioteca Nacional, Madrid
Codoin	*Colección de documentos inéditos para la historia de España*
IVDJ	Instituto Valencia de Don Juan
HHStA	Haus-, Hof-, und Staatsarchiv, Vienna
K	Karton
Leg.	Legajo
L.	Libro
Ms.	Manuscript
ÖNB	Österreichische Nationalbibliothek
PR	Patronato Real
RAH	Real Academia de la Historia
SDK	Spanien Diplomatische Korrespondenz
SHK	Spanien Hofkorrespondenz
SV	Spanien Varia

Notes

Introduction

1. BN, Madrid, Ms. 2751, "Historia de Joan Kevenhuller de Aichelberg," 1148–49.

2. ASV, Fondo Borghese, Ser. 2, no. 272, Nunziatura di Spagna, 1605–1606, fols. 58r–v.

3. Because her daughter, Anna, was Philip II's fourth wife, Empress María was also Philip III's grandmother.

4. John H. Elliott, *The Count-Duke of Olivares*; John H. Elliott and Angel García Sanz, *La España del Conde Duque de Olivares*; R. A. Stradling, *Philip IV and the Government of Spain, 1621–1665*.

5. Stradling, *Philip IV and the Government of Spain*, 18.

6. Ibid., 8. Stradling attributes this interpretation to Patrick Williams.

7. See, e.g., Ciriaco Pérez Bustamante, *La España de Felipe III*, vol. 24 of Menéndez Pidal's *Historia de España*, 105–10. The one historian to contradict this view is Patrick Williams, "Lerma, Old Castile, and the Travels of Philip III of Spain," 385 n. 22.

8. For brief discussions of the hostility between the queen and Lerma see Williams, "Lerma, Old Castile, and the Travels of Philip III," 389–90, 395; Stradling, *Philip IV and the Government of Spain*, 6; Antonio Feros Carrasco, "Gobierno de corte y patronazgo real en el reinado de Felipe III (1598–1618)." 44–47; and María Jesús Pérez Martín, *Margarita de Austria, Reina de España*.

9. Elliott, *The Count-Duke of Olivares*, 56–60; Peter Brightwell, "The Spanish Origins of the Thirty Years' War," 411–12; Bohdan Chudoba, *Spain and the Empire*, 219–20.

10. See Williams, "Lerma, Old Castile, and the Travels of Philip III," 396; Stradling, *Philip IV and the Government of Spain*, 7; and Magdalena S. Sánchez, "A House Divided: Spain, Austria, and the Bohemian and Hungarian Successions."

11. *Privanza* refers to an individual's enjoyment of royal favor. It also refers to the years that a royal favorite had influence with a monarch. It can broadly mean the power that a person such as Lerma gained by having a monarch's favor.

12. Antonio Feros, "The King's Favorite, the Duke of Lerma: Power, Wealth, and Court Culture in the Reign of Philip III of Spain, 1598–1621"; and Feros Carrasco, "Gobierno de corte y patronazgo real."

13. Margaret of Austria governed the Netherlands from 1507 to 1515 and again from 1519 to 1530. Upon her death she was replaced by María of Hungary, who ruled until 1555.

14. See Sharon Kettering, "The Patronage Power of Early Modern French Noblewomen"; Barbara J. Harris, "Women and Politics in Early Tudor England"; and Barbara A. Hanawalt, "Lady Honor Lisle's Networks of Influence," in Mary Erler and Maryanne Kowaleski, eds., *Women and Power in the Middle Ages*.

15. BN, Madrid, Ms. 2751, "Historia de Joan Kevenhuller de Aichelberg," 9 March 1604, 1049. In his diary, Hans Khevenhüller also recorded numerous incidents of meetings taking place in Juan de Borja's garden house (*huerta*) and in the Casa del Campo, during both Philip II's and Philip III's reigns. See, e.g., Hans Khevenhüller, *Geheimes Tagebuch*, 136, 145–46, 151, 168, 255, 261.

16. See RAH, Colección Salazar y Castro, Ms. 9/476, fol. 17, 12 May 1609; Ms. 9/476, fol. 3, 11 April; fols. 35v–36, 9 May; fol. 36, 11 May; fol. 36, 12 May. Diego de Guzmán noted that on 18 February 1610, in the gallery leading to the garden of the royal palace, the king met with the presidents of the Councils of Castile, the Indies, Finance, and Military Orders, along with Lerma, Philip's mayordomos and "los demas de la camara." See RAH, Colección Salazar y Castro, Ms. 9/476, fol. 128.

17. On the development of modern diplomacy see Garrett Mattingly, *Renaissance Diplomacy*. See also several of the essays in Malcolm R. Thorp and Arthur J. Slavin, eds., *Politics, Religion, and Diplomacy in Early Modern Europe*, in particular, Vincent Ilardi, "The First Permanent Embassy outside Italy: The Milanese Embassy at the French Court, 1464–1483," 1–18, and Gary M. Bell, "Elizabethan Diplomacy: The Subtle Revolution," 267–88.

18. The success of Spanish diplomacy in Central Europe during the reigns of Philip II and Philip III depended in large part upon the network of personal connections built up under the two skilled Spanish ambassadors to the imperial court, Guillén de San Clemente (1581–1608) and Baltasar de Zúñiga (1608–17). These two ambassadors were particularly valued for their skills in forming these networks; see Chudoba, *Spain and the Empire*, 195.

19. On this problem, see Charles Howard Carter, "The Ambassadors of Early Modern Europe: Patterns of Diplomatic Representation in the Early Seventeenth Century," in Charles Howard Carter, ed., *From the Renaissance to the Counter-Reformation*.

20. Karl Vocelka, "Matthias contra Rudolf. Zur politischen Propaganda in der Zeit des Bruderzwistes." See also R. J. W. Evans, *Rudolf II and His World*, 60.

21. Jonathan I. Israel, *The Dutch Republic and the Hispanic World, 1606–1661*, 12–14; Bernardo José García García, *La Pax Hispanica*, 27–30, 83–88; John H. Elliott, "Foreign Policy and Domestic Crisis: Spain, 1598–1659," in *Spain and Its World, 1500–1700*, 116–18; Brightwell, "The Spanish Origins of the Thirty Years' War," 423–24.

Chapter 1: Expanding the Spanish Court

1. John Elliott has argued that privacy was an essential aspect of Spanish kingship, and in fact Elliott describes Spanish kingship as "private kingship" as opposed to France's "public kingship." J. H. Elliott, "The Court of the Spanish Habsburgs: A Peculiar Institution?" in *Spain and Its World, 1500–1700*, 151. See also HHStA, SV, K 4, fols. 15r–v, 7 November 1601.

2. In 1607, the queen's private household alone numbered 285 individuals. See AGS, Dirección General del Tesoro, Inventario 24, Leg. 577, "Consignación de Gastos." See also Elliott, "The Court of the Spanish Habsburgs," 156.

3. The main question here is what in fact constituted an early modern court. As Jonathan Brown and John Elliott explain, the term *court* lacked a precise meaning. In their study of the Buen Retiro in Madrid, Brown and Elliott note the fluid characteristics of the seventeenth-century Spanish court: "The exact composition and size of the Spanish court therefore escape easy definition. Too many functions were duplicated, and there were too many blurred edges at the points where specific functions ended but privileged rights of access were nonetheless allowed. 'Court' was, by its nature, an imprecise word, expressing at once the place, the pomp and the persons associated with the presence of the king." Jonathan Brown and J. H. Elliott, *A Palace for a King*, 35–36. Norbert Elias defines the court as a place where "hundreds and often thousands of people were bound together in one place by peculiar restraints which they and outsiders applied to each other and to themselves." Norbert Elias, *The Court Society*, 35.

4. Borja was one of the Duke of Lerma's closest associates and regularly formed part of the juntas Lerma organized to discuss state matters. See Antonio Feros Carrasco, "Felipe III: Política interior," in *La Crisis del siglo xvii*, 40. On Borja, see his unedited correspondence, BL, Add. Mss. 28344; 28345; 28422; 28423; 28424; 28425.

5. See, for example, Hans Khevenhüller, *Geheimes Tagebuch*, 252 (13 October 1599); 255 (18 January 1600); 256 (6 February 1600); 270 (November 1600).

6. Luis Cabrera de Córdoba, *Relaciones de las cosas sucedidas en la corte de España desde 1599 hasta 1614*, 45–46, 6 November 1599; Khevenhüller, *Geheimes Tagebuch*, 252, 255, 256.

7. For a list of the places and homes outside Madrid which Philip III visited from 1599 to 1606 see BN, Madrid, Ms. 2347, fols. 343–58v: "Las jornadas q ha hecho Su Md desde el año de 1599 . . . hasta fin del de 1606."

8. RAH, Colección Salazar y Castro, Ms. 9/477, "Memorias del Cardenal Diego de Guzmán de los años 1610 y 1611," fols. 4r–v; Virginia Tovar Martín, "El pasadizo, forma arquitectónica encubierta en el Madrid de los siglos xvii y xviii," 34.

9. Many observers commented on Philip III's piety and his observation of religious duties. See, for example, Jacobo Sobieski's contemporary account of Philip III and

his court, "El reino de España," in José García Mercadal, ed., *Viajes de extranjeros por España y Portugal*, vol. 2: 333. See also "Relazione di Ottaviano Bon," 21 December 1602, in Nicolò Barozzi and Guglielmo Berchet, *Relazioni degli stati europei. Lette al Senato dagli ambasciatori Veneti nel secolo decimosettimo*, 246: "Il re Filippo . . . e . . . religiosissimo, di bonta e di costumi exemplare." See also Ana Castro Egas, *Eternidad del rey Don Felipe III* (Madrid, 1629).

10. Diego de Guzmán, Philip III's royal almoner, details the numerous religious activities of the queen. See RAH, Colección Salazar y Castro, Mss. 9/476 and 9/477. See also Diego de Guzmán, *Reina Católica: Vida y muerte de Doña Margarita de Austria, Reina de España*; María Jesús Pérez Martín, *Margarita de Austria*, 130–33, 139–42.

11. See RAH, Colección Salazar y Castro, Ms. 9/476, fols. 57–60.

12. Diego de Guzmán recorded occasions on which he said mass for the king or queen or for both monarchs. Ibid., fol. 94, 21 October 1609. Confessors to Philip III were: Gaspar de Córdoba (1598–1604); Diego de Mardones (1604–6); Jerónimo Javierre (1606–8); Luis de Aliaga (1608–21).

13. ASV, Correspondencia del Patriarca de Alexandria, nuncio in Spain, Fondo Borghese, Ser. 1, no. 649, fols. 21r–v, carta del nuncio a Cardenal Aldobrandino, Madrid, 10 January 1599; fols. 199r–v, carta del nuncio a Aldobrandino, 6 June 1599; fols. 391r–93v, carta del nuncio a Aldobrandino, Zaragoza, 28 September 1599. For the queen's friendship with nuns, see Luis Muñoz, *Vida y virtudes de la venerable Madre Mariana de San Joseph*, 222–23.

14. On the Encarnación, see María Leticia Sánchez Hernández, *El Monasterio de la Encarnación de Madrid: Un modelo de vida religiosa en el siglo xvii*.

15. For example, on 7 November 1601, the king and queen went together to Nuestra Señora de Santo Lorente to attend mass. HHStA, SV, K4, Avisos 1600–1604, fols. 11r, 15r.

16. On the importance, especially the political importance, of rituals, see Sean Wilentz, ed., *Rites of Power: Symbolism, Ritual, and Politics since the Middle Ages*.

17. RAH, Colección Salazar y Castro, Ms. 9/477, fols. 87v–88r.

18. Ibid., Ms. 9/476, fols. 7v, 17r–v.

19. Ibid., Ms. 9/476, fol. 28v, 1609.

20. Khevenhüller, *Geheimes Tagebuch*, passim.

21. Ibid., 2 (13 September 1600); BN, Madrid, Ms. 2751, "Historia de Joan Kevenhuller de Aichelberg," 1049.

22. The monarchs' visits were not limited to these religious occasions. Philip often went in the late evening to visit Empress María and Margaret of the Cross, especially when these women were sick. See, for example, Cabrera de Córdoba, *Relaciones de las cosas sucedidas*, 456, 22 November 1611.

23. From 1599 to 1601, Empress María also went to the royal apartments on a regular basis to visit Margaret of Austria. See BL, Add. Ms. 28422, fol. 278, 2 February 1600.

24. AGR, Sécretairerie d'État et de Guerre, no. 490, Correspondance de l'Archiduc Albert avec Juan Carrillo, fol. 47, 12 February 1600.

25. Although Lerma's power over the monarch in 1600 was sufficient to overrule Empress María, this power did not last throughout Philip III's reign.

26. RAH, Colección Salazar y Castro, Ms. 9/476, fols. 122v–23r, 6 January 1610.

27. Ibid., fol. 41, 30 May 1609. Feliciano Barrios includes Diego de Guzmán on the list of Philip III's councillors of state, but does not give a date of appointment. See Feliciano Barrios, *El Consejo de Estado de la monarquía española*, 349. On Diego de Guzmán, see "Memorias del Cardenal Diego de Guzmán," RAH, Colección Salazar y Castro, Mss. 9/476 and 9/477; and Diego Ortiz de Zúñiga, *Anales eclesiásticos y seculares de la muy noble y muy leal ciudad de Sevilla*, 645–59.

28. See, e.g., RAH, Colección Salazar y Castro, Ms. 9/476, fol. 94.

29. In January 1610, Guzmán was appointed teacher of the Infanta Anne (usually known by her more famous name, Anne of Austria), an office he filled until the princess went to France to marry Louis XIII.

30. BL, Add. Ms. 28424, fol. 236, Borja to Lerma, 12 December 1601.

31. RAH, Colección Salazar y Castro, Ms. 9/476, fol. 33.

32. Ibid., fol. 67. On the relationship between the queen and Diego de Guzmán, see Magdalena Sánchez, "Confession and Complicity: Margarita de Austria, Richard Haller, S.J., and the Court of Philip III," 133–49.

33. José Luis Saenz Ruiz-Olalde, O.A.R., *Las Agustinas Recoletas de Santa Isabel la Real de Madrid*, 46–95. For the original documents from the queen and Diego de Guzmán concerning the reformation of Santa Isabel, see AHN, Clero, Leg. 7677, "Relación que la reyna nuestra señora mando enbiar a Don Francisco de Castro," 8 folios, n.p.

34. See Diego de Guzmán, *Reina Católica: Vida y muerte de Doña Margarita de Austria, Reina de España*, fols. 142r–v.

35. RAH, Colección Salazar y Castro, Ms. 9/476, fol. 124, 19 January 1610.

36. For an excellent and thorough look at the role played by one confessor to a Habsburg prince, see Robert Bireley, S.J., *Religion and Politics in the Age of the Counterreformation*.

37. On these disagreements, see Ciriaco Pérez Bustamante, *La España de Felipe III*, 142–43.

38. John H. Elliott, *Imperial Spain, 1469–1716*, 250–51.

39. On the debate over the New World inhabitants' rights and Charles V's policies regarding them, see Lewis Hanke, *The Spanish Struggle for Justice in the Conquest of America*; José Antonio Fernández Santamaría, *The State, War, and Peace: Spanish Political Thought in the Renaissance, 1516–1559*, 75–119, 196–236; Anthony Pagden, *Spanish Imperialism and the Political Imagination*, 13–36; and James Muldoon, *The Americas in the Spanish World Order: The Justification for Conquest in the Seventeenth Century*.

40. Elliott, *Imperial Spain*, 250.

41. For Cardinal Trejo's recommendations, see AGS, Estado Alemania, Leg. 2865, 1 September 1614, n.p. On the Bohemian and Hungarian successions and on Trejo's role, see Magdalena S. Sánchez, "A House Divided: Spain, Austria, and the Bohemian and Hungarian Successions."

42. Sobieski, "El reino de España," in García Mercadal, *Viajes de extranjeros*, 332.

43. "Relazione di Ottaviano Bon," 21 December 1602, in Barozzi and Berchet, *Relazioni degli stati europei*, 229–30, 251.

44. AHN, Osuna, Leg. 571, nos. 138–39, fol. 138.

45. Cabrera de Córdoba, *Relaciones de las cosas sucedidas*, 54, 1 January 1600. The Duchess of Lerma, the Duke of Lerma's wife, replaced the Duchess of Gandía (who had been chosen by Philip II as Margaret of Austria's chief attendant).

46. See Khevenhüller, *Geheimes Tagebuch*, 264 (9 January 1601).

47. BL, Add. Ms. 28423, fol. 145, Borja to Lerma, 31 July 1600. Borja noted the royal confessor's intervention in the Council of Finance on his behalf.

48. On Aliaga, see Bernardo José García García, "Fray Luis de Aliaga y la conciencia del Rey," in Flavio Rurale, ed., *La presenza dei regolari nelle corti d'Antico Regime: religione, politica e diplomazia*. On Aliaga's attempts to control the king by discrediting others, see Matías de Novoa, "Memorias de Matías de Novoa (1580–1621)," in *Codoin*, vols. 60–61, 122. On Aliaga's and Uceda's influence over Philip III see BN, Madrid, Ms. 17858, "Relaciones de 1618–1621," particularly fol. 173. See also Stradling, *Philip IV and the Government of Spain*, 7–10.

49. See Sobieski, "El reino de España," in García Mercadal, *Viajes de extranjeros*, 332. On the rumor that Gaspar de Córdoba had died because of his disagreement with the Duke of Lerma, see Cabrera de Córdoba, *Relaciones de las cosas sucedidas*, 218, 12 June 1604.

50. BN, Madrid, Ms. 2751, "Historia de Joan Kevenhuller de Aichelberg," 1008–9.

51. Pérez Bustamante, *La España de Felipe III*, 142.

52. Antonio Feros Carrasco, "Gobierno de corte y patronazgo real," 110.

53. On the relationship between Margaret of Austria and Richard Haller, and specifically on the overlapping of a confessor's religious and political duties, see Sánchez, "Confession and Complicity."

54. RAH, Colección Salazar y Castro, Ms. 9/476, fol. 39, 21 May 1609.

55. "Relazione di Ottaviano Bon," 21 December 1602, in Barozzi and Berchet, *Relazioni degli stati europei*, 247; and "Relazione di Francesco Soranzo," 11 October 1602, ibid.

56. On Haller's career, see Bernhard Duhr, *Geschichte der Jesuiten in den Ländern deutscher Zunge*; and Carlos Sommervogel, *Bibliothèque de la Compagnie de Jesus*, 49–50.

57. BN, Madrid, Ms. 2577, Sepúlveda, "Tomo segundo de la historia de varios sucesos de España y otras naciones, y de la universal Iglesia Catholica Romana hasta el año 1605 por el Padre Sepúlveda," fol. 69; "Relazione di Ottaviano Bon," in Barozzi and Berchet, *Relazioni degli stati europei*, 247.

58. See BN, Madrid, Ms. 2577, Sepúlveda, "Tomo segundo de la historia de varios sucesos de España," fol. 69, 1600.

59. Among other things, Haller was instrumental in promoting Spanish support for the Catholic League against the Protestants in Germany. See Johann Andritsch, "Landesfürstliche Berater am Grazer Hof (1564–1619)," in *Innerösterreich, 1564–1619*, 105; Karl Mayr, ed., *Von den Rüstungen Herzog Maximilians von Bayern bis zum Aufbruch der Passauer*, vol. 8 of Felix Stieve, ed., *Briefe und Acten zur Geschichte des Dreissigjährigen Krieges*, 35–36, 163–64.

60. See Mayr, ed., *Von den Rüstungen Herzog Maximilians von Bayern*, 752, Zúñiga to Philip III, 17 December 1610.

61. See Hilary Dansey Smith, *Preaching in the Spanish Golden Age: A Study of Some Preachers of the Reign of Philip III*.

62. Cabrera de Córdoba, *Relaciones de las cosas sucedidas*, 549–50.

63. See, for example, the sermon delivered by Jerónimo de Florencia at Margaret of Austria's death. BN, Madrid, Varios Especiales, 54–93: "Sermón que predicó a la Magestad del Rey Don Felipe III en las honras que Su Magestad hizo a la sereníssima Reyna D. Margarita su muger, que es en gloria, en San Gerónimo el Real de Madrid a 18 de noviembre de 1611," 18 November 1611.

64. On Florencia's political influence, particularly in the last year of Philip III's reign, see Matías de Novoa, "Memorias de Matías de Novoa," in *Codoin*, 121, 132; BN, Madrid, Ms. 17858, "Relaciones de 1618–21," fol. 290; BN, Madrid, Ms. 2352, "Sucesos de . . . 1621," fol. 9r.

65. See, for example, Guzmán's numerous references to Florencia's sermons in RAH, Colección Salazar y Castro, Ms. 9/477, fol. 64v, 3 January 1611.

66. Florencia delivered two sermons at the queen's death, the first dedicated to Philip III and the second, to the Duke of Lerma. For the first sermon, see Jerónimo de Florencia, "Sermón que predicó a la Magestad del Rey Don Felipe III," 18 November 1611. For the second, see Florencia, "Sermón segundo que predicó el Padre Gerónimo de Florencia," 19 December 1612, in Micael Avellan, *Oración fúnebre*, BN, Madrid, R/24245.

67. BN, Madrid, Ms. 2348, "Sucesos desde el año 1611 hasta 1617," fol. 402v.

68. John H. Elliott, *The Count-Duke of Olivares*, 45, 105.

69. Jodi Bilinkoff, *The Ávila of Saint Teresa: Religious Reform in a Sixteenth-Century City*, 187–96.

70. Novoa, "Memorias de Matías de Novoa," in *Codoin*, 104.

71. For Lerma's patronage of a convent, see J. Maria Palomares Ibañez, *El patronato del Duque de Lerma sobre el convento de San Pablo en Valladolid*.

72. Lerma also tried to imitate royalty by patronizing art and acquiring a collection of paintings. His artistic taste closely followed that of Philip II. See Sarah Schroth, "The Private Picture Collection of the Duke of Lerma."

73. BL, Add. Ms. 28422, fol. 254, 17 January 1600.

74. Elliott, "The Court of the Spanish Habsburgs," in *Spain and Its World, 1500–1700*, 149.

75. See, for example, RAH, Colección Salazar y Castro, Ms. 9/476, fol. 17, 12 May 1609; fol. 72, 28 July 1609; Ms. 9/477, fol. 34, 13 August 1610; fol. 85, 24 May 1611.

76. In 1609, Philip III actually gave these houses to the Duke of Lerma. In 1613, however, the monarch bought them back from Lerma for 33,000 ducats. See AGS, PR, Caja 34-137, fol. 19.

77. Diego de Guzmán recorded numerous incidents in which Philip III went to eat at the Duke of Lerma's house. See RAH, Colección Salazar y Castro, Ms. 9/476, fol. 2, 1609; fol. 18, 15 March 1609; fol. 18v, 21 March 1609; fol. 19v, 29 March 1609. On occasion, the king and queen both ate at Lerma's house: ibid., Ms. 9/476, fol. 22, 5 April 1609; ibid., Ms. 9/477, fol. 115v, 8 June 1611. The king ate much less frequently at Lerma's house in 1610 and 1611 than he did in 1609.

78. There are a few references to the queen's lunches with the Duke of Lerma. See, for example, RAH, Colección Salazar y Castro, Ms. 9/476, fol. 19v, 29 March 1609.

79. On Lerma's use of hunting and travel to isolate and control the monarch, see "Relazione di Girolamo Soranzo," 11 January 1611, in Barozzi and Berchet, *Relazioni degli stati europei*, 457. For a record of the many trips taken by Philip III, see BN, Madrid, Ms. 2347, fols. 343–58, "Las jornadas que ha hecho S.M." See also Williams, "Lerma, Old Castile, and the Travels of Philip III," 379–97.

80. Williams, "Lerma, Old Castile, and the Travels of Philip III," 389–90.

81. In order to reconstruct Philip III's travels throughout these years, and in order to determine if and when the queen accompanied him, I have used the following accounts: BN, Madrid, Ms. 2347, fols. 343–58, "Las jornadas que ha hecho S.M."; Cabrera de Córdoba, *Relaciones de las cosas sucedidas*. Patrick Williams also used these accounts in his article, "Lerma, Old Castile, and the Travels of Philip III"; however, Williams concentrates primarily on where the king traveled and on his relationship with Lerma, not paying much attention to the queen. While I have profited from reading the article by Williams, my own conclusions come primarily from my detailed reading of Ms. 2347 and the account by Cabrera de Córdoba. I ultimately ascribe a more important role to the queen than does Williams.

82. See BN, Madrid, Ms. 2577, Sepúlveda, "Tomo segundo de la historia de varios sucesos de España," fol. 85.

83. Cabrera de Córdoba, *Relaciones de las cosas sucedidas*, 54, 102, 161, 216, and 273. Aristocrats in England also had the custom of giving deer as gifts to other aristocrats. See Barbara J. Harris, "Women and Politics in Early Tudor England," 267; Barbara A. Hanawalt, "Lady Honor Lisle's Network of Influence," 195.

84. See Cabrera de Córdoba, *Relaciones de las cosas sucedidas*, 101–2, 123.

85. Ibid., 292.

86. Ibid., 107, 149, 211, 425.

87. Although her full name was Maria Sidonia Riderer, she was usually referred to as Maria Sidonia. I therefore refer to her throughout the book as Maria Sidonia.

88. Cabrera de Córdoba, *Relaciones de las cosas sucedidas*, 149, 211, 226, 231, 262–63, 273, 281, 314, 334, 402, 425.

89. Ibid., 200, 29 December 1603.

90. See HHStA, SHK, K 2, fol. 147v, Margaret of the Cross to Rudolf II, 29 August 1610.

91. See, for example, Cabrera de Córdoba, *Relaciones de las cosas sucedidas*, 453.

92. On the Council of State, see Barrios, *El Consejo de Estado*; and José María Cordero Torres, *El Consejo de Estado: Su trayectoria y perspectivas en España*.

93. Barrios, *El Consejo de Estado*, 97.

94. On the reorganization of the Council of State, see Patrick Williams, "Philip III and the Restoration of Spanish Government, 1598–1603"; and Charles Howard Carter, "The Nature of Spanish Government after Philip II."

95. By the beginning of Philip III's reign, there were fourteen councils within the Spanish government. These were the Councils of Aragón, Castile, the Chamber of Castile, Crusade, Finance, Flanders, the Indies, the Inquisition, Italy, Military Orders, Navarre, Portugal, State, and War.

96. BN, Madrid, Ms. 1174, "Relación que hiço . . . Simon Contarini," fols. 5v–6.

97. Feros Carrasco, "Felipe III: Política interior," 40–42.

98. Antonio Feros, "The King's Favorite, the Duke of Lerma," 234–58.

99. For the Duke of Infantado's important say on Central Europe and Italy, see Magdalena S. Sánchez, "Dynasty, State, and Diplomacy in the Spain of Philip III," 258–63, 269–83.

100. On these changes see Williams, "Lerma, Old Castile, and the Travels of Philip III," 395–97; Feros Carrasco, "Gobierno de corte y patronazgo real," 105–14; and Stradling, *Philip IV and the Government of Spain*, 6–7.

101. Jacobo Sobieski explained that the Councils of State, War, and Finance were always resident at the Spanish court. By this Sobieski probably meant that the rooms in which these councils met were located permanently in the royal palace. See Sobieski, "El reino de España," in García Mercadal, *Viajes de extranjeros*, 332.

102. Elliott, "The Court of the Spanish Habsburgs," in *Spain and Its World, 1500–1700*, 145.

103. See, for example, Cabrera de Córdoba, *Relaciones de las cosas sucedidas*, 81. See also HHStA, SDK, K 13, fols. 262v–63r, Khevenhüller to Rudolf II, Valladolid, 8 October 1604; fols. 246v–47v, Khevenhüller to Rudolf II, 9 July 1604. All references to Khevenhüller's correspondence are taken from the typescript volumes compiled by Georg Graf Khevenhüller-Metsch, entitled *Die geheime Korrespondenz des kaiserlichen Botschafters am Königlich spanischen Hof in Madrid, Hans Khevenhüller, Graf von Frankenburg*. The typescript volumes are located within the Kartons of the Spanien Diplomatische Korrespondenz in the Haus-, Hof-, und Staatsarchiv in Vienna. There are six volumes and hereafter I refer to the correspondence with both the dates and the volumes in which the documents appear. The references for this note are taken from volume 6 of the typescript version.

104. When the monarchs went to eat the midday meal at Borja's summer house (*huerta*) in January 1600, the empress met them there for the afternoon meal (*merienda*). See BL, Add. Ms. 28422, fol. 254, 17 January 1600.

105. For Franqueza's rise to power and his fall from grace, see Feros, "The King's Favorite, the Duke of Lerma," 239–41, 263–74.

106. José Antonio Escudero, *Los secretarios de estado y del despacho*, 1:228.

107. "Relazione di Ottaviano Bon," in Barozzi and Berchet, *Relazioni degli stati europei*, 254–55.

108. BN, Madrid, Ms. 1174, "Relación que hiço . . . Simon Contarini," fol. 12.

109. Feros Carrasco, "Gobierno de corte y patronazgo real," 81.

110. Pérez Bustamante, *La España de Felipe III*, 131.

111. On the Junta de Desempeño, see Jean-Marc Pelorson, "Para una reinterpretación de la Junta de Desempeño General (1603–1606) a la luz de la 'visita' de Alonso Ramírez de Prado y de Don Pedro Franqueza, Conde de Villalonga."

112. Pérez Bustamante, *La España de Felipe III*, 131.

113. ASV, Fondo Borghese, Ser. 2, no. 272, Nunziatura di Spagna, 1605–1606, fols. 58r–v, 67r–v.

114. Feros Carrasco, "Gobierno de corte y patronazgo real," 105–9.

115. For a full list of these offices, see ibid., Appendix 2, 139.

116. Ibid., 110.

117. For the accusations against and the trial of Rodrigo Calderón, see BN, Madrid, Ms. 12851, fols. 274–84.

118. On the Real Alcázar, see Fernando Checa, *El real Alcázar de Madrid*; J. M. Barbeito, *El Alcázar de Madrid*.

119. See HHStA, SV, K 65 (B), "En un tratado que escrivio Juan Quevenhiller Conde de Franquenburg en lengua alemana de las cosas memorables que sucedieron en su tiempo, refiere en sustancia acerca de la jornada que el Ser^mo Archiduque Max^no hiço a España lo que sigue," n.p. See also Juan de Borja's account in BL, Add. Ms. 28423, fol. 167, 8 August 1600.

120. HHStA, SDK, K 13, vol. 6, fol. 47r, 15 August 1600. See also HHStA, SV, K 65 (B), "En un tratado que escrivio Juan Quevenhiller," n.p.

Chapter 2: Court Factions and Personal Networks

1. See, for example, Ciriaco Pérez Bustamante, *La España de Felipe III*.

2. See Antonio Feros Carrasco, "Gobierno de corte y patronazgo real," 105–33.

3. Antonio Feros, "The King's Favorite, the Duke of Lerma," 259–307; R. A. Stradling, *Philip IV and the Government of Spain*, 6–9; Patrick Williams, "Lerma, Old Castile, and the Travels of Philip III," 389–90.

4. Edouard Rott, "Philippe III et le Duc de Lerma (1598–1621): Étude historique d'après des documents inédits." For information on the factions at the Spanish court,

see Feros Carrasco, "Gobierno de corte y patronazgo real," 110–17; Stradling, *Philip IV and the Government of Spain*, 6–11; María Jesús Pérez Martín, *Margarita de Austria*, 146–55. For a discussion of the historiography of factions at the Spanish court, see Bernardo José García García, "El Duque de Lerma y la Pax Hispánica," 95–111. For a contemporary account of court factions, see Novoa, "Memorias de Matías de Novoa," in *Codoin*.

5. García García, *La Pax Hispanica: Política exterior del Duque de Lerma*, passim; and García Garía, "El Duque de Lerma y la Pax Hispánica," passim.

6. See, for example, Karl Mayr, ed., *Von den Rüstungen Herzog Maximilians von Bayern*, 35–37, Richard Haller to Duke Maximilian, 27 March 1610. See also Mayr, ed., *Von der Abreise Erzherzog Leopolds nach Jülich bis zu den Werbungen Herzog Maximilians von Bayern im März 1610*, 142–43, Lorenzo de Brindisi to Duke Maximilian, 7 November 1609.

7. See Johann Andritsch, "Landesfürstliche Berater am Grazer Hof (1564–1619)," 105.

8. On these divergent views, see García García, "Pacifismo y reformación en la política exterior del Duque de Lerma (1598–1618)," 218–21 n. 12. On the defense of reputation as a force motivating political policy, see John H. Elliott, "A Question of Reputation? Spanish Foreign Policy in the Seventeenth Century," and José Alcalá-Zamora y Queipo de Llano, "Zúñiga, Olivares y la política de reputación," in John H. Elliott and Angel García Sanz, *La España del Conde Duque de Olivares*, 103–8.

9. Ruth Kleinman, *Anne of Austria*, 13.

10. Feros, "The King's Favorite, the Duke of Lerma," 221.

11. On the changing nature of this junta and the functions of its various members, see ibid., 235–58.

12. See Feros Carrasco, "Gobierno de corte y patronazgo real," 73–82, 109. Feros Carrasco points out, however, that Lerma was unable to count on the loyalty of people such as Juan de Acuña (109).

13. By filling important positions with his dependents, Lerma was acting as most favorites would do. See Ronald G. Asch, "Introduction: Court and Household from the Fifteenth to the Seventeenth Centuries," in Ronald G. Asch and Adolf M. Birke, eds., *Princes, Patronage, and the Nobility*, 21.

14. Feros Carrasco, "Gobierno de corte y patronazgo real," 43.

15. Ibid., 42–43.

16. On Lerma's use of marriage to win prestige for his family, see Feros, "The King's Favorite, the Duke of Lerma," 192–95.

17. On the power and territorial holdings of the Infantado house, see Adolfo Carrasco Martínez, "El régimen señorial en la Castilla moderna."

18. Feros Carrasco, "Gobierno de corte y patronazgo real," 28–29.

19. Ibid.

20. Although some historians claim that Infantado was dependent upon Lerma and

supported the privado's positions on the Council of State, I have not found this to be true. For Infantado's opinion on Central European developments, see Magdalena S. Sánchez, "Dynasty, State, and Diplomacy in the Spain of Philip III," 258–63; and Sánchez, "A House Divided: Spain, Austria, and the Bohemian and Hungarian Successions," 894–98.

21. On the problems between Calderón and the Admiral of Aragón, see Feros Carrasco, "Gobierno de corte y patronazgo real," 110.

22. For Borja's observations of Empress María's activities, see his private correspondence with the Duke of Lerma in BL, Add. Mss. 28344; 28345; 28422; 28423; 28424; 28425.

23. See BN, Madrid, Ms. 1007. For the mayordomo's duties, see specifically 20v–34r. In 1606, Lerma instructed Juan de Borja (who was serving as the queen's mayordomo mayor) to record the names of all female servants in the queen's household. See BL, Add. Ms. 28425, fols. 421r–v, 19 July 1606.

24. On the camarera mayor's role and the etiquette governing the queen's household, see BN, Madrid, Ms. 1007; APR, Sección Histórica, Caja 50, "Ordenanzas y Etiquetas de Felipe II para la Casa de la Reina," fols. 314–58v; Dalmiro de la Válgoma y Díaz-Varela, *Norma y ceremonia de las reinas de la casa de Austria*, 33–35.

25. Pérez Martín, *Margarita de Austria*, 125.

26. See García García, "Honra, desengaño y condena de una privanza," 9–13, 17–18.

27. On his private collection and his patronage of the arts, see Sarah Schroth, "The Private Picture Collection of the Duke of Lerma." On convents and monasteries, see J. María Palomares Ibañez, *El patronato del Duque de Lerma sobre el convento de San Pablo en Valladolid*; Ventura Ginarte González, *El Duque de Lerma, Protector de la reforma Trinitaria (1599–1613)*. On the building of Lerma, see Luis Cervera Vera, *Lerma: Síntesis histórico-monumental*; and Cervera Vera, *El conjunto palacial de la villa de Lerma*.

28. Feros Carrasco, "Gobierno de corte y patronazgo real," 28. Observers noted Lerma's income and seemed almost obsessed with the amount he earned. For example, on 29 October 1605, the Bavarian ambassador at the Spanish court, Georg Huetter, reported that Lerma earned 60,000 ducats a year as contador mayor. On 18 March 1606, he also reported that the king had given Lerma the income from Gian Andrea Doria's estate, which brought Lerma's income to 14,000 ducats a year. See Felix Stieve, ed., *Vom Reichstag 1608 bis zur Gründung der Liga*, 16–17.

29. When Juan de Borja thanked Lerma for Ficallo, Lerma reassured him of his affection for him. BL, Add. Ms. 28422, fol. 40, 13 March 1599.

30. See García García, "Honra, desengaño y condena de una privanza," 4–6.

31. Feros Carrasco, "Gobierno de corte y patronazgo real," 111–12; Stradling, *Philip IV and the Government of Spain*, 7.

32. The list of Margaret of Austria's ladies-in-waiting says that the Countess of Porcia left the court and returned to her country in 1601. However, Cabrera de Córdoba lists her as being in Madrid in 1613. This seems to have been the same woman who

served the queen. For the list of Margaret of Austria's ladies-in-waiting, see APR, Histórica—Felipe III, Leg. 2914, Damas de la Reina Margarita de Austria.

33. Luis Cabrera de Córdoba, *Relaciones de las cosas sucedidas*, 532–33.

34. Lerma became increasingly melancholic and claimed to suffer from fevers and weakness. His health was such that he was unable to accompany the Infanta Anne on her betrothal trip to France. See García García, "Honra, desengaño y condena de una privanza," 2.

35. After the queen's death, in 1611, Margaret of the Cross emerged as the principal proponent of the Habsburgs in Madrid.

36. ASV, Fondo Borghese, Ser. 1, no. 649, Correspondencia del Patriarca de Alexandria, papal nuncio to Cardinal Aldobrandino, Madrid, fols. 21r–v, 10 January 1599.

37. See Juan de la Palma, *Vida de la sereníssima Infanta Sor Margarita de la Cruz, religiosa Descalza de Santa Clara*, fol. 123v. See also Pérez Martín, *Margarita de Austria*, 107. See HHStA, SDK, K 13, vol. 6, fol. 257r, Khevenhüller to Rudolf, Valladolid, 24 September 1604.

38. Cabrera de Córdoba, *Relaciones de las cosas sucedidas*, 45–46. See also BN, Madrid, Ms. 6751, "Relación de las joyas que se an entregado a Hernando de Espejo . . . 19 Hebrero . . . 1612," fols. 73–83.

39. BL, Add. Ms. 28423.

40. Mayr, ed., *Von der Abreise Erzherzog Leopolds nach Jülich*, 73–74, Richard Haller to Duke Maximilian, 19 September 1609; Felix Stieve, ed., *Die Politik Baierns, 1591–1607*, 513, no. 1.

41. For Khevenhüller and Nomi, see Hans Khevenhüller, *Geheimes Tagebuch*, 258 (15 May 1601), 264 (15 January 1601), 266 (27 June 1601), 273 (3 June 1602), 281 (18 April 1603), 284 (19 November 1603), 288 (26 June 1604), 292 (20 September 1604; with Nomi), 195 (8 January 1605), 302 (19 and 27 September 1605). For Castiglione, see Mayr, ed., *Von den Rüstungen Herzog Maximilians von Bayern*, 648–649, Castiglione to Rudolf II, Madrid, 23 October 1610. Rudolf II had instructed Francisco de Gonzaga, Prince of Castiglione, to greet the queen and to ask for her support. See ibid., 43, Instructions for Francisco de Gonzaga, Prague, 29 March 1610.

42. See BL, Add. Ms. 28424, fol. 78.

43. See, for example, BL, Add. Ms. 28422, fol. 40, 6 March 1599.

44. See ibid., fol. 106, 7 August 1599. Borja's letters throughout this period contain frequent references to Ledesma.

45. See ibid., fol. 261, 23 January 1600. Lerma's reply to Borja's letter was "Assi se hara luego" (24 January 1600).

46. For example, see ibid., fol. 206, 28 November 1599.

47. Borja often wrote Lerma telling him that the empress was very grateful for Lerma's assistance. See, among others, BL, Add. Ms. 28424, fol. 90, 7 July 1601; fol. 105, 14 July 1601.

48. These are Borja's words. Ibid., fol. 260, 5 January 1602.

49. See BL, Add. Ms. 28422, 6 May 1599.

50. For an example of how aristocratic women influenced political policy indirectly, see Barbara Hanawalt, "Lady Honor Lisle's Networks of Influence," 188–212.

51. Williams, "Lerma, Old Castile, and the Travels of Philip III," 379–97.

52. AGS, Hacienda, Consejo y Juntas de Hacienda, Leg. 428, Casa Real, no. 18, Valladolid, 13 September 1602.

53. Biblioteca Bartolomé March de Madrid, Ms. 23/II/I-II, fols. 292r–v, Richard Haller to a "titulado," 13 June 1609.

54. See Lerma's note on the consulta from 4 July 1609 transcribed in Stieve, ed., *Vom Reichstag 1608 bis zur Gründung der Liga*, 598–99, no. 1.

55. See Ferdinand's letter (Graz, 29 May 1609), ibid., 597–98.

56. Transcribed in Stieve, ed., *Die Politik Baierns, 1591–1607*, 513, no. 1.

57. BL, Add. Ms. 28423, fol. 289, 29 October 1600. See also ibid., fol. 306.

58. Georg Huetter, Maximilian of Bavaria's ambassador to the Spanish court, reported on 3 September 1605 that Maria Sidonia was given 6,000 ducats and that rumor had it that she had already received about 120,000 ducats through the queen's intercession. See Stieve, ed., *Vom Reichstag 1608 bis zur Gründung der Liga*, 16. See also Cabrera de Córdoba, *Relaciones de las cosas sucedidas*, 165.

59. On the cooperation between Haller and Magdalena de Guzmán, see Juan Carrillo's report to Archduke Albert. AGR, Sécretairerie d'État et de Guerre, no. 490, Juan Carrillo to Archduke Albert, fol. 82, 10 April 1600.

60. See Cabrera de Córdoba, *Relaciones de las cosas sucedidas*, 165.

61. So, for example, the queen's accounts show payments to several women in her household. See AGS, Estado, Corona de Castilla, Leg. 187, 2 August 1600. See also APR, Sección Histórica, Caja 190, "Quenta de los bestidos que Bar.ᵐᵉ Dominguez sastre de la Reyna Nra Sra a echo por mandado de Su Magd. por quenta de mercedes en el ano de 1599," fols. 1–7r.

62. Palma, *Vida de la sereníssima Infanta*, fols. 106v–107v.

63. BN, Madrid, Ms. 687, fol. 705 (n.d.), fols. 707r–v (20 September 1609), fol. 709r (29 October 1608), 713 (n.d.), 715r (31 March 1610).

64. Feros, "The King's Favorite, the Duke of Lerma," 300.

65. There might have been regular contact between Margaret of the Cross and Baltasar de Zúñiga during the last years of Philip III's reign. In fact, Margaret wrote to Archduke Albert in favor of a petition from Zúñiga. See AGR, Sécretairerie d'État et de Guerre, no. 502, Margarita de la Cruz a Alberto, n.f., n.d.

66. In her will, Empress María expressly asked Philip III to continue to assist and favor Archduke Albert. See AGS, PR, Caja 31-28, fol. 63v. The empress also left Archduke Albert as one of the principal executors of her testament.

67. For examples, see Antonio de León Pinelo, *Anales de Madrid de León Pinelo, reinado de Felipe III, Años 1598 a 1621* (1931 ed.), 64. See also Diego de Guzmán, *Reina Católica*, 134v–135r, 136v–137r.

68. For one of these requests see BL, Add. Ms. 28422, fol. 296, 9 February 1600.

69. On Lerma's problems with melancholy, see BN, Madrid, Ms. 1174, "Relación que hiço . . . Simón Contarini," fol. 8v; Feros, "The King's Favorite, the Duke of Lerma," 142 n. 102.

70. See García García, "Honra, desengano y condena de una privanza," 13–17; Patrick Williams, "Lerma, 1618: Dismisssal or Retirement?"

71. See García García, "Honra, desengaño y condena de una privanza," 8–9.

72. Antonio Feros argues that the struggle between Lerma and Uceda for control of the palace began as early as 1606 and became quite open by 1610. See Feros, "The King's Favorite, the Duke of Lerma," 283–85.

73. John H. Elliott, *The Count-Duke of Olivares*, 34.

74. RAH, Colección Salazar y Castro, Ms. 9/477, fols. 75v–76, 14 February 1611.

75. See BN, Madrid, Ms. 17858, "Relaciones de 1618 a 1621," fol. 142v.

76. Feros, "The King's Favorite, the Duke of Lerma," 285–86.

77. Ibid.

78. García García, "Honra, desengaño y condena de una privanza," 5.

79. See Feros, "The King's Favorite, the Duke of Lerma," 298–99.

80. See, for example, BN, Madrid, Ms. 17858, "Relaciones de 1618 a 1621," fols. 27v–28r.

81. On Santa María's influence at the court during the years 1618–21, see ibid., fols. 28r–v, 103v, 105v, 161v.

82. On the influence of preachers at the court, see ibid., fol. 53v.

83. Feros, "The King's Favorite, the Duke of Lerma," 312.

84. Ibid., 295.

Chapter 3: Fashioning Female Models from Royal Women

1. For the history of the Descalzas Reales, see Elías Tormo, *En las Descalzas Reales*; Juan de Carrillo, *Relación histórica de la real fundación del Monasterio de las Descalzas Reales de Santa Cruz de la villa de Madrid*; and María Teresa Ruiz Alcón, *Monasterio de las Descalzas Reales*.

2. Jerónimo de Florencia, "Sermón que predicó el Padre Gerónimo de Florencia, religioso de la Compañia de Jesús, a las honras de la S.C. Magestad de la Emperatriz Doña María." On preachers during Philip III's reign see Hilary Dansey Smith, *Preaching in the Spanish Golden Age*.

3. See also Fernando Checa Cremades, "Monasterio de las Descalzas Reales: Orígenes de su colección artística."

4. Florencia, "Sermón que predicó el Padre Gerónimo de Florencia," fol. 40.

5. Moralists argued that a widow often had to act like a father and a mother and assume masculine characteristics in order to discipline her children and control her household. See, for example, Gaspar de Astete, *Tratado del gobierno de la familia y estado de las viudas y donzellas*, 2–3.

6. Juan de la Cerda, *Vida política de todos los estados de mujeres*, fol. 434.

7. ARMEN, Testimonios, Leg. 1, tomo I: Relación de testigos que convivieron con la Madre Mariana de San José, fols. 3, 17. For a discussion of how female virgins rose above their sex and assumed masculine attributes, see Jane Tibbetts Schulenburg, "The Heroics of Virginity: Brides of Christ and Sacrificial Mutilation," 32; and Rosemary Radford Ruether, "Misogynism and Virginal Feminism in the Fathers of the Church," 159–61, 176.

8. On early modern ideas about the nature of women, see Merry E. Wiesner, *Women and Gender in Early Modern Europe*, 9–29; Ian Maclean, *The Renaissance Notion of Woman*; Linda Woodbridge, *Women and the English Renaissance*, passim; Theodora A. Jankowski, *Women in Power in the Early Modern Drama*, 22–53; and Constance Jordan, *Renaissance Feminism*, 11–64.

9. Juan Luis Vives, *De los deberes del marido*, 616. Juan de la Cerda, in his *Vida política*, added that women should be quiet because they are "not wise" (*poco sabias*), fol. 317. For prescriptive literature for English women, see Suzanne Hull, *Chaste, Silent, and Obedient*. See also the influential book by Leon Battista Alberti, *The Family in Renaissance Florence*, 77–99.

10. Rodrigo Mendes Silva, *Admirable vida*.

11. Ibid., fol. 21v.

12. Ibid., fol. 28v.

13. See David P. Daniel, "Piety, Politics, and Perversion," 83–84.

14. Barbara Harris has reached similar conclusions for aristocratic women in early modern England. See Harris, "Women and Politics in Early Tudor England," especially 281.

15. Cerda, *Vida política*, fols. 306v–7.

16. Juan de la Cerda pointed out that when a wife saw to her duties and served her husband, all functioned well. Ibid., fol. 307.

17. Mendes Silva, *Admirable vida*, fol. 33.

18. Ibid., fol. 33v. For another example of a nun in Philip III's Spain who was praised in a similar fashion for her charitable and flagellating practices, see Luis Muñoz, *Vida y virtudes de la venerable Madre Mariana de San Joseph*, 312. The language used by Mendes Silva and by Muñoz is similar to that used by medieval and early modern religious women who tended to the poor and the ill literally by starving themselves and mutilating their bodies. On this issue, see Caroline Walker Bynum, *Holy Feast and Holy Fast*, especially 219–44. See also Jane Tibbets Schulenburg, "The Heroics of Virginity."

19. Some Spaniards even suspected that while he was governor in Castile, Maximilian had begun the Lutheran group that was discovered in Valladolid eight years after his departure from the Spanish kingdoms. See Bohdan Chudoba, *Spain and the Empire*, 103. On Maximilian's Protestant leanings, see Viktor Bibl, "Zur Frage der religiösen Haltung Kaiser Maximilians II."; Chudoba, *Spain and the Empire*, 103–4, 107–12.

20. On this issue see R. J. W. Evans, *The Making of the Habsburg Monarchy*, 52–57. On the conflict between Emperor Rudolf II and Archduke Matthais, see Karl Vocelka, "Matthias contra Rudolf: Zur politischen Propaganda in der Zeit des Bruderzwistes"; and H. Sturmberger, "Die Anfänge des Bruderzwistes in Habsburg."

21. On acceptable behavior for widows, see Cerda, *Vida política*; Juan Luis Vives, *La mujer cristiana* (1523); and Astete, *Tratado del gobierno de la familia*.

22. Quoted in Mariló Vigil, *La vida de las mujeres en los siglos xvi y xvii*, 196.

23. Mendes Silva, *Admirable vida*, fol. 36v.

24. Ibid., fol. 37.

25. R. J. W. Evans, *Rudolf II and His World*, 59.

26. Chudoba, *Spain and the Empire*, 158–59. Rudolf II's volatile personality might have been a symptom of mental disorder. See H. C. Erik Midelfort, *Mad Princes of Renaissance Germany*, 125–40.

27. At her death, Empress María had at least 102 individuals in her household. See Tormo, *En las Descalzas Reales*, 229 n. 38. Tormo reproduces the list of María's household; the original list is in BL, Add. Ms. 28707, fol. 68. For the empress's visitors, see, for example, "Diario de la relación del viaje de Monseñor Camilo Borghese," in José García Mercadal, *Viajes de extranjeros por España y Portugal*, vol. 1, 1472.

28. For the empress's art collection, see Checa Cremades, "Monasterio de las Descalzas Reales," 21–30.

29. Midelfort, *Mad Princes of Renaissance Germany*, 125–26.

30. Cerda, *Vida política*, fol. 436v.

31. Mendes Silva, *Admirable vida*, fol. 44.

32. Ibid., fol. 43v. Juan Carrillo says the same in his *Relación histórica*, fol. 197.

33. Mendes Silva, *Admirable vida*, fol. 44v.

34. See the discussion of this event in Juan de la Palma, *Vida de la serenísima Infanta Sor Margarita de la Cruz*, fols. 95–96v.

35. Quoted in Vigil, *La vida de las mujeres*, 196.

36. See, for example, Electa Arenal, "The Convent as Catalyst for Autonomy." See also Craig A. Monson, ed., *The Crannied Wall*.

37. A recent examination of the years in which Maximilian and María governed Castile still ignores María's role. See Ana Díaz Medina, "El gobierno en España de Maximiliano II (1548–1551)." Díaz Medina even claims that the eight months during which María governed by herself (because Maximilian had left for Central Europe) can still be seen as a continuation of Maximilian's rule (38).

38. Mendes Silva, *Admirable vida*, fol. 33.

39. Juan Carrillo, *Relación histórica*, fol. 197v.

40. AGR, Sécretairerie d'État et de Guerre, no. 490, Correspondance de l'Archiduc Albert avec Juan Carrillo, fol. 106, 8 June 1600.

41. Diego de Guzmán, *Reina Católica*, fols. 39v–40.

42. Elke Roth comments that Margaret's father, Archduke Karl of Styria, played

no role in the education of his daughters. See Roth, "Erzherzogin Anna von Innerösterreich, Königin von Polen und Schweden," 18.

43. ÖNB, Handschriftensammlung, Ms. 8219, fol. 67v. See also, for example, the
case of her sister Anna, who became queen of Poland. Roth, "Erzherzogin Anna von
Innerösterreich," 15.

44. Guzmán, *Reina Católica*, fol. 40.

45. ÖNB, Handschriftensammlung, Ms. 8219, fol. 67v.

46. Ibid.

47. María Jesús Pérez Martín, *Margarita de Austria, Reina de España*, 22.

48. On the Rodrigo Calderón trial, see Angel Ossorio y Gallardo, *Los hombres de
toga en el proceso de Don Rodrigo Calderón*. See also AGS, Cámara de Castilla, Diversos
de Castilla, Legs. 34–36.

49. See BN, Madrid, Ms. 20260^{30}, fols. 124–27.

50. Jerónimo de Florencia, "Sermón segundo que predicó el Padre Gerónimo de
Florencia," fol. A2.

51. Guzmán, *Reina Católica*. See Philip's letter, transcribed by Gil González Dávila,
Historia de la vida y hechos del ínclito monarca, amado y santo Don Felipe Tercero, 191. On
Guzmán's tutoring the Infanta Anne, see Martha K. Hoffman-Strock, "'Carved on
Rings and Painted in Pictures': The Education and Formation of the Spanish Royal
Family, 1601–1634," 109–15.

52. Guzmán, *Reina Católica*, fols. 112v–13.

53. Florencia delivered two sermons at the queen's death. See Florencia, "Sermón
que predicó a la Magestad del Rey Don Felipe III en las honras que Su Magestad hizo
a la sereníssima Reyna D. Margarita su muger," and "Sermón segundo que predicó
el Padre Gerónimo de Florencia."

54. See the rules for a religious novice in Cerda, *Vida política*; Vives, *Formación de
la mujer cristiana* (1523). The biographies written about nuns such as Sor Margaret
of the Cross and Sor Mariana de San José emphasize their obedience to their confessors. See Palma, *Vida de la sereníssima Infanta*, and Muñoz, *Vida y virtudes de la venerable Sor Mariana de San Joseph*.

55. See Anna Coreth, *Pietas Austriaca*, 23.

56. Florencia, "Sermón segundo que predicó el Padre Gerónimo de Florencia," fol.
14v.

57. See, for example, the advice of Galindo, quoted in Vigil, *La vida de las mujeres*,
98. Galindo's book is from 1678, but the advice he gave was standard for sixteenth-
and seventeenth-century Spain.

58. Guzmán, *Reina Católica*, fol. 100v.

59. Ibid., fols. 134v–135.

60. Ibid., fols. 136v–137.

61. Florencia, "Sermón segundo que predicó el Padre Gerónimo de Florencia,"
fol. 11.

62. Ibid., fol. 11v. See also Mary Elizabeth Perry, "The Manly Woman"; Mary Beth Rose, "Women in Men's Clothing"; and Melveena McKendrick, *Woman and Society in the Spanish Drama of the Golden Age.*

63. For a discussion of reason as a male characteristic, see Jankowski, *Women in Power in the Early Modern Drama*, 59–60.

64. Andrés de Espinosa, "Sermón a las honras de Su Magestad de la Reina Doña Margarita de Austria N.S. que la muy insigne universidad de Salamanca hizo en los 9. dias del mes de noviembre del año de 1611," fols. 1–31v.

65. Ibid., fols. 16 and 17.

66. Jordan, *Renaissance Feminism*, 29–34; Jankowski, *Women in Power*, 54–60.

67. Espinosa, "Sermón a las honras de Su Magestad," fol. 1v.

68. Ibid., fol. 15.

69. This love of truth was also supposedly characteristic of Margaret of Austria's mother, Archduchess Maria of Bavaria. See Pedro Salazar de Mendoza, *Successión de la ínclyta casa de Baviera con la vida de la seteníssima Señora Archiduquesa María*, fol. 63r.

70. Guzmán, *Reina Católica*, fol. 116v.

71. Florencia, "Sermón que predicó a la Magestad del Rey Don Felipe III en las honras que Su Magestad hizo a la seteníssima Reyna D. Margarita su muger," fol. 11v.

72. Guzmán, *Reina Católica*, fol. 116v.

73. Ibid., fols. 149r–v.

74. Cabrera de Córdoba, court chronicler to Philip III, recorded a similar incident in which Margaret of Austria requested the office of Inquisitor General for Cardinal Zapata, the brother-in-law of the queen's closest friend, Maria Sidonia. The office, however, went to the Cardinal of Toledo, the Duke of Lerma's uncle. Cabrera de Córdoba explained that the queen favored Cardinal Zapata because of his familial tie to her privada, Maria Sidonia. Luis Cabrera de Córdoba, *Relaciones de las cosas sucedidas*, 344, 2 August 1608. Cabrera de Córdoba's account does not specify the queen's reaction to the appointment of the Cardinal of Toledo, but it helps confirm the picture presented by Guzmán and Florencia of a queen who intervened when her friends and relatives were involved.

75. Florencia, "Sermón que predicó a la Magestad del Rey Don Felipe III en las honras que Su Magestad hizo a la seteníssima Reyna D. Margarita su muger," fols. 17r–v.

76. This image of women is clearly elaborated in Vives, *Formación de la mujer cristiana*. The significance of a cult of female intercessors during the medieval period is discussed in Jo Ann McNamara, "A Legacy of Miracles."

77. See Florencia, "Sermón que predicó el Padre Gerónimo de Florencia."

78. This fourth wife was Anna, Margaret's sister, Empress María's daughter, and mother of Philip III.

79. Palma, *Vida de la seteníssima Infanta*. Philip IV requested a biography of his

aunt, Margaret of the Cross, from her confessor, Fray Juan de la Palma. The final biography may have been written, however, by Juan de Palafox y Mendoza, who held the title of Chronicler of Castile and the Indies at Philip IV's court. Palafox y Mendoza claimed he wrote the book and that Palma's only role in the project was to provide information about Margaret of the Cross. But Palma claimed to have written the book himself at the specific request of Philip IV. For this controversy, see the introduction to Palafox y Mendoza, "Libro de la vida de la sereníssima señora Infanta Sor Margarita de la Cruz," 115.

80. Tormo, *En las Descalzas Reales*, 160–61. Tormo argues, among other things, that Philip considered asking Empress María to govern Portugal for him. Tormo's arguments are in part corroborated by the account of the imperial ambassador in Madrid, Hans Khevenhüller, who reported a rumor that Philip II wanted Empress María to govern Portugal. See BN, Madrid, Ms. 2751, "Historia de Joan Kevenhuller de Aichelberg," fol. 404.

81. BN, Madrid, Ms. 2751, "Historia de Joan Kevenhuller de Aichelberg," fol. 400.

82. Palma, *Vida de la sereníssima Infanta*, fols. 43v–46v.

83. Ibid., fol. 46.

84. Elías Tormo reproduces a letter from Margaret of the Cross to Philip II in which she states her unwillingness to marry him. Tormo does not give any reference for this document, so it is difficult to judge the historical validity of this letter. See Tormo, *En las Descalzas Reales*, 186–87. Tormo probably transcribed the letter from a source that he used often but that now seems to be lost, namely Abellan, "Espejo de las sereníssimas infantas de la agustíssima casa de Austria. Vida de la sereníssima Infanta del Imperio de Alemania."

85. BN, Madrid, Ms. 2751, "Historia de Joan Kevenhuller de Aichelberg," fol. 400.

86. See Hortensio Felix Paravicino's eulogy about Margaret of the Cross entitled "Margarita o oración funebre . . . Esposa de Jesu Christo, rey de reyes, y señor de señores," in *Oraciones evangélicas, y panegíricos funerales que a diversos intentos dixo*.

87. Ibid., fol. 175v.

88. Ibid., fol. 172v.

89. This idea that women could speak directly to God through meditation is well known to scholars of medieval and early modern visionaries. See Elizabeth Alvilda Petroff, *Body and Soul*, 211–21, and *Medieval Women's Visionary Literature*, 11–14.

90. Paravicino, "Margarita o oración funebre," fols. 180v–81.

91. Ibid., fol. 181v.

92. Ibid., fol. 177v. Juan de la Palma notes a similar incident in his biography of Margaret of the Cross. Palma claimed that the nun heard of a man who had sold his soul to the devil and, in retaliation for such a direct affront to God, cut her breast with a knife in order to show that there were still individuals who would gladly give their blood for Christ. See Palma, *Vida de la sereníssima Infanta*, fol. 154v.

93. In the dedication to his book, Cerda noted that Margaret of the Cross was "the honor and the crown of all female religious." Cerda, *Vida política*, n.f.

94. Ibid., fols. 121v–122.

95. Ibid., fol. 122.

96. Palma, *Vida de la sereníssima Infanta*, fol. 173v.

97. Ibid.

98. For the nuncio's report of Empress María's request to the pope to allow the queen to enter the Descalzas, see ASV, Fondo Borghese, Ser. 1, no. 649, Correspondencia del Patriarca de Alexandria, papal nuncio to Cardinal Aldobrandino, Madrid, fols. 21r–v, 10 January 1599.

99. Palma, *Vida de la sereníssima Infanta*, fol. 120.

100. Florencia, "Sermón segundo que predicó el Padre Gerónimo de Florencia," fol. 11v. On the Duke of Lerma's pursuit of pacifistic policies, see Bernardo José García García, *La Pax Hispanica*, passim.

101. In turn, the pursuit of pacifistic policies was often associated with effeminacy. See Woodbridge, *Women and the English Renaissance*, 160–65.

102. See Cerda, *Vida política*, fols. 306v–7.

103. Florencia, "Sermón segundo que predicó el Padre Gerónimo de Florencia," fol. 11v.

Chapter 4: Correcting the Image

1. Some prominent historians have assumed that Empress María was confined to the monastery and rarely ventured from its cloistered walls. See, for example, Patrick Williams, "Lerma, Old Castile, and the Travels of Philip III," 385 n. 22.

2. See, for example, Hans Khevenhüller, *Geheimes Tagebuch*, 129 (18 April 1583); 130 (12 July 1583); 135–36 (3 March 1584); 136 (14 March, 21 April 1584); 139 (19 October 1584); 140 (24 November 1584); 141 (19 December 1584); 141 (16 January 1585); 144 (27 April 1585); 146 (August 1585); 150 (8 April 1586); 154 (12 November, 23 November 1586); 155 (15 December 1586); 155 (12 January 1587); 159 (7 June 1587); 160 (6 July, 10 July, 31 July 1587); 161–64 (August-November 1587); 164 (23 November 1587). These regular visits continued after Philip II's death, into the reign of Philip III.

3. BN, Madrid, Ms. 1255, Antonio de León Pinelo, "Anales de Madrid," fol. 78v.

4. On the numerous visits of Empress María to this huerta, see Khevenhüller, *Geheimes Tagebuch*, 136, 137, 139, 144, 145–46. See also BL, Add. Ms. 28422, fol. 254, 17 January 1600. Juan de Borja sold this huerta to Philip III in 1600 for 2,000 ducats. See AGR, Sécretairerie d'État et de Guerre, no. 490, Correspondance de l'Archiduc Albert avec Juan Carrillo, fol. 97, Juan Carrillo to Archduke Albert, 17 May 1600.

5. See, for example, Khevenhüller, *Geheimes Tagebuch*, 258 (25 May 1600); 263 (26

November 1600); 275 (21 December 1602). See also BN, Madrid, Ms. 2751, "Historia de Joan Kevenhuller de Aichelberg," 963.

6. On this portrait and the art collection of the monastery of the Descalzas Reales, see Fernando Checa Cremades, "Monasterio de las Descalzas Reales," 21–30.

7. Checa Cremades emphasized that this is a political portrait of the empress because in it she adopts the pose and the attributes of a political statesman. See ibid., 27.

8. BL, Add. Ms. 28422, fol. 106, 7 August 1599.

9. Ibid.

10. BL, Add. Ms. 28422, fol. 220, 30 December 1599. See a further plea on Borja's part, ibid., fol. 261, 23 January 1600. Lerma's reply (24 January) was "assi se hara luego."

11. BL, Add. Ms. 28424, fol. 345, 8 June 1602.

12. BL, Add. Ms. 28422, fol. 122, 21 August 1599; but Lerma's reply is dated 30 August 1599.

13. Ibid., fol. 284, 4 February 1600.

14. Ibid., fol. 114, 14 August 1599.

15. Ibid.

16. BL, Add. Ms. 28423, fol. 139.

17. Ibid., fol. 447, 18 March 1601. For other occasions on which the empress was informed about events in Flanders, see BL, Add. Ms. 28424, fol. 5, 5 April 1601; fol. 232v, 15 December 1601; fol. 260, 5 January 1602; fol. 349, 10 June 1602.

18. See H. C. Erik Midelfort, *Mad Princes of Renaissance Germany*, 131.

19. BL, Add. Ms. 28423, fol. 306, 6 November 1600. See also Midelfort, *Mad Princes of Renaissance Germany*, 131–32.

20. BL, Add. Ms. 28424, fol. 129, 22 August 1601. Empress María made this request through Borja.

21. See BN, Madrid, Ms. 2751, "Historia de Joan Kevenhuller de Aichelberg," 433–34 (1583).

22. See, for example, entries for 6 January 1585 and 16 and 17 April 1586, Khevenhüller, *Geheimes Tagebuch*, 141, 150.

23. Ibid., 126.

24. Ibid., 135.

25. See, for example, "Relazione di Francesco Soranzo," 11 October 1602, in Nicolò Barozzi and Guglielmo Berchet, *Relazioni degli stati europei*, 163–64.

26. Ibid.

27. For examples of some of the empress's debts, see AGS, Estado España, Leg. 649, no. 40, "Memorial de las deudas que la señora reyna de Bohemia hizo en España y después en Alemania"; Moravský Zemský Archiv (formerly Státní Archiv) Brno, Rodinnký Archiv Ditrichštejnů, K 423/1898–163, "Lo que debe la emperatriz, nuestra señora, al baron Dietristan, mayordomo del emperador."

28. See Tomás Contarini, "Relación de la estancia en España," in José García Mercadal, ed., *Viajes de extranjeros por España y Portugal*, vol. 1, 1460.

29. See BN, Madrid, Ms. 2751, "Historia de Joan Kevenhuller de Aichelberg," 404.

30. See, for example, John H. Elliott, *Imperial Spain*, 207–8, 285–87. See also A. W. Lovett, *Early Habsburg Spain*, 227–35; Geoffrey Parker, *Philip II*, 121–27.

31. BN, Madrid, Ms. 2751, "Historia de Joan Kevenhuller de Aichelberg," 1149–50.

32. Ibid., 1139.

33. For this conversation see ibid., 1150–51.

34. See, for example, BL, Add. Ms. 28422, fol. 11, Borja to Lerma, 1 November 1598; fol. 32, Borja to Lerma, 17 February 1599; fol. 220, Borja to Lerma, 5 March 1600; BL, Add. Ms. 28423, fol. 95, Borja to Lerma, 10 July 1600; fol. 396, 1 February 1601; fol. 429, Borja to Lerma, 10 March 1601; fol. 447, Borja to Lerma, 18 March 1601; fol. 457, Borja to Lerma, 21 March 1601; BL, Add. Ms. 28425, fol. 19, Borja to Lerma (letter has no date but was received 12 February 1603).

35. In June 1601, Empress María petitioned on behalf of the abbess of the Descalzas, Sor Mariana. See BL, Add. Ms. 28424, fol. 76, Borja to Lerma, 16 June 1601.

36. Ibid., fol. 111, Borja to Lerma, 18 July 1601.

37. Ibid., fol. 383, Borja to Lerma, 24 August 1602.

38. For a complete list of Margaret of Austria's siblings, see Friedrich von Hurter, *Bild einer christlichen Fürstin*, 72–73.

39. "Relazione di Ottaviano Bon," 21 December 1602, in Barozzi and Berchet, *Relazioni degli stati europei*, 247.

40. "Relazione de Francesco Soranzo," 11 October 1602, ibid., 162.

41. "Relazione di Ottaviano Bon," 21 December 1602, ibid., 247.

42. "Relazione di Francesco Priuli," 1608, ibid., 358.

43. "Relazione de Girolamo Soranzo," ibid., 457.

44. "Relazione de Girolamo Soranzo," ibid., 473.

45. See Jean-Marc Pelorson, "Para una reinterpretación de la Junta de Desempeño General," 613–27.

46. Matías de Novoa, "Memorias de Matías de Novoa," in *Codoin*, vol. 60, 1611, 438–39.

47. Ibid., 442. Juan de Santa María was the author of *República y policía cristiana*, a political treatise that was highly critical of privados. For Novoa's criticism of Mariana de San José and Juan de Santa María, see Novoa, "Memorias de Matías de Novoa," in *Codoin*, vol. 61, 101–2.

48. Ibid., vol. 60, 442; vol. 61, 101–2, 121.

49. BL, Add. Ms. 28422, fols. 129–31, Borja to Lerma, 4 September 1599.

50. Ibid.

51. Ibid., fol. 217, 22 December 1599.

52. BN, Madrid, Ms. 2751, "Historia de Joan Kevenhuller de Aichelberg," 1140–41.

53. Ibid.

54. On this meeting, see Fidel Pérez Mínguez, "La Condesa de Castellar, fundadora del convento 'Las Carboneras,'" 392–418.

55. For contemporary accounts of the events surrounding the Marquesa del Valle, see Luis Cabrera de Córdoba, *Relaciones de las cosas sucedidas*, 204, 215, 236, 334, 338, 376; BN, Madrid, Ms. 2577, Sepúlveda, "Tomo segundo de la historia de varios sucesos de España," fols. 178v–80. See also the marquesa's statements to the judges sent to question her: BN, Madrid, Ms. 18191, "Declaración dada por la Marquesa del Valle en la prision en que se hallava, por cierta traicion que acaeció en palacio," fols. 192–201v. The marquesa's story is retold and analyzed in detail in Luis Fernández Martín, "La Marquesa del Valle."

56. See BN, Madrid, Ms. 2577, Sepúlveda, "Tomo segundo de la historia de varios sucesos de España," fols. 202v–3.

57. Pérez Mínguez, "La condesa de Castellar," 414–15.

58. BN, Madrid, Ms. 18191, "Declaración dada por la Marquesa del Valle," fol. 196v.

59. Fernández Martín, "La Marquesa del Valle," 601.

60. Ibid., 606; and Cabrera de Córdoba, *Relaciones de las cosas sucedidas*, 89. The camarera mayor, the Duchess of Lerma, had to leave because she was suffering from melancholy.

61. AGR, Sécretairerie d'État et de Guerre, no. 490, Correspondance de Juan Carrillo avec l'Archiduc Albert, fol. 13v, 8 November 1599.

62. BN, Madrid, Ms. 3207, "A la Marquesa del Valle Doña Magdalena de Guzmán del Marqués de Montesclaro," fols. 694–95, Mexico, 20 November 1603.

63. For the marquesa's declaration see BN, Madrid, Ms. 18191, "Declaración dada por la Marquesa del Valle," fols. 192–201v.

64. Ibid., fol. 199v.

65. Ibid., fols. 196r–v.

66. See BN, Madrid, Ms. 12859, fols. 113–14, Don Diego de Alderese to Rodrigo Calderón, 2 September 1609.

67. Archivio di Stato, Naples, Carte Farnesiane, Corrispondenza dal Duca di Poli (1606–1606), fascio 25, fols. 290r–v, 17 February 1606.

68. See the letter written to the Marquis of Velada in 1611 by a friend in Oropesa. Biblioteca/Archivo Zabálburu, Colección Altamira, Carpeta 194-117, n.f., 19 September 1610. The observations about the queen's love of truth correspond to what Diego de Guzmán and Jerónimo de Florencia wrote. See Guzmán, *Reina Católica*, fol. 116v; and Florencia, "Sermón que predicó a la Magestad del Rey Don Felipe III en las honras que Su Magestad hizo a la sereníssima Reyna D. Margarita su muger," fol. 11v.

69. HHStA, SDK, K 14, fol. 1, deciphered letter from the Prince of Castiglione from 1611, n.d.

70. HHStA, SDK, K 13, vol. 6, fol. 278r, Khevenhüller to Rudolf II, 8 January 1605.

71. Ibid., fol. 217v, Khevenhüller to Rudolf II, 22 November 1603.

72. See Barbara J. Harris, "Women and Politics in Early Tudor England," 259–81, especially 260–62.

73. HHStA, SDK, K 13, vol. 6, fol. 222r, Khevenhüller to Rudolf II, 20 December 1603.

74. Ibid., fols. 57r–v, Khevenhüller to Rudolf II, letter from 11 October 1600.

75. HHStA, Familienakten, K 106, fol. 86.

76. On the Bohemian and Hungarian issue, see Otto Gliss, *Der Oñate Vertrag*; Magdalena S. Sánchez, "A House Divided," 887–903; Magdalena S. Sánchez, "Dynasty, State, and Diplomacy," chap. 7. For San Clemente's recommendation, see AGS, Estado Alemania, Leg. 707, fol. 235, 31 January 1603. For Zúñiga's advice, see ibid., Leg. 709, fol. 152, Prague, 10 February 1611.

77. HHStA, SHK, K 2, no. 7, fol. 155, Margaret of the Cross to Rudolf II, 18 December 1610.

78. HHStA, SDK, K14, fol. 1, deciphered letter from the Prince of Castiglione, 1611.

79. Transcribed in Gil González Dávila, *Historia de la vida y hechos del ínclito monarca, amado y santo Don Felipe Tercero*, 189. For an insightful discussion of Philip's advice to Anne, see Martha K. Hoffman-Strock, "'Carved on Rings and Painted in Pictures,'" 219–35.

80. Transcribed in González Dávila, *Historia de la vida*, 191.

81. Ibid.

82. Ibid.

83. BN, Madrid, Ms. 2348, fols. 441v–42, Philip III to Anne, 16 November 1616.

84. Ibid., fol. 443v, 17 February 1616.

85. Ibid., fol. 444v, 7 April 1617.

86. Ibid., fols. 441v–42, 16 November 1616.

87. HHStA, SDK, K 13, vol. 6, fol. 304v, Khevenhüller to Rudolf II, Valladolid, 30 May 1605.

88. For Margaret's letters to Archduke Albert, see AGR, Sécretairerie d'État et de Guerre, no. 502, Correspondance de Margarita de la Cruz avec l'Archiduc Albert. For her letters to Philip III, see BN, Madrid, Ms. 915, fols. 93r–120v. For her letters to the Duke of Lerma, see BN, Madrid, Ms. 687, fols. 705–15.

89. HHStA, SHK, K 2, fols. 147r–48r, Margaret of the Cross to Rudolf II, 29 August 1610.

90. Ibid., fols. 153r–v, Margaret to Rudolf II, 19 April 1610.

91. BN, Madrid, Ms. 687, fols. 705r–v, Margaret of the Cross to the Duke of Lerma, n.d.

92. Ibid.

93. See, for example, HHStA, SDK, K 15, no. 11, fol. 276, 2 September 1617.

94. Cabrera de Córdoba, *Relaciones de las cosas sucedidas*, 172, 197, 227–28, 453.

95. AGS, Estado Alemania, Leg. 711, fol. 110 (2). No date is given, but from the subjects discussed I would place it around 1618.

96. BN, Madrid, Ms. 2348, fol. 29v; BN, Madrid, Ms. 17858, "Relaciones de 1618–21," fols. 129r–v; Mateo Escagedo Salmón, "Los Acebedos," *Boletín de la Biblioteca Menéndez Pelayo* 8, no. 2 (1926): 23.

97. BN, Madrid, Ms. 17858, "Relaciones de 1618–21," fols. 129r–v.

98. BN, Madrid, Ms. 2348, "Sucesos desde el año 1611 hasta 1617," fol. 29r.

99. Cristóbal Pérez de Herrera, "Carta apologética al Doctor Luis del Valle defendiendo su buena intención al publicar su obra sobre los males y remedios del Reino," Madrid, 1 November 1610, in *Codoin*, vol. 18 (Madrid, 1874), 564–74.

100. Ibid., 566.

101. Ibid.

Chapter 5: Family, Affection, and Politics

1. Rodrigo Mendes Silva, *Admirable vida*, fol. 21v. Margaret of the Cross's biographer, Juan de la Palma, also referred to Empress María as "the daughter, mother, and sister of so many emperors and kings." See Juan de la Palma, *Vida de la sereníssima Infanta*, fol. 105.

2. Mendes Silva, *Admirable vida*.

3. The inscription emphasized not only the empress's familial connections but also her piety and pious deeds. See Marqués de Ayerbe, *Correspondencia inédita de Don Guillén de San Clemente*, vi n. 2.

4. Palma, *Vida de la sereníssima Infanta*, fols. 107v, 112r.

5. See Hortensio Felix Paravicino, "Margarita o oración funebre."

6. See Blas Orejón, "Sermón que predicó Blas Orejón."

7. For the power exercised by aristocratic women and the ties between familial and political power, see Barbara A. Hanawalt, "Lady Honor Lisle's Networks of Influence," 188–212; Barbara J. Harris, "Property, Power, and Personal Relations"; and Harris, "Women and Politics in Early Tudor England."

8. On the definition of the "House of Austria" see Alphons Lhotsky, "Was heißt 'Haus Österreich.'"

9. Peter Brightwell claimed that the two Habsburg branches constituted a system that held political and economic hegemony over Europe in the late sixteenth and early seventeenth centuries. See Brightwell, "The Spanish System and the Twelve Years' Truce."

10. See, for example, "Relazione di Francesco Priuli," in Nicolò Barozzi and Guglielmo Berchet, *Relazioni degli stati europei*, 389.

11. On the role of family in the making of political decisions during the reign of Philip III, see Magdalena S. Sánchez, "Dynasty, State, and Diplomacy."

12. On Habsburg marriages, see Karl Vocelka, *Habsburgische Hochzeiten 1550–1600*; see also Paula S. Fichtner, "Dynastic Marriage in Sixteenth-Century Habsburg Diplomacy and Statecraft."

13. See Harris, "Power, Profit, and Passion"; and Garrett Mattingly, *Renaissance Diplomacy*.

14. See Ruth Kleinman, *Anne of Austria*, 18, 40; Martha K. Hoffman-Strock, "'Carved on Rings and Painted in Pictures,'" 220–24; and especially Ricardo Martorell Téllez-Girón, ed., *Cartas de Felipe III a su hija Ana, Reina de Francia*. For a similar example from England (namely, the circle around Charles I's French queen, Henrietta Maria), see Caroline M. Hibbard, "The Role of a Queen Consort," 403–5; and Kevin Sharpe, "The Image of Virtue," 256–57.

15. See Harris, "Women and Politics in Early Tudor England," 260–61.

16. For Margaret of Austria, see Ghislaine de Boom, *Marguerite d'Autriche*; Eleanor E. Tremayne, *The First Governess of the Netherlands*; Jane de Iongh, *Margaret of Austria, Regent of the Netherlands*; Shirley Harrold Bonner, "Margaret of Austria"; and Pierre Guerin, *Marguerite d'Autriche-Bourgogne*. For Maria of Hungary, see the following publications by Gernot Heiß: "Königin Maria von Ungarn und Böhmen (1505–1558)"; "Politik und Ratgeber der Königin Maria von Ungran in den Jahren 1521–1531"; and "Die ungarischen, böhmischen Besitzungen der Konigin Maria (1505–1558)." See also Laetitia V. G. Gorter-van Royen, *Marie van Hongarije*; and Ghislaine de Boom, *Marie de Hongrie*.

17. Joan Kelly-Gadol, "The Social Relation of the Sexes," 818–19.

18. See Louise Lamphere, "Strategies, Cooperation, and Conflict among Women in Domestic Groups," 100.

19. Paul C. Allen, "The Strategy of Peace," 3–4, 470–88.

20. Ibid., 488.

21. See Bernardo José García García, *La Pax Hispanica*, 84–88.

22. On this issue, see José A. Fernández Santamaría, *Reason of State and Statecraft in Spanish Political Thought, 1595–1640*; and Robert Bireley, S.J., *The Counter-Reformation Prince*.

23. On these marriages, see F. Tommy Perrens, *Les mariages espagnols sous le regne de Henri IV*; and Francisco Silvela, *Matrimonios de España y Francia en 1615*.

24. Kleinman, *Anne of Austria*, 13.

25. See Samuel R. Gardiner, *Prince Charles and the Spanish Marriage, 1612–1623*.

26. On this issue, see Brightwell, "Spain and Bohemia"; Brightwell, "The Spanish Origins of the Thirty Years' War"; and Magdalena S. Sánchez, "A House Divided."

27. Barbara Harris reaches the same conclusion about English aristocratic women. See her article "Women and Politics in Early Tudor England," 281.

28. For the responsibilities that motherhood brought to aristocratic women, see Harris, "Property, Power, and Personal Relations." For an interesting case of an aristocratic widow who exercised a great deal of influence through her skillful negotiations on behalf of her children, see Robert J. Kalas, "The Noble Widow's Place in the Patriarchal Household."

29. Juan de Mora, *Discursos morales* (Madrid, 1589), fol. 135.

30. Fray Mauro de Valencia, "Sermón . . . en las honras de D. Margarita de Austria," 17.

31. BN, Madrid, Ms. 2348, fols. 441v–42, Philip III to his daughter Anne, 16 November 1616.

32. BN, Madrid, Ms. 915, fol. 117v, All Saints' Day, 1606; HHStA, SHK, K 2, fols. 147r–v, Margaret of the Cross to Rudolf II, 29 August 1610.

33. John Elliott says that Philip IV feared Margaret of the Cross more than he did the Count of Olivares. See Elliott, *The Count-Duke of Olivares*, 430.

34. Margaret L. King, *Women of the Renaissance*, 54.

35. See Viktor Bibl, *Maximilian II.*, 50, 365–83.

36. The Habsburg archdukes were also sent to the Spanish court for political training because at the time, Philip II's only son, Carlos, was infirm, and the monarch looked to the Austrian Habsburg archdukes as possible heirs to his throne. See Helga Widern, "Die Spanischen Gemahlinnen," 34. See also Bibl, *Maximilian II.*, 113.

37. See "Minuta de carta de S. M. al Conde de Monteagudo, en su mano," Madrid, 18 February 1571, in *Codoin*, vol. 110, 167.

38. Widern, "Die Spanischen Gemahlinnen," 33; "Carta original del Conde de Monteagudo á Su Magestad," Speyer, 15 August 1570, in *Codoin*, vol. 110, 52; "Carta del Conde de Monteagudo á S. M.," Vienna, 5 July 1572, ibid., 464.

39. Widern, "Die Spanischen Gemahlinnen," 32. "Minuta de la instrucción que se dió al Conde de Monteagudo," Madrid, 12 January 1570, in *Codoin*, vol. 110, 8–9.

40. "Minuta de la instrucción que se dió al Conde de Monteagudo," Madrid, 12 January 1570, in *Codoin*, vol. 110, 9.

41. See, for example, "Carta del Conde de Monteagudo á S. M.," Prague, 22 May 1571, ibid., 227.

42. See ibid., Vienna, 9 December 1571, 328.

43. Widern, "Die Spanischen Gemahlinnen," 31. Widern cites a letter from Luis Vanegas to Philip II, 30 October 1567, in *Codoin*, vol. 101, 290.

44. See "Carta original del Conde de Monteagudo á S. M.," Speyer, 30 October 1570, in *Codoin*, vol. 110, 98–110; "Carta original del Conde de Monteagudo á S. M.," Nuremberg, 31 December 1570, ibid., 140–141; "Carta original del Conde de Monteagudo á S. M.," Vienna, 19 January 1572, ibid., 349.

45. "Carta original del Conde de Monteagudo á Su Magestad," Speyer, 15 August 1570, ibid., 50–51.

46. "Minuta de carta de S. M. al Conde de Monteagudo," Madrid 27 January 1571, ibid., 156.

47. Gaspar de Astete, *Tratado del gobierno de la familia y estado de las viudas y donzellas*, 2–3.

48. HHStA, SDK, K 13, vol. 6, fols. 57r–v, Khevenhüller to Rudolf II, 11 October 1600.

49. "Relazione di Ottaviano Bon," in Barozzi and Berchet, *Relazione degli stati europei*, 258.

50. The letter is reproduced in Felix Stieve, ed., *Vom Reichstag 1608 bis zur Gründung der Liga*, 590 n. 4. (The original letter is from AGS, Estado Alemania, Leg. 2495, fol. 53.) Ferdinand also wrote the queen asking for financial assistance from Spain. See Stieve, ed., *Vom Reichstag 1608 bis zur Gründung der Liga*, 597–98, no. 374, Ferdinand to Queen of Spain, Graz, 29 March 1609. (The original is from AGS, Estado Alemania, Leg. 2495, fol. 54.)

51. AGS, Estado Alemania, Leg. 2452, Minutas de Despachos, fol. 259, 13 August 1609.

52. Archivio di Stato, Venice, Spagna 52, "Relazione di Francesco Soranzo," fol. 59, Madrid, 9 January 1600.

53. "Relazione di Girolamo Soranzo," in Barozzi and Berchet, *Relazione degli stati europei*, 473.

54. AGS, Estado Alemania, Leg. 707, fol. 139, "Copia de lo q le escrivio El Emp. a Su Magd de la Reyna en carta dada en Praga a 27 de abril de 1602."

55. HHStA, SHK, K 2, fols. 12r–v (to Empress María) and 14r–v (to Margaret of Austria), 18 March 1601.

56. AGS, Estado Alemania, Leg. 707, n.d., n.f.

57. HHStA, SDK, K 12, vol. 5, part 2, fols. 5r–10r, 17 April 1597; HHStA, SV, K 3, fols. 280r–v.

58. HHStA, SHK, K 2, fols. 54r–v, 30 March 1598.

59. BN, Madrid, Ms. 687, fols. 705r–6r, Margaret of the Cross to Lerma.

60. See H. C. Erik Midelfort, *Mad Princes of Renaissance Germany*, 129.

61. For information on the portraits, see María Teresa Ruiz Alcón, *Monasterio de las Descalzas Reales*, 80, 82.

62. Kleinman, *Anne of Austria*, 13.

63. Palma, *Vida de la serenissima Infanta*, fols. 89r–90v; Elías Tormo, *En las Descalzas Reales*, 195–97.

64. AGS, Estado Alemania, Leg. 711, Consejo de Estado, 1 June 1617.

65. See BL, Add. Ms. 28707, n.f.

66. See Sharon Kettering, "The Patronage Power of Early Modern French Noblewomen," 825.

67. Luis Cabrera de Córdoba, *Relaciones de las cosas sucedidas*, 113–14, 26 September 1601.

68. See Widern, "Die Spanischen Gemahlinnen," 50.

69. Empress María left a large sum to the Jesuit school in Madrid, and Margaret of Austria gave money to the Jesuit college in Salamanca.

70. For Margaret of the Cross's testament, see *Testamentos de 43 personas del Madrid de los Austrias*, ed. and trans. Antonio Matilla Tascón, 141–48, dated 9 September 1633.

71. See Margaret of Austria's will in RAH, Colección Salazar y Castro, M63, fols. 316v, 318r; Cabrera de Córdoba, *Relaciones de las cosas sucedidas*, 451.

72. In her will, Margaret of Austria left 15,000 ducats to Maria Amelia, her lady-in-waiting and Maria Sidonia's sister. She left Maria Sidonia's brother Wolfgang Alberto 10,000 ducats. She also left 5,000 ducats for each of Maria Sidonia's other siblings (two brothers and one sister), who were still in Central Europe. See RAH, Colección Salazar y Castro, M63, fol. 316v.

73. Ayerbe, *Correspondencia inédita de Don Guillén de San Clemente*, vi n. 2.

74. The exceptions are the endowments of the Jesuit college in Madrid by Empress María and the Jesuit university in Salamanca by Margaret of Austria.

75. On the burial preferences of early modern aristocratic women, see King, *Women of the Renaissance*, 56.

76. Stanley Chojnacki, "The Power of Love," 139.

77. On this issue, see Palma, *Vida de la seren*í*ssima Infanta*, fols. 106v–12v.

78. See HHStA, SHK, K 2, fol. 106, 1585. Barbara Harris has seen similar cases of mothers' preferential treatment of daughters and younger sons among English aristocratic women. See Harris, "Property, Power, and Personal Relations," 631.

79. On Finale, see Friedrich Edelmayer, *Maximilian II., Philipp II. und Reichsitalien*; José L. Cano de Gardoqui, *Incorporación del marquesado del Finale (1602)*; Sánchez, "Dynasty, State, and Diplomacy," 200–209.

80. HHStA, SV, K 3, fol. 298, 5 March 1599, "Lo que Su Magd es servido que se responda de su parte a lo que el Embaxador Kevenhiler le a propuesto de la del Emperador."

81. AGS, Estado Alemania, Leg. 2323, fols. 133–34, 3 October 1600.

82. Ibid., fol. 166, 18 June 1602.

83. AGS, Estado Alemania, Leg. 707, fol. 246, Prague, San Clemente to Philip III, 15 March 1603.

84. Ibid., fol. 138, "Copia de la que escrive el Emperador Rudolfo a Su Magd en carta fechada en Praga a 27 de abril de 1602."

85. Ibid., fol. 139, Prague, 27 April 1602.

86. AGS, Estado Alemania, Leg. 2323, Consulta Original, fol. 199, 19 March 1603.

87. HHStA, Familienakten, K 106, fol. 86, instructions from April 1613.

88. On the Bohemian and Hungarian successions, see Otto Gliss, *Der Oñate Vertrag*; and Sánchez, "A House Divided."

89. On this issue, see Sánchez, "Dynasty, State, and Diplomacy," 75–83.

90. HHStA, Familienkorrespondenz A, K 10, fol. 105, Ferdinand to Philip III, 1618.

91. See, for example, Archduke Albert to the Duke of Lerma, Brussels, 18 April 1607, in *Codoin*, vol. 43, 46–58.

92. HHStA, Familienkorrespondenz A, K 5, no. 12, fol. 70, 17 April 1625.

93. AGS, Estado Alemania, Leg. 707, n.d.

94. HHStA, SHK, K 3, no. 3, fol. 81, 30 July 1618. Philip III regularly used the lan-

guage of family and affection when writing to his relatives. For example, see ibid., fol. 88.

95. HHStA, SHK, K 3, fol. 112, 20 March 1619.

96. HHStA, SDK, K 12, vol. 5, part 1, fol. 71r, Khevenhüller to Rudolf II, 22 February 1591.

97. Ibid., part 2, fol. 409r, 21 May 1599.

98. HHStA, SDK, K 13, vol. 6, fol. 74r, 29 March 1601.

99. Ibid.

100. Ibid., fol. 275r, Khevenhüller to Rudolf II, 22 December 1604.

101. Ibid., fol. 260v, 30 September 1604; and fol. 256v, 24 September 1604.

102. Ibid., fol. 205, 13 September 1603.

103. AGR, Sécretairerie d'État et de Guerre, no. 490, fol. 229v, Carrillo to Albert, 20 November 1600.

104. BN, Madrid, Ms. 2751, "Historia de Joan Kevenhuller de Aichelberg," 1149.

105. BN, Madrid, Ms. 2577, Sepúlveda, "Tomo segundo de la historia de varios sucesos de España," fol. 79r.

106. BL, Add. Ms. 28423, fol. 428, Borja to Lerma, 10 March 1601.

107. See HHStA, Familienkorrespondenz A, K 5, fol. 27, 29 May 1600.

108. HHStA, SHK, K 2, fol. 50v.

109. See HHStA, SDK, K 12, vol. 5, part 2, fol. 301v, 3 September 1596.

110. AHN, Estado, Leg. 2661, fol. 107, 1 November 1608.

111. Ibid., fol. 108, 1 November 1608.

112. Archivio di Stato, Florence, Mediceo 4941, Madrid, Orso d'Elci, fol. 270, 20 October 1609. On Brindisi's mission to Spain, see P. Arthur M. de Carmignano de Brenta, O.F.M. Cap., *Mission diplomatique de Laurent de Brindes.* For Baltasar de Zúñiga's instructions to Brindisi on how best to negotiate at the Spanish court, see AGS, Estado Alemania, Leg. 709, fol. 56, Prague, 8 June 1609.

113. BN, Madrid, Ms. 915, fols. 104r–v, Margaret of the Cross to Philip III, All Saints' Day, 1603.

114. Ibid., fols. 107r–v, Margaret of the Cross to Philip III, 20 July 1605.

115. Ibid., fols. 109r–v, Margaret of the Cross to Philip III, July 1605.

116. Ibid., fols. 111r–v, Margaret of the Cross to Philip III, 12 November 1605.

Chapter 6: Pious Women and Court Politics

1. See Jerónimo de Florencia, "Sermón que predicó el Padre Gerónimo de Florencia, religioso de la Compañia de Jesús, a las honras de la S.C. Magestad de la Emperatriz Doña María"; Rodrigo Mendes Silva, *Admirable vida.*

2. Juan de la Palma, *Vida de la sereníssima Infanta*; Hortensio Felix Paravicino, "Margarita o oración funebre."

3. See Diego de Guzmán, *Reina Católica*; Florencia, "Sermón que predicó a la

Magestad del Rey Don Felipe III en las honras que Su Magestad hizo a la sereníssima Reyna D. Margarita su muger, que es en gloria, en San Gerónimo el Real de Madrid a 18 de noviembre de 1611."

4. See BN, Madrid, Ms. 20260[30], fols. 124–27.

5. See David P. Daniel, "Piety, Politics, and Perversion," 75–76. On the various forms of religious devotion that particularly appealed to the Habsburgs, see Anna Coreth, *Pietas Austriaca.*

6. See, for example, the cases of Lucrecia de León and María de Santo Domingo in Richard L. Kagan, *Lucrecia's Dreams*; Jodi Bilinkoff, "A Spanish Prophetess and Her Patrons."

7. On this issue, see Phyllis Mack, "Women as Prophets during the English Civil War"; and Keith Thomas, *Religion and the Decline of Magic*, 138–39.

8. See AGS, Estado España, Leg. 184, fols. 258–59. For Philip III's letter to the papal nuncio requesting permission for Margaret of the Cross to leave the Descalzas, see BL, Add. Ms. 28707, fol. 25, 2 August 1599.

9. For Archduchess Maria's devotional practices, see Pedro Salazar de Mendoza, *Successión de la ínclyta casa de Baviera*, fols. 64v–67v. The account of her visits to convents is on fol. 65r.

10. ASV, Correspondence of Patriarch of Alexandria, nuncio in Spain, Fondo Borghese, Ser. 1, no. 649, fols. 391r–93v, letter from nuncio to Cardinal Aldobrandino, Zaragoza, 28 November 1599. See also the letter of Archduchess Maria to Ferdinand, which mentions their visit to a cloistered convent close to Valencia, in Friedrich von Hurter, *Bild einer christlichen Fürstin*, 257. See also P. Enrique Flórez de Setien, *Memorias de las reinas católicas de España*, 476.

11. RAH, Colección Salazar y Castro, Ms. 9/476, fols. 17–31v.

12. See Palma, *Vida de la seteníssima Infanta,* fols. 123v, 124v.

13. Luis Cabrera de Córdoba, *Relaciones de las cosas sucedidas*, 197, 200; Guzmán, *Reina Católica*, fols. 134v–135; Elías Tormo, *En las Descalzas Reales*, 197–98.

14. See Juan Luis Vives, *Formación de la mujer cristiana*, 282–85. The moralist Juan de la Cerda argued that even an aristocratic woman was subject to her husband. See Cerda, *Vida política*, fol. 324v. It is noteworthy that Cerda dedicated his book to Margaret of the Cross. He claimed that the life of a nun was the highest calling for women and that Margaret of the Cross was the "crown of all religious women."

15. On the convent of Santa Isabel, see José Luis Saenz Ruiz-Olalde, O.A.R., *Las Agustinas Recoletas de Santa Isabel*, 63–66, 102–10.

16. See AHN, Clero, Leg. 7677, n.f., "Relación que la Reyna Nuestra Señora mando embiar a Don Francisco de Castro embaxador de Su Magestad en Roma."

17. Ibid.

18. See Saenz Ruiz Olalde, *Las Agustinas Recoletas de Santa Isabel*, 40–43. See also APR, Real Capilla, Caja 100, expediente 7, "Carta de todo el convento de Sta Isabel de 24 agosto de 1610, enq dan gracias a Su Magd de averlas dejado con sus constitu-

ciones"; expediente 8, "Parecer q se pueden mudar las monjas de Sᵗᵃ Isabel a otro monasterio," 30 December 1610, "Carta de F. Jn de Camargo . . . a la reyna," "Consulta q se hizo para bolver a su convento de Sᵗᵃ Ysabel a la Mᵉ Cathalina de Espiritu Santo," 1631, "Consulta qe se hizo sobre si la comunidad de religiosas del Real Convento de Sᵗᵃ Isabel," 1632; expediente 41, "cuentas de Santa Isabel"; and expediente 44, "Memorial, Vall.," 14 March 1601.

19. On the convent of the Encarnación, see María Leticia Sánchez Hernández, *El Monasterio de la Encarnación de Madrid*.

20. See Cabrera de Córdoba, *Relaciones de las cosas sucedidas*, 432, 12 May 1611.

21. BN, Madrid, Ms. 1255; Antonio de León Pinelo, *Anales de Madrid*, 90. Philip III gave money to the Royal Convent of Santa Isabel which had come from the goods confiscated from the Moriscos who were expelled from Spain. See APR, Real Capilla, Caja 100, expediente 13, Madrid, 22 November 1612. By the time of their final expulsion, which occurred without much incident, the Moriscos had been under siege for almost a century.

22. See Saenz Ruiz-Olalde, *Las Agustinas Recoletas de Santa Isabel*, 94–102.

23. See APR, Real Capilla, Caja 100, expediente 5, "Carta de Mariana de San José," 4 June, n.d.

24. See Saenz Ruiz-Olalde, *Las Agustinas Recoletas de Santa Isabel*, 96–97. Although Philip III agreed in 1615 to allow the convent to begin taking novices, the nuns had to wait to do so until 1619, when a papal bull was issued granting them permission and stating the exact guidelines.

25. On Teresa of Ávila, see Jodi Bilinkoff, *The Ávila of Saint Teresa*; Alison Weber, *Teresa of Ávila and the Rhetoric of Femininity*; and John Sullivan, O.C.D., ed., *Carmelite Studies*.

26. Margaret of Austria indeed had two books about Teresa of Ávila, who was canonized in 1622. See APR, Sección Histórica, Registro 239, nos. 165, 278.

27. On Mariana de Jesús, see Jodi Bilinkoff, "Self-Identity and Urban Identity in Early Modern Madrid."

28. See Luis de Granada, *Historia de Sor María de la visitación y sermón de las caídas públicas*, ed. Bernardo Velado García; Ramón Robres Lluch and José Ramón Ortolá, "La Monja de Lisboa"; Alvaro Huerga, "La vida seudomística y el proceso inquisitorial de Sor María de la Visitación"; and by the same author, "La Monja de Lisboa y Fray Luis de Granada."

29. Diane Willen argues that women often formed very close ties to other women through religion. See Willen, "Women and Religion in Early Modern England," 152.

30. See Palma, *Vida de la sereníssima Infanta*, fol. 57.

31. Ibid., fol. 123v. See also BN, Madrid, Ms. 2751, "Historia de Joan Kevenhuller de Aichelberg," 1148–49; and María Jesús Pérez Martín, *Margarita de Austria*, 107.

32. See HHStA, SDK, K 13, vol. 6, fol. 257r, Khevenhüller to Rudolf II, Valladolid, 24 September 1604.

33. See Ruth Kleinman, *Anne of Austria*, 38–42; Caroline M. Hibbard, "The Role of a Queen Consort," 404–7; Kevin Sharpe, "The Image of Virtue," 247–48, 256–57.

34. León Pinelo, *Anales de Madrid de León Pinelo*, 97.

35. See "Testamento de Doña Margarita de Austria (9 September 1633)," in *Testamentos de 43 personas del Madrid de los Austrias*, 143–44; "Testamento de Margarita de Austria," RAH, Colección Salazar y Castro, M63, fols. 312v–13r; BL, Add. Ms. 28707, n.f.

36. Mendes Silva, *Admirable vida*, fol. 46. Mendes Silva paraphrased what Jerónimo de Florencia had already preached: see Florencia, "Sermón que predicó el Padre Gerónimo de Florencia," fol. 35.

37. *Testamento de Felipe III*, 7.

38. "Testamento de Doña Margarita de Austria (9 September 1633)," in *Testamentos de 43 personas del Madrid de los Austrias*, 143.

39. Ibid.

40. Ibid., 144.

41. BL, Add. Ms. 28707, n.f.

42. For the important political and cultural ramifications of the patronage conducted by aristocratic women, see Sharon Kettering, "The Patronage Power of Early Modern French Noblewomen." See also June Hall McCash, ed., *The Cultural Patronage of Medieval Women*.

43. Mendes Silva, *Admirable vida*, fol. 33. For Florencia's similar comments, see Florencia, "Sermón que predicó el Padre Gerónimo de Florencia," fol. 32v.

44. "Testamento de Margarita de Austria," RAH, Colección Salazar y Castro, M63, fol. 313v and 314r.

45. Ibid., fol. 313v.

46. See Salazar de Mendoza, *Successión de la ínclyta casa de Baviera*, fol. 67r.

47. "Testamento de Margarita de Austria," RAH, Colección Salazar y Castro, M63, fol. 312.

48. The queen also named the Duke of Lerma as an executor. The queen probably chose Lerma because she recognized that he had the power to see to the speedy execution of her will; the queen was motivated more by pragmatic concerns than the affectionate ones that she alludes to in her will. Moreover, by naming Lerma as one of the executors, the queen was also forcing Lerma to comply with her wishes. See ibid., fol. 318v.

49. The term "mutual dependence" comes from Bilinkoff. See Bilinkoff, *The Ávila of Saint Teresa*, 193.

50. BL, Add. Ms. 28707, n.f.

51. Barbara J. Harris, "A New Look at the Reformation," 91.

52. Willen, "Women and Religion in Early Modern England," 147.

53. On Catholic women's involvement in charitable activities, see Elizabeth Rapley, *The Dévotes*.

54. "Relazione di Francesco Soranzo," 11 October 1602, in Nicolò Barozzi and Guglielmo Berchet, *Relazioni degli stati europei*, 163–64.

55. Florencia, "Sermón que predicó el Padre Gerónimo de Florencia," fol. 35. For Empress María's testament see AGS, PR, L. 31-28. For the settlement of her testament see, for example, AHP, no. 2016, fols. 1535–47, "Fundación del Colegio Imperial de Madrid," 17 March 1614.

56. See AGS, Hacienda, Contaduría de Mercedes, Leg. 683, no. 39, fol. 4.

57. Patrick Williams, "Lerma, Old Castile, and the Travels of Philip III," 385 n. 22.

58. BL, Add. Ms. 28422, fol. 206, 28 November 1599; fol. 254, 17 January 1600; fol. 278, February 1600.

59. For example, Juan de Zúñiga visited the empress on 20 October 1583; HHStA, SV, K 3, fol. 18. Juan de Idiáquez, councillor of state and one of Philip II's closest advisers, saw the empress on 18 April 1590; see HHStA, SDK, K 12, vol. 5, part 1, fol. 19v. The papal nuncio had an audience with Empress María on 3 February 1594; see ibid., fol. 167. In October 1600, the French ambassador visited Empress María at the Descalzas convent; see Cabrera de Córdoba, *Relaciones de las cosas sucedidas*, 85.

60. See Hans Khevenhüller, *Geheimes Tagebuch*, 241–64.

61. Palma, *Vida de la serenísima Infanta*, fols. 111, 119v–20.

62. For a discussion of the advantages that convent life and virginity offered women, see Theodora A. Jankowski, *Women in Power in the Early Modern Drama*, 25–31.

63. For a list of the individuals in the empress's court, see BL, Add. Ms. 28707, fol. 68. This list is reproduced and discussed in Tormo, *En las Descalzas Reales*, 226–29 n. 38. See also José Simón Díaz, *Historia del Colegio Imperial de Madrid*, vol. 1, 34.

64. See BL, Add. Ms. 28422, fol. 296, Borja to Lerma, 9 February 1600.

65. BN, Madrid, Ms. 2751, "Historia de Joan Kevenhuller de Aichelberg," 404; AGS, Estado Venecia, Leg. 1527, fol. 120, Cardinal Granvela to Cristóbal Salazar, Madrid, 4 August 1582.

66. See, for example, AGS, Estado Venecia, Leg. 1527, fol. 102, Madrid, 19 February 1582. See also ibid., fol. 104, Cardinal Granvela to Cristóbal Salazar, 2 March 1582. In arguing that the empress had to subordinate her own desires to those of the Spanish monarchy, Granvela was merely echoing what most people (including the Habsburgs) expected of royal women.

67. Hortensio Felix Paravicino, "Margarita o oración funebre," fols. 173v, 179v, 181v.

68. Palma, *Vida de la serenísima Infanta*, fol. 154v. Hortensio Felix Paravicino, undoubtedly following Palma's account, recounts the same incident. See Paravicino, "Margarita o oración funebre," fols. 177r–v.

69. See Caroline Walker Bynum, *Holy Feast and Holy Fast*, 165–86.

70. Paravicino, "Margarita o oración funebre," fols. 170v, 177v.

71. Mendes Silva, *Admirable vida*, fols. 21v, 33, 44. Mendes Silva claimed that the empress slept only two hours each night. He may have misread Florencia, his obvi-

ous source, who wrote that the empress would retire to her bedroom and pray for two hours before going to sleep. See Florencia, "Sermón que predicó el Padre Gerónimo de Florencia," fol. 34.

72. Palma, *Vida de la seteníssima Infanta*, fol. 104.

73. See Fidel Pérez Mínguez, "La Condesa de Castellar," 394.

74. Cabrera de Córdoba, *Relaciones de las cosas sucedidas*, 499–500.

75. Cristóbal Pérez de Herrera, "Carta apologética al Doctor Luis del Valle," 1 November 1610, in *Codoin*, vol. 18, 564–74.

76. BN, Madrid, Ms. 2577, Sépulveda, "Tomo segundo de la historia de varios sucesos de España," fol. 79 (1600).

77. Jo Ann McNamara, "The Need to Give," 200.

78. This is in sharp contrast to the historiographical depiction of the king as pacifistic. See Bernardo José García García, "El Duque de Lerma y la Pax Hispánica," 84–86, 127 n. 10.

79. See BN, Madrid, Ms. 20260[30], fols. 124r–v.

80. See Juan Gómez de Mora, "Relación de las honras funerales," fol. 3r.

81. Palma, *Vida de la seteníssima Infanta*, fols. 107, 108v.

82. See Guzmán, *Reina Católica*, fols. 142r–v.

83. See Flórez de Setien, *Memorias de las reinas católicas de España*, 467–68.

84. This was true for aristocratic women in France as well. See Rapley, *The Dévotes*, 77.

85. Andrés de Espinosa, "Sermón que predicó a la Magestad del Rey Don Felipe III en las honras que Su Magestad hizo a la seteníssima Reyna D. Margarita su muger," fol. 15.

86. Rosemary Radford Ruether, "Misogynism and Virginal Feminism in the Fathers of the Church," 159–61, 175–76; Clarissa Atkinson, "'Precious Balsam in a Fragile Glass.'"

87. See Florencia, "Sermón que predicó el Padre Gerónimo de Florencia," fol. 40; and Florencia, "Sermón segundo que predicó el Padre Gerónimo de Florencia," fol. 11.

88. See the portrait by the studio of Sir Anthony Van Dyck, c. 1628–34, in the Walker Art Museum in London.

89. McNamara, "The Need to Give," 214.

90. P. Agustín de Castro, "Sermón q. predicó el Padre Agustín de Castro de la Compañia de Jesús, en las exequias que el colegio imperial desta corte hizo a la seteníssima Infanta Soror Margarita de la Cruz," n.f. The sermon was dedicated to Philip IV.

91. Agustín de Castro related approximately the same story. Ibid., n.f.

92. Paravicino, "Margarita o oración funebre," fol. 185r.

93. Ibid., fol. 182v. (This should really be folio 184v; the folios are misnumbered and contain two folios numbered 182v.)

94. Florencia, "Sermón que predicó a la Magestad del Rey Don Felipe III en las honras que Su Magestad hizo a la seteníssima Reyna D. Margarita su muger," fol. 20v;

and Florencia, "Sermón segundo que predicó el Padre Gerónimo de Florencia," fol. 21v.

95. On specific saints who believed that they had the power to free souls from purgatory, see Bynum, *Holy Feast and Holy Fast*, 127, 129, 133, 171, 227, 234, 242, 281. Bynum's book also details the numerous other ways (particularly, fasting, self-denial, and suffering) through which medieval women acquired a reputation for holiness.

96. On these paintings, see Juan Miguel Serrera, "Alonso Sánchez Coello," 39–40.

97. Ibid.

98. On Queen Elizabeth's use of Marian imagery, see Peter McClure and Robin Headlam Wells, "Elizabeth I as a Second Virgin Mary"; Frances Yates, *Astraea*, 76–80; Carole Levin, *The Heart and Stomach of a King*, 26–28.

99. See BN, Madrid, Ms. 2751, "Historia de Joan Kevenhulller de Aichelberg," 1140.

100. BN, Madrid, Ms. 687, fol. 709r, Margaret of the Cross to the Duke of Lerma, 29 October 1608.

101. BN, Madrid, Ms. 915, fols. 100r–v, Margaret of the Cross to Philip III, 1605.

102. Ibid., fol. 117v, Margaret of the Cross to Philip III, All Saints' Day, 1606.

103. Ibid., fols. 104r–v, Margaret of the Cross to Philip III, All Saints' Day, 1603.

Chapter 7: Melancholy and Infirmity

1. Tomé Pinheiro da Veiga, *Fastiginia*, 112, 118. Pinheiro da Veiga described a banquet that Lerma gave for visiting English notables in which 2,200 different entrees were served.

2. Magdalena and Balthasar Paumgartner are good examples of early modern individuals who were extremely concerned about their health. See Steven Ozment, *Magdalena and Balthasar*.

3. See, for example, Juan Carrillo's report to Archduke Albert in 1599 on Margaret of the Cross's health. AGR, Sécretairerie d'État et de Guerre, no. 490, fol. 38, Carrillo to Albert, 17 December 1599.

4. On melancholy, see Lawrence Babb, *The Elizabethan Malady*; Raymond Klibansky, Erwin Panofsky, and Fritz Saxl, *Saturn and Melancholy*; Wolf Lepenies, *Melancholy and Society*; Bridget Gellert Lyons, *Voices of Melancholy*; Juliana Schiesari, *The Gendering of Melancholia*; Teresa Scott Soufas, *Melancholy and the Secular Mind in Spanish Golden Age Literature*; Jean Starobinski, *History of the Treatment of Melancholy from the Earliest Times to 1900*.

5. See Michael MacDonald, *Mystical Bedlam*, 150–60. MacDonald analyzed the manuscripts of a seventeenth-century English doctor, Richard Napier, and found that two-thirds of Napier's aristocratic patients complained of melancholy (151). For the popularity of melancholy in Elizabethan England, see Babb, *The Elizabethan Malady*.

6. Giovanni Botero, *Descripción de todas las provincias y reynos del mundo*, fol. 4r.

7. Lepenies, *Melancholy and Society*, 31–32. Lepenies argues that boredom caused

many rulers to become melancholic. See also H. C. Erik Midelfort, *Mad Princes of Renaissance Germany*, 73–155; and Richard L. Kagan, *Lucrecia's Dreams*, 93.

8. On Rudolf II's melancholy, see Midelfort, *Mad Princes of Renaissance Germany*, 125–40. R. J. W. Evans's portrait of Rudolf II is essentially that of a melancholic ruler. See Evans, *Rudolf II and His World*. For melancholy, see also José Antonio Maravall, *Culture of the Baroque*, 150–51.

9. BN, Madrid, Ms. 1174, "Relación que hiço . . . Simón Contarini," fol. 8v; Luis Cabrera de Córdoba, *Relaciones de las cosas sucedidas*, 89, 113, 161, 210, 211, 212, 299.

10. Cabrera de Córdoba, *Relaciones de las cosas sucedidas*, 89.

11. HHStA, SDK, K 13, vol. 6, fol. 324v, Khevenhüller to Rudolf II, Valladolid, 22 December 1605.

12. Cabrera de Córdoba, *Relaciones de las cosas sucedidas*, 362.

13. Midelfort, *Mad Princes of Renaissance Germany*, 21–23.

14. Cabrera de Córdoba, *Relaciones de las cosas sucedidas*, 211.

15. On the empress's overall health, see AGR, Sécretairerie d'État et de Guerre, no. 490, Correspondance de l'Archiduc Albert avec Juan Carrillo, fol. 102, 3 June 1600; fol. 114v, 19 June 1600; fol. 126, 8 July 1600. For an account of Empress María's jealousy, see BL, Add. Ms. 28424, fol. 217, Borja to Lerma, 21 November 1601. For a seventeenth-century discussion of the symptoms of melancholy, see Robert Burton, *The Anatomy of Melancholy (A Selection)*, 132–46.

16. ASV, Spagna 49, fol. 417v, 20 November 1598.

17. AGR, Sécretairerie d'État et de Guerre, no. 490, Correspondance de l'Archiduc Albert avec Juan Carrillo, fol. 114v, 3 June 1600.

18. Ibid., fol. 92, 17 May 1600.

19. BN, Madrid, Ms. 687, fol. 189, Albert to Lerma, 30 November 1600.

20. AGR, Sécretairerie d'État et de Guerre, no. 490, Correspondance de l'Archiduc Albert avec Juan Carrillo, fol. 106, 8 June 1600.

21. BL, Add. Ms. 28423, fol. 35, Borja to Lerma, 4 June 1600.

22. Ibid.

23. BL, Add. Ms. 28424, fol. 94, Borja to Lerma, July 1601.

24. Ibid., fol. 95, Lerma to the Duke of Alburquerque, July 1601.

25. Ibid., fol. 221, Borja to Lerma, 29 November 1601.

26. Ibid., fol. 217, Borja to Lerma, 21 November 1601.

27. Ibid., fol. 223, Lerma to Borja, 5 December 1601; fol. 226, Borja to Lerma, 8 December 1601. I do not have Borja's original letter reporting the empress's complaints, but it was written before 29 November 1601.

28. Ibid., fol. 236, Borja to Lerma, 12 December 1601.

29. Ibid., fol. 228, Borja to Lerma, 15 December 1601.

30. HHStA, SV, K 4 (B), Fasz. 3, "Inventario de los bienes que se an de llebar a Alemania," fol. 535r, 5 June 1606.

31. Ibid., fol. 536r.

32. See BN, Madrid, Ms. 2752, "Historia de Joan Kevenhuller de Aichelberg," 1150–51.

33. In her study of female illness in eighteenth-century Germany, Barbara Duden argues that aristocratic women often chose their own remedies for illness and relied on their personal physicians to confirm these remedies. See Barbara Duden, *The Woman beneath the Skin*, 95. This might also have been true for Spanish royal women in the early modern period. Their medical doctors were often members of their households and were dependent upon them for employment and for their position at court.

34. HHStA, Familienakten, K 65, Madrid, 26 February 1603.

35. On the connection between choler and melancholy, see Soufas, *Melancholy and the Secular Mind*, 8, 20–24.

36. "Relazione di Ottaviano Bon," 21 December 1602, in Nicolò Barozzi and Guglielmo Berchet, *Relazioni degli stati europei*, 247.

37. Cabrera de Córdoba, *Relaciones de las cosas sucedidas*, 123–24. The queen had given birth to a daughter on 22 September 1601.

38. Ibid., 124.

39. BN, Madrid, Ms. 2577, Sepúlveda, "Tomo segundo de la historia de varios sucesos de España," fol. 115.

40. Cabrera de Córdoba, *Relaciones de las cosas sucedidas*, 124.

41. Ibid., 60.

42. Ibid., 201.

43. Ibid., 217, 224, 266, 350.

44. Ibid., 113. By 1610, the queen was willing to give birth at Lerma's house. Patrick Williams has quite convincingly interpreted this as a sign of a reconciliation between Lerma and the queen. As he writes: "The 1610 journey saw a reconciliation between Lerma and Margaret. The queen at last consented to give birth under Lerma's roof and on 24 May a daughter was born to her who seems [to] have been named jointly after herself and her host, Margarita Francisca. Lerma's crisis was over." See Williams, "Lerma, Old Castile, and the Travels of Philip III," 395. However, I would take Williams's observations a step further. The incident also shows the queen's confidence in her influence over the king. She was no longer threatened by the Duke of Lerma and could bestow this favor on him.

45. Cabrera de Córdoba, *Relaciones de las cosas sucedidas*, 367.

46. Ibid., 149–55.

47. Ibid., 123. When the queen became very sick in 1601 and the doctors could not seem to help her, the populace turned to spiritual remedies.

48. See HHStA, SDK, K 12, vol. 5, part 2, fol. 447v, 3 December 1599.

49. AGS, Estado Corona de Castilla, Leg. 205, 26 June 1606.

50. Ibid.

51. Khevenhüller often noted her "regular indisposition." See, for example, HHStA, SDK, K 12, vol. 5, part 2, fol. 294r, 12 June 1596; HHStA, SDK, K 13, vol. 6, fol. 304v, 30 May 1605.

52. See, for example, Khevenhüller, *Geheimes Tagebuch*, 289–90. See also HHStA, SDK, K 12, vol. 5, part 2, no. 2, fol. 415v, 19 June 1599; HHStA, SDK, K 13, vol. 6, fols. 240v–41v, 9 June 1604.

53. Juan de la Palma, *Vida de la sereníssima Infanta*, fol. 142.

54. AGR, Sécretairerie d'État et de Guerre, no. 502, Margaret of the Cross to Albert, n.f., 14 March. This letter is probably from 1609 or 1610 judging from the dates on subsequent letters.

55. See AGR, Sécretairerie d'État et de Guerre, no. 502, n.f., 10 June 1617.

56. On suffering and sanctity, see Donald Weinstein and Rudolf M. Bell, *Saints and Society*, 156.

57. St. Teresa advised prioresses to deal harshly with melancholic nuns, to discipline and even imprison them. See Teresa of Ávila, *Book of the Foundations*, 36–40. See also Alison Weber, *Teresa of Ávila and the Rhetoric of Femininity*, 139–47.

58. Schiesari, *The Gendering of Melancholia*; see especially chap. 2, 96–159.

59. See Anne Laurence, "Women's Psychological Disorders in Seventeenth-Century Britain," 205–6, 208–11.

60. Juan Huarte de San Juan, *Examen de ingenios para las sciencias donde se muestran*, 110–11.

61. Schiesari claims that the melancholic voice "historically has been the culturally empowered expression of loss and sorrow by men (190)." See Schiesari, *The Gendering of Melancholia*, 186–90.

62. Cabrera de Córdoba, *Relaciones de las cosas sucedidas*, 113–14.

63. HHStA, SDK, K 13, vol. 6, fol. 229v, Khevenhüller to Rudolf II, 17 March 1604; fols. 234v–36r, 31 March 1604; and fol. 242r, 15 June 1604.

64. On Magdalena de Guzmán, Marquesa del Valle, see Luis Fernández Martín, "La Marquesa del Valle," 559–638; Fidel Pérez Mínguez, "La Condesa de Castellar," 400–409. For the Marquesa del Valle's declaration to the committee sent to question her about her activities at the court, see BN, Madrid, Ms. 18191, fols. 192r–201v.

65. Lerma had other severe bouts with melancholy in 1611–12 when his close associate Rodrigo Calderón came under attack and investigation. See Patrick Williams, "Lerma, 1618: Dismissal or Retirement?" 313.

66. See ASV, Fondo Borghese, Ser. 2, no. 272, Nunziatura di Spagna 1605–6, fols. 58r–v, 67r–v.

67. See Bernardo José García García, "Paz, desempeño y reputación en la política exterior del Duque de Lerma (1598–1618)," 485 n. 53. For a discussion of Lerma's desire to enter a monastery, see Williams, "Lerma, 1618," 307–32.

68. Bleeding was a common treatment in early modern Spain for melancholy and

other diseases of the humors. See Soufas, *Melancholy and the Secular Mind*, 94–95.

69. For a list of gifts the queen received on one occasion in 1602, see AGS, Hacienda, Consejos y Juntas de Hacienda, Leg. 428, no. 18, Casa Real.

70. Cabrera de Córdoba also claimed that the custom was spreading to gentlemen (*señores*). See Cabrera de Córdoba, *Relaciones de las cosas sucedidas*, 155.

71. BL, Add. Ms. 28423, fol. 88, Borja to Lerma, 9 July 1600.

72. Pinheiro da Veiga, *Fastiginia*, 77.

73. For a seventeenth-century reference to diamonds as a cure for melancholy, see H. J. C. von Grimmelshausen, *The Adventures of a Simpleton*, 135.

74. Pinheiro da Veiga, *Fastiginia*, 77.

75. Cabrera de Córdoba, *Relaciones de las cosas sucedidas*, 113.

76. AGR, Sécretairerie d'État et de Guerre, no. 490, Correspondance de l'Archiduc Albert avec Juan Carrillo, fol. 48, 12 February 1600.

77. Ibid., fol. 127, 8 July 1600. For Juan de Borja's account, see BL, Add. Ms. 28423, fol. 88, Borja to Lerma, 9 July 1600.

78. AGR, Sécretairerie d'État et de Guerre, no. 490, Correspondance de l'Archiduc Albert avec Juan Carrillo, fol. 48, 12 February 1600.

79. "Viaje hecho por Bartolomé Joly, consejero y limosnero del Rey en España" (1603–4), in José García Mercadal, ed., *Viajes de extranjeros por España y Portugal*, 2: 100.

Conclusion: Women and Spanish Policy at the Court of Philip III

1. For the political influence of one early modern Jesuit confessor, see Robert Bireley, S.J., *Religion and Politics in the Age of the Counterreformation*.

2. Margaret of Austria was also undoubtedly following the example of her mother, Archduchess Maria of Bavaria, who was from the Wittelsbach family. What I assert about the Habsburg women is certainly true of women in other royal households. Archduchess Maria of Bavaria is a very good example of how a royal woman exerted tremendous political influence. Among other things, she was instrumental in the education and political training of her son, Archduke Ferdinand. Margaret of Austria therefore had examples of strong, politically active women on both her mother's and her father's side.

3. See, for example, Caroline Walker Bynum, *Holy Feast and Holy Fast*; Gerda Lerner, *The Creation of Feminist Consciousness from the Middle Ages to Eighteen-Seventy*, 65–87.

4. See BN, Madrid, Ms. 20260[30], fols. 124–27.

5. See Judith Brown, *Immodest Acts*; Bynum, *Holy Feast and Holy Fast*; Craig Harline, *The Burdens of Sister Margaret*; Ronald E. Surtz, *The Guitar of God*.

6. On this issue, see Magdalena S. Sánchez, "A House Divided," 887–903.

7. See BN, Madrid, Ms. 17858, "Relaciones de los años 1618 a 1621."

8. See AGS, Estado Alemania, Leg. 709, fol. 152.

9. By the terms of the treaty of Oñate, which Philip III and Archduke Ferdinand signed in 1617, Philip agreed to help Ferdinand if any revolt broke out in Bohemia. For the terms of the treaty, see ÖNB, Handschriftensammlung, Ms. 15188.

10. For a recent, excellent overview of historians' obsession with the "decline of Spain," see Richard L. Kagan, "Prescott's Paradigm."

Bibliography

Archival Sources

SPAIN

Archivo General de Simancas (AGS)

Cámara de Castilla

   Casa Real: Leg. 303
   Diversos de Castilla: Legs. 34–36
   Memoriales y Expedientes: Legs. 305, 831, 841, 850, 854–56

Estado

   Alemania: Legs. 688, 692, 706–12, 2323–27, 2450–54, 2492–2505, 2865, 2868
   Corona de Castilla: Legs. 162–69, 176, 180, 182, 186–87, 205, 250, 257
   España: Legs. 184, 649, 2636, 2652, 2706
   Estados Pequeños de Italia: Legs. 1453, 1484–95, 1942–44
   Genoa: Legs. 1401, 1414–15, 1430–37, 1932–34
   Milán y Saboya: Legs. 1285, 1287–1306, 1896–1916, 1918–19, 1921, 1938–39
   Venecia: Legs. 1527, 1928, 1929

Hacienda

   Consejo y Juntas de Hacienda: Legs. 385, 386–90, 412, 417, 419, 428–29, 431–32, 442–45, 454, 456, 458–59, 462–63, 481
   Contaduría Mayor de Cuentas, 3° Época: Legs. 669, 683, 1140, 1146–47, 1166–67, 1746, 1785, 1817, 2420, 2550, 2465, 2550, 2717, 2903, 3000
   Contaduría de Mercedes: Legs. 541, 606, 683, 728, 1140, 1146, 1148, 1746, 1785, 2082, 2465, 2550, 2962, 3000, 3519
   Dirección General del Tesoro: Legs. 577–79, 1001, 1288

Patronato Real (PR)

   Cajas 31-28; 34-137; 38-68; 78, 188-306

Archivo Histórico Nacional (AHN)

Clero: Leg. 7677
Consejo de Hacienda: Legs. 33.899, 33.900
Consejos: Leg. 16.244; L. 2605
Consejos/Patronato de Castilla: Legs. 17.249–53
Consejos Suprimidos: Legs. 4410–12, 4415–22
Diversos/Títulos de Castilla: Leg. 2181
Estado: Legs. 678, 2661; L. 76, 81, 162, 613, 692, 712, 832
Jesuítas: Legs. 1180, 1288; L. 1324, 1326, 1348, 1383, 1384, 1437
Osuna: Leg. 571

Archivo Histórico de Protocoles (AHP)

Nos. 2016, 2606, 2607, 2633

Archivo del Palacio Real (APR)

Expedientes Personales: Cajas 13/3, 47/13, 96/19, 135/49–50, 147/37, 209/1–5, 494/29,
  7303/26–28
Histórico—Felipe III: Legs. 2913, 2914
Real Capilla: Caja 100
Sección Descalzas: 7140
Sección Histórica: Registro 239; Cajas 49, 50, 56, 190

Archivo del Real Monasterio de la Encarnación (ARMEN)

Matritense sobre la M. Mariana de San José

Cartas: Leg. 65
Cuentas de Conciencia: Leg. 61
Diario Espiritual: Leg. 62
Escritos Impresos
Testimonios: Legs. 1, 2, 6, 7, 9, 32, 60

Biblioteca/Archivo Zabálburu

Colección Altamira: Carpeta 194

Biblioteca Bartolomé March de Madrid,

Ms. 23/11/1–II

Biblioteca del Palacio Real

Mss. II/1445, III/4056, III/6492, IX/6842

Biblioteca Nacional, Madrid (BN, Madrid)

Mss. 290, 300, 687, 861, 915, 981, 989, 1007, 1174, 1255, 1431, 1440, 1492, 1761, 1881, 1923, 2035, 2036, 2347, 2348, 2349, 2352, 2509, 2551, 2577, 2751, 2989, 3207, 3657, 5570, 5627, 5628, 5913, 6043, 6494, 6751, 6933, 6955, 7423, 8526, 9087, 9855, 10259, 10305, 10454, 10623, 10818, 10861, 11124, 11773, 12851, 12859, 17858, 18191, 18716, 18718, 18725, 19706, 20260

Instituto Valencia de Don Juan (IVDJ)

Colección Altamira: Envíos 7, 37, 40, 41, 44, 47, 48

Real Academia de la Historia (RAH)

Colección Jesuítas: Tomo 57, 72, 86, 91, 96, 101, 132, 195
Colección Pellicer: Tomo 14, 22, 23, 28, 32
Colección Salazar y Castro: A63, A64, A75, A76, I35, K106, L12, M63; Mss. 9/476, 9/477, 9/3507

AUSTRIA

Haus-, Hof-, und Staatsarchiv, Vienna (HHStA)

Belgische Korrespondenz: K 7, 8, 9, 10
Familienakten: K 15, 23, 65, 86, 106, 109
Familienkorrespondenz A: K 4, 5, 6, 8, 10, 31, 40, 42, 43, 44, 49, 53
Spanien Diplomatische Korrespondenz (SDK): K 10–17
Spanien Hofkorrespondenz (SHK): K 2, 3
Spanien Varia (SV): K 3, 4, 5, 6, 65

Österreichische Nationalbibliothek (ÖNB)

Handschriftensammlung: Mss. 1/32-1; 15/21-1; 670/51-2; 8219; 15188; Codex 6024

BELGIUM

Archives Générales du Royaume, Brussels (AGR)

Sécretairerie d'État et de Guerre: nos. 489, 490, 502

ENGLAND

British Library (BL)

Add. Mss. 28343; 28344; 28345; 28346; 28349; 28358; 28422; 28423; 28424; 28425; 28707

ITALY

Archivio di Stato, Florence

Mediceo: 4933, 4937, 4941–44

Archivio di Stato, Naples

Archivio Farnesiano-Spagna: Fasci 25, 27, 30

Archivio di Stato, Venice

Spagna: 52

Archivio Segreto Vaticano (ASV)

Fondo Borghese: Ser. 1, no. 649; Ser. 2, no. 272
Spagna: 49, 52, 59, 327, 335

CZECH REPUBLIC

Moravský Zemský Archiv (formerly Státní Archiv) Brno, Rodinný Archiv
Ditrichštejnů K 423/1898-163

Printed Primary Sources

Aguilar, Gaspar de. *Expulsión de los moriscos de España*. Valencia, 1610.

Alamos de Barrientos, Baltasar. *Discurso político al Rey Felipe III al comienzo de su reinado*. Barcelona: Anthropos, 1990.

Alberti, Leon Battista. *The Family in Renaissance Florence* (Book Three). Trans. Renée Neu Watkins. Park Heights, Ill.: Waveland Press, 1994.

Alidosi, Roderico. *Relazione di Germania e della corte di Rodolfo II*. Modena, 1872.

Almansa y Mendoza, Andrés de. *Cartas de Felipe III*. Madrid, 1886.

Astete, Gaspar de. *Tratado del gobierno de la familia y estado de la viudas y donzellas*. Burgos, 1603.

Ayerbe, Marqués de. *Correspondencia inédita de Don Guillén de San Clemente, Embajador en Alemania de los Reyes Don Felipe II y III sobre la intervención de España en los sucesos de Polonia y Hungría, 1581–1608*. Zaragoza: La Derecha, 1892.

Aznar Cardona, Pedro. *Vida y muerte de Doña Margarita de Austria*. Madrid, 1617.

Barozzi, Nicolò, and Guglielmo Berchet. *Relazioni degli stati europei: Lette al senato dagli ambasciatori veneti nel secolo decimosettimo*. Serie 1: *Spagna*, vol. 1. Venice, 1856.

Botero, Giovanni. *Descripción de todas las provincias y reynos del mundo*. Barcelona: Gabriel Graells y Giraldo Dotil, 1603.

Burton, Robert. *The Anatomy of Melancholy (A Selection)*, ed. Lawrence Babb. East Lansing: Michigan State University Press, 1965.

Cabrera de Córdoba, Luis. *Relaciones de las cosas sucedidas en la corte de España desde 1599 hasta 1614*. Madrid: J. Martín Alegria, 1857.

Carrillo, Fray Juan de. *Relación histórica de la real fundación del Monasterio de las Descalzas Reales de Santa Clara de la Villa de Madrid*. Madrid, 1616.

Castro, P. Agustín de. "Sermón q. predicó el Padre Agustín de Castro de la Compañia de Jesús, en las exequias que el colegio imperial desta corte hizo a la seceníssima Infanta Soror Margarita de la Cruz." Madrid, 1633.

Castro Egas, Ana. *Eternidad del Rey Don Felipe III: Discurso de su vida y santas costumbres*. Madrid, 1629.

Cerda, Juan de la. *Vida política de todos los estados de mujeres*. Alcalá de Henares, 1599.

Colección de documentos inéditos para la historia de España [Codoin]. Vols. 18, 43, 60, 61, 110. Madrid: Academia de la Historia, 1842–95.

Escagedo Salmón, Mateo. "Los Acebedos." *Boletín de la Biblioteca Menéndez Pelayo* 6, no. 1 (1924): 108–24; 6, no. 3 (1924): 224–41; 7, no. 1 (1925): 50–64; 7, no. 2 (1925): 181–88; 7, no. 3 (1925): 211–24; 8, no. 1 (1926): 15–29; 8, no. 2 (1926): 156–62; 8, no. 3 (1926): 243–63; 8, no. 4 (1926): 333–42.

Espinosa, Andrés de. "Sermón a las honras de Su Magestad de la Reyna Doña Margarita de Austria N. S. que la muy insigne Universidad de Salamanca hizo en los 9. dias del mes de noviembre del año de 1611." Fols. 1–31v.

Florencia, Jerónimo de. "Sermón que predicó a la Magestad del Rey Don Felipe III en las honras que Su Magestad hizo a la seceníssima Reyna D. Margarita su muger, que es en gloria, en San Gerónimo el Real de Madrid a 18 de noviembre de 1611." Madrid, 1611.

———. "Sermón que predicó a la Magestad . . . del Rey Don Felipe IV . . . en las honras que hizo al Rey Felipe III su padre . . . en San Gerónimo en Real de Madrid a 4 de mayo de 1621." Madrid, 1621.

———. "Sermón que predicó el Padre Gerónimo de Florencia, religioso de la Compañia de Jesús, a las honras de la S.C. Magestad de la Emperatriz Doña María." In *Libro de las honras que hizo el colegio de la Compañia de Jesús de Madrid, a la M.C. de la Emperatriz Doña María de Austria, fundadora del dicho colegio, que se celebraron a 21 de abril de 1603*. Madrid: Luis Sánchez, 1603.

———. "Sermón segundo que predicó el Padre Gerónimo de Florencia de la Compañia de Jesus, y predicador del Rey N.S. en las honras que hizo á la Magestad de la seteníssima Reyna Doña Margarita N.S. (que Dios tiene) la nobilíssima villa de Madrid en Santa Maria, á los 19. de Diziembre de 1611." Madrid: Luis Sánchez, 1612.

Gans, Joannes P. *Österreichisches Frauenzimmer das ist, das Leben aller gebornen Erzherzoginnen von Österreich von den zeiten Rudolfs I., des Erzhauses Erhebers, bis auf unsere Zeit*. Cologne, 1638.

García Mercadal, José, ed. *Viajes de extranjeros por España y Portugal*. 2 vols. Madrid: Aguilar, 1952, 1959.

Gómez de Mora, Juan. "Relación de las honras funerales que se hizieron por la Reyna Doña Margarita de Austria nuestra s^ra en esta villa de Madrid por su Magestad del Rey Don Felipe nuestro señor." N.p., n.d.

González Dávila, Gil. *Historia de la vida y hechos del ínclito monarca, amado y santo D. Felipe Tercero*. Madrid: D. Joachin de Ibarra, 1771.

———. *Teatro de las grandezas de la villa de Madrid, corte de los reyes católicos de España*. Madrid: Thomas Iunti, 1623.

González de Cellorigo, Martín. *Memorial de la política necessaria y útil restauración de la república de España*. Valladolid, 1619.

Granada, Luis de. *Historia de Sor María de la Visitación y sermón de las caídas públicas*. Ed. Bernardo Velado García. Barcelona: J. Flors, 1962.

Grimmelshausen, H. J. C. von. *The Adventures of a Simpleton*. New York: Ungar Publishing Co., 1986.

Guzmán, Diego de. *Reina Católica: Vida y muerte de Doña Margarita de Austria, Reina de España*. Madrid, 1617.

Hinojosa y Naveros, Ricardo. *Despachos de la diplomacia pontificia en España*. Madrid: B. A. de la Fuente, 1896.

Huarte de San Juan, Juan. *Examen de ingenios para las sciencias donde se muestran la diferencia de habilidades que ay en los hombres; y el genero de letras, que a cada uno responde en particular*. Baeza, 1575.

Khevenhüller, Hans. *Geheimes Tagebuch, 1548–1605*. Graz, Akademische Druck- und Verlagsanstalt, 1971.

Khull, Ferdinand. *Sechsundvierzig Briefe der Erzherzogin Maria an ihren Sohn Ferdinand aus den Jahren 1598–99*. Graz, 1898.

Klarwill, Victor von, ed. *The Fugger News Letters: A Selection, 1566–1605*. Trans. Pauline de Chary. London, 1924.

Lhermite, Jehan. *Le passetemps de Jehan Lhermite*. 2 vols. Antwerp: Ch. Ruelens, 1890–96.

León Pinelo, Antonio de. *Anales de Madrid de León Pinelo, reinado de Felipe III, Años 1598 a 1621*. Ed. Ricardo Martorell Tellez-Girón. Madrid: E. Maestre, 1931.

Malvezzi, Virgilio. *Historia del Marqués Virgilio Malvezzi.* In Yáñez Fajardo y Montroy, *Memorias.* Madrid, 1723.

Martorell Téllez-Girón, Ricardo, ed. *Cartas de Felipe III a su hija Ana, Reina de Francia.* Madrid: Imprenta Helénica, 1929.

Matilla Tascón, Antonio, trans. and ed., *Testamentos de 43 personas del Madrid de los Austrias.* Madrid: Instituto de Estudios Madrileños, 1983.

Mendes Silva, Rodrigo. *Admirable vida y heroicas virtudes de aquel glorioso blasón de España . . . la enclarecida Emperatriz María, hija del siempre invicto Emperador Carlos V.* Madrid, 1655.

Muñoz, Luis, *Vida de la venerable virgen Luisa de Carvajal.* Madrid, 1632.

————. *Vida y virtudes de la venerable Madre Mariana de San Joseph.* Madrid, 1643.

Orejón, Blas. "Sermón que predicó Blas Orejón, canonigo de la Santa Iglesia de Segovia, en las honras que aquella insigne ciudad hizo, a la seteníssima Reyna Doña Margarita de Austria nuestra señora en la Iglesia mayor, jueves 1 diciembre 1611." Valladolid, 1612.

Ortiz, Antonio. *A Relation of the Solemnite.* Trans. Francis River. N.p., 1601. Reprinted in vol. 341, *English Recusant Literature 1558–1640,* ed. D. M. Rogers. London: The Scholar Press, 1977.

Ortiz de Zúñiga, Diego. *Anales eclesiásticos y seculares de la muy noble y muy leal ciudad de Sevilla.* Madrid: en la Imprenta Real, por I. Garcia Infanzon, 1677.

Osuna, Francisco de. *Nortes de los estados en que se da regla de vivir a los mancebos, y a los casados, y a los viudos, y a todos los continentes y se tratan muy por extenso los remedios del desastrado casamiento, enseñando que tal ha de ser la vida del cristiano casado.* Seville, n.d.

Palafox y Mendoza, Juan de. "Libro de la vida de la serenissíma señora Infanta Sor Margarita de la Cruz." In *Tomo quarto de las obras del ilustrísimo Señor Don Juan de Palafox y Mendoza.* Madrid, 1664.

Palma, Juan de la. *Vida de la serenissíma Infanta Sor Margarita de la Cruz, religiosa Descalza de Santa Clara.* Seville, 1653.

Paravicino, Hortensio Felix. "Margarita o oración funebre en las honras de la seteníssima Infanta del Imperio de Alemania, Reynos de Bohemia, Ungria, Moravia, etc. Sor Margarita de la Cruz. Hija, hermana, prima, tía de sacras, católicas, cesareas, reales, christianíssimas magestades del Imperio Romano, monarquía de España, y reyno de Francia. Esposa de Jesu Christo, rey de reyes, y señor de señores." In *Oraciones evangélicas, y panegíricos funerales que a diversos intentos dixo.* Madrid, 1641.

————. *Panegyrico funeral . . . a Felipe Tercero el piadoso.* Madrid, 1625.

————. *Sermones cortesanos.* Ed. Francis Cerdan. Madrid: Castalia, 1994.

Paz y Meliá, Antonio, ed. "Correspondencia del Conde de Lemos con Don Francisco de Castro, su hermano, y con el Príncipe de Esquilache (1613–1620)." *Bulletin Hispanique* 5 (1903).

Pérez de Herrera, Cristóbal. "Carta apologética al Doctor Luis del Valle defendiendo su buena intención al publicar su obra sobre los males y remedios del Reino." In *Colección de documentos inéditos para la historia de España [Codoin]*, vol. 18. Madrid, 1874.

Pidal, Pedro José de, et al., eds. *Continuación de los documentos relativos al Archiduque Alberto de Austria*. Vol. 43 of *Colección de documentos inéditos para la historia de España [Codoin]*. Madrid: Imprenta de la viuda de Calero, 1863.

Pinheiro da Veiga, Tomé. *Fastiginia: Vida cotidiana en la corte de Valladolid*. Trans. Narciso Alonso Cortés. Valladolid: Ambito, 1989.

Porreño, Baltasar. *Dichos y hechos de Felipe III*. In Yáñez Fajardo y Montroy, *Memorias*. Madrid, 1723.

Quevedo, Francisco de. *Política de Dios y gobierno de Cristo Señor*. Madrid, 1617. Reprinted in *Biblioteca de Autores Españoles*, ed. D. Aureliano Fernández-Guera y Orbe. Madrid: Librería y Casa Editorial Hernando, 1930, 23:10–110.

———. *Grandes anales de quince días*. Madrid, n.d. Reprinted in *Biblioteca de Autores Españoles*, ed. D. Aureliano Fernández-Guera y Orbe. Madrid: Librería y Casa Editorial Hernando, 1930, 23:193–220.

Ramírez de Arellano, Feliciano, ed. *Correspondencia de los príncipes de alemania con Felipe II y de los embajadores de éste en la corte de Viena (1556 á 1598)*. Vol. 110 of *Colección de documentos inéditos para la historia de España [Codoin]*. Madrid: Imprenta de José Perales y Martínez, 1894.

Ramírez de Arellano, Feliciano, and Sancho Rayón, José, eds. *Historia de Felipe III, Rey de España*. Vol. 60 of *Colección de documentos inéditos para la historia de España [Codoin]*. Madrid: Imprenta de Muguel Ginesta, 1875.

———. *Historia de Felipe III, Rey de España, desde Libro V*. Vol. 61 of *Colección de documentos inéditos para la historia de España [Codoin]*. Madrid: Imprenta de Muguel Ginesta, 1875.

Rodríguez Villa, Antonio, ed. *Correspondencia de la Infanta Archiduquesa D. Isabel Clara Eugenia con el Duque de Lerma y otros personajes*. Madrid, 1906.

Salazar de Mendoza, Pedro. *Successión de la ínclyta casa de Baviera con la vida de la sereníssima Señora Archiduquesa María*. Toledo, 1608.

Salazar y Castro, Luis de. *Advertencias históricas sobre las obras de algunos doctos escritores modernos*. Madrid, 1688.

Salva y Munar, Miguel, and Sainz de Baranda, Pedro, eds. *Colección diplomática*. Vol. 18 of *Colección de documentos inéditos para la historia de España [Codoin]*. Madrid: Imprenta de la viuda de Calero, 1851.

Seco Serrano, Carlos, ed. *Cartas de Sor María de Ágreda y de Felipe IV*. 2 vols. In *Biblioteca de Autores Españoles*, vols. 108 and 109. Madrid: Ediciones Atlas, 1958.

Símon Díaz, José, ed. *Relaciones breves de actos públicos celebrados en Madrid (1541–1650)*. Madrid: Instituto de Estudios Madrileños, 1982.

Testamento de Felipe III (facsimile edition). Introduction by Carlos Seco Serrano. Madrid: Colección Documenta, 1982.

Teresa of Ávila. *Book of the Foundations.* In *The Complete Works of St. Teresa of Jesús,* ed. E. Allison Peers. London: Sheed and Ward, 1975.

Valencia, Mauro de. "Sermón . . . en las honras de D. Margarita de Austria." Madrid, 1626.

Vives, Juan Luis. *Formación de la mujer cristiana.* In *Obras completas,* ed. Lorenzo Riber. Madrid: Aguilar, 1947.

———. *La mujer cristiana. De los deberes del marido. Pedagogia pueril.* 1523. Ed. Lorenzo Riber. Madrid: Aguilar, 1949.

Winwood, Ralph. *Memorials of Affairs of State in the Reigns of Queen Elizabeth and James I.* 3 vols. London: T. Ward, 1725.

Yáñez Fajardo y Montroy, Juan Isidro. *Memorias para la historia de Don Felipe III, Rey de España.* Madrid: N. Rodríguez Franco, 1723.

Secondary Sources

Aguilera Schil, P. Cesar. "Franz Christopher Khevenhüller, embajador imperial." Ph.D. diss., Universidad Complutense, Madrid, n.d.

Alcalá-Zamora y Queipo de Llano, José. "En torno a los planteamientos hegemónicos de la monarquía hispana de los Felipes." *Revista de la Universidad de Madrid, Homenaje a Menéndez Pidal,* vol. 3, 19, no. 73 (1970): 57–106.

———. "Iniciativa, desaciertos, y posibilidades en la política exterior española bajo Felipe III." *Estudios del Departamento de Historia Moderna* (Universidad de Zaragoza), 1976: 191–224.

Allen, Paul C. "The Strategy of Peace: Spanish Foreign Policy and the 'Pax Hispanica,' 1598–1609." Ph.D. diss., Yale University, 1995.

Alonso, Carlos, O.S.A., ed. "Cartas de la Madre Mariana de San José y otras prioras del Monasterio de la Encarnación de Madrid a los Barberino." *Recollectio* 11 (1988): 565–94.

Alvar Ezquerra, Alfredo. *Felipe II, la corte y Madrid en 1561.* Madrid: Consejo Superior de Investigaciones Científicas, 1985.

Álvarez Solar-Quintes, Nicolás. *Reales cédulas de Felipe II y adiciones de Felipe III en la escritura fundacional del Monasterio de las Descalzas de Madrid.* Madrid: Instituto de Estudios Madrileños, 1962.

Andritsch, Johann. "Landesfürstliche Berater am Grazer Hof (1564–1619)." In *Innerösterreich, 1564–1619,* 73–117. Graz: Universitätsbuchdruckerai, 1968.

Arco, Ricardo del. *La idea del imperio en la política y la literatura española.* Madrid: Espasa-Calpe, 1944.

Arenal, Electa. "The Convent as Catalyst for Autonomy: Two Hispanic Nuns of the

Seventeenth Century." In *Women in Hispanic Literature: Icons and Fallen Idols*, ed. Beth Miller, 147–83. Berkeley: University of California Press, 1983.

Asch, Ronald G., and Adolf M. Birke, eds. *Princes, Patronage, and the Nobility: The Court at the Beginning of the Modern Age, c. 1450–1650*. Oxford: Oxford University Press, 1991.

Asensio, José María. *El Conde de Lemos*. Madrid, 1880.

Atkinson, Clarissa. "'Precious Balsam in a Fragile Glass': The Ideology of Virginity in the Later Middle Ages." *Journal of Family History* 8, no. 2 (1983): 131–43.

Babb, Lawrence. *The Elizabethan Malady*. East Lansing: Michigan State University Press, 1951.

Barbeito, José Manuel. *El Alcázar de Madrid*. Madrid: Colegio Oficial de Arquitectos de Madrid, Comisión de Cultura, 1992.

Barbeito Carneiro, María Isabel. "Escritoras madrileñas del siglo xvii (Estudio bibliográfico-crítico)." Ph.D. diss., Universidad Complutense, Madrid, 1986.

Barrios, Feliciano. *El Consejo de Estado de la monarquía española, 1521–1812*. Madrid: Consejo de Estado, 1984.

Bennett, Judith. *Women in the Medieval English Countryside: Gender and Household in Brigstock before the Plague*. New York: Oxford University Press, 1987.

Bibl, Viktor. "Zur Frage der religiösen Haltung Kaiser Maximilians II." *Archiv für Österreichische Geschichte* 106, no. 2 (1918): 298–426.

———. *Maximilian II. Der Rätselhafte Kaiser: Ein Zeitbild*. Dresden: Avalun, 1929.

Bilinkoff, Jodi. *The Ávila of Saint Teresa: Religious Reform in a Sixteenth-Century City*. Ithaca: Cornell University Press, 1989.

———. "Self-Identity and Urban Identity in Early Modern Madrid: Mariana de Jesús (1565–1624)." Paper delivered at the Ninth Berkshire Conference on the History of Women, Vassar College, Poughkeepsie, New York, 12 June 1993.

———. "A Spanish Prophetess and Her Patrons: The Case of María de Santo Domingo." *Sixteenth Century Journal* 23, no. 1 (1992): 21–34.

Bireley, Robert, S.J. *The Counter-Reformation Prince: Anti-Machiavellianism or Catholic Statecraft in Early Modern Europe*. Chapel Hill: University of North Carolina Press, 1990.

———. *Religion and Politics in the Age of the Counterreformation: Emperor Ferdinand II, William Lamormaini, S.J., and the Formation of Imperial Policy*. Chapel Hill: University of North Carolina Press, 1981.

Blas y Diaz-Jiménez, María del Carmen. "La Emperatriz Doña María de Austria." Ph.D. diss., Universidad Complutense, Madrid, 1950.

Bonner, Shirley Harrold. "Margaret of Austria: Her Life and Learning in Europe's Renaissance." Ph.D. diss., University of Pittsburgh, 1981.

Boom, Ghislaine de. *Marguerite d'Autriche*. Brussels: La Renaissance du Livre, 1945.

———. *Marie de Hongrie*. Brussels: La Renaissance du Livre, 1956.

Bottineau, Yves. "Aspects de la cour d'Espagne au xviiᵉ siècle. L'étiquette de la chambre du roi." *Bulletin Hispanique* 74 (1972): 138–57.

Bouza Álvarez, Fernando J. *Cartas de Felipe II as sus hijas*. Madrid: Turner, 1988.

Boyden, James M. *The Courtier and the King: Ruy Gómez de Silva, Philip II, and the Court of Spain*. Berkeley: University of California Press, 1995.

Bravo-Villasante, Carmen. *La mujer vestida de hombre en el teatro español (siglos xvi–xvii)*. Madrid: Sociedad General Española de Librería, 1976.

Breisach, Ernst. *Caterina Sforza: A Renaissance Virago*. Chicago: University of Chicago Press, 1967.

Brightwell, Peter. "Spain and Bohemia: The Decision to Intervene." *European Studies Review* 12 (1982): 117–41.

———. "The Spanish Origins of the Thirty Years' War." *European Studies Review* 9 (1979): 409–31.

———. "The Spanish System and the Twelve Years' Truce." *English Historical Review* 89 (1974): 270–92.

Brink, Jean R., Allison P. Coudert, and Maryanne C. Horowitz, eds. *The Politics of Gender in Early Modern Europe*. Kirksville, Mo.: Sixteenth Century Journal Publishers, 1989.

Brown, Jonathan, and J. H. Elliott. *A Palace for a King: The Buen Retiro and the Court of Philip IV*. New Haven: Yale University Press, 1980.

Brown, Judith. *Immodest Acts: The Life of a Lesbian Nun in Renaissance Italy*. New York: Oxford University Press, 1986.

Bynum, Caroline Walker. *Holy Feast and Holy Fast: The Religious Significance of Food to Medieval Women*. Berkeley: University of California Press, 1987.

Caeiro, Francisco. *O Archiduque Alberto de Áustria*. Lisbon, 1961.

Camara, Alicia. "El Escorial de Felipe III. Historia y arquitectura." *Fragmentos*, nos. 4–5 (1985): 32–45.

Cano de Gardoqui, José Luis. "España y la 'escalada de Ginebra' (1602)." In *Homenaje al Profesor Alarcos*, vol. 2. Valladolid, 1966.

———. "España y los estados italianos independientes en 1600." *Hispania* 23, no. 92 (1963): 3–34.

———. "El incidente del embajador francés en Valladold (1601)." *Revista de Investigaciones Históricas* (Valladolid) 5 (1985): 37–53.

———. *Incorporación del marquesado del Finale (1602)*. Valladolid: Facultad de Filosofía y Letras de la Universidad de Valladolid, Escuela de Historia Moderna del C.S. de I.C., 1955.

———. "La orientación italiana del ducado de Saboya. Primera fase (1603–1604)." *Hispania* 33, no. 125 (1973): 505–95.

———. "Saboya en la política del Duque de Lerma, 1601–1602." *Hispania* 26, no. 101 (1966): 41–60.

Cánovas del Castillo, Antonio. *Bosquejo histórico de la Casa de Austria en España*. Madrid, 1911.

———. *Historia de la decadencia española*. Madrid, 1854.

———. *Matías de Novoa, monografía de un historiador español desconocido*. Madrid, 1876.

———. "Sobre las ideas políticas de los Españoles durante la Casa de Austria." *Revista de España* 6–7 (1968–69).

Carmignano de Brenta, P. Arthur M. de, O.F.M. Cap. *Mission diplomatique de Laurent de Brindes auprès de Philippe III en faveur de la Ligue Catholique Allemande (1609)*. Padua: Ex Officina Typographica Seminarii, 1964.

Carrasco Martínez, Adolfo. "El régimen señorial en la Castilla moderna: las tierras de la Casa de Infantado en los siglos xvii y xviii." Ph.D. diss., Complutense University, Madrid, 1991.

Carter, Charles Howard. "The Ambassadors of Early Modern Europe: Patterns of Diplomatic Representation in the Early Seventeenth Century." In *From the Renaissance to the Counter-Reformation. Essays in Honour of Garrett Mattingly*. New York: Random House, 1965.

———. "The Nature of Spanish Government after Philip II." *Historian* 26 (Nov. 1963): 1–18.

Castoviejo, J. M., and F. Fernández de Córdoba. *El Conde de Gondomar, un azor entre ocasos*. Madrid: Editorial "Prensa Española," 1967.

Castro, Cristóbal de. *Felipe III: Idea de un príncipe cristiano*. Madrid: Biblioteca Nueva, 1944.

Catálogo iv centenario de la real fundación del Convento de Santa Isabel de Madrid. Madrid: Patrimonio Nacional, 1990.

Ceredo, F., S.J. "La vocación Jesuítica del Duque de Lerma." *Razon y Fe*, 1948, no. 605, 512–23.

Cervera Vera, Luis. *El conjunto palacial de la villa de Lerma*. Valencia: Editorial Castilia, 1967.

———. *Lerma: Síntesis histórico-monumental*. Lerma, 1982.

Checa [Cremades], Fernando. *El Real Alcázar de Madrid*. Madrid: Nerea, 1994.

———. "Monasterio de las Descalzas Reales: Orígenes de su colección artística." *Reales Sitios* 26, no. 102 (1989): 30 n. 27.

Chojnacki, Stanley. "The Power of Love: Wives and Husbands in Late Medieval Venice." In *Women and Power in the Middle Ages*, ed. Mary Erler and Maryanne Kowaleski. Athens: University of Georgia Press, 1988.

Chudoba, Bohdan. *Spain and the Empire*. Chicago: University of Chicago Press, 1962.

Chueca Goitia, Fernando. *Casas reales en monasterios y conventos españoles*. Bilbao: Xarait Ediciones, 1982.

Claretta Gaudenzio, Barone. *Il Principe Emanuele Filiberto di Savoia alla corte di Spagna* [Storici sul Regno di Carlo Emanuele I]. Turin: G. Civelli, 1872.

Clavero, Bartolomé. *Tantas personas como estados: Por una Antropología de la historia europea*. Madrid: TECHNOS, Fundación Cultural Enrique Luño Peña, 1986.

Contreras, Juan de (Marqués de Lozoya). *Las Descalzas Reales*. Madrid: Instituto de Estudios Madrileños del Consejo Superior de Investigaciones Científicas, 1970.

Cordero Torres, José María. *El Consejo de Estado: Su trayectoria y perspectivas en España.* Madrid: Instituto de Estudios Políticos, 1944.

Coreth, Anna. *Pietas Austriaca: Österreichische Frömmigkeit im Barock.* Vienna: Verlag für Geschichte und Politik Wien, 1982.

Dadson, Trevor J. "La biblioteca del poeta y político Diego de Silva y Mendoza, conde de Salinas (1564–1630)." *Journal of Hispanic Research* 3 (1994–95): 181–216.

———. "The Duke of Lerma and the Count of Salinas: Politics and Friendship in Early Seventeenth-Century Spain." *European History Quarterly* 25 (1995): 5–38.

Daniel, David P. "Piety, Politics, and Perversion: Noblewomen in Reformation Hungary." In *Women in Reformation and Counter-Reformation Europe*, ed. Sherrin Marshall, 68–88. Bloomington: Indiana University Press, 1989.

Danvila y Burguero, Alfonso. *Don Cristóbal de Moura, primer Marqués de Castel Rodrigo (1583–1613).* Madrid, 1900.

Danvila y Collado, Manuel. "Nuevos datos para escribir la historia de las Cortes de Castilla en el reinado de Felipe III." *Boletín de la Real Academia de la Historia* 8 (1886).

Dean, Trevor. "The Courts." *Journal of Modern History* 67, Supplement (Dec. 1995): S136–51.

Dennis, Amarie. *Philip III: The Shadow of a King.* Madrid: A. W. Dennis, 1985.

Díaz Medina, Ana. "El gobierno en España de Maximiliano II (1548–1551)." In *Kaiser Maximilian II. Kultur und Politik im 16. Jahrhundert*, ed. Friedrich Edelmayer and Alfred Kohler, 38–54. Munich: Verlag für Geschichte und Politik Wien, 1992.

Domínguez Ortiz, Antonio. *Crisis y Decadencia de la España de los Austrias.* Barcelona: Editorial Ariel, 1969.

Duden, Barbara. *The Woman beneath the Skin: A Doctor's Patients in Eighteenth-Century Germany.* Trans. Thomas Dunlap. Cambridge: Harvard University Press, 1991.

Duhr, Bernhard. *Geschichte der Jesuiten in den Ländern deutscher Zunge.* Freiburg im Breisgau: Herder, 1907.

Echevarría Bacigalupe, Miguel Angel. *La diplomacia secreta en Flandes, 1598–1643.* Leioa-Vizcaya: Servicio Editorial Universidad del País Vasco, 1984.

Edelmayer, Friedrich. "Die Beziehungen zwischen Maximilian II. und Philipp II." Unpublished Diplomarbeit, University of Vienna, 1982.

———. *Maximilian II., Philipp II. und Reichsitalien: Die Auseinandersetzungen um das Reichslehen Finale in Ligurien.* Stuttgart: Franz Steiner Verlag Wiesbaden GMBH, 1988.

Egido, Teófanes, ed. *Sátiras políticas de la España moderna.* Madrid: Alianza, 1973.

Eiras Roel, Antonio. "Política francesa de Felipe III." *Hispania* 31, no. 118 (1971): 245–336.

Elias, Norbert. *The Court Society.* Trans. Edmund Jephcott. New York: Pantheon Books, 1983.

Elliott, John H. *The Count-Duke of Olivares: The Statesman in an Age of Decline.* New Haven: Yale University Press, 1986.

———. *Imperial Spain, 1469–1716.* New York: Penguin Books, 1990.

———. "Poder y propaganda en la España de Felipe IV." In *Homenaje a José Antonio Maravall.* Madrid, 1985.

———. "A Question of Reputation? Spanish Foreign Policy in the Seventeenth Century." *Journal of Modern History* 55 (1983).

———. *Spain and Its World, 1500–1700.* New Haven: Yale University Press, 1989.

Elliott, John H., and Angel García Sanz. *La España del Conde Duque de Olivares. Encuentro internacional sobre la España del Conde Duque de Olivares Celebrado en Toro los días 15–18 de septiembre 1987.* Valladolid: Secretariado de Publicaciones, Universidad de Valladolid, 1990.

Entrambasaguas, Joaquín de. *Una familia de ingenios: Los Ramírez de Prado.* Madrid, 1943.

Escudero, José Antonio. *Los secretarios de estado y del despacho.* 4 vols. Madrid: Instituto de Estudio Administrativos, 1976.

Espejo de Hinojosa, Cristóbal. *El Consejo de Hacienda durante la presidencia del Marqués de Poza.* Madrid, 1924.

———. *Las dificultades económicas en España en el primer tercio del siglo xvii y las soluciones particulares.* Madrid: Imprenta Municipal, 1926.

Etreros Mena, Mercedes. *La sátira política en el siglo xvii.* Madrid: Fundación Universitaria Española, 1983.

Evans, R. J. W. *Rudolf II and His World: A Study in Intellectual History.* New York: Oxford University Press, 1973.

———. *The Making of the Habsburg Monarchy.* New York: Oxford University Press, 1979.

Fernández Albaladejo, Pablo. *Fragmentos de monarquía.* Madrid: Alianza, 1992.

Fernández Álvarez, Manuel. "Las instrucciones políticas de los Austrias mayores. Problemas e interpretaciones." In *Gesammelte zur Kulturgeschichte Spaniens* (Münster) 3 (1967): 171–88.

Fernández Cuesta, N. "Felipe III y los principales sucesos de su reinado." *Revista de España* 12, vol. 67 (1879).

Fernández de Bethencourt, Francisco. *Historia genealógica y heráldica de la monarquía española, casa real y grandes de España.* 10 vols. Madrid: E. Teodoro, 1897–1920.

Fernández de Velasco, Recaredo. *La doctrina de la razón de estado en los escritores españoles anteriores al siglo xix.* Madrid, 1925.

Fernández Duro, Cesareo. *Don Pedro Enríquez de Acevedo, Conde de Fuentes* (Memorias de la Academia de la Historia, vol. 10). Madrid: M. Tello, 1884.

Fernández Martín, Luis. "La Marquesa del Valle: Una vida dramática en la corte de los Austrias." *Hispania* 39, no. 143 (1979): 559–638.

Fernández Santamaría, José Antonio. *Reason of State and Statecraft in Spanish Political Thought, 1595–1640*. New York: University Press of America, 1983.

——. *The State, War, and Peace: Spanish Political Thought in the Renaissance, 1516–1559*. Cambridge: Cambridge University Press, 1977.

Feros [Carrasco], Antonio. "The King's Favorite, the Duke of Lerma: Power, Wealth, and Court Culture in the Reign of Philip III of Spain, 1598–1621." Ph.D. diss., The Johns Hopkins University, Baltimore, Maryland, 1994.

——. "Felipe III: Política interior." In *La Crisis del siglo xvii*. Vol. 6 of *Historia de España*, ed. Antonio Domínguez Ortiz. Barcelona: Planeta, 1988.

——. "Gobierno de corte y patronazgo real en el reinado de Felipe III (1598–1618)." Memoria de Licenciatura, Universidad Autonoma, Madrid, 1986.

Ffolliott, Sheila. "Catherine de' Medici as Artemisia: Figuring the Powerful Widow." In *Rewriting the Renaissance: The Discourses of Sexual Difference in Early Modern Europe*, ed. Margaret W. Ferguson, Maureen Quilligan, and Nancy J. Vickers, 227–41. Chicago: University of Chicago Press, 1986.

Fichtner, Paula S. "Dynastic Marriage in Sixteenth-Century Habsburg Diplomacy and Statecraft: An Interdisciplinary Approach," *American Historical Review* 81 (1976): 243–65.

Flórez de Setien, P. Enrique. *Memorias de las reinas católicas de España*. 3d ed. Madrid: Aguilar, 1959. Reprinted from 1761 ed.

Fraser, Antonia. *The Warrior Queens: The Legends and the Lives of the Women Who Have Led Their Nations in War*. New York: Vintage Books, 1990.

Frye, Susan. *Elizabeth I: The Competition for Representation*. New York: Oxford University Press, 1993.

Fullerton, Georgiana. *The Life of Luisa de Carvajal*. Leipzig: B. Tauchnitz, 1881.

Gaillard, Claude. *Le Portugal sous Philippe III d'Espagne: L'action de Diego de Silva y Mendoza*. Grenoble: Université des Langues et Lettres de Grenoble, 1982.

García García, Bernardo José. "La cuestión morisca y la restauración de la milicia (1595–1614)." In *L'expulsió dels moriscos: Conseqències en el món islàmic i en el món cristià*, 1–5. Barcelona: Generalitat de Catalunya, 1994.

——. "El Duque de Lerma y la Pax Hispánica. Auge y crisis del pacifismo en la política exterior de la monarquía (1607–1615)." Memoria de Licenciatura, Universidad Complutense, Madrid, 1991.

——. "Fray Luis de Aliaga y la conciencia del Rey." In *La presenza dei regolari nelle corti d'Antico Regime: religione, politica e diplomazia*, ed. Flavio Rurale. Roma: Bulzoni Editore, forthcoming.

——. "La 'Guarda del Estrecho' durante el reinado de Felipe III." *II Congreso Internacional El Estrecho de Gibraltar*, 4:247–58. Actas. Madrid: U.N.E.D., 1995.

——. "Honra, desengaño y condena de una privanza. La retirada de la corte del Cardenal Duque de Lerma." Paper presented at VI Reunión Científica de la Asociación Española de Historia Moderna (AEHM), Alicante, 27–30 May 1996.

———. "Pacifismo y reformación en la política exterior del Duque de Lerma (1598–1618). Apuntes para una renovación historiográfica pendiente." *Cuadernos de Historia Moderna*, no. 12 (1991): 207–22.

———. *La Pax Hispanica: Política exterior del Duque de Lerma*. Leuven: Leuven University Press, 1996.

———. "Paz, desempeño y reputación en la política exterior del Duque de Lerma (1598–1618)." Ph.D. diss., Universidad Complutense, Madrid, 1994.

Gardiner, Samuel R. *Prince Charles and the Spanish Marriage, 1612–1623*. London: Hurst and Blackett, 1869.

Gerlo, Alöis, and Vervliet, H. D. V. *Inventaire de la correspondance de Juste Lipse, 1564–1606*. Antwerp: Editions Scientifiques Erasme, 1968.

Ginarte González, Ventura. *El Duque de Lerma, protector de la reforma Trinitaria 1599–1613*. Madrid: Rodagraf, 1982.

Gliss, Otto. *Der Oñate Vertrag*. Frankfurt am Main, 1934.

González Hontoria, A. *Los embajadores de Felipe III en Venecia*. N.p.: Conferencias de la Escuela Diplomática, 1945–46.

González Palencia, Angel, ed. *La Junta de Reformación*. Valladolid, 1932.

Gorter-van Royen, Laetitia V. G. *Maria van Hongarije: Regentes der Nederlanden*. Hilversum: Veloren, 1995.

Greer, Margaret. *The Play of Power: Mythological Court Dramas of Calderón de la Barca*. Princeton: Princeton University Press, 1991.

Guerin, Pierre. *Marguerite d'Autriche-Bourgogne*. Lyons: Editions Bellier, 1992.

Hanawalt, Barbara A. "Lady Honor Lisle's Networks of Influence." In *Women and Power in the Middle Ages*, ed. Mary Erler and Maryanne Kowaleski, 188–212. Athens: University of Georgia Press, 1988.

Hanke, Lewis. *The Spanish Struggle for Justice in the Conquest of America*. Philadelphia: University of Pennsylvania Press, 1949.

Harline, Craig. *The Burdens of Sister Margaret: Private Lives in a Seventeenth-Century Convent*. New York: Doubleday, 1994.

Harris, Barbara J. "A New Look at the Reformation: Aristocratic Women and Nunneries, 1450–1540." *Journal of British Studies* 32, no. 2 (1993): 89–113.

———. "Power, Profit, and Passion: Mary Tudor, Charles Brandon, and the Arranged Marriage in Early Tudor England." *Feminist Studies* 15, no. 1 (1989): 59–88.

———. "Property, Power, and Personal Relations: Elite Mothers and Sons in Yorkist and Early Tudor England." *Signs* 15, no. 3 (1990): 606–32.

———. "Women and Politics in Early Tudor England." *Historical Journal* 33, no. 2 (1990): 259–81.

Heiß, Gernot. "Königin Maria von Ungarn und Böhmen (1505–1558)." Ph.D diss., University of Vienna, 1971.

———. "Politik und Ratgeber der Königin Maria von Ungarn in den Jahren 1521–1531." *Mitteilungen des Instituts für österreichische Geschichtsforschung* 82 (1974): 119–80.

———. "Princes, Jesuits, and the Origins of Counter-Reformation in the Habsburg Lands." In *Crown, Church, and Estates: Central European Politics in the Sixteenth and Seventeenth Centuries*, ed. R. J. W. Evans and T. V. Thomas, 92–109. London: St. Martin, 1991.

———. "Die ungarischen, böhmischen Besitzungen der Konigin Maria (1505–1558)." *Mitteilungen des österreichischen Staatsarchiv* 27 (1974): 61–100; 29 (1976): 52–121.

Hermida Balado, M. *La Condesa de Lemos y la corte de Felipe III*. Madrid: Paraninfo, 1950.

Herrero García, Miguel. "La poesía satírica contra los políticos del reinado de Felipe III." *Hispania* 6, no. 23 (1946): 267–96.

Herrero Salgado, Felix. *Aportación bibliográfica a la oratoria sagrada española*. Madrid: Consejo Superior de Investigaciones Científicas, 1971.

Hespanha, Antonio Manuel. *História das instituiçoes*. Coimbra: Almedina, 1982.

Hibbard, Caroline M. "The Role of a Queen Consort: The Household and Court of Henrietta Maria, 1625–1642." In *Princes, Patronage, and the Nobility*, ed. Ronald G. Asch and Adolf M. Birke, 404–9.

Hoffman-Strock, Martha K. "'Carved on Rings and Painted in Pictures': The Education and Formation of the Spanish Royal Family, 1601–1634." Ph.D. diss., Yale University, 1996.

Hofmann, Christina. *Das spanische Hofzeremoniell von 1500–1700*. Frankfurt am Main: Lang, 1985.

Huerga, Alvaro. "La vida seudomística y el proceso inquisitorial de Sor María de la Visitación." *Hispania Sacra* 12 (1959): 35–96.

———. "La Monja de Lisboa y Fray Luis de Granada." *Hispania Sacra* 12 (1959): 333–56.

Hull, Suzanne. *Chaste, Silent, and Obedient: English Books for Women, 1475–1640*. San Marino, Calif.: Huntington Library, 1982.

Hurter, Friedrich von. *Bild einer christlichen Fürstin. Maria, Erzherzogin zu Öesterreich, Herzogin von Bayern*. Schaffhausen: Fr. Hurter'sche Buchhandlung, 1860.

———. *Geschichte Kaiser Ferdinands II. und seiner Eltern bis zu dessen Krönung in Frankfurt*. 11 vols. Schaffhausen: Fr. Hurter'sche Buchhandlung, 1850–64.

Imirizaldu, Jesús de. *Monjas y beatas embaucadoras*. Madrid: Editora Nacional, 1977.

Iongh, Jane de. *Margaret of Austria, Regent of the Netherlands*. New York: Norton, 1953.

Israel, Jonathan I. *The Dutch Republic and the Hispanic World, 1606–1661*. Oxford: Clarendon Press, 1986.

Ives, Eric. *Anne Boleyn*. Oxford: Oxford University Press, 1986.

Jankowski, Theodora A. *Women in Power in the Early Modern Drama*. Urbana: University of Illinois Press, 1992.

Jordan, Constance. *Renaissance Feminism*. Ithaca: Cornell University Press, 1990.

———. "Woman's Rule in Sixteenth-Century British Political Thought." *Renaissance Quarterly* 40, no. 3 (1987): 421–51.

Juan Gómez de Mora. (1586–1648): Arquitecto y trazador del rey y maestro mayor de obras de la villa de Madrid, 381–83. Madrid: Ayuntamiento de Madrid, 1996.

Juderías, Julián. "Los comienzos de una privanza." *La Lectura* 15 (1915): 62–71, 405–14.

———. "Los favoritos de Felipe III. Don Pedro Franqueza, Conde de Villalonga y secretario de estado." *Revista de Archivos, Bibliotecas y Museos* 13 (1909).

———. "Un proceso político en tiempo de Felipe III: Don Rodrigo de Calderón, Marqués de Siete Iglesias. Su vida, su proceso y su muerte." *Revista de Archivos, Bibliotecas y Museos* 9–10 (1905–6).

Kagan, Richard L. *Lucrecia's Dreams: Politics and Prophecy in Sixteenth-Century Spain*. Berkeley: University of California Press, 1990.

———. "Prescott's Paradigm: American Historical Scholarship and the Decline of Spain." *American Historical Review* 101, no. 2 (1996): 423–46.

Kagan, Richard L., and Geoffrey Parker. *Spain, Europe, and the Atlantic World: Essays in Honour of John H. Elliott*. Cambridge: Cambridge University Press, 1995.

Kalas, Robert J. "The Noble Widow's Place in the Patriarchal Household: The Life and Career of Jeanne de Gontault." *Sixteenth Century Journal* 24, no. 3 (1993): 519–39.

Kelly-Gadol, Joan. "The Social Relation of the Sexes: Methodological Implications of Women's History." *Signs* 1, no. 4 (1976): 819–22.

Kettering, Sharon. "The Patronage Power of Early Modern French Noblewomen." *Historical Journal*, 32, no. 4 (1989): 817–41.

King, Margaret L. *Women of the Renaissance*. Chicago: University of Chicago Press, 1991.

Klapisch-Zuber, Christiane. "The 'Cruel Mother': Maternity, Widowhood, and Dowry in Florence in the Fourteenth and Fifteenth Centuries." In *Women, Family, and Ritual in Renaissance Italy*, trans. Lydia G. Cochrane, 116–31. Chicago: University of Chicago Press, 1987.

Klarwill, Victor (Ritter von). *Fugger-Zeitungen. Ungedruckte Briefe an das Haus aus den Jahren 1568–1605*. Vienna: Rikola, 1923.

Kleinman, Ruth. *Anne of Austria: Queen of France*. Columbus: Ohio State University Press, 1985.

———. "Social Dynamics at the French Court: The Household of Anne of Austria." *French Historical Studies* 16 (1990): 517–35.

Klibansky, Raymond, Erwin Panofsky, and Fritz Saxl. *Saturn and Melancholy: Studies in the History of Natural Philosophy, Religion, and Art*. New York: Basic Books, 1964.

Laínez Alcalá, Rafael. *Don Bernardo de Sandoval y Rojas, Protector de Cervantes (1546–1615)*. Salamanca, 1958.

Lamphere, Louise. "Strategies, Cooperation, and Conflict among Women in Domestic Groups." In *Woman, Culture, and Society*, ed. Michelle Zimbalist Rosaldo and Louise Lamphere, 97–112. Stanford: Stanford University Press, 1993.

Lasso de la Vega y López de Tejada, Miguel, Marqués del Saltillo. *La embajada en Alemania del Conde de Oñate y la elección de Fernando II Rey de Romanos (1616–1620)*. Oviedo, 1929.

Laurence, Anne. "Women's Psychological Disorders in Seventeenth-Century Britain." In *Current Issues in Women's History*, ed. Arina Angerman, Geerte Binnema, Annemieke Keunen, Vefie Poels, and Jacqueline Zirkzee, 109–23. New York: Routledge, 1989.

Lee, Patricia-Ann. "Reflections of Power: Margaret of Anjou and the Dark Side of Queenship." *Renaissance Quarterly* 39 (1986): 183–217.

LeFévre, Joseph. "Les ambassadeurs d'Espagne á Bruxelles sous le règne de l'Archiduc Albert (1598–1621)." *Revue Belge de Philosophie et d'Histoire* 2 (1923): 61–80.

———. *Spinola et la Belgique (1601–1627)*. Brussels: La Renaissance du Livre, 1947.

Le Flem, Jean-Paul, et al. *La frustración de un imperio*. Barcelona: Labor, 1982.

Lepenies, Wolf. *Melancholy and Society*. Trans. Jeremy Gaines and Doris Jones. Cambridge: Harvard University Press, 1992.

Lerner, Gerda. *The Creation of Feminist Consciousness from the Middle Ages to Eighteen-Seventy*. New York: Oxford University Press, 1993.

Levin, Carole. *The Heart and Stomach of a King: Elizabeth I and the Politics of Sex and Power*. Philadelphia: University of Pennsylvania Press, 1994.

Levin, Carole, and Patricia A. Sullivan, eds. *Political Rhetoric, Power, and Renaissance Women*. Albany: State University of New York Press, 1995.

Levine, Mortimer. "The Place of Women in Tudor government." In *Tudor Rule and Tudor Revolution: Essays for G. R. Elton from his American Friends*, ed. Delloyd J. Guth and John McKenna, 109–23. Cambridge: Cambridge University Press, 1982.

Lhotsky, Alphons. "Was heißt 'Haus Österreich.'" In *Europäisches Mittelalter das Land Österreich*, 344–64. Vienna: Verlag für Geschichte und Politik, 1970.

Lisón Tolosana, Carmelo. *La imagen del rey: Monarquía, realeza y poder ritual en la casa de los Austrias*. Madrid: Espasa-Calpe, 1991.

Liss, Peggy K. *Isabel the Queen: Life and Times*. New York: Oxford University Press, 1992.

Llanos y Torriglia, Felix. *Santas y reinas*. 2d ed. Madrid: Ediciones Fax, 1943.

Lovett, A. W. *Early Habsburg Spain, 1517–1598*. New York: Oxford University Press, 1986.

Lunenfeld, Marvin. "Isabella I of Castile and the Company of Women in Power." *Historical Reflections* 4 (1977): 207–29.

Lyons, Bridget Gellert. *Voices of Melancholy: Studies in Literary Treatments of Melancholy in Renaissance England*. New York: Barnes and Noble, 1971.

MacDonald, Michael. *Mystical Bedlam: Madness, Anxiety, and Healing in Seventeenth-Century England*. Cambridge: Cambridge University Press, 1981.

Mack, Phyllis. *Visionary Women: Ecstatic Prophecy in Seventeenth-Century England*. Berkeley: University of California Press, 1992.

——. "Women as Prophets during the English Civil War." *Feminist Studies* 8, no. 1 (1982): 19–45.

Maclean, Ian. *The Renaissance Notion of Woman*. Cambridge: Cambridge University Press, 1980.

Maravall, José Antonio. *Culture of the Baroque: Analysis of a Historical Structure*. Trans. Terry Cochran. Minneapolis: University of Minnesota Press, 1986.

Martínez Bara, José Antonio. "Los Cabrera de Córdoba, Felipe II y El Escorial." *Revista de Archivos, Bibliotecas y Museos* 71, nos. 1–2 (1963): 203–33.

Martínez Millán, José, ed. *La corte de Felipe II*. Madrid: Alianza, 1994.

Mattingly, Garrett. *Catherine of Aragon*. Boston: Little, Brown, 1941.

——. *Renaissance Diplomacy*. London: Jonathan Cape, 1955.

Mayr, Karl, ed. *Von der Abreise Erzherzog Leopolds nach Jülich bis zu den Werbungen Herzog Maximilians von Bayern im März 1610* and *Von den Rüstungen Herzog Maximilians von Bayern bis zum Aufbruch der Passauer*. Vols. 7 and 8, *Briefe und Acten zur Geschichte des Dreissigjährigen Krieges*, ed. Felix Stieve. Munich: M. Rieger'sche Universitäts-Buchhandlung, 1905–8.

McCash, June Hall, ed. *The Cultural Patronage of Medieval Women*. Athens: University of Georgia Press, 1996.

McClure, Peter, and Robin Headlam Wells. "Elizabeth I as a Second Virgin Mary." *Renaissance Studies* 4, no. 1 (1980): 38–70.

McKendrick, Melveena. *Theatre in Spain, 1490–1700*. Cambridge: Cambridge University Press, 1992.

——. *Woman and Society in the Spanish Drama of the Golden Age: A Study of the Mujer Varonil*. Cambridge: Cambridge University Press, 1974.

McNamara, Jo Ann. "A Legacy of Miracles: Hagiography and Nunneries in Merovingian Gaul." In *Women of the Medieval World*, ed. Julius Kirshner and Suzanne F. Wemple, 36–52. New York: Basil Blackwell, 1985.

——. "The Need to Give: Suffering and Female Sanctity in the Middle Ages." In *Images of Sainthood in Medieval Europe*, ed. Renate Blumenfeld-Kosinski and Timea Szell, 199–221. Ithaca: Cornell University Press, 1991.

Midelfort, H. C. Erik. *Mad Princes of Renaissance Germany*. Charlottesville: University Press of Virginia, 1994.

Monson, Craig A., ed. *The Cranned Wall: Women, Religion, and the Arts in Early Modern Europe*. Ann Arbor: University of Michigan Press, 1992.

Montrose, Louis. "'Eliza, Queen of Shepeardes,' and the Pastoral of Power." *English Literary Renaissance* 10 (1980): 153–82.

Moreno Villa, José, and F. J. Sánchez Cantón. "Noventa y siete retratos de la familia de Felipe III por Bartolomé González." *Archivo Español de Arte y Arqueología* 38 (1937).

Muldoon, James. *The Americas in the Spanish World Order: The Justification for Conquest in the Seventeenth Century.* Philadelphia: University of Pennsylvania Press, 1994.

Muñoz, Angela, and Maria del Mar Grana, eds. *Religiosidad feminina: Expectativas y realidades (SS. viii–xviii).* Madrid: Asociación Cultural AL-MUDAYNA, 1991.

Nader, Helen. "Habsburg Ceremony in Spain: The Reality of the Myth." *Historical Reflections/Reflexions Historiques* 15, no. 1 (1988): 293–309.

Niederkorn, Jan Paul. *Die europäischen Mächte und der 'Lange Türkenkrieg' Kaiser Rudolf II. (1593–1606).* Vienna: Österreichische Akademie der Wissenschaften, 1993.

———. "Das 'negotium secretum' der Familie Cicala." *Mitteilungen des Instituts für österreichische Geschichtsforschung* 101 (1993): 425–34.

———. "Spanische Subsidien für den Türkenkrieg, die Markgrafschaft Finale und der Sturz eines Ministers am Hof König Philipps III. *Römische historische Mitteilungen* 36 (1994): 143–52.

Ollero, Julio, ed. *Los Austrias: Grabados de la Biblioteca Nacional.* Madrid: Ministerio de Cultura, 1993.

Orso, Steven N. *Philip IV and the Decoration of the Alcázar de Madrid.* Princeton: Princeton University Press, 1986.

Ossorio y Gallardo, Angel. *Los hombres de toga en el proceso de Don Rodrigo Calderón.* Madrid: Biblioteca Nueva, 1918.

Ozment, Steven. *Magdalena and Balthasar: An Intimate Portrait of Life in Sixteenth-Century Europe Revealed in the Letters of a Nuremberg Husband and Wife.* New York: Simon and Schuster, 1986.

Pagden, Anthony. *The Languages of Political Theory in Early Modern Europe.* Cambridge: Cambridge University Press, 1987.

———. *Spanish Imperialism and the Political Imagination.* New Haven: Yale University Press, 1990.

Palomares Ibañez, J. María. *El patronato del Duque de Lerma sobre el convento de San Pablo en Valladolid.* Valladolid: Universidad de Valladolid, Secretariado de Publicaciones, 1970.

Pardo Manuel de Villena, Alfonso. *El Conde de Lemos: Noticia de su vida.* Madrid: J. Ratés Martin, 1911.

Parker, Geoffrey. *Philip II.* 3d ed. Chicago: Open Court, 1995.

Pelorson, Jean-Marc. "Para una reinterpretación de la Junta de Desempeño General (1603–1606) a la luz de la 'visita' de Alonso Ramírez de Prado y de Don Pedro Franqueza, Conde de Villalonga." *Actas del IV Symposium de Historia de la Administración,* 613–27. Madrid: Instituto Nacional de Administración Pública, 1983.

Pérez Bustamante, Ciriaco. *La correspondencia diplomática entre los Duques de Parma y sus agentes o embajadores en la corte de Madrid durante los siglos xvi, xvii y xviii. Notas para su estudio*. Madrid: Tip. de Archivos, 1934.

———. *La España de Felipe III*. 3d ed. Vol. 24 of Menéndez Pidal's *Historia de España*. Madrid: Espasa-Calpe, 1983.

———. *Felipe III. Semblanza de un monarca y perfiles de una privanza*. Madrid, 1950.

———. "La política internacional española durante el reinado de Felipe III (1598–1621)." *Investigación y Progreso* 6 (1932).

Pérez Martín, María Jesús. *Margarita de Austria, Reina de España*. Madrid: Espasa-Calpe, 1961.

Pérez Mínguez, Fidel. "La Condesa de Castellar, fundadora del convento 'Las Carboneras.'" *Revista de la Biblioteca, Archivo, y Museo del Ayuntamiento de Madrid* 8, no. 31 (1931): 253–73; 8, no. 32 (1931): 392–418; 9, no. 34 (1932): 150–80; 9, no. 36 (1932): 409–27.

———. *Don Juan de Idiáquez: Embajador y consejero de Felipe II*. San Sebastián: Imprenta de la Diputacion de Guipúzcoa, 1934.

———. "Infancia y juventud de Doña Beatriz Ramírez de Mendoza." *Revista de la Biblioteca, Archivo, y Museo del Ayuntamiento de Madrid* 8, no. 30 (1931): 152–70.

———. "Un rincón romántico de Madrid." *Revista de la Biblioteca, Archivo, y Museo del Ayuntamiento de Madrid* 8, no. 29 (1931): 41–52.

Perrens, F. Tommy. *Les mariages espagnols sous le régne de Henri IV et la régence de Marie de Medicis*. Paris: Didier, 1869.

Perry, Mary Elizabeth. *Gender and Disorder in Early Modern Seville*. Princeton: Princeton University Press, 1990.

———. "The Manly Woman: A Historical Case Study." *American Behavioral Scientist* 31, no. 1 (1987): 86–100.

Petroff, Elizabeth Alvilda. *Body and Soul: Essays on Medieval Women and Mysticism*. New York: Oxford University Press, 1994.

———. *Medieval Women's Visionary Literature*. New York: Oxford University Press, 1986.

Pulido Bueno, Ildefonso. *La real hacienda de Felipe III*. Huelva: I. Pulido Bueno, 1995.

Queíroz Velloso, J. M. *Doña Francisca de Aragón: Condessa de Mayalde e de Ficalho*. Barcelos: Portucalense Editora, 1931.

Rapley, Elizabeth. *The Dévotes. Women and Church in Seventeenth-Century France*. Montreal: McGill-Queen's University Press, 1993.

Robres Lluch, Ramón, and José Ramón Ortolá, "La Monja de Lisboa. Sus fingidos estigmas. Fray Luis de Granada y el Patriarca Ribera." *Boletín de la Sociedad Castellonense de Cultura* 23 (1947): 182–214, 230–78.

Roco de Campofrío, Juan. *España en Flandes: Trece años de gobierno del Archiduque Alberto (1595–1608)*. Madrid, 1973.

Rodríguez Moñino, A., and M. Brey Mariño. "Luisa de Carvajal." *Revista de la Biblioteca, Archivo, y Museo del Ayuntamiento de Madrid* 10, no. 39 (1933): 321–44.

Rodríguez Raso, Rafaela. *Maximiliano y María de Austria, Gobernadores de España (1548–1551). Estudio a través de su correspondencia con Carlos V.* Ph.D. diss., Universidad Complutense, Madrid, 1957.

Rodríguez-Salgado, M. J. "The Court of Philip II of Spain." In *Princes, Patronage, and the Nobility*, ed. Ronald G. Asch and Adolf M. Birke. Oxford: Oxford University Press, 1991.

Rodríguez Villa, Antonio. *Etiquetas de la Casa de Austria.* Madrid: J. Ratés, 1913.

Rose, Mary Beth. "Women in Men's Clothing: Apparel and Social Stability in *The Roaring Girl.*" *English Literary Renaissance* 14 (1984): 367–91.

Roth, Elke. "Erzherzogin Anna von Innerösterreich, Königin von Polen und Schweden." Ph.D. diss., University of Graz, 1957.

Rott, Edouard. "Philippe III et le Duc de Lerme (1598–1621): Étude historique d'après des documents inédits." *Revue d'Histoire Diplomatique* Paris, 1887, 1–38.

Rubin, Nancy. *Isabella of Castile: The First Renaissance Queen.* New York: St. Martin, 1991.

Ruether, Rosemary Radford. "Misogynism and Virginal Feminism in the Fathers of the Church." In *Religion and Sexism: Images of Woman in the Jewish and Christian Traditions*, ed. Rosemary Radford Ruether, 150–83. New York: Simon and Schuster, 1974.

Ruiz Alcón, María Teresa. *Monasterio de las Descalzas Reales.* Madrid: Editorial Patrimonio Nacional, 1987.

Ruiz Martín, Felipe. "La hacienda y los grupos de presión en el siglo XVII." In *Estado, Hacienda, y Sociedad en la Historia de España*, ed. Bartolome Bennassar et al., 95–122. Valladolid: Instituto de Historia Simancas, Universidad de Valladolid, 1989.

Saenz Ruiz-Olalde, José Luis, O.A.R. *Las Agustinas Recoletas de Santa Isabel la Real de Madrid.* Madrid: Editorial Augustinus, 1990.

Saltillo, Marqués de. "El Real Monasterio de la Encarnación y artistas que allí trabajaron, 1614–1621." *Revista de Bibliotecas, Archivos, y Museos* 8, no. 50 (1944).

Sánchez, Magdalena S. "Confession and Complicity: Margarita de Austria, Richard Haller, S.J., and the Court of Philip III." *Cuadernos de Historia Moderna*, no. 14 (1993): 133–49.

———. "Dynasty, State, and Diplomacy in the Spain of Philip III." Ph.D. diss., The Johns Hopkins University, Baltimore, Maryland, 1988.

———. "Empress María and the Making of Political Policy in the Early Years of Philip III's Reign." In *Religion, Body, and Gender in Early Modern Spain*, ed. Alain Saint-Saëns, 139–47. San Francisco: Mellen Research University Press, 1991.

———. "A House Divided: Spain, Austria, and the Bohemian and Hungarian Successions." *Sixteenth Century Journal* 25, no. 4 (1994): 887–903.

———. "Melancholy and Female Illness: Habsburg Women and Politics at the Court of Philip III." *Journal of Women's History* 8, no. 2 (1996): 81–102.

Sánchez, Magdalena S., and Alain Saint-Saëns, eds. *Spanish Women in the Golden Age: Images and Realities*. Westport, Conn.: Greenwood Press, 1996.

Sánchez Hernández, María Leticia. *El Monasterio de la Encarnación de Madrid: Un modelo de vida religiosa en el siglo xvii*. Salamanca: Ediciones Escurialenses, 1986.

Sánchez Lora, José Luis. *Mujeres, conventos y formas de la religiosidad barroca*. Madrid: FUE, 1988.

Schiesari, Juliana. *The Gendering of Melancholia: Feminism, Psychoanalysis, and the Symbolics of Loss in Renaissance Literature*. Ithaca: Cornell University Press, 1992.

Schroth, Sarah. "The Private Picture Collection of the Duke of Lerma." Ph.D. Diss., New York University, 1990.

Schulenburg, Jane Tibbetts. "The Heroics of Virginity: Brides of Christ and Sacrificial Mutilation." In *Women in the Middle Ages and the Renaissance: Literary and Historical Perspectives*, ed. Mary Beth Rose, 29–72. New York: Syracuse University Press, 1986.

Seco Serrano, Carlos. "Los comienzos de la privanza de Lerma a través de los embajadores florentinos." *Boletín de la Real Academia de la Historia* 144 (1959).

———. "El Marqués de Bedmar y la "Conjuración" española de 1618." *Revista de la Universidad de Madrid* 4, no. 15 (1955): 299–342.

———. "Los antecedentes de la 'Conjuración' de Venecia de 1618." *Boletín de la Real Academia de la Historia* 136 (1955): 37–73.

Serrera, Juan Miguel. "Alonso Sánchez Coello y la mecénica del retrato de corte." In *Alonso Sánchez Coello y el retrato en la corte de Felipe II*. Madrid: Museo del Prado, 1990.

Sharpe, Kevin. "The Image of Virtue: the Court and Household of Charles I, 1625–1642." In *The English Court*, ed. David Starkey et al., 226–60.

Silvela, Francisco. *Matrimonios de España y Francia en 1615*. Madrid: Discurso de Ingreso en la Real Academia de la Historia, 1901.

Simón Díaz, José. *Historia del Colegio Imperial de Madrid*. 2 vols. Madrid: Consejo Superior de Investigaciones Scientíficas, Instituto de Estudios Madrilenos, 1952.

Smith, Hilary Dansey. *Preaching in the Spanish Golden Age: A Study of Some Preachers of the Reign of Philip III*. Oxford: Oxford University Press, 1978.

Sommervogel, Carlos. *Bibliothèque de la Compagnie de Jésus*. Vol. 9. Paris, 1900.

Soufas, Teresa Scott. *Melancholy and the Secular Mind in Spanish Golden Age Literature*. Columbia: University of Missouri Press, 1990.

Starkey, David, D. A. L. Morgan, John Murphy, Pam Wright, Neil Cuddy, and Kevin Sharpe, eds. *The English Court: From the Wars of the Roses to the Civil War*. London: Longman, 1987.

Starobinski, Jean. *History of the Treatment of Melancholy from the Earliest Times to 1900*. Basel: J. R. Geigy, 1962.

Stieve, Felix, ed. *Die Politik Baierns, 1591–1607*. Vols. 4 and 5, *Briefe und Acten zur Geschichte des Dreissigjährigen Krieges*. Munich: M. Rieger'sche Universitäts-Buchhandlung, 1878–83.

———. *Vom Reichstag 1608 bis zur Gründung der Liga*. Vol. 6, *Briefe und Acten zur Geschichte des Dreissigjährigen Krieges*. Munich: M. Rieger'sche Universitäts-Buchhandlung, 1895.

Stradling, R. A. *Europe and the Decline of Spain: A Study of the Spanish System, 1580–1720*. London: George Allen and Unwin, 1981.

———. *Philip IV and the Government of Spain, 1621–1665*. New York: Cambridge University Press, 1988.

Strakosch-Grassmann, Gustav. *Erziehung u. Unterricht im Hause Habsburg*. Korneuburg, 1903.

Sturmberger, H. "Die Anfänge des Bruderzwistes in Habsburg." *Mitteilungen des Oberösterreichischen Landesarchivs*, 1957, 143–88.

Sullivan, John, O.C.D., ed. *Carmelite Studies: Centenary of St. Teresa*. Washington, D.C.: Institute of Carmelite Studies, 1984.

Surtz, Ronald E. *The Guitar of God: Gender, Power, and Authority in the Visionary World of Mother Juana de la Cruz (1481–1534)*. Philadelphia: University of Pennsylvania Press, 1990.

Thomas, Keith. *Religion and the Decline of Magic*. New York: Charles Scribner's Sons, 1971.

Thorp, Malcolm R., and Arthur J. Slavin, eds. *Politics, Religion, and Diplomacy in Early Modern Europe*. Kirksville, Mo.: Sixteenth Century Journal Publishers, 1994.

Tormo, Elías. *En las Descalzas Reales: Estudios históricos, iconográficos, y artísticos*. Madrid: Junta de Iconografía Nacional, 1915–17.

Tovar Martín, Virginia. "El pasadizo, forma arquitectónica encubierta en el Madrid de los siglos xvii y xviii." *Villa de Madrid* 29, no. 87 (1986–1): 31–42.

———. "La entrada triunfal en Madrid de doña Margarita de Austria (24 de octubre de 1599)." *Archivo Español de Arte* 61 (1988).

Tremayne, Eleanor E. *The First Governess of the Netherlands: Margaret of Austria*. London: Methuen, 1908.

Válgoma y Díaz-Varela, Dalmiro de la. *Norma y ceremonia de las reinas de la Casa de Austria*. Madrid: Real Academia de Historia, 1958.

Varela, Javier. *La muerte del rey. El Ceremonial funerario de la monarquía española (1500–1850)*. Madrid: Turner, 1990.

Vigil, Mariló. *La vida de las mujeres en los siglos xvi y xvii*. Mexico: Siglo Veintiuno Editores, 1986.

Vocelka, Karl. *Habsburgische Hochzeiten 1550–1600: Kulturgeschichtliche Studien zum manieristichen Repräsentationsfest*. Vienna: Veröffentlichungen der Komission für neuere Geschichte Österreichs, 1976.

———. "Matthias contra Rudolf: Zur politischen Propaganda in der Zeit des Bruderzwistes." *Zeitschrift für Historische Forschung* 10 (1983): 341–51.

Warnicke, Retha M. *The Rise and Fall of Anne Boleyn: Family Politics at the Court of Henry VIII*. New York: Cambridge University Press, 1989.

Watson, Robert. *The History of the Reign of Philip the Third*. London, 1839.

Weber, Alison. *Teresa of Ávila and the Rhetoric of Femininity*. Princeton: Princeton University Press, 1990.

Weinstein, Donald, and Rudolf M. Bell. *Saints and Society: The Two Worlds of Western Christendom, 1000–1700*. Chicago: University of Chicago Press, 1982.

Wemple, Suzanne F. *Women in Frankish Society: Marriage and the Cloister, 500 to 900*. Philadelphia: University of Pennsylvania Press, 1981.

Widern, Helga. "Die Spanischen Gemahlinnen der Kaiser Maximilian II., Ferdinand III., und Leopold I." Ph.D. diss., University of Vienna, 1959.

Wiesner, Merry E. *Women and Gender in Early Modern Europe*. Cambridge: Cambridge University Press, 1993.

Wilentz, Sean, ed. *Rites of Power: Symbolism, Ritual, and Politics since the Middle Ages*. Philadelphia: University of Pennsylvania Press, 1985.

Willen, Diane. "Women and Religion in Early Modern England." In *Women in Reformation and Counter-Reformation Europe*, ed. Sherrin Marshall, 140–65. Bloomington: Indiana University Press, 1989.

Williams, Patrick. "Lerma, 1618: Dismissal or Retirement?" *European History Quarterly* 19, no. 3 (1989): 307–32.

———. "Lerma, Old Castile, and the Travels of Philip III of Spain." *History* 73, no. 239 (1988): 379–97.

———. "Philip III and the Restoration of Spanish Government, 1598–1603." *English Historical Review* 88 (1973): 751–69.

———. "Política Interior." In *La Crisis de la hegemonia española, S. XVII*. Vol. 8, *Historia General de España y América*, 419–43. Madrid: Rialp, 1986.

Woodbridge, Linda. *Women and the English Renaissance: Literature and the Nature of Womankind*. Urbana: University of Illinois Press, 1984.

Yates, Frances. *Astraea: The Imperial Theme in the Sixteenth Century*. London: Ark, 1985.

Index

Library of Congress Cataloging-in-Publication Data

Sánchez, Magdalena S.
  The empress, the queen, and the nun : women and power at the court of Phillip III
of Spain / Magdalena S. Sánchez.
      p.   cm. — (The Johns Hopkins University studies in historical and political
  science : 116th ser., 2)
  Includes bibliographical references and index.
  ISBN 0-8018-5791-0 (alk. paper)
      1. Spain—Politics and government—1598–1621. 2. Philip III, King of Spain,
1578–1621—Family. 3. Habsburg, House of. 4. Women in politics—Spain—History—
17th century. 5. Power (Social sciences)—Spain—History—17th century.
  I. Title. II. Series.
DP183.S26 1998
946'.051—dc21   97–42171 CIP